History of Medieval India

D1724010

History of Medieval India
(800–1700)

SATISH CHANDRA

Orient BlackSwan

The external boundary and coastline of India as depicted in the maps in this book are neither correct nor authentic.

HISTORY OF MEDIEVAL INDIA

ORIENT BLACKSWAN PRIVATE LIMITED

Registered Office
3-6-752 Himayatnagar, Hyderabad 500 029 (A.P.), INDIA
Email: centraloffice@orientblackswan.com

Other Offices
Bangalore, Bhopal, Bhubaneshwar, Chennai, Ernakulam, Guwahati, Hyderabad, Jaipur, Kolkata, Lucknow, Mumbai, New Delhi, Patna

© Satish Chandra 2007
First published by Orient Longman Private Limited 2007
First Orient Blackswan impression 2009
Reprinted 2009, 2010, 2011

ISBN 13: 978 81 250 3226 7
ISBN 10: 81 250 3226 6

Maps by Cartography Department,
Sangam Books (India) Private Limited,
Hyderabad

Typeset by
Bukprint
Delhi

Printed in India at
B.B. Press
Noida

Published by
Orient Blackswan Private Limited
1/24 Asaf Ali Road
New Delhi 110 002
Email: delhi@orientblackswan.com

Contents

Classes: The Nobles and Zamindars • Zamindars and
the Rural Gentry • The Middle Strata • Organization of
Trade and Commerce • Foreign Trade and the European
Traders

List of Maps

Preface

As a nation grows, it is bound to review its past to see what part of its legacy is relevant, or an inhibiting factor, for growth. The medieval period of Indian history has often been equated to the period of Turkish and Mughal rule over the country. This meant that primacy was given to political factors rather than societal ones. This attitude was also based on the assumption that there has been little change in Indian society down the centuries. This attitude has now begun to change. Historians have traced the evolution of tribe-based society in India to the rise of territorial states, and the gradual formation of classes and castes within this state system. It has also been shown that with the growing trend towards ownership of land, and the desire to dominate and control those engaged in cultivation, a new form of society arose—that is, the feudal mode. It has, however, been recognized that there were vital differences between this social order and the feudal order in Europe.

Without trying to investigate these differences in detail, an attempt has been made to trace the evolution of social, economic, political and cultural trends in India from the eight century to the end of the seventeenth century. It is a daunting task to bring all these aspects together in a single volume. An attempt has been made in the hope that the summation of the efforts of many historians during the last four decades to give a new orientation to medieval Indian history would stimulate public interest, and also put in better perspective recent controversies regarding the nature of the state in medieval India, the extent of religious freedom to peoples within it, and the nature of the economic growth during the period.

A point has been made in the book that the emergence of large empires followed by their breakdown into smaller components and vice versa did not necessarily mean economic stagnation and cultural decay. Even when larger states emerged subsequently, there was often an active interchange between the new center and the regional states.

Thus, Indian history is not just an endless story of the rise and fall of empires without any institutional and cultural growth, as Sir Charles Elliot had postulated in his introduction to the eight-volume *History of India as Told by its Own Historians*. Indian history is a much more complex web with the center of gravity shifting from north to east, or to the south, and back again, and finally, for a long period the forces of growth triumphing under the Mughals over the forces of disintegration. The process of disintegration during the eighteenth century, and a re-integration under vastly different circumstances under the British and its harmful consequences have not been touched upon here.

In the end, I would like to thank Orient Longman for bringing out this work, despite many difficulties.

Satish Chandra
New Delhi
January 2007

ONE

India and the World

The thousand year period between the eighth and the eighteenth century saw important changes in India and the world. New social and political forms rose in Europe as well as Asia. The new forms also had profound effects on the thinking and living patterns of the peoples. These changes had an impact on India also since India had long-standing trade and cultural relations with countries around the Mediterranean Sea, and the various empires which arose in the area, including the Roman and Persian empires.

EUROPE

In Europe, the mighty Roman empire had broken into two by the third quarter of the sixth century. The western part with its capital at Rome had been overwhelmed by the Slav and Germanic tribesmen coming from the side of Russia and Germany. These tribes came in many waves, and indulged in a great deal of ravaging and plundering in the territories of the old Roman empire. But, in course of time, these tribes settled down in different parts of Europe, profoundly changing the character of the old population as well as the languages and pattern of governments. The foundations of many of the modern European nations were laid during this period as a result of the commingling of these tribesmen with the local population.

The eastern part of the old Roman empire had its capital at Byzantium or Constantinopole. This empire which was called the Byzantine empire included most of eastern Europe as well as modern Turkey, Syria and North Africa, including Egypt. It continued many of the traditions of the Roman empire such as a strong monarchy and a highly centralized administration. However, in belief and ritual, it had many differences with the Catholic Church in the West which had its head quarters at Rome. The church in the East was called the Greek Orthodox Church. It was due to its efforts and those of the Byzantine rulers that Russia was converted to Christianity. The

Byzantine empire was a large and flourishing empire which continued to trade with Asia after the collapse of the Roman empire in the West. It created traditions of government and culture many of which were later absorbed by the Arabs when they overran Syria and Egypt. It also acted as a bridge between the Greco-Roman civilization and the Arab world, and later helped in the revival of Greek learning in the West. It disappeared finally in the middle of the fifteenth century when Constantinopole fell to the Turks.

For centuries after the collapse of the Roman empire in the West, the cities virtually disappeared in western Europe. One cause of this was the absence of gold which the Romans had obtained from Africa and used for trade with the Orient. The period between the sixth and tenth centuries was for long called a 'Dark Age' by historians. However, this was also a period of agricultural expansion which prepared the way for the revival of city life from the tenth century, and growth of foreign trade. Between the twelfth and the fourteenth century, western Europe was again able to attain a high level of prosperity. A notable feature of the period was the growth of science and technology, growth of towns, and the establishment of universities in a number of cities, such as Padua and Milan in Italy. The universities played an important part in the growth of new learning and new ideas which were gradually to lead to the Renaissance and the rise of a new Europe.

Growth of Feudalism

A new type of society and a new system of government rose in western Europe, following the breakup of the Roman empire. The new order that gradually emerged is called feudalism. This is derived from the Latin word *feudum* which in English became fief. In this society the most powerful elements were the chiefs who, with their military following, dominated large tracts of land and also played an important part in government. The king was just like one of the more powerful feudal chiefs. In course of time, the monarchy became stronger and an attempt was made to limit the power of the chiefs, who constantly fought each other leading to a state of social anarchy. One method of controlling this was that the king swore the chiefs to an oath of loyalty to him as his vassals, and, in return, recognized the tract of land dominated by the chiefs as their fiefs. The chiefs, in turn, could appoint sub-chiefs as vassals, and allot a tract out of their fief to them. The king could, in theory, resume the fief of a disloyal vassal, but, in practice, this was rarely done. Thus, in the feudal system, government was dominated by a landed aristocracy. The aristocracy soon became hereditary and tried its best not to admit outsiders to its fold. But it was never a completely closed aristocracy, with disloyal chiefs being removed, and new ones being appointed, or rising to power.

The feudal system is associated with two other features. First is the system of serfdom. A serf was a peasant who worked on the land but could not change his profession, or migrate to any other area or marry without the permission of his lord or master. Associated with this system was the manor. The manor was the house or castle where the lord lived. In many of the European countries, large tracts of land were owned by the lords of these manors. A part of the land was cultivated by the lord directly with the help of serfs who had to divide their time between cultivating their own fields and the fields of their master. The land belonged theoretically to the lord, and the serf had to pay him other dues in cash and kind. The lord of the manor also had the responsibility of maintaining law and order, dispensing justice, etc. Since there was a great deal of lawlessness in those days, even free peasants were sometimes prepared to accept the vassalage of the lord of the manor in return for protection.

Some historians think that the system of serfdom and the manor system are vital parts of feudalism, and that it is wrong to speak of feudalism for societies in which these two did not exist. In India, for instance, there was no serfdom and no manor system as such. But the local landed elements (*samantas*) exercised many of the powers of the feudal lords, and the peasantry was in a dependent position to them. In other words, what mattered was not whether the peasantry was formally free, but the manner and the extent to which it could exercise its freedom. In many countries of western Europe, the manor system, and the system of labour dues by the peasants disappeared after the fourteenth century.

The second feature associated with the feudal system in Europe is the system of military organization. The most typical symbol of the feudal system was the armoured knight on horseback. Actually, the system of cavalry warfare can roughly be traced back in Europe only to the eighth century. In the Roman times, the chief wings of the army were the heavy and light infantry, armed with long spears and short swords. Horses were used to draw chariots in which the officers rode. It is generally believed that the mode of warfare changed with the arrival of the Arabs. The Arabs had a large supply of horses and their swift movements and mounted archers made the infantry largely ineffective. The problem of developing and maintaining the organization needed for the new mode of warfare helped in the growth of feudalism in Europe. No king could hope to maintain out of his own resources the large body of cavalry that was needed, and to provide them with armour and equipment. Hence, the army was decentralized, assigning to the fief-holders the responsibility of maintaining a fixed force of cavalry and infantry for the service of the king.

Cavalry warfare became the principal mode of warfare on account of two inventions which, though much older, began to be used on a large scale during this period. The first was the iron stirrup. The iron stirrup made it possible for a heavily armoured person to sit firmly on a horse without falling off. It also made possible a cavalry charge with lances held tightly to the body, without the rider being thrown off by the shock of the impact. The earlier device was either a wooden stirrup or a piece of rope which only provided a toe-hold. Another invention was a new type of harness which enabled a horse to draw twice the amount of load it pulled earlier. It is believed that both these inventions came to Europe from the East, possibly from East Asia. They spread in India from the tenth century onwards.

Thus, many factors, political, economic and military, were responsible for the growth of feudalism in Europe. Even when stronger governments emerged after the eleventh century, the tradition had become too strong for the king to reduce easily the power of the feudal chiefs.

Apart from the system of feudalism, the pattern of life in Europe during what is called the medieval period was also shaped by the Christian Church. We have already referred to the role of the Greek Orthodox Church in the Byzantine empire and in Russia. In the absence of a powerful empire in the West, the Catholic Church took on some of the functions of the government as well. The Pope, who was the head of the Catholic Church, became not only a religious head, but also a figure who exercised a great deal of political and moral authority. In Europe, as in West Asia and in India, the Medieval Age was an age of religion, and those who spoke on behalf of religion exercised a great deal of power and influence. With the help of grants of land from the princes and feudal chiefs, and donations from rich merchants, many monastic orders and monasteries were set up. Some of these orders, such as that of the Franciscans, served the needy and the poor. Many monasteries, gave medical help, or shelter to the travellers. They also served as centres for education and learning. In this way, the Catholic Church played an important role in the cultural life of Europe.

However, some of the monasteries which became exceedingly wealthy began to behave like feudal lords. This led to internal discord, and conflict with the rulers who resented the worldly power of the Church and of the Popes. This conflict was reflected in the Renaissance and Reform movements later on.

THE ARAB WORLD

The rise of Islam from the seventh century onwards was instrumental in uniting the warring Arab tribes into a powerful empire. The Arab empire founded by the early caliphs embraced, apart from Arabia, Syria, Iraq, Iran, Egypt, North Africa and Spain.

Following internal differences and civil war among the Arab tribes, in the middle of the eighth century the caliph at Damascus was displaced, and a new dynasty, called the Abbasids came to power. They set up their capital at the newly founded city of Baghdad. The Abbasids claimed to belong to the same tribe to which the Prophet Muhammad belonged, and were for that reason considered holy. For about 150 years the Abbasid empire was one of the most powerful and flourishing empire in the world. At its height, it included all the important centres of civilization in the area, viz., parts of North Africa, Egypt, Syria, Iran and Iraq. The Abbasids controlled not only some of the most important regions of West Asia and North Africa but also commanded the important trade routes linking the Mediterranean world with India. The safety and security which the Abbasids provided to these trade routes was an important factor for the wealth and prosperity of the people in the area, and of the splendour and magnificence of the Abbasid court. The Arabs were keen merchants and quickly emerged as the most enterprising and wealthy merchants and seafarers in the world during the period. Numerous cities, with magnificent buildings, both private and public, arose. The standard of living and the cultural environment of the Arab towns could hardly be paralled in any country in the world during the period. The Arabs also established the gold *dinar* and the silver *dirham* which became the currency of trade all over the world. This was made possible by the Arab access to African gold. The Arabs also established double entry book-keeping, advanced accountancy, and large scale and elaborate banking and credit, including bills of exchange (*hundis*).

The most famous caliphs of this period were al-Mamun and Harun al-Rashid. The splendour of their court and their palaces, and of their patronage to men of science and learning, became subjects of numerous stories and legends. During the early period, the Arabs displayed a remarkable capacity of assimilating the scientific knowledge and administrative skills of the ancient civilizations they had overrun. For managing the administration, they had no hesitation in employing non-Muslims, such as Christians and Jews, and also non-Arabs, particularly the Iranians, many of whom were Zoroastrians or even Buddhists. Although the Abbasid caliphs were orthodox Muslims, they opened wide the gate of learning from all quarters as long as it did not challenge the fundamental tenets of Islam. The Caliph al-Mamun set up a 'House of Wisdom' (*bait-ul-hikmat*) at Baghdad for translating into Arabic the learning from various civilizations—Greek, Byzantine, Egyptian, Iranian and Indian. The example set by the Caliphs was followed by individual nobles. In a short space of time, almost all the important scientific works of the various countries had become available in Arabic. We know a good deal about the impact of Greek science and philosophy on the Arabs, largely due to the work done in recent years by a devoted band of European scholars. We are also beginning to have a better idea of the impact of Chinese science and philosophy on the Arab world. Many Chinese inventions such as the compass, paper, printing, gun-powder and even the humble wheel-barrow travelled from China to Europe via the Arabs during this period. The famous Venetian traveller, Marco Polo, travelled to China in order to know more about it, and to breach the Arab monopoly of Europe's trade with China.

Unfortunately, we have only a limited knowledge of India's economic and cultural relations with the Arab world during the period, and India's scientific contribution to it. After its conquest by the Arabs in the eighth century, Sind did become a conduit of scientific and cultural links between India and the Arab world. The decimal system which is the basis of modern mathematics and which had developed in India in the fifth century, travelled to the Arab world during this period. During the ninth century it was popularized in the region by the Arab mathematician al-Khwarizmi. It was introduced to Europe in the twelfth century by a monk, Abelard, and became known as the system of Arab numerals! Many Indian works dealing with astronomy and mathematics were also translated into Arabic. The famous work on astronomy, *Surya Siddhanta*, which had been revised and reformed by Aryabhatta was one of these. Works of Charak and Sushruta dealing with medicine were also translated. Indian traders and merchants continued to visit the marts of Iraq and Iran, and Indian physicians and master-craftsmen were received at the caliph's court at Baghdad. A number of Sanskrit literary works, such as *Kalila wa Dimma* (*Panchatantra*) were also translated into Arabic and formed the basis of *Aesop's Fables* in the West. A more detailed study of the impact of Indian sciences and philosophy on the Arab world and of the Arab sciences on India is now being made.

By the beginning of the tenth century, the Arabs had reached the stage when they could make their own contribution to the various sciences. The growth of geometry, algebra, geography, astronomy, optics, chemistry, medicine, etc., in the Arab world during this period made it the leader in the field of science. The writings of Arab geographers, and their maps advanced knowledge about the world. The Arabs also helped to develop new devices for travelling across the open sea. These devices continued to be used till the fifteenth century. The accounts of the Arab traders about India and the neighbouring countries during this period is a useful source of information for us.

Some of the best stocked libraries in the world, and the leading scientific laboratories were established in the Arab world during the period. However, it is necessary to remember that many of these achievements were the result of work done by people outside Arabia, in Khurasan, Egypt, Spain, etc. The Arab science was truly international. It has been called Arab science because Arabic was the language of literature and thought in the entire area, and the people from various countries could move freely and work or settle down anywhere they liked. The remarkable degree of intellectual and personal freedom enjoyed by scientists and scholars as well as the patronage extended to them was an important factor in the remarkable growth of Arab science and civilization. Such freedom was not available in Europe at that time due to the rigid attitude of the church. Perhaps, conditions in India were similar, for hardly any of the Arab sciences could filter into India, and the growth of Indian science slowed down during the period.

Arab science began to decline after the twelfth century partly due to political and economic developments affecting the area, but even more on account of growing orthodoxy which stifled free thought. But it continued to grow in Spain until the fourteenth century.

AFRICA

The Arabs also brought Africa more closely into the Indian Ocean and Middle Eastern trade. Arab migrations and mercantile activity along the east coast of Africa increased enormously, extending upto Malindi, Zanzibar etc. However, the Arab trade included large scale export of slaves, as also gold, ivory, etc. There was in Africa a powerful Ethiopian kingdom of long standing which had many towns. The Ethiopians were engaged in the Indian Ocean trade across Aden to India. The Ethiopians, called Habshis, were Christians. They were closely allied to the Byzantine empire in the Indian Ocean trade. Their economic position weakened with the decline of the Byzantine empire.

EAST AND SOUTHEAST ASIA

China's society and culture had attained a climax in the eighth and ninth centuries under Tang rule. The Tang rulers extended their overlordship over large parts of Sinkiang in Central Asia, including Kashgar. This helped in giving a fillip to the overland trade across what is called the Silk Road. Not only silk, but fine quality porcelain, and works in jade—a semi-precious stone—were exported to West Asia, Europe and India across this road. Foreign traders were welcome in China. Many of them—Arabs, Persians and Indians—came to South China, across the land and the seas, and settled down in Canton.

The Tang empire declined in the middle of the ninth century, and was replaced in the tenth century by another dynasty, the Sung, which ruled over China for about one hundred years. Its growing weakness gave an opportunity to the Mongols to conquer China in the thirteenth century. The Mongols wrought great death and destruction in China. But due to their highly disciplined and mobile cavalry forces, the Mongol rulers were able to unify north and south China under one rule for the first time. For some time, they also brought under their sway Tonkin (north Vietnam) and Annam (south Vietnam). In the north, they overran Korea. Thus, the Mongols established one of the largest empires in East Asia.

The Venetian traveller, Marco Polo, who spent some time at the court of Kublai Khan, the most famous of the Mongol rulers of China, has left a picturesque account of his court. Marco Polo returned to Italy by sea, visiting Malabar in India on the way. Thus, already different parts of the world were coming closer together, and their commercial and cultural contacts were increasing.

The countries of Southeast Asia had to meet the expansionist urges of some of the Chinese rulers, China having developed a strong navy by this time. But during most of the time, the Southeast Asian states remained independent. The two most powerful kingdoms which flourished in the region during the period were the Sailendra and Kambuja empires.

The Sailendra dynasty which arose in the seventh century, and largely displaced the Sri Vijaya empire, flourished till the tenth century. At its height, the empire included Sumatra, Java, the Malaya peninsula, parts of Siam (modern Thailand) and even the Philippines. According to a ninth century Arab writer, the empire was so large that even the fastest vessel could not complete a round trip of it in two years. The Sailendra rulers had a powerful navy, and dominated the sea trade to China. The Pallavas of south India also had a powerful navy. The Pallava navy was especially active in the Bay of Bengal. The sea trade with the countries of Southeast Asia and China was so important that in the tenth century, a Chola ruler sent a series of naval expeditions to Sumatra and Malaya to keep the sea lanes of communications open. Since the early centuries of the Christian era and even before, India had close trade and cultural contacts with the countries of the area. Many Chinese and Indian scholars visited Palembang, the capital of the empire, which was located in Sumatra, and which had been a Sanskrit and Buddhist centre of study even earlier. The rulers built magnificent temples during the period, the most famous of them being the temple of Borobodur in east Java dedicated to the Buddha. It is a whole mountain carved into nine stone terraces, surmounted by a stupa. Indian epics, such as the *Ramayana* and the *Mahabharata* are displayed in the panels of the temple. These epics continued to provide the themes for literature, folk-art, puppet-plays, etc.

The Kambuja empire extended over Cambodia and Annam (south Vietnam) and replaced the Hinduized kingdom of Funan which had dominated the area earlier. The Kambuja empire flourished till the fifteenth century and attained a high level of cultural development and prosperity. Its most magnificent achievement may be considered the group of temples near Ankor Thom in Cambodia. Begun in the tenth century, each ruler built a new temple there to commemorate his memory till about two hundred temples were built in an area of 3.2 square kilometres. Of these, the largest is the temple of Ankor Wat. It has three kilometres of covered passages containing beautiful statues of Hindu gods, goddesses and nymphs (*apsaras*), and skillfully executed panels containing scenes from the *Ramayana* and the *Mahabharata*. This entire group of buildings had been completely forgotten by the outside world and been largely taken over by the jungle, till it was 'discovered' by a Frenchman in 1860. It is interesting to note that the most vigorous period of temple building activity was the period from the tenth to the twelfth century, which was also the most magnificent period of temple building activity in India.

Many Indian traders went to south China, after travelling overland from the port of Takkala in the Malaya peninsula to the South China Sea. Many brahmans, and later Buddhist monks settled in countries of Southeast Asia and in south China. Buddhism travelled from China to Korea and Japan. Indian monks reached Korea and influenced the evolution of a Korean script near to the Indian one. While Buddhism declined in India, in course of time, it continued to flourish in Southeast Asia. In fact, it assimilated the Hindu gods into the Buddhist fold, and even took over the Hindu temples—a movement opposite to what was happening in India at that time.

Thus, India had close commercial and cultural contacts both with the West, Southeast Asia, China, as also Madagascar and countries on the east coast of Africa. The various kingdoms in Southeast Asia acted as a kind of a bridge for commercial and cultural contacts between India and China, and the outside world. Though deeply influenced by Indian civilization and culture, they were able to attain a distinctive culture of their own of a very high order. Arab traders who had been trading with south India and with the countries of Southeast Asia earlier, became even more active after the establishment of the Abbasid empire. But the Arabs did not displace the Indian traders and preachers. In the early phase, they did not make any special effort to convert the people of the area to Islam. Thus, a remarkable degree of religious freedom and tolerance, and the commingling of various cultures marked these countries, a characteristic they have retained even today. The conversion of Indonesia and Malaya to Islam took place gradually, after Islam had consolidated its position in India. Elsewhere, Buddhism continued to flourish. Commercial and cultural contacts between India and these countries were snapped only with the establishment of the Dutch rule in Indonesia, the English rule in India, Burma and Malaya, and later, the French rule in Indo-China.

Two

Northern India: Age of the Three Empires (800–1000)

After the decline of Harsha's empire in the seventh century, a number of large states arose in north India, the Deccan and south India. Unlike the Gupta and Harsha's empire in north India, none of the other kingdoms in north India were able to bring the entire Ganga valley under its control. The Ganga valley with its population and other resources was the basis on which the Gupta rulers and Harsha had been able to extend their control over Gujarat which, with its rich sea ports and manufacturers, was important for overseas trade. Malwa and Rajasthan were the essential links between the Ganga valley and Gujarat. This defined the geographical limits of an empire in north India. In south India, the Cholas were able to bring the Krishna, Godavari and the Kaveri deltas under their control. This was the basis of their supremacy in south India.

Large states arose in north India and the Deccan between AD 750 and 1000. These were the Pala empire, which dominated eastern India till the middle of the ninth century; the Pratihara empire, which dominated western India and the upper Gangetic valley till the middle of the tenth century, and the Rashtrakuta empire, which dominated the Deccan and also controlled territories in north and south India at various times. Each of these empires, although they fought among themselves, provided stable conditions of life over large areas, extended agriculture, built ponds and canals, and gave patronage to arts and letters, including temples. Of the three, the Rashtrakuta empire lasted the longest. It was not only the most powerful empire of the time, but also acted as a bridge between north and south India in economic as well as in cultural matters.

THE STRUGGLE FOR DOMINATION IN NORTH INDIA: THE PALAS

The period following the death of Harsha was a period of political confusion. For some time, Lalitaditya, the ruler of Kashmir brought the Punjab under his control and even controlled Kanauj which, since the days of Harsha, was considered the symbol of the sovereignty of north India—a position which Delhi was to acquire later. Control of Kanauj also implied control of the upper Gangetic valley and its rich resources in trade and agriculture. Lalitaditya even invaded Bengal or Gaud, and killed its reigning king. But his power waned with the rise of the Palas and the Gurjara-Pratiharas.

The Palas and the Pratiharas clashed with each other for the control of the area extending from Banaras to south Bihar which again had rich resources and well developed imperial traditions. The Pratiharas also clashed with the Rashtrakutas of the Deccan.

The Pala empire was founded by Gopala, probably in AD 750 when he was elected king by the notable men of the area to end the anarchy prevailing there. Gopala was not born in a high, much less a royal family, his father probably being a soldier. He unified Bengal under his control, and even brought Magadha (Bihar) under his control. Gopala was succeeded in AD 770 by his son, Dharamapala, who ruled till AD 810. His reign was marked by a tripartite struggle between the Palas, the Pratiharas and the Rashtrakutas for the control of Kanauj and north India. The Pratihara ruler advanced upon Gaud (Bengal), but before a decision could be taken, the Pratihara ruler was defeated by the Rashtrakuta ruler, Dhruva, and was forced to seek refuge in the deserts of Rajasthan. Dhruva then returned to the Deccan. This left the field free for Dharmapala who occupied Kanauj and held a grand darbar which was attended by vassal rulers from Punjab, eastern Rajasthan, etc. We are told that the rule of Dharmapala extended upto the furthest limit of India in the northwest and, perhaps, included Malwa and Berar. Apparently, this implied that the rulers of these areas accepted the suzerainty of Dharmapala.

The triumphal career of Dharmapala may be placed between AD 790 and 800. Dharmapala could not, however, consolidate his power in north India. The Pratihara power revived under Nagabhatta II. Dharmapala fell back, but was defeated near Mongyr. Bihar and modern east Uttar Pradesh remained a bone of contention between the Palas and the Pratiharas. However, Bihar, in addition to Bengal, remained under the control of the Palas for most of the time.

Failure in the north compelled the Pala rulers to turn their energies in other directions. Devapala, the son of Dharmapala, who succeeded to the throne in AD 810 and ruled for 40 years, extended his control over Pragjyotishpur (Assam) and parts of Orissa. Probably a part of modern Nepal was also brought under Pala suzerainty.

Thus, for about a hundred years, from the middle of the eighth to the middle of the ninth century, the Pala rulers dominated eastern India. For some time, their control extended upto Varanasi. Their power is attested to by an Arab merchant, Sulaiman, who visited India in the middle of the ninth century, and wrote an account of it. He calls the Pala Kingdom Ruhma, (or Dharma, short for Dharmapala), and says that the Pala ruler was at war with his neighbours, the Pratiharas and the Rashtrakutas, but his troops were more numerous that his adversaries. He tells us that it was customary for the Pala king to be accompanied by a force of 50,000 elephants, and that 10,000–15,000 men in his army were employed 'in fulling and washing clothes'. Even if these figures may be exaggerated, we can assume that the Palas had a large military force at their disposal. But we do not know whether they had a large standing army, or whether their forces consisted largely of feudal levies. Information about the Palas is also provided to us by Tibetan chronicles, although these were written in the seventeenth century. According to these, the Pala rulers were great patrons of Buddhist learning and religion. The Nalanda university which had been famous all over the eastern world was revived by Dharmapala, and 200 villages were set apart for meeting its expenses. He also founded the Vikramasila university which became second only to Nalanda in fame. It was located on the top of a hill, on the banks of the Ganga in Magadha, amidst pleasant surroundings. The Palas built many *viharas* in which a large number of Buddhist monks lived.

The Pala rulers also had close cultural relations with Tibet. The noted Buddhist scholars, Santarakshita and Dipankara (called Atisa), were invited to Tibet, and they introduced a new form of Buddhism there. As a result, many Tibetan Buddhists flocked to the universities of Nalanda and Vikramsila for study. Although the Palas were supporters of Buddhism, they also extended their patronage to Saivism and Vaishnavism. They gave grants to large numbers of brahmans from north India who flocked to Bengal. Their settlements helped in the extension of cultivation in the area, and the transformation of many pastoralists and food-gatherers to settle down to cultivation. The growing prosperity of Bengal helped in extending trade and cultural contacts with countries of Southeast Asia—Burma, Malaya, Java, Sumatra, etc.

The trade with Southeast Asia was very profitable and added greatly to the prosperity of the Pala empire and led to the incursion of gold and silver from these countries into Bengal. The powerful Sailendra dynasty, which was Buddhist in faith and which ruled over Malaya, Java, Sumatra and the neighbouring islands, sent many embassies to the Pala court and sought permission to build a monastery at Nalanda, and also requested the Pala ruler, Devapala, to endow five villages for its upkeep. The request was granted and bears testimony to the close relations between the two empires.

THE PRATIHARAS

The Pratiharas who ruled over Kanauj for a long time are also called Gurjara-Pratiharas. Most scholars consider that they originated from the Gurjaras who were pastoralists and fighters, like the Jats. The Pratiharas established a series of principalities in central and eastern Rajasthan. They clashed with the Rashtrakutas for the control of Malwa and Gujarat, and later for Kanauj which implied control of the upper Ganga valley. The Pratiharas who first had their capital at Bhinmal gained prominence under Nagabhatta I who offered stout resistance to the Arab rulers of Sind who were trying to encroach on Rajasthan, Gujarat, the Punjab, etc. The Arabs made a big thrust towards Gujarat but were decisively defeated by the Chalukyan ruler of Gujarat in 738. Although small Arab incursions continued, the Arabs ceased to be a threat thereafter.

The efforts of the early Pratihara rulers to extend their control over the upper Ganga valley and Malwa were defeated by the Rashtrakuta rulers Dhruva and Gopal III. In 790 and again in 806–07, the Rashtrakutas defeated the Pratiharas, and then withdrew to the Deccan, leaving the field free for the Palas. Perhaps the main interest of the Rashtrakutas was the domination of Malwa and Gujarat. The real founder of the Pratihara empire and the greatest ruler of the dynasty was Bhoja. We do not know much about the early life of Bhoja, or when he ascended the throne. He rebuilt the empire, and by about AD 836 he had recovered Kanauj which remained the capital of the Pratihara empire for almost a century.

Bhoja tried to extend his sway in the east, but he was defeated and checkmated by the Pala ruler, Devapala. He then turned towards central India and the Deccan and Gujarat. This led to a revival of the struggle with the Rashtrakutas. In a sanguinary battle on the bank of the Narmada, Bhoja was able to retain his control over considerable parts of Malwa, and some parts of Gujarat. But he could progress no further in the Deccan. Hence, he turned his attention to the north again. According to an inscription, his territories extended to the western side of the river Sutlej. Arab travellers tell us that the Pratihara rulers had the best cavalry in India. Import of horses from Central Asia and Arabia was an important item of India's trade at that time. Following the death of Devapala and the weakening of the Pala empire, Bhoja also extended his empire in the east.

The name of Bhoja is famous in legends. Perhaps, the adventures of Bhoja in the early part of his life, his gradual reconquest of his lost empire, and his final recovery of Kanauj struck the imagination of his contempories. Bhoja was a devotee of Vishnu, and adopted the title of 'Adivaraha' which has been found inscribed in some of his coins. He is sometimes called Mihir Bhoja to distinguish him form Bhoja Paramara of Ujjain who ruled a little later.

Bhoja probably died in about 885. He was succeeded by his son Mahendrapala I. Mahendrapala, who ruled till about 908–09 maintained the empire of Bhoja and extended it over Magadha and north Bengal. His inscriptions have also been found in Kathiawar, east Punjab and Awadh. Mahendrapala fought a battle with the king of Kashmir but had to yield to him some of the territories in the Punjab won by Bhoja.

The Pratiharas, thus, dominated north India for over a hundred years, from the early ninth to the middle of the tenth century. Al-Masudi, a native of Baghdad, who visited Gujarat in 915–16, testifies to the great power and prestige of the Pratihara rulers and the vastness of their empire. He calls the Gurjara-Pratihara kingdom al-Juzr (a corrupt form of Gurjara), and the king Baura, probably a mispronounciation of Adivaraha the title used by Bhoja, although Bhoja had died by that time. Al-Masudi says that the empire of Juzr had 1,80,000 villages, cities and rural areas and was about 2000 km in length and 2000 km in breadth. The king's army had four divisions, each consisting of 7,00,000 to 9,00,000 men: 'with the army of the north he fights against the ruler of Multan and other Muslims who align themselves with him.' The army of the south fought against the Rashtrakutas, and that of the east against the Palas. He had only 2000 elephants trained for war, but the best cavalry of any king in the country.

The Pratiharas were patrons of learning and literature. The great Sanskrit poet and dramatist, Rajashekhar, lived at the court of Mahipala, a grandson of Bhoja. The Pratihara also embellished Kanauj with many fine buildings and temples.

During the eighth and ninth centuries, many Indian scholars went with embassies to the court of the caliph at Baghdad. These scholars introduced Indian sciences, especially mathematics, algebra and medicine to the Arab world. We do not know the names of the Indian kings who sent these embassies. The Pratiharas were well-known for their hostility to the Arab rulers of Sind. Despite this, it seems that the movement of scholars and goods between India and West Asia continued even during this period.

Between 915 and 918, the Rashtrakuta king, Indra III, again attacked Kanauj, and devastated the city. This weakened the Pratihara empire, and Gujarat probably passed into the hands of the Rashtrakutas, for al-Masudi tells us that the Pratihara empire had no access to the sea. The loss of Gujarat, which was the hub of the overseas trade and the main outlet for north Indian goods to West Asian countries, was another blow to the Pratiharas. Another Rashtrakuta ruler, Krishna III, invaded north India in about 963 and defeated the Pratihara ruler. This was followed by the rapid dissolution of the Pratihara empire.

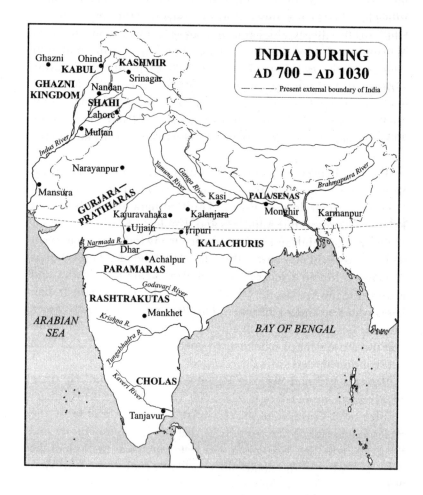

INDIA DURING
AD 700 – AD 1030
– – – – – – Present external boundary of India

Ghazni   Ohind   **KASHMIR**
KABUL   Srinagar
GHAZNI   Nandan
KINGDOM
SHAHI
Lahore
Multan
Indus River
Narayanpur
Mansura
GURJARA–
PRATIHARAS
Yamuna River   *Ganga River*   Kasi   **PALA/SENAS**
Kajuravahaka   Kalanjara   Monghir   Karmanpur
Ujjain   Tripuri   *Brahmaputra River*
Narmada R.   **KALACHURIS**
Dhar
Achalpur
PARAMARAS
Godavari River
RASHTRAKUTAS
Krishna R.   Mankhet
ARABIAN
SEA   *Tungabhadra R.*
BAY OF BENGAL
Kaveri River   **CHOLAS**
Tanjavur

THE RASHTRAKUTAS

While the Palas and the Pratiharas were ruling over north India, the Deccan was being ruled by the Rashtrakutas, a remarkable dynasty which produced a long line of warriors and able administrators. The kingdom was founded by Dantidurga who set up his capital at Manyakhet or Malkhed near modem Sholapur. The Rashtrakutas soon dominated the entire area of northern Maharashtra. They also engaged with the Pratiharas for the overlordship of Gujarat and Malwa as we have seen above. Although their raids did not result in the extension of the Rashtrakuta empire to the Ganga valley, they brought rich plunder, and added to the fame of the Rashtrakutas. The Rashtrakutas also fought constantly against the eastern Chalukyas of Vengi (in modern Andhra Pradesh) and in the south against the Pallavas of Kanchi and the Pandyas of Madurai.

Probably the greatest Rashtrakuta rulers were Govinda III (793–814) and Amoghavarsha (814–878). After a successful expedition against Nagabhatta of Kanauj and the annexation of Malwa, Govinda III turned to the south. We are told in an inscription that Govinda 'terrified the Kerala, Pandya and the Chola kings and caused the Pallavas to wither. The Ganga (of Karnataka), who became dissatisfied through baseness, were bound down with fetters and met with death.' The king of Lanka and his minister who had been negligent of their own interests, were captured and brought over as prisoners to Halapur. Two statues of the lord of Lanka were carried to Manyakhet, and installed like pillars of victory in front of a Siva temple.

Amoghavarsha ruled for 64 years but by temperament he preferred the pursuit of religion and literature to war. He was himself an author and is credited with writing the first Kannada book on poetics. He was a great builder, and is said to have built the capital city Manyakhet so as to excel the city of Indra.

There were many rebellions in the far flung Rashtrakuta empire under Amoghavarsha. These could be barely contained, and began afresh after his death. His grandson, Indra III, (915–927) re-established the empire. After the defeat of Mahipala and the sack of Kanauj in 915, Indra III was the most powerful ruler of his times.

According to al-Masudi who visited India at that time, the Rashtrakuta king, Balhara or Vallabharaja, was the greatest king of India and most of the Indian rulers accepted his suzerainty and respected his envoys. He possessed large armies and innumerable elephants.

Krishna III (934–963) was the last in a line of brilliant rulers. He was engaged in a struggle against the Paramaras of Malwa and the eastern Chalukyas of Vengi. He also launched a campaign against the Chola ruler of Tanjore, who had supplanted the Pallavas of Kanchi. Krishna III defeated the Chola king, Parantaka I (AD 949), and annexed the northern part of the Chola empire. He then pressed down to Rameshwaram and set up a pillar of victory there and built a temple. After his death, all his opponents united against his successor. The Rashtrakuta capital, Malkhed, was sacked and burnt in 972. This marked the end of the Rashtrakuta empire.

The Rashtrakuta rule in the Deccan thus lasted for almost two hundred years, till the end of the tenth century. The Rashtrakuta rulers were tolerant in their religious views and patronised not only Saivism and Vaishnavism but Jainism as well. The famous rock-cut temple of Siva at Ellora was built by one of the Rashtrakuta kings, Krishna I, in the ninth century. His successor, Amoghavarsha, is said to have been a Jain but be also patronised other faiths. The Rashtrakutas allowed Muslim traders to settle, and permitted Islam to be preached, in their dominions. We are told that the Muslims had their own headman, and had large mosques for their daily prayers in many of the coastal towns in the Rashtrakuta empire. This tolerant policy helped to promote foreign trade which enriched the Rashtrakutas.

The Rashtrakuta kings were great patrons of arts and letters. In their courts, we find not only Sanskrit scholars, but also poets and others who wrote in Prakrit and in the *apabhramsha*, the so-called corrupt languages which were the fore-runners of the various modern Indian languages. The great *apabharamsha* poet, Svayambhu, and his son probably lived at the Rashtrakuta court.

POLITICAL IDEAS AND ORGANISATION

The system of administration in these empires was based on the ideas and practices of the Gupta empire, Harsha's kingdom in the north, and the Chalukyas in the Deccan. As before, the monarch was the centre of all affairs. He was the head of the administration as well as the commander-in-chief of the armed forces. He sat in a magnificent darbar. Squadrons of infantry and cavalry were stationed in the courtyard. Captured war-elephants and horses were paraded before him. He was attended by royal chamberlains, who regulated the coming and going of vassal chiefs, feudatories, ambassadors, and other high officials who regularly waited on the king. The king also dispensed justice. The court was not only a centre of political affairs and justice, but cultural life as well. Dancing girls and skilled musicians attended the court. Women of the King's household also attended the darbar on festive occasions. In the Rashtrakuta empire, according to Arab writers, women did not veil their faces.

The king's position was generally hereditary. Thinkers of the time emphasized absolute loyalty and obedience to the king because of the insecurity of the times. Wars were frequent between kings, and between kings and their vassals. While kings strove to maintain law and order within their kingdoms, their arms rarely extended far enough. Vassal rulers and autonomous chiefs often limited the area of the direct administration of the king, although the kings adopted high sounding titles such as *Maharajadiraj param-bhattaraka* etc., and claimed to be *chakravartin*, or supreme, of all Indian rulers. A contemporary writer, Medhatithi, thinks that it was the right of an individual to bear arms in order to defend himself against thieves and assassins. He also thinks that it was right to oppose an unjust king. Thus, the extreme view of royal rights and privileges, put forward mainly in the *Puranas*, was not accepted by all the thinkers.

The rules about succession were not rigidly fixed. The eldest son often succeeded, but there are many instances when the eldest son had to fight his younger brothers, and sometimes lost to them. Thus, the Rashtrakuta rulers Dhruva and Govinda IV, deposed their elder brothers. Sometimes, rulers designated the eldest son or another favourite son as their Yuvaraj or successor. In that case, the Yuvaraj stayed at the capital and helped in the task of administration. Younger sons were sometimes appointed provincial governors. Princesses were rarely appointed to government posts, but we do have an instance when a Rashtrakuta princess, Chandrobalabbe, a daughter of Amoghavarsha I, administered the Raichur doab for sometime.

Kings were generally advised by a number of ministers. The ministers were chosen by the king, generally from leading families. Their position was often hereditary. Thus, in the case of the Pala kings, we hear that a brahmana family supplied four successive chief ministers to Dharmapala and his successors. In such cases, the minister could become very powerful. Although we hear of a number of departments of the central government, we do not know how many of them were there and how they worked. From epigraphic and literary records, it appears that in almost every kingdom, there was a minister of correspondence which included foreign affairs, a revenue minister, treasurer, chief of the armed forces (*senapati*), chief justice, and *purohita*. More that one post could be combined in one person, and perhaps one of the ministers was considered the chief or the leading minister on whom the king leaned more than the others. All the ministers, except the *purohita*, were expected to lead military campaigns as well when called upon to do so. We also hear of officials of the royal household (*antahpur*). Since the king was the fountain head of all power, some of the officers of household became very powerful.

The armed forces were very important for the maintenance and expansion of the empire. We have already cited evidence from Arab travellers that the Pala, Pratihara and Rashtrakuta kings had large and well-organised infantry and cavalry, and large number of war-elephants. Elephants were supposed to be elements of strength and were greatly prized. The largest number of elephants was maintained by the Pala kings. Large numbers of horses were imported both by Rashtrakuta and Pratihara kings by sea from Arabia and West Asia, and over land from Khurasan (east Persia), and Central Asia. The Pratihara kings are believed to have had the finest cavalry in the country. There are no reference to war-chariots which had fallen out of use. Some of the kings, especially the Rashtrakutas, had a large number of forts. They were garrisoned by special troops, and had their own independent commanders. The infantry consisted of regular and irregular troops, and of levies provided by the vassal chiefs. The regular troops were often hereditary and sometimes drawn from different regions all over India. Thus, the Pala infantry consisted of soldiers from Malwa, Khasa (Assam), Lata (south Gujarat) and Karnataka. The Pala kings, and perhaps the Rashtrakutas, had their own navies, but we do not know much about their strength and organisation.

The empires consisted of area administered directly and areas ruled over by the vassal chiefs. The latter were autonomous as far as their internal affairs were concerned, and had a general obligation of loyalty, paying a fixed tribute and supplying the quota of troops to the overlord. Sometimes, a son of a vassal chief was required to stay in attendance of the overlord to guard against rebellion. The vassal chiefs were required to attend the darbar of the overlord on special occassions, and sometimes they were required to marry one of their daughters to the overlord or to one of his sons. But the vassal chiefs always aspired to be independent and wars between them and the overlord were frequent. Thus, the Rashtrakutas had to fight constantly against the vassal chiefs of Vengi (Andhra) and Karanataka; the Pratiharas had to fight against the Paramaras of Malwa and the Chandellas of Bundelkhand.

The directly administered territories in the Pala and Pratihara empires were divided into *bhukti* (provinces), and *mandala* or *visaya* (districts). The governor of a province was called *uparika* and the head of a district, *visayapati*. The *uparika* was expected to collect land revenue and maintain law and order with the help of the army. The *visayapati* was expected to do the same within his jurisdiction. During the period, there was an increase of smaller chieftains, called *samantas* or *bhogapatis*, who dominated over a number of villages. The *visayapatis* and these smaller chiefs tended to merge with each other, and later on the word *samanta* began to be used indiscriminately for both of them.

In the Rashtrakuta kingdom, the directly administered areas were divided into *rashtra* (provinces), *visaya* and *bhukti*. The head of *rashtra* was called *rashtrapati*, and he performed the same functions as the *uparika* did in the Pala and Pratihara empires. The *visaya* was like a modern district, and the *bhukti* was a smaller unit to it. In the Pala and Pratihara empires, the unit below the *visaya* was called *pattala*. The precise role of these smaller units is not known. It seems that their main purpose was the realization of land revenue and some attention to law and order. Apparently all the officials were paid by giving them grants of rent-free land. This tended to blur the distinction between local officials and the hereditary chiefs and smaller vassals. Similarly, the *rashtrapati* or governor sometimes enjoyed the status and title of a vassal king.

Below these territorial divisions was the village. The village was the basic unit of administration. The village administration was carried on by the village headman and the village accountant whose posts were generally hereditary. They were paid by grants of rent-free lands.

The head man was often helped in his duties by the village elders called *grama mahajana* or *grama mahattara*. In the Rashtrakuta kingdom, particularly in Karnataka, we are told that there were village committees to manage local schools, tanks, temples and roads. They could also receive money or property in trust, and manage them. These sub-committees worked in close cooperation with the headman and received a percentage of the revenue collection. Simple disputes were also decided by these committees. Towns had similar committees, to which the heads of trade guilds were also associated. Law and order in the towns and in areas in their immediate vicinity was the responsibility of the *koshta pala* or *kotwal*—a figure made familiar through many stories.

An important feature of the period was the rise in the Deccan of hereditary revenue officers called *nad gavundas* or *desa gramakutas*. They appear to have discharged the same functions as the deshmukhs and deshpandes of later times in Maharashtra. This development, along with the pettry chieftainships in north India which we have just mentioned, had an important bearing on society and politics. As the power of these hereditary elements grew, the village committees became weaker. The central ruler also found it difficult to assert his authority over them and to control them. This is what we mean when we say that the government was becoming 'feudalised'.

Another point to bear in mind is the relationship of state and religion during the time. Many of the rulers of that time were devout followers of Siva or Vishnu, or they followed the teachings of Buddhism or Jainism. They made handsome donations to the Brahmans, or the Buddhist *viharas* or the Jain temples. But, generally, they gave patronage to all the faiths, and did not persecute anyone for his or her religious beliefs. Muslims were also welcomed and allowed to preach their faith by the Rashtrakuta kings. Normally, a king was not expected to interfere with the customs, or with the code of conduct prescribed by the law books called the *Dharmashastras*. But he did have the general duty of protecting Brahmans and maintaining the division of society into four states or *varnas*. The *purohita* was expected to guide the king in this matter. But it should not be thought that the *purohita* interfered with state affairs or dominated the king. Medhatithi, the foremost expounder of *Dharmashastra* in this period, says that the king's authority was derived both from the *Dharmashastras*, including the *Vedas*, and from *Arthashastra* or the science of polity. His public duty or *rajadharma* was to be based on the *Arthshastra*, that is, on principles of politics. This really meant that politics and religion were, in essence, kept apart, religion being essentially a personal duty of the king. Thus, the kings were not dominated by the priests, or by the sacred law expounded by them. Religion was, however important for legitimizing and strengthening the position of the rulers. Many of the rulers therefore built grand temples, often at their capitals, and gave handsome land-grants for the maintenance of the temples and to the Brahmans.

THREE

South India: The Chola Empire (900–1200)

Powerful kingdoms had risen in south India during the sixth and eighth centuries. The most important among them were the Pallavas and the Pandyas who dominated modern Tamil Nadu, the Cheras of modern Kerala, and the Chalukyas who dominated the Maharashtra area or the Deccan. It was the Chalukyan king, Pulakesin II, who had defeated Harsha and not allowed him to expand his kingdom towards the Deccan. Some of these kingdoms, such as the Pallava and Pandya, had strong navies. They also played an important role in strengthening economic, religious and cultural relations with the countries of Southeast Asia, and with China. Their navies enabled them to invade and rule some parts of Sri Lanka for some time.

The Chola empire which arose in the ninth century brought under its control a large part of the peninsula. The Cholas developed a powerful navy which enabled them to conquer Sri Lanka and the Maldives. Its impact was felt even by the countries of Southeast Asia. The Chola empire may be said to mark a climax in south Indian history.

THE RISE OF THE CHOLA EMPIRE

The founder of the Chola empire was Vijayalaya, who was at first a feudatory of the Pallavas. He captured Tanjore in AD 850. And by the end of the ninth century, the Cholas had defeated both the Pallavas of Kanchi (Tondaimandalam) and weakened the Pandyas, bringing the southern Tamil country under their control. But the Cholas were hard put to defend their position against the Rashtrakutas. As we have noted in a previous chapter, Krishna III defeated the Chola king, and annexed the northern part of the Chola empire. This was a serious set-back to the Cholas, but they rapidly recovered, particularly after the death of Krishna III in 965 and the downfall of the Rashtrakuta empire.

The greatest Chola rulers were Rajaraja (985–1014) and his son Rajendra I (1014–1044). Rajaraja destroyed the Chera navy at Trivandrum, and attacked Quilon. He then conquered Madurai and captured the Pandyan king. He also invaded Sri Lanka and annexed its northern part to his empire. These moves were partly motivated by his desire to bring the trade with the Southeast Asian countries under his control. The Coromandel coast and Malabar were the centres for India's trade with the countries of Southeast Asia. One of his naval exploits was the conquest of the Maldives. Rajaraja, annexed the northwestern parts of the Ganga kingdom in Karnataka, and overran Vengi.

Rajendra had been appointed heir apparent in his father's lifetime, and had considerable experience in administration and warfare before his accession to the throne. He carried forward the annexationist policy of Rajaraja by completely overrunning the Pandya and Chera countries and including them in his empire. The conquest of Sri Lanka was also completed, with the crown and royal insignia of the king and the queen of Sri Lanka being captured in a battle. Sri Lanka was not able to free herself from the Chola control for another 50 years.

Rajaraja and Rajendra I marked their victories by erecting a number of Siva and Vishnu temples at various places. The most famous of these was the Brihadishwara temple at Tanjore which was completed in 1010. The Chola rulers adopted the practice of having inscriptions written on the walls of these temples, giving a historical narrative of their victories. That is why we know a great deal more about the Cholas that their predecessors.

One of the most remarkable exploits in the reign of Rajendra I was the march across Kalinga to Bengal in which the Chola armies crossed the river Ganga, and defeated two local kings. This expedition, which was led by a Chola general, took place in 1022 and followed

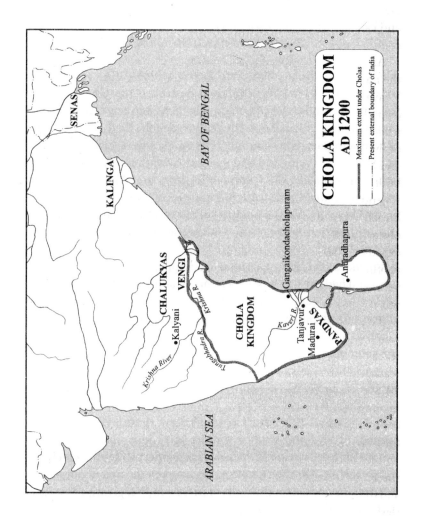

in reverse the same route which the great conqueror Samudragupta had followed. To commemorate this occasion, Rajendra I assumed the title of Gangaikondachola ('the Chola who conquered the Ganga'). He built a new capital near the mouth of the Kaveri river and called it Gangaikondacholapuram ('the city of the Chola who conquered the Ganga').

An even more remarkable exploit in the time of Rajendra I were the naval expeditions against the revived Sri Vijaya empire. The Sri Vijaya empire, which had been revived in the 10th century, extended over the Malay peninsula, Sumatra, Java and the neighbouring islands, and controlled the overseas trade route to China. The rulers of the Sailendra dynasty of the Sri Vijaya kingdom were Buddhists and had cordial relations with the Cholas. The Sailendra ruler had built a Buddhist monastery at Nagapatnam and, at his instance, Rajendra I had endowed a village for its upkeep. The cause of the breach between the two apparently was the Chola eagerness to remove obstacles to Indian traders, and to expand trade with China. The expeditions led to the conquest of Kadaram or Kedah and a number of other places in the Malay peninsula and Sumatra. The Chola navy was the strongest in the area, and for some time the Bay of Bengal was converted into a 'Chola lake'.

The Chola rulers also sent a number of embassies to China. These were partly diplomatic and partly commercial. Chola embassies reached China in 1016 and 1033. A Chola embassy of 70 merchants reached China in 1077 and, according to a Chinese account, received '81,800 strings of copper-cash', that is, more than four lakhs of rupees in return for the articles of 'tribute' comprising 'glass-ware, camphor, brocades, rhinoceros horns, ivory, etc.' Tribute was the word used by the Chinese for all articles brought for trade.

The Chola rulers fought constantly with the Chalukyas who had succeeded the Rashtrakutas. These are called the later Chalukyas and their capital was at Kalyani. The Cholas and the later Chalukyas clashed for the overlordship of Vengi (Rayalaseema), the Tungabhadra doab, and the Ganga ruled country in northwest Karnataka. Neither side was able to gain a decisive victory in this contest and ultimately it exhausted both the kingdoms. It also appears that the wars were becoming harsher during this time. The Chola rulers sacked and plundered Chalukyan cities including Kalyani, and massacred the people, including Brahmans and children. They adopted a similar policy in the Pandya country, settling military colonies to overawe the population. They destroyed Anuradhapura, the ancient capital of the rulers of Sri Lanka, and treated their king and queen harshly. These are blots in the history of the Chola empire. However, once they had conquered a country, the Cholas tried to set up a sound system of administration in it. One of the remarkable features of the Chola administration was their encouragement to local self-government in the villages all over their empire.

The Chola empire continued to flourish during the twelfth century, but it declined during the early part of the thirteenth century. The later Chalukyan empire in the Maharashtra area had also come to an end during the twelfth century. The place of the Cholas was taken by the Pandyas and the Hoysalas in the south, and the later Chalukyas were replaced by the Yadavas and the Kakatiyas. All these states extended patronage to arts and architecture. Unfortunately, they weakened themselves by continually fighting against each other, sacking the towns and not even sparing the temples. Ultimately, they were destroyed by the sultans of Delhi at the beginning of the fourteenth century.

Chola Government—Local Self Government

The king was the most important person in the Chola administration. All authority rested in his hands, but he had a council of ministers to advise him. The kings often went on tours in order to oversee the administration. The Cholas maintained a large army consisting of elephants, cavalry and infantry which were called the three limbs of the army. The infantry was generally armed with spears. Most of the kings had bodyguards who were sworn to defend the kings even at the cost of their lives. The Venetian traveller, Marco Polo, who visited Kerala in the thirteenth century, says that all the soldiers who were bodyguards burnt themselves in the funeral pyre of the monarch when he died—a statement which may well be an exaggeration. The Cholas also had a strong navy, as we have seen, which dominated the Malabar and Coromandel coast and, for some time, the entire Bay of Bengal.

The Chola state included area of central control, and loosely administered areas under different types of local control. The state was interpersed with hill people and tribals. The basic unit of administration was the *nadu* which consisted of a number of villages having close kinship ties and other close associations. The number of *nadus* increased as fresh lands were brought under cultivation by means of irrigation works such as ponds, wells, etc., and by converting hill or tribal people into agriculturists. Grants to Brahmans and temples increased, both of which helped in expanding cultivation.

In the Chola kingdom, *nadus* were grouped into *valanadus*. The Chola state was divided into four *mandalams* or provinces. Sometimes, princes of the royal family were appointed governors of provinces. Officials were generally paid by giving them assignments of revenue-bearing lands.

The Chola rulers built a network of royal roads which were useful for trade as well as for the movement of the army. Trade and commerce flourished in the Chola empire, and there were some gigantic trade guilds which traded with Java and Sumatra.

The Cholas also paid attention to irrigation. The river Kaveri and other rivers were used for the purpose. Many tanks for irrigation were built. Some of the Chola rulers carried out an elaborate survey of land in order to fix the government's share of the land revenue. We do not know what precisely the government's share was.

In addition to land tax, the Chola rulers drew their income from tolls on trade, taxes on professions, and also from the plunder of the neighbouring territories. The Chola rulers were wealthy, and could afford to build a number of towns and magnificent monuments, including temples.

We have already referred to local self-government in the villages in some areas in the Rashtrakuta empire. We know more about village government in the Chola empire from a number of inscriptions. We hear of two assemblies, called the *ur*, and the *sabha* or *mahasabha*. The *ur* was a general assembly of the village. However, we know more about the working of the *mahasabha*. This was a gathering of the adult men in the Brahman villages which were called *agraharams*. These were villages with Brahman settlements in which most of the land was rent-free. These villages enjoyed a large measure of autonomy. The affairs of the village were managed by an executive committee to which educated persons owning property were elected either by drawing lots or by rotation. These members had to retire every three years. There were other committees for helping in the assessment and collection of land revenue, for maintenance of law and order, justice, etc. One of the important committees was the tank committee which looked after the distribution of water to the fields. The *mahasabha* could distribute new lands, and exercise ownership rights over them. It could also raise loans for the village and levy taxes.

The self-government enjoyed by these Chola villages was a very fine system. To some extent this system worked in the other villages as well. However, the growth of feudalism which is discussed in an earlier chapter, restricted their autonomy.

CULTURAL LIFE

The Chola rule saw the further growth and climax of the bhakti movement which we have discussed separately. The movement was closely linked to temples. The extent and resources of the Chola empire enabled the rulers to build great capitals, such as Tanjore, Gangaikondacholapuram, Kanchi, etc. The rulers maintained large households and large palaces with banquet halls, spacious gardens and terraces. Thus, we learn of seven or five-storeyed houses for their chiefs. Unfortunately, none of the palaces of the period have survived. The Chola capital, Gangaikondacholapuram, is now just a small village near Tanjore. However, descriptions of the magnificent palaces of the rulers and their ministers, and of equally magnificent houses in which the wealthy merchants lived, are to be found in the literature of the period.

Temple architecture in the south attained its climax under the Cholas. The style of architecture which came into vogue during this period is called Dravida, because it was confined largely to south India. The main feature of this style was the building of many storeys above the *garbhagriha* (the innermost chamber where the chief deity resides). The number of storeys varied from five to seven, and they had a typical style which came to be called the *vimana*. A pillared hall called *mandap*, with elaborately carved pillars and a flat roof, was generally placed in front of the sanctum. It acted as an audience hall and was a place for various other activities such as ceremonial dances which were performed by the *devadasis*—the women dedicated to the service of the gods. Sometimes, a passage ran around the sanctum so that the devotees could go round it. Images of many other gods could be put in this passage. This entire structure was enclosed in a courtyard surrounded by high walls, which were pierced by lofty gates called *gopurams*. In course of time, the *vimanas* rose higher and higher, the number of courtyards were increased to two or three, and the *gopurams* also became more and more elaborate. Thus the temple became a miniature city or a palace, with living-rooms for priests and many others being provided in it. The temples generally enjoyed revenue-free grants of lands for their expenses. They also received grants and rich donations from the wealthy merchants. Some of the temples became so rich that they entered business, lent money, and took part in business enterprises. They also spent money on improving cultivation, digging tanks, wells, etc., and providing irrigation channels.

An early example of the Dravida style of temple architecture is the eighth century temple of Kailasanath at Kanchipuram. One of the finest and most elaborate examples of the style is, however, provided by the Brihadiswara temple at Tanjore built by Rajaraja I. This is also called the Rajaraja temple because the Cholas were in the habit of installing images of kings and queens in the courtyards of the temples. The temple at Gangaikondacholapuram, though in a dilapidated condition, is another fine example of temple architecture under the Cholas. A large number of temples were also built at other places in south India. However, it may be well to remember that the proceeds for some of these activities were obtained from the plunder of the population of the neighbouring areas by the Chola rulers.

After the fall of the Cholas, temple building activity continued under the Chalukyas of Kalyani and the Hoysalas. The district of Dharwar and the Hoysala capital, Halebid, had a large number of temples. The most magnificent of these is the Hoysalesvara temple. It is the best example of what is called the Chalukyan style. Apart from the images of gods and their attendants, both men and women (*yaksha* and *yakshini*), the temples contain finely sculptured panels which show a busy panorama of life, including dance, music and scenes of war and love. Thus, life was closely integrated with religion. For the common man, the temples were not merely a place for worship but the hub of social and cultural life as well.

The art of sculpture attained a high standard in south India during this period. One example of this was the giant statue of Gomateswara at Sravana Belgola. Another aspect was image-making which reached its zenith in the dancing figure of the Siva, called Nataraja. The Nataraja figures of this period, particularly those in bronze, are considered masterpieces. Many fine examples of this are to be found in museums in India and abroad.

The rulers of the various dynasties also patronized arts and letters during this period. While Sanskrit was regarded as the language of high culture and a number of kings as well as scholars and court poets wrote in it, a remarkable feature of the period was the growth of literature in the local languages of India. A number of popular saints called *Nayanmars* and *Alvars* who were devotees of Siva and Vishnu respectively, flourished in the Tamil kingdoms between the sixth and the ninth centuries. They composed their works in Tamil. The writings of the Saivite saints, which were collected into eleven volumes under the name *Tirumurai* in the early part of the twelfth century, are considered sacred and are looked upon as the fifth Veda. The age of Kamban who is placed in the second half of the eleventh and the early part of the twelfth century is regarded as a golden age in Tamil literature. Kamban's *Ramayana* is considered a classic in Tamil literature. Kamban is believed to have lived at the court of a Chola king. Many others too took their themes from the *Ramayana* and *Mahabharata*, thus bringing these classics nearer to the people.

Though younger than Tamil, Kannada also became a literary language during this period. The Rashtrakuta, the Chalukya and the Hoysala rulers patronized Kannada as well as Telugu. The Rashtrakuta king, Amoghavarsha, wrote a book on poetics in Kannada. Many Jain scholars also contributed to the growth of Kannada. Pampa, Ponna and Ranna are regarded as the three gems of Kannada poetry. Although they were under the influence of

Jainism, they also wrote on themes taken from the *Ramayana* and *Mahabharata*. Nanniah, who lived at the court of a Chalukyan king began the Telugu version of the *Mahabharata*. The work begun by him was completed in the thirteenth century by Tikkanna. Like the Tamil *Ramayana*, the Telugu *Mahabharata* is a classic which inspired many subsequent writers. Many folk or popular themes are also to be found in these literatures. Popular themes which were not derived from Sanskrit and which reflect popular sentiments and emotions are called *desi* or rural in Telugu.

We can, thus, see that the period from the eighth to the twelfth century was not only remarkable for the growth of regional kingdoms and regional integration, but was also a period of cultural growth, and the development of trade and commerce and agriculture in south India.

FOUR

Economic and Social Life, Education and Religious Beliefs (800–1200)

Although we have not yet studied political developments in north India from 1000 to 1200, the entire period from 800 to 1200 may be regarded as one for the purpose of studying economic and social life, and religious beliefs. Economic and social life, ideas and beliefs change much more slowly than political life. That is why many of the earlier features which existed before the ninth century continued during this period also. At the same time, there were a number of new factors which made the period different from the earlier one. Generally speaking, new elements as well as elements of continuity are found in every historical period, but the extent and direction of change varies.

TRADE AND COMMERCE

The economic situation, especially trade and commerce in the country during this period is a matter of debate among historians. Some consider it to be a period of stagnation and decline, a set back both of foreign trade and long distance trade within the country, decline of towns, and greater localism and regionalism. The virtual absence of gold coins till the tenth century is considered to be a proof of this.

We can hardly examine here all these points in detail. Suffice it to say that the fall of the Roman empire did not seriously affect India's trade with the West since two large empires, the Byzantine empire with its base in Constantinople, and the Sassanid empire based in Iran rose during the subsequent period. Both of them took keen interest in trade with India and the Indian Ocean region. After the rise of the Arab empire in the seventh century, the Arabs expanded the trade of the West to India, Southeast Asia and China.

There is no reason to believe that Indian traders were excluded from this expanded trade. Hence, gold and silver continued to come to India in return for its favourable trade. That is why India continued to be considered a country full of gold and silver, and hence an attractive prize for foreigners to invade and trade with. Why the gold and silver was used for decorating temples and palaces, or for jewellery, or simply buried for future use, and not used for coinage, is a question to which no satisfactory answer is available.

We have seen how a large number of states arose in the country during the period, and the growing power and authority of those holding superior rights in land. Many of these kingdoms expanded agriculture by building bunds, wells, etc. In some instances, as in Bengal, Sind and the Tamil country, in order to strengthen their own positions, the rulers invited Brahmans to settle down by giving them grants of rent-free lands. Since the bulk of these lands were uncultivated, many tribesmen who were nomads, or cattle-rearers or food-gatherers were induced to settle down to agriculture. Such expansion of cultivation further strengthened the position of the local chiefs, *samantas*, etc.

We do not know the impact of this development on internal trade. The growth of small towns which catered to local trade, along with greater local self-sufficiency seems to have gone hand in hand. In north India, in particular, the decline of long distance trade within the country apparently led to the decline of trade guilds or *shrenis* and *sanghs*. The guilds had often consisted of people belonging to different castes. They had their own rules of conduct which the members were legally bound to obey, and were entitled to lend or borrow money or receive endowments. With the decline of long distance trade and commerce, these bodies lost their former importance. We find very few references in north India during the period to guilds receiving endowments. In the course of time, some of the older *shrenis* emerged as sub-castes. For example, the *Dvadasa-shreni*, which was a guild, became a subcaste of the Vaishyas. Jainism, which was patronized by the mercantile sections, also received a set back in north India.

In some of the Dharamshastras which were written during this period, a ban is put on travel beyond the areas where the *munja* grass does not grow or where the black gazelle does not roam, that is, outside India proper. Travel across the salt seas was also considered polluting. These bans were not taken seriously, for we have accounts of Indian merchants, philosophers, medical men and craftsmen visiting Baghadad and other Muslim towns in West Asia during this period. Perhaps, the ban was meant for Brahmans only, or was meant to discourage too many Indians going to the areas dominated by Islam in the West and Buddhism in the East for fear of their bringing back heretical religious ideas which may be embarrassing and unacceptable to the Brahmans and the ruling groups.

The ban on sea travel did not interfere with the growth of India's overseas trade with the countries of Southeast Asia and China. A brisk trade between south India and the countries of Southeast Asia had started from the sixth century onwards. The growing geographical knowledge about the countries of the area is reflected in the literature of that time. The peculiar features of the languages of the area, their dresses, etc., are mentioned in the books of the period such as Harisena's *Brihatkatha-kosh*. There are many stories about the adventures of the Indian merchants in the magical waters of the area, stories which became the basis of the well-known story of Sindbad the Sailor. The Indian merchants were organised in guilds, the most famous of them being the *Manigraman* and the *Nandesi* which had been active since early times. These guilds displayed a spirit of enterprise, engaging in retail and whoselsale trade in many foreign countries. They also gave handsome grants to temples, which became centres of social and cultural life, and sometimes also advanced money for trade. Many of the Indian traders settled down in these countries. Some of them took wives from the local population. The priests followed the traders. In this way, both Buddhist and Hindu religious ideas were introduced in the area. The Buddhist temple of Borobudur in Java and the Hindu temple of Angkor Wat in Cambodia testify to the spread of both these religions there. Some of the ruling families of the area were semi-Hinduized, and they welcomed trade and cultural relations with India. In this way, Indian culture mingled with the local culture to establish new literary and cultural forms. Some observers think that the material prosperity of the Southeast Asian countries, the growth of civilization, and establishment of large states was based in large measure on the introduction of the Indian technique of irrigated rice cultivation.

The chief Indian port for sailing to Java, Sumatra, etc., was Tamralipti (Tamluk) in Bengal. In most of the stories of the period, merchants start for Suvarnadvipa (modern Indonesia) or to Kataha (Kedah in Malaya) from Tamralipti. A fourteenth century writer in Java speaks of people from Jambudvipa (India), Karnataka (south India), and Gaud (Bengal) coming unceasingly in big numbers in large ships. Traders from Gujarat also took part in this trade.

On account of its prosperity, China had become a main focus of trade in the Indian Ocean. The Chinese consumed enormous quantities of spices, which were imported from Southeast Asia and India. They also imported ivory, the best of which came from Africa, and glassware which came from West Asia. To these were added medicinal herbs, lac, incense, and all types of rare commodities. Generally, products from Africa and West Asia did not go beyond Malabar in South India. Nor did many Chinese ships go beyond the Moluccas in Southeast Asia. Thus, both India and Southeast Asia were important staging centres for trade between China and the countries of West Asia and Africa. Indian traders – especially from the Tamil country and Kalinga (modern Orissa and Bengal) – played an active role in this trade, along with Persians, and at a later stage, the Arabs. Much of the trade to China was carried in Indian ships, the teakwood of Malabar, Bengal and Burma providing the basis of a strong tradition of ship building. The weather conditions were also such that it was not possible for a ship to sail straight from the Middle East to China. The ships would have to wait for a long period in ports in between for favourable winds which blew from the west to the east before the monsoon, and from east to west after the monsoon. Indian and Southeast Asian ports were preferred by the merchants for the purpose.

The main seaport for foreign trade in China during this period was Canton, or Kanfu as the Arab travellers called it. Buddhist scholars went from India to China by the sea route. The Chinese chroniclers tell us that the number of Indian monks in the Chinese court towards the close of the tenth and the beginning of the eleventh century was the highest in Chinese history. A Chinese account of a slightly earlier period tells us that the Canton river was full of ships from India, Persia and Arabia. It says that in Canton itself there were three Hindu temples in which Indians resided. The presence of Indians in the Chinese Sea is testified to by Japanese records which give the credit of introducing cotton into Japan to two Indians who were carried over to the country by the black current.

Indian rulers, particularly the Pala and Sena rulers of Bengal, and the Pallava and Chola rulers of south India, tried to encourage this trade by sending a series of embassies to the Chinese emperors. The Chola ruler, Rajendra I, sent a naval expedition against Malaya and the neighbouring countries to overcome their interference in the trade with China. The embassy sent to China by Rajendra I travelled in an Indian ship. There is evidence to show that there were many shipyards which were located on the west coast, including Gujarat. Thus, growth of India's foreign trade in the area was based on a strong maritime tradition, including ship building, and the skill and enterprise of its traders. The Chinese trade was very favourable to the countries engaged in it, so much so that in the thirteenth century, the Chinese government tried to restrict the export of gold and silver from China. Indian ships gradually gave way to the Arabs and the Chinese ships which were bigger and faster. We are told that the Chinese ships were several storeys high and carried 600 passengers apart from 400 soldiers. An important factor in the growth of the Chinese ships was the use of the mariner's compass—an invention which later travelled from China to the West. Already Indian science and technology were being left behind.

Thus, India's trade with the western areas and with Southeast Asia and China grew steadily. The lead in this trade was taken by south India, Bengal and Gujarat. This was an important factor in the wealth and prosperity of these areas.

Condition of the People

There was no decline in the high standard of Indian handicrafts such as textiles, work on gold and silver, metallurgy, etc., during the period. Indian agriculture also continued to be in a flourishing condition.

Many of the Arab travellers testify to the fertility of the soil and the skill of the Indian peasant.

All the literary works of the period tell us that the ministers, officials and feudal chiefs lived in great ostentation and splendour. They aped the ways of the king in having fine houses which sometimes were three to five storeys high. They used costly foreign apparel such as imported woollen clothes, Chinese silk, and costly jewels and ornaments made of gold and silver to adorn their bodies. They maintained a large number of women in their households and had a train of domestic servants to look after them. Whenever they moved out, a large number of attendants accompanied them. They assumed high-sounding titles, such as *mahasamantadhipati*, and had their own distinctive symbols, such as banners, decorated umbrellas and the yak-tail to whisk away flies.

Big merchants also aped the ways of the king, and sometimes their living was quite royal. Of a millionare (*kotisvara*) in the Chalukyan empire, we are told that huge banners with ringing-bells were hoisted over his house, and that he owned a large number of horses and elephants. The main building was approached by a staircase of crystal, and had a temple of crystal floor and walls which were adorned by religious paintings containing an image in crystal. Vastupala and Tejahpala who were ministers in Gujarat are reputed to have been the richest merchants of their times.

We cannot, however, assume from the above that there was prosperity all round. While food stuffs were cheap, there were many poor people in the cities who could not get enough to eat. The author of the *Rajatarangini* (written in Kashmir in the twelfth century) has them in mind when he says that whereas the courtiers ate fried meat and drank cooled wine perfumed with flowers, the ordinary people had to be content with rice and *utpala-saka* (a wild vegetable of bitter taste). There are many stories of the hard lot of poor men and women, some of whom took to a life of robbery and plunder. As for the villages where the large bulk of the population lived, we have to get information about the life of the peasants from literary works, grants of land, inscriptions, etc. The commentators on Dharmashastras tell us that the rate of the revenue demand from the peasant was one-sixth of the produce as before. However, from some of the grants we learn of a large number of additional cesses, such as grazing tax, tax on ponds, etc. The peasants had to pay these taxes over and above the land-revenue. In addition, some of the grants gave the grantees the right to levy fixed or unfixed, proper or improper taxes on the peasants. The peasants also had to render forced labour (*vishti*). In some cases, as in central India and Orissa, we find some villages being given to the Brahmans, and other donees along with artisans, herdsmen and cultivators who were tied to the soil like serfs in medieval Europe. In literary works we hear of chiefs realising money on every opportunity that offered itself. We are told of a Rajput chief that he made money even from sparrows, dead birds, pig dung and the shrouds of dead bodies. Another writer tells us of a village which was depopulated due to the actions of a chief (*samanta*).

To this may be added the frequent recurrence of famines and wars. In the wars, destruction of water reservoirs, burning of villages, seizure by force of all the cattle or the grains stored in granaries and destruction of cities were normal features, so much so that they are considered legitimate by the writers of the period.

Thus, the growth of a society which may be called feudal increased the burdens on the common man.

Nature of Society

A number of important changes took place in Indian society during this period. One of these was the growing power of a class of people who are variously called *samanta, ranak, rautta* (rajput), etc., by the contemporary writers. Their origins were very different. Some were government officers who were increasingly paid not in cash but by assigning to them revenue-bearing villages. Others were defeated rajas and their supporters who continued to enjoy the revenue of limited areas. Still others were local hereditary chiefs or military adventurers who had carved out a sphere of authority with the help of armed supporters. Still others were tribal or clan leaders. Thus, there was a hierarchy among them. But their actual position varied, depending on the situation. Some of them were only village chiefs, some of them dominated a tract comprising a number of villages, while a few dominated an entire region. They constantly contended against each other, and tried to enhance their sphere of authority and privileges.

The revenue assignments (called *bhoga* or fief) granted by a ruler to his officers and supporters were temporary in theory and were liable to be resumed whenever the ruler wanted. However, in practice this was rarely done, except in the case of outright rebellion or disloyalty. According to current notions, it was a sin to deprive even a defeated ruler of his lands.

As a result, the kingdoms of this period included large areas dominated by defeated and subordinate rulers who were constantly on the look out for reasserting their independence. Within the territories of these rulers, again, various officers looked upon their assignments as hereditary fiefs. In course of time, even various government offices began to be considered hereditary. We have in an earlier chapter seen a case in Bengal where members of a family held the office of *mahamantri* for four generations. Similarly, most offices began to be considered the monopoly of a few families. The hereditary chiefs gradually assumed many of the functions of the government. They not only assessed and collected land revenue, but also assumed more and more administrative powers, such as the right of awarding punishments and exacting fines on their own, which earlier were generally considered royal privileges. They assumed the right to sublet their land to their followers without the prior permission of the ruler, thus increasing the number of people who drew sustenance from land without working on it themselves.

Some historians call this type of a society 'feudal', although features of European feudalism, such as vassalge, serfdom, and manors did not exist in India. It is emphasized that the common feature between the two was that the society was dominated by a class of people who derived their income from the surplus produced by the peasant, but did not work on the land themselves. Also, that the position of the primary producer, the peasant, was a dependent one. A number of other historians prefer to call this society a 'medieval society'. They consider feudalism to be the specific feature of 'medieval' European society, only, as we have mentioned earlier.

Without giving into this controversy further, we may note that a new type of society grew in India from the eighth century onwards, emphasizing localism and sub-regionalism. This is important for understanding the political and cultural developments during this and the subsequent period.

THE CASTE SYSTEM

(a) Brahmans and Rajputs

The caste system, which had been established much earlier, continued to be the basis of the society. But there were important changes within the caste system. Thus, there was considerable strengthening of the position of the Brahmans. As we have seen, the ruler of Sind who was himself a Brahman, and the rulers of Bengal and south India, invited Brahmans and gave large scale revenue-free lands to them to settle down. These Brahmans not only expanded cultivation, but also acted as local revenue officials, ministers, accountants, etc. Some of them also played as active role in military affairs. Education, and production of literary works was another important field of their activities. The *smriti* writers of the period appear to reflect the growing importance of the Brahmans by further exalting their position. Some of them argue that the ancient caste of Kshatriyas having disappeared, and the Vaishyas having sunk to the position of Shudras, the only *dvija* (twice born or privileged) section in society were the Brahmans!

But this vein of thinking in the *shastras* did not necessarily reflect social reality. We have already referred to the existence of rich merchants, Hindu and Jain, and the rise of a powerful class of landed chiefs. In this connection, we have the rise of a new section, called the Rajputs. During this period, a large numbers of states were being ruled by Rajputs. These Rajputs were considered leaders of clans which dominated certain tracts of land, and provided the core of the armed forces. The leaders of the clan, most of whom were related to the ruler by ties of blood, considered the state to be ruled jointly by them.

There is a good deal of controversy among scholars about the origin of the Rajputs. Some of them consider them to be of mixed origin, some being descendents of foreigners, such as Shakas, Hunas, etc., and indigenous tribes, and even Brahmans. On the other hand, many of the Rajputs clans, traditionally numbering thirty-six, trace their geneology to the solar and lunar families of the Kshatriyas which are mentioned in the *Mahabharata*. Modern scholarship lays emphasis on the process by which people belonging to different social groups tried to legitimize their newly acquired power and position by being accorded the status of Kshatriyas. Sometimes a mixed Brahman-Kshatriya status was sought by claiming descent through a Brahman mother. Scholars consider this to be a part of a complex process of social growth. Thus, in some areas of Rajasthan, tribal lands were colonized, and Brahmans, traders and warriors settled on the land. In many areas, this was accompanied by introducing a superior type of economy based on irrigation through wells, bunds, etc. and bringing in superior crops. In the process, some of the cultivators became Rajputs, while some remained Shudras.

What is called 'Rajputization' is accompanied by the growth of the agrarian economy, and also of acquisition of political power by some sections. The Brahmans played an important role in this process. Thus, there was the *agnikula* legend, traced to the eleventh century, whereby the sage, Vashishtha, produced four Rajput clans— the Pratiharas, Solanki or Chalukyas, Parmar or Pawar, and Chahamans or Chauhan out of the sacrifical fire. During the period, Brahmans wrote many geneologies of ruling families, linking them to ancient kshatriya families. Thus, the Gurjar-Pratiharas, who are reputed to originate from the Gurjar stock, were linked to Lakshman who had acted as the door-keeper (*pratihar*) of Rama.

This Brahman-Rajput alliance had many political and cultural consequences. The Rajputs, acting as champions of the newly expansionist Hinduism, symbolized their power by building grand temples, and endowed them and the Brahman priests with large grants of lands, gifts, endowments, etc.

It will thus be seen that caste (*jati*) is not as rigid as has sometimes been believed: individuals and groups could rise in the *varna* scale, and they could also fall. Sometimes, it was found difficult to classify new castes in the *varna* scale. An instance of this is the Kayastha caste, which begins to be mentioned more prominently from this period. It seems that originally people from different castes, including Brahmans and Shudras, who worked in the royal establishments, were called Kayastha. In course of time, they emerged as a distinct caste. Hinduism was expanding rapidly during the period. It not only absorbed large numbers of Buddhists and Jains within its fold, but also many indigenous tribes. Foreigners such as Hunas were also Hinduized. These new sections formed new castes and sub-castes, the tribals often continuing their own customs, rituals of marriage ceremonies, and even their own tribal gods and goddesses who were often made subordinate to Hindu gods. Thus, society and religion became more and more complex.

(b) Shudras, Dalits and Slaves

According to the law-giver Yagyavalkya, it was possible for a Brahman to have food with his farmer, barber, milkman and family friends. According to a modern historian, D.C. Sircar, an important feature of the caste system during this period, was 'the gradual elevation of the social position of the Shudras'. Although they were not allowed to study the Vedas, they became eligible for *smarta* rituals, like birth, death, name giving, etc. As agriculture expanded, many of the tribals were included in this category. The Jats who were a pastoral nomadic tribe in Sind gradually moved to the Punjab and became agriculturists cum warriors. Although in the *varna* system they were classified as shudras, they formed a higher section and considered themselves on par with the Rajputs.

Marriages between the higher castes and the shudras were frowned upon, but that they existed is shown by dubbing the marriage of a high caste man with a lower caste woman as *anulom* (according to norm), and the marriage of a low caste man and a high caste woman as *pratilom* (against norm). The origin of new castes, which often consisted of professional groups such as potters, weavers, barbers, etc., or tribals, were explained as the result of such mixed marriages.

As compared to the Shudras, the position of the Dalits seems to have deteriorated. The Dalits included those following professions such as scavenging, skinning dead animals, shoe-makers, hunters, etc. These people were called the *antyaja* or untouchables, and formed the fifth social grade, outside the four-fold *varna* system. They were often required to live away from the areas inhabited by the upper castes. There is even a discussion in the *smritis* on whether the shadow of an *antyaja* was polluting or not. In some parts of the country, the *Chandals* were required to hit a wooden board on a stick as they walked so that upper caste people would not come into contact with them. In most areas of the country, these sections were not allowed to be owners of cultivated land.

Slavery also existed during the period. Prisoners of war, debtors unable to pay their stakes could be sold into slavery. During famines, many farmers sold themselves or their wife and children for food. Women were also purchased for domestic work or for company. But there were no systematic slave raids as in the case of the Turks. In general, slaves were treated better than people from the *antyaja* or despised castes.

Though slaves were not used for fighting, they could fight because we are told that if a slave saved his master's life, he became free and was entitled to get a share of his master's property. A female slave bearing a child to his master also became free. In general, emancipation of a slave was considered a good deed, and there were rules prescribed for doing so.

CONDITION OF WOMEN

As in the earlier period, women were generally considered to be mentally inferior. Their duty was to obey their husbands blindly. A writer illustrates the wife's duty of personal service towards her husband by saying that she shall shampoo his feet and render him such other services as befits a servant. But he adds the condition that the husband should follow the righteous path and should be free from hatred as well as jealousy towards a wife. Women continued to be denied the right to study the Vedas. Furthermore, the marriageable age for girls was lowered, thereby destroying their opportunities for higher education. The omission of all reference to women teachers in the dictionaries written during the period shows the poor state of higher education among women. However, from some of the dramatic works of the period, we find that the court ladies and even the queen's maids-in-waiting were capable of composing excellent Sanskrit and Prakrit verses. Various stories point to the skill of princesses in the fine arts, specially in paining and music. Daughters of high officials, courtesans and concubines were also supposed to be highly skilled in various arts, including poetry.

As for marriage, the *smriti* writers say that girls were to be given away by their parents, between the ages of six and eight, or between their eighth year and attaining puberty. Remarriage was allowed under certain conditions when the husband had deserted (i.e. was not heard of) or died, or adopted the life of a recluse, or was impotent, or had become an outcaste.

In general, women were distrusted. They were to be kept in seclusion and their life was to be regulated by the male relations—father, brother, husband or son. However, within the home they were honoured. If a husband abandoned even a wife guilty of offensive behaviour, she was to be given maintenance. With the growth of property rights in land, the property rights of women also increased. In order to preserve the property of a family, women were give the right to inherit the property of their male relations. With some reservations, a widow was entitled to the entire estate of her husband if he died sonless. Daughters also had the right to succeed to the properties of a widow. Thus, the growth of feudal society strengthened the concept of private property.

The practice of *sati* was made obligatory by some writers, but condemned by others. According to an Arab writer, Sulaiman, wives of kings sometimes burnt themselves on the funeral pyre of their husbands, but it was for them to exercise their option in the matter. It appears that with the growth of the practice of large number of women being maintained by the leading chiefs, and with the resultant disputes about property, there was a tendency for the rite of *sati* to spread.

Upper class women lived in seclusion and generally were kept away from public gaze. There was, however, no system of *purdah* or veiling of women. Abu Zaid, a tenth century Arab traveller, noted that most Indian princes while holding court, allowed their women to be seen unveiled by all the men present, not excluding even foreigners. In Orissa and Kashmir many women ruled as queens in their own right. Among these may be mentioned Prabhavati Gupta of the Vakataka dynasty who ruled for at least thirteen years as the mother of the *yuvaraja*; Queen Didda ruled Kashmir for fifty years, and withstood all intrigues against her.

We have little information on the lives of ordinary women. They must have worked hard, side by side with their men, in addition to looking after the household, and tending children.

Dress, Food and Amusements

There were no significant changes in the style of dress of men and women during the period, the *dhoti* and the *sari* remaining the normal dress for men and women in most parts of the country. In north India, men use the jacket, and women the bodice (*choli*). From sculptures it appears that long coats, trousers and shoes were worn by upper class men in north India. According to *Rajatarangini*, Harsha introduced into Kashmir a general dress befitting a king. This included the long coat; we are told that a former chief minister, having worn a short coat, incurred the king's displeasure. Woollen blankets were used in winter. While cotton was the material most commonly used, the upper classes also used silk cloth and fine muslin.

The Arab travellers testify to the fondness of both men and women for wearing ornaments. Both men and women wore gold bracelets and earrings, sometimes set with costly stones. A Chinese writer, Chau Ju Kua, says that in Gujarat, both men and women wore double earrings and close-fitting clothes, with hoods on their heads, as well as red-coloured shoes on their feet. Another famous traveller, Marco Polo, tells us that in Malabar men and women wore only a loin-cloth, the king being no exception, and that the profession of the tailor was unknown. Loin-cloth was also the dress of men and women in Quilon. But though their clothes were scanty, the kings of southern India were fond of jewellery. According to Chau Ju Kua, the king of Malabar was dressed in cotton loin-cloth and was bare-footed like his subjects, but when going out on an elephant in procession he wore a golden hat ornamented with pearls and gems, as well as golden armlets and anklets. Marco Polo says, 'What this king wears between gold and gems and pearls is worth more than a city's ransom.'

As far as food is concerned, while vegetarianism appeared to have been the rule in many areas and among sections of the population, the leading *smriti* writer of the times describes at great length the occasions on which the eating of meat was lawful. From this it appears that the peacock, the horse, the wild ass, the wild cock and the wild pig were regarded lawful food.

Arab writers compliment the Indians for the absence of the use of intoxicants among them. However, this appears to be an idealized picture. In literary works of the period, we have many references to wine-drinking. Wine was drunk on ceremonial occasions, including marriages and feasts, and outings which were very popular among some classes of citizens. Even women in the king's train indulged freely in wine. While some *smriti* writers forbid wine-drinking to the three upper castes, some others forbid it only to the Brahmans, the Kshatriyas and the Vaishyas being permitted to indulge in it with some exceptions.

The literature of the time shows that the people of the towns were fun-loving. Apart from fairs and festivals, excursions to gardens, swimming parties, etc. were widely popular. Fights among various types of animals, such as rams, cocks, etc., as well as wrestling bouts were popular among the masses. The upper classes continued to be fond of dicing, hunting and a kind of Indian polo which was regarded as a royal pastime.

EDUCATION, SCIENCE AND RELIGIOUS LEARNING

The system of education which had been gradually developed in the earlier period continued during this period without much change. There was no idea of mass education at that time. People learnt what they felt was needed for their livelihood. Reading and writing was confined to a small section, mostly Brahmans and some sections of the upper classes, specially Kayasthas.

Sometimes temples made arrangements for education at a higher level as well. Generally, a student had to go to the house of a teacher or had to live with him for getting initiation into higher education. In such a case, he had to pay fees to his teacher, or give him a gift at the end of his education. Students, particularly those who were too poor to pay fees, were expected to do personal service to the teacher. The main subjects studied were the various branches of the Vedas and grammar. Logic and philosophy were also studied. The study of politics which included political morality was popular among the nobility. A notable contribution to this branch of study was Kamandaka's *Nitisara*.

The Kayasthas had their own system of teaching the system of administration, including accountancy. Science, including mathematics, astronomy and medicine were also taught at many centres. Thus, the Arab astronomer, Abu Maashir of Balkh, studied at Banaras for ten years during the ninth century.

The responsibility for giving education for a craft or profession was generally left to the guilds, or to individual families. For instance, we have a detailed description of the careful manner in which a merchant trained his son for his profession.

Education of a more formal kind, with greater emphasis on secular subjects, continued to be provided at some of the Buddhist *viharas* (monasteries). Nalanda in Bihar was the most famous of these. Other such centres of learning included Vikramsila, and Uddandapur which also were in Bihar. All these drew students from distant places, including Tibet. In these centres, education for most of the residents was free. For meeting the expenses, lavish grants of money and land were given to these educational centres by the rulers. Thus, Nalanda had a grant of 200 villages.

Kashmir was another important centre of education. Many Saiva sects and centres of learning flourished in Kashmir during the period. A number of important *maths* were set up in south India, for example, at Madurai and Sringeri. The various centres of education provided a great impetus to discussions, religion and philosophy being the main topics. The numerous *maths* and other centres of education in various parts of India enabled ideas to flow freely and quickly from one part of the country to another. Philosophical education was not considered complete till the philosopher had visited the various centres of learning in different parts of the country, and held discussions with the scholars there. The manner in which ideas could be transmitted throughout the country was important in upholding and strengthening the cultural unity of India.

The growth of science in the country slowed down during the period so that in course of time, it was no longer regarded as a leading country in the field of science. Thus, surgery declined because the dissection of dead bodies was regarded as fit only for people of low castes. In fact, surgery became the profession of barbers. Astronomy was gradually pushed into the background by astrology. However, some advance was made in the field of mathematics. The *Lilawati* of Bhaskar II which was written during this period, remained a standard text for a long time. Some advance was made in the field of medicine by the use of minerals, especially mercury. Many books were written on plant sciences and for the treatment of animals (e.g. horses, elephants, etc.). But no way was found for breeding fine quality horses so that India remained dependent on the import of such horses from Central Asia, including Arabia and Iran. With the conquest of these areas by Muslim rulers, the Indian rulers had to face many difficulties in securing the supply of good horses.

There were many reasons for the stagnation of Indian science during the period. Experience suggests that the growth of science is closely connected with the growth of society as a whole. As we have seen, during the period society was becoming increasingly rigid and narrow in character. There had been a setback in urban life and communications, with growing religious orthodoxy.

Another reason was the tendency for the Indians to isolate themselves from the main currents of scientific thought outside India. This is reflected in the writings of al-Biruni, a noted scientist and scholar from Central Asia who lived in India for about ten years during the early part of the eleventh century. Although a great admirer of Indian science and learning, al-Biruni noted the insular attitude of the learned people of the country, viz., the Brahmans. He says: 'They are haughty, foolish, vain, self-conceited, stolid. They are by nature niggardly in communicating that which they know, and they take the greatest possible care to withhold it from men of another caste among their own people, still much more, of course, from any foreigners. According to their belief, no other created beings besides them have any knowledge of science whatsoever.'

RELIGIOUS MOVEMENTS AND BELIEFS

The period is marked by a revival and expansion of Hinduism, and a continued decline of Buddhism and Jainism. Not only were the tenets of Buddhism and Jainism challenged at the intellectual level, but on occasions, the Buddhist and Jain monks were persecuted. According to tradition, the Pandya king at Madurai executed large numbers of Jain monks at the instance of a Saivite preacher, Sambandar. In some instances, their temples were also taken over. Thus, the temple of

Puri was once a Buddhist temple. The temple near the Qutub Minar had once been a Jain temple, then converted into a Vishnu temple. We do not know how widespread such instances were, but even if they were few and far between, they can hardly be defended. However, they were not part of a misplaced religious philosophy of temple-destruction, as in the case of the early Arab and Turkish invaders later on.

During this period, Buddhism was gradually confined to eastern India. The Pala rulers were patrons of Buddhism. The decline of the Pala power after the tenth century was a blow to Buddhism in the area. But even more serious were the internal developments in Buddhism. Buddha had preached a practical philosophy, with a minimum of priesthood and speculation about God. This worship now became more elaborate. The belief grew that a worshipper could attain what he desired by uttering magical words (*mantra*), and making various kinds of mystic gestures. They also believed that by these practices, and by various kinds of austerities and secret rites, they could attain supernatural powers, such as the power to fly in the air, to become invisible, to see things at a distance, etc. Man has always yearned for control over nature in this manner. It is only with the growth of modern science that many of these yearnings have been fulfilled. Many Hindu yogis also adopted these practices. The most famous among them was Gorakhnath. The followers of Gorakhnath were called Nath-Panthis, and at one time they were popular all over north India. Many of these yogis belonged to the lower castes. They denounced the caste system and the privileges claimed by the Brahamans. The path they preached was called *tantra* which was open to all, irrespective of caste distinctions.

Thus, Buddhism did not so much decline, as it assumed forms which made it indistinguishable from Hinduism.

Jainism continued to be popular, particularly among the trading communities. The Chalukyan rulers of Gujarat patronized Jainism. It was during this time that some of the most magnificent Jain temples, such as the Dilwara temple at Mt. Abu, were built. The Paramara rulers of Malwa also built many huge images of Jain saints and of Mahavira who began to be worshipped as a god. The magnificent Jainalayas which were built in various parts also acted as resting places for travellers. In south India, Jainism attained its high water-mark during the ninth and tenth centuries. The Ganga rulers of Karnataka were great patrons of Jainism. During this period, many Jain *basadis* (temples) and *mahastambhas* (pillars) were set up in different parts. The colossal image at Sravana Belgola was set up during this time. The statue is about 18 meters high and was cut out of granite rock. It shows the saint standing up, practising rigid austerities, unmindful of the snakes coiled around his feet, and the anthills which had grown up. The Jain doctrine of the four gifts (learning, food, medicine and shelter) helped to make Jainism popular among the people. In course of time, the growing rigidity of Jainism and the loss of royal patronage led to the decline of Jainism.

The revival and expansion of Hinduism took many forms. Siva and Vishnu became the chief gods and magnificent temples were built to proclaim their supremacy. In the process, many local gods and goddesses, including the gods and goddesses of tribals who had been Hinduized, became subordinate or their consorts. In eastern India, the consorts—Tara the consort of Buddha, Durga and Kali the consort of Siva became themselves the chief objects of worship. Nevertheless, the rise of the worship of Siva and Vishnu signified the growth of a process of cultural synthesis. Thus, in an era of disintegration, religion played a positive part. But the religious revival also increased the power and arrogance of the Brahmans. This resulted in a series of popular movements which targeted the Brahmans, and emphasized the element of human equality and freedom.

We have already referred to the growth of tantrism in North India in which anyone irrespective of caste, could be enrolled. But far more important and broad based was the growth of bhakti movement in south India. The bhakti movement was led by a series of popular saints called Nayanmars and Alvars. These saints rejected austerities. They looked upon religion not as a matter of cold, formal worship but as a living bond based on love between the god and the worshipper. The chief objects of their worship were Siva and Vishnu. They spoke and wrote in Tamil, the language which everyone could understand. These saints went from place to place carrying their message of love and devotion. Some of them belonged to the lower classes. There was also a woman saint, Andal. Almost all of them disregarded the inequalities of caste, though they did not try to oppose the caste system as such. The lower castes had been excluded from Vedic scholarship and Vedic worship. The path of bhakti advocated by these saints was open to all, irrespective of caste.

The bhakti movement not only won to the fold of Hinduism many adherents of Buddhism and Jainism, they also won over many tribals. A series of *acharyas*, led by Nathamuni, collected and systematised the teachings of the Alvars and declared them equivalent to the Vedas. These early saints and their writings began to be worshipped in the temples, and a whole set of rituals and ceremonies were elaborated. Many of these are followed to this day.

Another popular movement which arose during the twelfth century was the Lingayat or Vir Saiva movement. Its founders were Basava and his nephew, Channabasava, who lived at the court of the Kalachuri kings of Karnataka. They established their faith after bitter disputes with the Jains. The Lingayats are worshippers of Siva. They strongly opposed the caste system, and rejected fasts, feasts, pilgrimages and sacrifices. In the social sphere, they opposed child marriage and allowed remarriage of widows.

Thus, both in south and north India, the revival and expansion of Hinduism took two forms—a renewed emphasis on the Vedas and Vedic worship, on the one hand, accompanied by a powerful literary and intellectual movement, and, on the other, a popular movement based on tantra in north India, and on bhakti in south India. Both tantra and bhakti disregarded caste inequalities and were open to all.

At the intellectual level, the most serious challenge to Buddhism and Jainism was posed by Sankara who reformulated the Hindu philosophy. Sankara was born in Kerala, probably in the ninth century. His life is shrouded in obscurity, and many legends have grown around his life. Persecuted by the Jains, it is said that he undertook thereafter a triumphant visit to north India where he worsted his opponents in debate. The victory was completed by a warm welcome by the king on his return to Madurai, and the banishment of the Jains from the court.

Sankara's philosophy is called *advaitavada* or the doctrine on non-dualism. According to Sankara, God and the created world are one:

the differences were apparent but not real, and arose due to ignorance, *maya* being a part of it. The way to salvation was devotion to God, strengthened by the knowledge that God and the created beings were one and the same. This philosophy is called *vedanta*. Thus, Sankara upheld the Vedas as the fountainhead of true knowledge.

The path of knowledge put forward by Sankara could be followed by only a few. Sankara did not reject the path of bhakti by which the devotee merged with God. But for this, the heart had to be cleaned through *jnana* or knowledge. It could not, thus, influence the masses. The *acharyas* from Nathamuni onwards were all orthodox Brahmans, and had argued that the path of bhakti was open only to the three upper castes, and that for the purpose, dutifully following rituals prescribed by Brahmans, and the study of the scriptures was necessary.

In the eleventh century, another famous *acharya*, Ramanuja, tried to assimilate bhakti to the tradition of the Vedas. He argued that in order to attain salvation, grace of God was more important than knowledge about Him. Ramanuja emphasized that the path of *prapatti* or total reliance on, or surrender to God was open to all, including the Shudras and the Dalits. Thus, Ramanuja tried to build a bridge between the popular movement based on bhakti, and the upper caste movement based on the Vedas.

The tradition established by Ramanuja was followed by a number of thinkers such as Madhvacharya (tenth century), and in north India by Ramananda, Vallabhacharya and others. In this way, bhakti in its popular form became acceptable to all sections of Hindu society by the early sixteenth century.

FIVE

The Age of Conflict
(*Circa 1000–1200*)

The period from 1000 to 1200 saw rapid changes both in West and Central Asia, and in north India. It were these developments which led to the incursion of the Turks into northern India leading to their rule towards the end of the period.

By the end of the ninth century, the Abbasid caliphate was in decline. Its place was taken by a series of states ruled by Islamized Turks. The Turks had entered the Abbasid empire during the ninth century as palace-guards and mercenary soldiers. Soon they emerged as the king-makers. As the power of the central government declined, provincial governors started assuming independent status, though for sometime the fiction of unity was kept up by the caliph formally granting the title of *amir-ul-umra* (Commander of Commanders) on generals who were able to carve out a separate spheres of authority. These new rulers assumed the title of 'amir' at first, and of 'sultan' later on.

The continuous incursion of the Turkish tribesmen from Central Asia, the mercenary character of the Turkish soldiers who were prepared to switch loyalties and abandon an unsuccessful ruler without much thought, the strife between different Muslim sects, and between different regions made the period a restless one. Empires and states rose and fell in rapid succession. In this situation, only a bold warrior and leader of men, a person who was as adept in warfare as in withstanding intrigues could come to the surface.

The Turkish tribesmen brought with them the habit of ruthless plunder. Their main mode of warfare consisted of rapid advance and retreat, lightning raids, and attacking any loose body of stragglers. They could do this because of the excellent quality of their horses as also their hardihood so that they could cover incredible distances on horseback.

Meanwhile, the break-up of the Gurjara-Pratihara empire led to a phase of political uncertainty in north India, and a new phase of struggle for domination. As a result, little attention was paid to the emergence of aggressive, expansionist Turkish states on the northwestern border of India and in West Asia.

Kabul, Qandahar, and its neighbouring area to the south called Zabul or Zamindawar, were considered parts of al-Hind or India till the end of the ninth century. There were many Buddhist and Hindu shrines in the area, the most important being the 53.5 m colossal statue of Buddha at Bamiyan, with caves for residence of a thousand monks. The area upto the river Oxus was ruled by many dynasties, some of them claiming descent from Kanishka. These kingdoms, backed by a mixed population of local tribes, Hunas, Turks, exiled Iranians and Indians (such as Bhati Rajputs) offered stiff resistance to the Arab effort to enter the area for tribute, plunder and slaves. Consequently, there was continuous skirmishing on both sides of the border.

THE GHAZNAVIDS

Towards the end of the ninth century, Trans-Oxiana, Khu san and parts of Iran were being ruled by the Samanids who were I. nians by descent. The Samanids had to battle continually with the on-Muslim Turkish tribesmen on their northern and eastern frontiei.. It was during this struggle that a new type of soldier, the *ghazi*, was born. The battle against the Turks, most of whom worshipped the forces of nature and were heathens in the eyes of the Muslims, was a struggle for religion as well as for the safety of the state. Hence, the *ghazi* was as much a missionary as a fighter. He acted as a loose auxiliary of the regular armies, and made up for his pay by plunder. It was the resourcefulness of the *ghazi* and his willingness to undergo great privations for the sake of the cause which enabled these infant Muslim states to hold their own against the heathen Turks. In course of time, many Turks became Muslims, but the struggle against renewed incursions of the non-Muslim Turkish tribes continued. The Islamized Turkish tribes were to emerge as the greatest defenders and crusaders of Islam. But the love of plunder went side by side with defence of Islam.

Among the Samanid governors was a Turkish slave, Alp-tigin, who, in course of time, established an independent kingdom with its capital at Ghazni. The Samanid kingdom soon ended, and the Ghaznavids took over the task of defending the Islamic lands from the Central Asian tribesmen.

It was in this context that Mahmud ascended the throne (998–1030) at Ghazni. Mahmud is considered a hero of Islam by medieval Muslim historians because of his stout defence against the Central Asian Turkish tribal invaders. The *ghazi* spirit, therefore, further increased during his reign. Secondly, Mahmud was closely associated with the renaissance of the Iranian spirit which grew rapidly during this period. The proud Iranians had never accepted the Arabic language and culture. The Samanid state had also encouraged the Persian language and literature. A high watermark in the Iranian renaissance was reached with Firdausi's *Shah Namah*. Firdausi was the poet laureate at the court of Mahmud. He transported the struggle between Iran and Turan to mythical times, and glorified the ancient Iranian heroes. There was a resurgence of Iranian patriotism, and Persian language and culture became the language and culture of the Ghaznavid empire, so much so that Mahmud himself claimed descent from the legendary Iranian king, Afrasiyab. Thus, the Turks became not only Islamized but Persianized. It was this culture that they were to bring with them to India two centuries later.

While Mahmud played an important role in the defence of the Islamic states against the Turkish tribes and in the Iranian cultural renaissance, in India his memory is only that of a plunderer and a destroyer of temples. Mahmud is said to have made seventeen raids into India. The initial raids were directed against the Hindushahi rulers who at the time held Peshawar and the Punjab. Their capital was at Udbhanda or Waihind (Peshawar). The Hindushahi rulers had been quick to see the danger to them of the rise of an aggressive, expansionist state on their southwestern border. The Hindushahi ruler, Jayapala had, in alliance with the displaced Samanid governor of Ghazni, the Bhatti ruler of the area around Multan, and the amir of Multan, invaded Ghazni. But he had to suffer a defeat and the coalition built by him collapsed. In retaliation, the Ghaznavid ruler of the times laid waste the area upto Kabul and Jalalabad.

In about 990–91, under Sabuk-tigin, the Shahis suffered a serious defeat. Following this, the provinces of Kabul and Jalalabad were annexed to Ghazni. As a prince, Mahmud had taken part in these battles. After his accession to the throne (AD 998), he resumed the offensive against the Shahis. The Shahi ruler, Jayapala, had, in the meantime, strengthened his position by bringing Lohavar (Lahore) under his control. Thus, the Shahi rule extended from Peshawar to Punjab.

In a furious battle near Peshawar in 1001, Jayapala was again defeated. Mahmud advanced to the Shahi capital, and thoroughly ravaged it. Peace was made by ceding the territory west of the Indus to Mahmud. Soon after, Jayapala died and was succeeded by his son, Anandpala. According to some later accounts, Jayapala had entered a funeral pyre following his defeat because he felt he had disgraced himself. The story that he had been taken prisoner by Mahmud and then released seems doubtful.

Despite these setbacks, the Shahis were still strong enough to offer serious resistance to Mahmud's efforts to penetrate into the Punjab. Mahmud also had to counter the attacks of non-Muslim Turks from Central Asia. However, in a decisive battle near the Indus in 1009, Anandpala was defeated and Mahmud devastated his new capital, Nandana, in the Salt Ranges, and overran his fort called Nagarkot (wrongly confused with Nagarkot in Himachal which Mahmud never reached). Anandpal was allowed for some time to rule from Lahore as a feudatory. But in 1015, Mahmud advanced upto Lahore, plundered it, and ousted Anandpal. Soon, Ghazanvid territories extended upto the river Jhelum. Earlier, the Muslim kingdom of Multan had also been overrun. However, an attack on Kashmir by Mahmud in 1015 was foiled due to weather conditions.

Thus, the struggle against the Shahis was a prolonged one, and the Shahis put up stout resistance. In this struggle, the Shahis were supported only by the Muslim ruler of Multan who had been harrassed by slave taking raids from Ghazni, and belonged to a sect which Mahmud considered heretical, and hence an enemy. It is noteworthy that apparently none of the Rajput rulers came to the aid of the Shahis, although in order to exaggerate the scale of Mahmud's victory, the seventeenth century historian, Ferishta, mentions that many Rajputs rulers, including those from Delhi, Ajmer and Kanauj aided Jayapala in 1001. However, Ajmer had not been founded by then, and Delhi (Dhillika) was a small state. Likewise, the Gurjara-Pratiharas of Kanauj whose sway had extended upon Thanesar at one time, were in a much weakened condition. Thus, the Shahis fought virtually alone.

By 1015, Mahmud was poised for an attack on the Indo-Gangetic valley. During the next half a dozen years, Mahmud launched a series of expeditions into the Indo-Gangetic plains. These raids were aimed at plundering the rich temples and the towns which had amassed wealth over generations. The plundering of this wealth also enabled him to continue his struggle against his enemies in Central Asia. He also did not want to give time to the princes in India to regroup, and to combine against him. Mahmud's raids into India alternated with battles in Central Asia. For his plundering raids into India the *ghazis* came handy to him. Mahmud also posed as a great *but shikan* or 'destroyer of the images' for the glory of Islam. From the Punjab, Mahmud raided Thanesar the old capital of Harsha. His most daring raids, however, were against Kanauj in 1018, and against Somnath in Gujarat in 1025. In the campaign against Kanauj, he sacked and plundered both Mathura and Kanauj. The following year, he invaded Kalinjar in Bundelkhand, and returned loaded with fabulous riches. He was able to do all this with impunity due to the fact that no strong state existed in north India at that time. No attempt was made by Mahmud to annex any of these states.

Between 1020, and 1025, Mahmud was engaged in Central Asian affairs. In 1025, he made a plan for raiding Somnath which had a fabulously rich temple and attracted lakhs of pilgrims. It was also a rich port. The objective was also to create a sense of awe and shock among the Rajputs because he marched via Multan and Jaisalmer with a regular cavalry of 30,000. Meeting light opposition on the way, he reached Somnath. The commander of the city fled at his approach, but the citizens put up a stout resistance. Mahmud broke the *Sivalingam*, and ordered parts of it brought back with him to Ghazni. Evading the attempt of some Rajput rulers to block him on his way back, he had to counter the marauding bands of Jats in Sind. He returned to Ghazni loaded with immense wealth.

It is difficult to say whether Mahmud's attack on Somnath presaged an attack on Rajasthan and Gujarat. Mahmud returned the following year to punish the Jats who had harried him on his return to Ghazni. He died at Ghazni in 1030.

It is not correct to dismiss Mahmud as just a raider and plunderer. The Ghaznavid conquest of the Punjab and Multan completely changed the political situation in north India. The Turks had crossed the chain of mountains defending India in the northwest and could make a deeper incursion into the Gangetic heartland at any time. The reason why they were not able to extend their conquests into the area for the next 150 years was due to the rapid changes which took place in Central Asia as well as in north India during the period.

Following the death of Mahmud, a powerful empire, the Seljuk empire, came into being. The Seljuk empire included Syria, Iran and Trans-Oxiana, and contended with the Ghaznavids for the control of Khurasan. In a famous battle, Masud, the son of Mahmud, was completely defeated and had to flee to Lahore for refuge. The Ghaznavid empire now shrank to Ghazni and the Punjab. Although the Ghaznavids continued to make plundering raids into the Gangetic valley and Rajputana, they were no longer in a position to pose a serious military danger to India. Simultaneously, a number of new states arose in north India which could counter the Ghaznavid raids.

THE RAJPUT STATES

The rise of a new section called the Rajputs and the controversy about their origins have already been mentioned. With the break-up of the Pratihara empire, a number of Rajput states came into existence in north India. The most important of these were the Gahadavalas of Kanauj, the Paramaras of Malwa, and the Chauhans of Ajmer. There were other smaller dynasties in different parts of the country, such as the Kalachuris in the area around modern Jabalpur, the Chandellas in Bundelkhand, the Chalukyas of Gujarat, the Tomars of Delhi, etc. Bengal remained under the control of the Palas and, later, under the Senas. The Gahadavalas of Kanauj gradually squeezed the Palas out of Bihar.

At its height, the Gahadvar kingdom extended from Mongyr in Bihar to Delhi. The greatest ruler in the dynasty was Govind Chandra who ruled in the first half of the twelfth century. He made Kanauj his capital, with Banaras remaining a second capital. Persian sources of the time call Govind Chandra the greatest ruler of Hindustan. The Gahadvars are reputed to be the biggest defenders against the continued Ghaznavid raids into the doab. Govind Chandra was succeeded by Jai Chandra who had to contend with the rising power of the Chauhans.

The Chauhans who had served under the rulers of Gujarat established their capital at Nadol towards the end of the tenth century. The greatest ruler in the dynasty was, perhaps, Vigraharaj who captured Chittor, and established Ajmer (Ajayameru), and made it his capital. He built a Sanskrit College at Ajmer, and the Anasager lake there. Like the Gahadvars, the Chauhans, too, offered stout resistance to the Ghazanavid raids. Vigraharaj captured Delhi (Dhillika) from the Tomars in 1151, but allowed them to rule it as feudatories. Vigraharaj also came into conflict with the Paramars of Malwa where the most famous ruler, known in legend, was Bhoja. Both Vigraharaj and Bhoja were patrons of poets and scholars. Vigraharaj himself wrote a Sanskrit drama. Bhoja had to fight his neighbours to the north as well to the south. He is credited with writing books on philosophy, poetics, yoga and medicine.

The most famous among the Chauhan rulers was Prithviraj III who ascended the throne at the young age of eleven in or about 1177, but took the reins of administration in his hands when he was sixteen. He immediately embarked on a vigorous polity of expansion, and brought many of the smaller Rajput states under his sway. However, he was not successful in his struggle against the Chalukyan ruler of Gujarat. This forced him to move towards the Ganga valley. He led an expedition in Bundelkhand against its capital Mahoba. It was in this struggle that the famous warriors, Alha and Udal, lost their lives. The Chandel ruler of Mahoba is said to have been supported in this struggle by Jai Chandra of Kanauj. The Gahadvars had also contested the attempt of the Chauhans to control Delhi and the Punjab. It was these rivalries which made it impossible for the Rajput rulers to join hands to oust the Ghaznavids from the Punjab.

The basis of Rajput society was the clan. Every clan traced its descent from a common ancestor, real or imaginary. The clans generally dominated a compact territory. Sometimes, these settlements were based on units of 12 or 24 or 48 or 84 villages. The chief would allot land in the villages to his sub-chiefs who, in turn, would allot it to individual Rajput warriors for the maintenance of their family and the horses. Attachment to land, family and honour (*maan*) was a characteristic of the Rajputs. Each Rajput state was supposed to be ruled over by the *rana or rawat* in conjunction with his chiefs who were generally his blood brothers. Though their fiefs were supposed to be held at the pleasure of the ruler, the Rajput notion of sanctity of land did not permit their resumption by the ruler, except in special circumstances, such as rebellion, absence of an heir, etc.

The Rajput organisation of society had both advantages and disadvantages. One advantage was the sense of brotherhood and egalitarianism which prevailed among the Rajputs. But the same trait made it difficult to maintain discipline among them. Feuds which continued for several generations were another weakness of the Rajputs. But their basic weakness was their tendency to form exclusive groups, each claiming superiority over the others. They were not prepared to extend the sense of brotherhood to non-Rajputs. This led to a growing gap between the Rajput ruling groups and the people most of whom were non-Rajputs. The Rajputs form only about ten per cent of the population in Rajasthan even today. The proportion of the Rajputs to the total population of the areas they dominated could not have been much higher during the eleventh and twelfth centuries.

The Rajputs treated war as a sport. This and struggle for land and cattle led to continuous warfare among the various Rajput states. The ideal ruler was one who led out his armies after celebrating the Dussehra festival to invade the territories of his neighbours. The people, both in the villages and in the cities, suffered the most from this policy.

Most of the Rajput rulers of the time were champions of Hinduism, though some of them also patronized Jainism. They gave rich donations and grants of land to Brahmans and temples. The Rajput

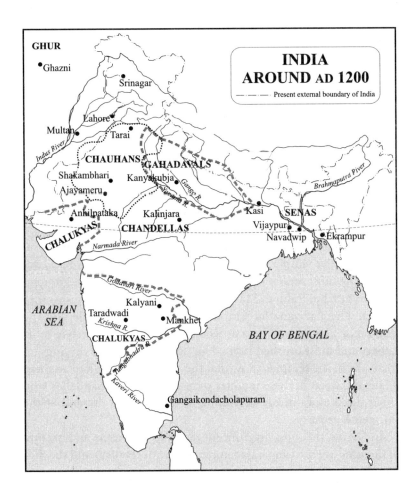

GHUR

• Ghazni

• Srinagar

Lahore•

Multan•
• Tarai

Indus River

CHAUHANS **GAHADAVALS**

Shakambhari•   Kanyakubja•

Ajayameru•

Anhilpataka•   • Kasi   **SENAS**

CHALUKYAS   Kalinjara•   Vijaypur•

                 CHANDELLAS   Navadwip   •Ekrampur

Narmada River

Brahmaputra River

Godavari River

Kalyani•

Taradwadi•
              •Mankhet

Krishna R.

CHALUKYAS

Tungabhadra R.

Kaveri River

•Gangaikondacholapuram

INDIA AROUND AD 1200

––––– Present external boundary of India

ARABIAN SEA

BAY OF BENGAL

rulers stood forth as protectors of the privileges of the Brahmans and of the caste system. Thus, the system of charging a lower rate of land revenue for Brahmans continued in some Rajput states till their merger in the Indian Union. In return for these and other concessions, the Brahmans were prepared to recognise the Rajputs as descendants of the old lunar and solar families of the kshatriyas which were believed to have become extinct.

The period after the eighth century, and particularly between the tenth and twelfth centuries, may be regarded as marking a climax in temple building activity in north India. Some of the most magnificent temples that we have today can be traced back to this period. The style of temple construction which came into prominence was called the *nagara*. Though found almost all over India, the main centres of constructions in this style were in north India and the Deccan. Its main characteristic feature was the tall curved spiral roof over the *garbhagriha* or the deity room (deul). The main room was generally a square, though projections could be made from each of its sides. An anteroom (*mandapa*) was added to the sanctum sanctorum and sometimes the temple was enclosed by high walls which had lofty gates. The most representative temples of this type are the group of temples at Khajuraho in Madhya Pradesh and at Bhubaneshwar in Orissa. The Parsvanatha temple, the Visvanatha temple and the Kandarya Mahadeo temple at Khajuraho illustrate this style in its richest and most finished form. The rich and elaborate carvings on the walls of the temples show that the art of sculpture had attained its height. Most of these temples were built by the Chandellas who ruled the area from the beginning of the ninth to the end of the thirteenth century.

In Orissa, the most magnificent examples of temple architecture of the time are the Lingaraja temple (eleventh century) and the Sun temple of Konark (thirteenth century). The famous Jaganatha temple at Puri also belongs to this period.

A large number of temples were built at various other places in north India—Mathura, Banaras, Dilwara (Abu), etc. Like the temples in south India, temples in north India also tended to become more and more elaborate. They were the centres of social and cultural life. Some of them, such as the temple of Somnath, became extremely wealthy. They ruled over many villages, and took part in business activities. In addition to temples, the Rajput rulers also built many fine·palaces, powerful forts, and works of public benefits, such as stepped wells (*baolis*), bunds, etc.

The Rajput rulers also patronized arts and letters. Many books and plays were written in Sanskrit during the period under their partonage. Vastupala, the famous minister of the Chalukyan ruler Bhima in Gujarat, was a writer and a patron of scholars and the builder of the beautiful Jain temple at Mt. Abu. Ujjain and Dhara, the capitals of the Paramara rulers, were famous centres for Sanskrit learning. Many works were written in Apabhramsha and Prakrit which represented the languages of the region. The Jain scholars made significant contributions in this direction, the most famous among them being Hemachandra who wrote both in Sanskrit and Apabhramsha. With the revival of Brahmanism, Sanskrit supplanted Apabhramsha and Prakrit among the upper classes. However, literature in these languages, which were nearer to the spoken languages, continued to be produced. The modern north Indian languages, such as Hindi, Bengali and Marathi began to emerge out of these popular languages during this period.

THE TURKISH CONQUEST OF NORTH INDIA

After the Ghaznavid conquest of the Punjab, two distinct patterns of relations between the Muslims and the Hindus were at work. One was the lure for plunder which resulted in raids into the Gangetic valley and Rajputana by the successors of Mahmud. The rulers of the Rajput states put up a spirited resistance against these raids and won victories against the Turks on a number of occasions. But the Ghaznavid state was no longer a very powerful state, and the gaining of a number of victories against it in local battles made the Rajput rulers more complacent. At the second level, Muslim traders were allowed even welcomed in the country since they helped in strengthening and augmenting India's trade with the Central and West Asian countries, and thus increasing the income of the state. Colonies of Muslim traders sprang up in some of the towns in north India. In the wake of these came a number of Muslim religious preachers called the Sufis to Punjab. The Sufis preached the gospel of love, faith and dedication to the one God. They directed their preachings mainly towards the Muslim settlers but they influenced some Hindus also. Thus, a process of interaction between Islam and Hindu religion and society was started. Lahore became a centre of Arabic and Persian languages and literature. Hindu generals, such as Tilak, a barber by caste, commanded the Ghaznavid armies in which Hindu (Jat) soldiers also were recruited.

These two processes might have continued indefinitely but for another large-scale change in the political situation in Central Asia. Towards the middle of the twelfth century, another group of Turkish tribesmen, who were partly Buddhist and partly pagan, shattered the power of the Seljuk Turks. In the vacuum, two new powers rose to prominence, the Khwarizmi empire based in Iran, and the Ghurid empire based in Ghur in northwest Afghanistan. The Ghurids had started as vassals of Ghazni, but had soon thrown off their yoke. The power of the Ghurids increased under Sultan Alauddin who earned the title of 'the world burner' (*jahan-soz*) because during the middle of the twelfth century he ravaged Ghazni and burnt it to the ground in revenge for the treatment that had been meted out to his brothers at Ghazni. The rising power of the Khwarizmi empire severely limited the Central Asian ambition of the Ghurids. Khurasan, which was the bone of contention between the two, was soon conquered by Khwarizm Shah. This left no option for the Ghurids but to look for expansion towards India.

In 1173, Shahabuddin, Muhammad (1173–1206) (also known as Muizzuddin Muhammad bin Sam) ascended the throne at Ghazni, while his elder brother was ruling at Ghur. Proceeding by way of the Gomal pass, Muizzuddin Muhammad conquered Multan and Uchch. In 1178, he attempted to penetrate into Gujarat by marching across the Rajputana desert. But the Gujarat ruler completely routed him in a battle near Mount Abu, and Muizzuddin Muhammad was lucky in escaping alive. He now realised the necessity of creating a suitable base in the Punjab before venturing upon the conquest of India. Accordingly, he launched a campaign against the Ghaznavid possessions in the Punjab. By 1190, Muizzuddin Muhammad had conquered Peshawar, Lahore and Sialkot, and was poised for a thrust towards Delhi and the Gangetic doab.

Meanwhile, events had not been standing still in north India. The Chauhan power had been steadily growing. The Chauhan rulers had defeated and killed a large number of Turks who had tried to invade Rajasthan, most probably from the Punjab side. They had also captured Delhi (called Dhillika) from the Tomars around the middle of the century. The expansion of the Chauhan power towards the Punjab brought them into conflict with the Ghaznavid rulers of the area.

THE BATTLE OF TARAIN

Thus, a battle between these two ambitious rulers, Muizzuddin Muhammad and Prithviraj was inevitable. The conflict started with rival claims for Tabarhinda. In the battle which was fought at Tarain in 1191, the Ghurid forces were completely routed, Muizzuddin Muhammad's life being saved by a young Khalji horseman. Prithviraj now pushed on to Tabarhinda and conquered it after a twelve-month siege. Little attempt was made by Prithviraj to oust the Ghurids from the Punjab. Perhaps, he felt that this was another of recurrent Turkish raids, and that the Ghurid ruler would be content to rule over the Punjab. This gave Muizzuddin Muhammad time to regroup his forces and make another bid for India the following year. He rejected the proposal said to be made by Prithviraj to leave Punjab under the possession of the Ghurid ruler.

The second battle of Tarain in 1192 is regarded as one of the turning points in Indian history. Muizzuddin Muhammad had made careful preparations for the contest. It is said that he marched with 1,20,000 men, including a force of heavy cavalry, fully equipped with steel coats and armour; and 10,000 mounted archers. It is not correct to think that Prithviraj was negligent of the affairs of the state, and awoke to the situation when it was too late. It is true that at that time Skanda, the general of the last victorious campaign, was engaged elsewhere. As soon as Prithviraj realised the nature of the Ghurid threat, he appealed to all the rajas of northern India for help. We are told many rajas sent contingents to help him, but Jaichandra, the ruler of Kanauj, stayed away. The legend that this was because Prithviraj had abducted Jaichandra's daughter, Sanyogita, who was in love with him, is not accepted by many historians. The story was written much later as a romance by the poet, Chand Bardai, and includes many improbable events. As we have seen, there had been an old outstanding rivalry between the two states. Hence, it is not surprising that Jaichandra stayed away.

Prithviraj is said to have fielded a force of 3,00,000 including a large body of cavalry and 300 elephants. The strength of the forces on both sides may have been exaggerated. The numerical strength of the Indian forces was probably greater, but the Turkish army was better organised and led. The battle was mainly a battle between cavalry. The superior organisation skill and speed of movements of the Turkish cavalry and their mounted archers and heavy cavalry ultimately decided the issue. A large number of Indian soldiers lost their lives. Prithviraj escaped, but was captured near Saraswati (Sirsa). The Turkish armies captured the fortresses of Hansi, Saraswati and Samana. Then they attacked and captured Ajmer. Prithviraj was allowed to rule over Ajmer for some time, for we have coins of this period giving the date and the legend 'Prithvirajadeva' on one side and the words 'Sri Muhammad Sam' on the other.

Soon after, Prithviraj was executed on a charge of 'conspiracy', and Prithviraj's son succeeded him. Delhi also was restored to its Tomar ruler. But this policy was reversed soon after. The ruler of Delhi was ousted and Delhi was made a base for further Turkish advance into the Ganga valley. Following a rebellion, a Muslim army recaptured Ajmer and installed a Turkish general there. Prithviraj's son moved to Ranthambor and founded a new powerful Chauhan kingdom there.

Thus, the Delhi area and eastern Rajasthan passed under the Turkish rule.

TURKISH CONQUEST OF THE GANGA VALLEY

Bihar and Bengal

Between 1192 and 1206, Turkish rule was extended over the Ganga-Jamuna doab and its neighbouring area. Bihar and Bengal were also overrun. In order to establish themselves in the doab, the Turks had first to defeat the powerful Gahadavala kingdom of Kanauj. The Gahadavala ruler, Jaichandra, had been ruling over the state peacefully for two decades. Perhaps, he was not a very capable warrior because he had earlier suffered a reverse at the hands of the Sena king of Bengal.

After Tarain, Muizzuddin returned to Ghazni leaving the affairs in India in the hands of one of his trusted slaves, Qutbuddin Aibak. During the next two years, the Turks overran parts of upper doab, without any opposition from the Gahadavalas. In 1194, Muizzuddin returned to India. He crossed the Jamuna with 50,000 cavalry and moved towards Kanauj. A hotly contested battle between Muizzuddin and Jaichandra was fought at Chandawar near Kanauj. We are told that Jaichandra had almost carried the day when he was killed by an arrow, and his army was totally defeated. Muizzuddin now moved on to Banaras which was ravaged, a large number of temples there being destroyed. The Turks established their hold over a huge territory extending up to the borders of Bihar.

Thus, the battles of Tarain and Chandawar laid the foundations of the Turkish rule in north India. The task of consolidating the conquest thus won proved, however, to be an onerous task which occupied the Turks for almost fifty years. We shall study this in a subsequent chapter.

Muizuddin lived till 1206. During this period, he occupied the powerful forts of Bayana and Gwaliyar to guard the southern flank of Delhi. A little later, Aibak conquered Kalinjar, Mahoba and Khajuraho from the Chandel rulers of the area.

With a base in the doab the Turks launched a series of raids in the neighbouring areas. Aibak defeated Bhima III, the ruler of Gujarat, and Anhilwara and a number of other towns were ravaged and plundered. Though a Muslim governor was appointed to rule the place he was soon ousted. This showed that the Turks were not yet strong enough to be able to rule over such far-flung areas.

The Turks, however, were more successful in the east. A Khalji officer, Bakhtiyar Khalji, whose uncle had fought at the battle of Tarain, had been appointed in charge of some of the areas beyond Banaras. He had taken advantage of this to make frequent raids into Bihar, which was at the time in the nature of a no-man's land. During these raids, he had attacked and destroyed some of the famous Buddhist monasteries of Bihar, Nalanda and Vikramasila, which had no protector left. He had also accumulated much wealth and gathered many followers around him. During his raids, he also collected information about the routes to Bengal. Bengal was a rich prize because its internal resources and flourishing foreign trade had given it the reputation of being fabulously rich.

Making careful preparations, Bakhtiyar Khalji marched with an army towards Nadia, a pilgrim centre where the Sena ruler, Lakshmana Sena, had built a palace, and to which he had gone on pilgrimage. Turkish horse-merchants had become a common sight in those days. Pretending to be a horse-merchant, Bakhtiyar Khalji made a sudden attack on the palace, and created a great confusion. The Sena ruler Lakshmana Sena had been a noted warrior. However, taken by surprise and thinking that the main Turkish army had arrived, he slipped away by a back door. The Turkish army must have been near, for they soon arrived and overpowered the garrison. All the wealth of the ruler, including his wives and children were captured. These events are placed in 1204. Bakhtiyar then marched and occupied the Sena capital, Lakhnauti, without any opposition. Lakshmana Sena moved to Sonargaon in south Bengal where he and his successors continued to rule.

Although Bakhtiyar Khalji was formally appointed the governor of Bengal by Muizzuddin, he ruled over it as a virtually independent ruler. But he was not to enjoy this position for long. He foolishly undertook an expedition into the Brahmaputra valley in Assam, though writers say that he wanted to lead an expedition into Tibet. The Magh rulers of Assam retreated and allowed the Turkish armies to come in as far as they could. At last the tired and exhausted armies found they could advance no further and decided to retreat. They could find no provisions on the way, and were constantly harassed by the Assamese armies. Tired and weakened by hunger and illness, the Turkish army had to face a battle in which there was a wide river in front and the Assamese army at the back. The Turkish armies suffered a total defeat. Bakhtiyar Khalji was able to come back with a few followers with the help of some mountain tribes. But his health and spirits were broken. He was mortally sick and confined to the bed when one of his own amirs stabbed him to death.

While Aibak and the Turkish and Khalji chief were trying to expand and consolidate the Turkish gains in north India, Muizzuddin and his brother were trying to expand the Ghurid empire into Central Asia. The imperialistic ambitions of the Ghurids brought them into headlong conflict with the powerful Khwarizmi empire. In 1203, Muizzuddin suffered a disastrous defeat at the hands of the Khwarizmi ruler. This defeat came as a blessing in disguise to the Turks, for they had to big goodbye to their Central Asian ambitions and to concentrate their energies exclusively on India. This paved the way for the emergence after some time of a Turkish state based exclusively in India. In the immediate context, however, the defeat of Muizzuddin emboldened many of his opponents in India to rebel. The Khokhars, a warlike tribe in western Punjab, rose and cut off the communications between Lahore and Ghazni. Muizzuddin led his last campaign into India in 1206 in order to deal with the Khokhar rebellion. He resorted to large-scale slaughter of the Khokhars and cowed them down. On his way back to Ghazni, he was killed by a Muslim fanatic belonging to a rival sect.

Muizzuddin Muhammad bin Sam has often been compared to Mahmud of Ghazni. As a warrior, Mahmud Ghazni was more successful than Muizzuddin, having never suffered a defeat in India or in Central Asia. He also ruled over a larger empire outside India. But it has to be kept in mind that Muizzuddin had to contend with larger and better organised states in India than Mahmud. Though less successful in Central Asia, his political achievements in India were greater. But it was Mahmud's conquest of the Punjab which paved the way for Muizzuddin's successes in north India. Considering that the conditions facing the two were very different, no useful comparison can be made between the two. The political and military motives of the two in India were also different in important respects.

Neither was really concerned with Islam. Once a ruler submitted, he was allowed to rule over his territories unless, for some other reasons, it was necessary to annex his kingdom in part or in whole. Hindu officers and soldiers were used by Mahmud as well as by Muizzuddin. But neither scrupled to use the slogan of Islam for their purposes, and to justify their plunder of Indian cities and temples in the name of religion.

CAUSES OF THE DEFEAT OF THE RAJPUTS

The defeat of the leading states of north India within a short space of about 15 years by the Turkish armies also needs some explanation. It may be stated as an axiom that a country is conquered by another only when it suffers from social and political weaknesses, or become, economically and militarily backward compared to its neighbours. Recent research shows that the Turks did not have any superior weapons at their disposal as compared to the Indians. The iron-stirrup which had changed the mode of warfare in Europe, as we have noted earlier, had spread in India from the 8th century onwards. The Turkish bows could shoot arrows to a longer distance, but the Indian bows were supposed to be more accurate and more deadly, the arrowheads being generally dipped in poison. In hand to hand combat the Indians swords were considered to be best in the world. The Indians also had the advantage of elephants. Perhaps the Turks had horses which were swifter and more sturdy than the horses imported into India.

The weakness of the Indians were social and organizational. The growth of feudalism, i.e., rise of the local landed elements and chiefs had weakened the administrative structure and military organisation of the Indian states. The rulers had to depend more on the various chiefs who rarely acted in coordination, and quickly dispersed to their areas after battle. On the other hand, the tribal structure of the Turks, and the growth of the *iqta* and *khalisa* systems, enabled the Turks to maintain large standing armies which could be kept in the field for a long time. Also, the Indians were not accustomed to move as an organized body of horsemen which could cover long distances and fight and manoeuvre. Nor, does it seem, the Rajputs had large bodies of mounted archers, or heavily armed cavalry. But for these factors, the Rajput states, many of which had greater human and physical resources at their disposal than the Ghaznavid and Ghurid empires, would not have suffered defeat, or would have been able to recover if they had been defeated in a battle.

The social and organizational structure of the Turks also gave them many advantages. The *iqta* system which grew slowly in West Asia, implied that a Turkish chief was allotted a piece of land as *iqta* from which he could collect the land revenues and taxes due to the state. In return, he had to maintain a body of troops for the service of the ruler. The grant was not hereditary, and was held at the pleasure of the sultan who could transfer him to any place. The sultan drew revenues directly from pieces of land which were called *khalisa*. This enabled him to maintain a large standing army. While states rose and fell in West Asia as in India, in West Asia, unlike the Rajput states, in each state the armed forces were more highly centralized. Many of the Turkish officers were slaves, who had been trained for warfare, and grew in the Sultan's service, and on whom the Sultan could place total trust.

In terms of personal bravery, the Rajputs were in no way inferior to the Turks. In this context, the role of religion and caste in the military organization should not be unduly exaggerated. While the Turks were imbued with the *'ghazi'* spirit, the Rajputs considered retreat in battle to be a dishonour. Also, caste did not prevent non-Rajputs, or the *kuvarna* (lower castes) from taking part in the battles so that Rajput armies were larger in numbers to those fielded by the Turks.

Finally, the Rajput defeat at the hands of Muizzuddin Muhammad should be seen in the context of the past few centuries. From the end of the tenth century, the Turks had started reconnoitering India. The Rajputs did put up spirited and prolonged resistance, and defeated the Turkish armies a number of times. But the Rajputs lacked what might be called 'strategic vision'. Once the outer bastions of India— Kabul and Lahore, had fallen to the Turks, no concerted attempt was made by the Rajputs to recover them. Thus, little effort was made to push the Ghaznavids out of the Punjab. The gaze of the Rajputs remained fixed on India, and they paid little attention to developments outside, specially to Central Asia which had often played a key-role in shaping the history of India.

SIX

The Delhi Sultanat—I
(*Circa 1200–1400*)

I. THE MAMELUK[1] SULTANS (THIRTEENTH CENTURY)

Some of the factors which enabled the Turks to extend their conquest from the Punjab and Multan into the Ganga valley and even to overrun Bihar and parts of Bengal have been mentioned in the previous chapter. For almost one hundred years after that, the Delhi sultanat, as the state ruled over by these invaders was called, was hard pressed to maintain itself in the face of foreign invasions, internal conflicts among the Turkish leaders and the attempts of the dispossessed and subordinate Rajput rulers and chiefs to regain their independence and, if possible, to oust the Turks. The Turkish rulers were successful in overcoming these difficulties, and by the end of the century, were in a position to extend their rule over Malwa and Gujarat, and to penetrate into the Deccan and south India. The effects of the establishment of the Turkish rule in northern India, thus began to be felt within a hundred years all over India, and resulted in far-reaching changes in society, administration and cultural life.

STRUGGLE FOR THE ESTABLISHMENT OF A STRONG MONARCHY

Muizzuddin (Muhammad of Ghur) was succeeded by Qutbuddin Aibak, a Turkish slave in 1206; he had played an important part in the expansion of the Turkish Sultanat in India after the battle of Tarain. Another slave of Muizzuddin, Yalduz, succeeded at Ghazni. As the ruler of Ghazni, Yalduz claimed to rule over Delhi as well.

---

1 An Arabic word meaning 'owned'. It was used to distinguish the imported Turkish slaves meant chiefly for military service, from the humble slaves used for domestic or economic purposes.

This, however, was not accepted by Aibak who ruled from Lahore. But from this time, the Sultanat severed its links with Ghazni. This was fortunate, since it helped to prevent India being drawn into Central Asian politics. It also enabled the Delhi Sultanat to develop on its own without depending on countries outside India.

ILTUTMISH (1210–36)

In 1210, Aibak died of injuries received in a fall from his horse while playing *chaugan* (polo). He was succeeded by Iltutmish who was the son-in-law of Aibak. But before he could do so, he had to fight and defeat the son of Aibak. Thus, the principle of heredity, of son succeeding his father, was checked at the outset.

Iltutmish must be regarded as the real consolidator of the Turkish conquests in north India. At the time of his accession, Ali Mardan Khan had declared himself the king of Bengal and Bihar, while Qubacha, a fellow slave of Aibak, had declared himself an independent ruler of Multan and seized Lahore and parts of the Punjab. At first, even some of the fellow officers of Iltutmish near Delhi were reluctant to accept his authority. The Rajputs found an opportunity to assert their independence. Thus, Kalinjar, Gwaliyar and the entire eastern Rajasthan, including Ajmer and Bayana, threw off the Turkish yoke.

During the early years of his reign, Iltutmish's attention was concentrated on the northwest. A new danger to his position arose with the conquest of Ghazni by Khwarizm Shah. The Khwarizmi empire was the most powerful state in Central Asia at this time, and its eastern frontier now extended up to the Indus. In order to avert this danger, Iltutmish marched to Lahore and occupied it. In 1218, the Khwarizmi empire was destroyed by the Mongols who founded one of the strongest empires in history, which at its height extended from China to the shores of the Mediterranean Sea, and from the Caspian Sea to the river Jaxartes. The danger it posed to India and its effects on the Delhi Sultanat will be discussed in a subsequent section. While the Mongols were busy elsewhere, Iltutmish also ousted Qubacha from Multan and Uchch. The frontiers of the Delhi Sultanat, thus, reached up to the Indus once again.

Secure in the west, Iltutmish was able to turn his attention elsewhere. In Bengal and Bihar, a person called Iwaz who had taken the title of Sultan Ghiyasuddin had assumed independence. He was a generous and able ruler, and built many public works. While he made raids on the territories of his neighbours, the Sena rulers of East Bengal, and the Hindu rulers of Orissa and Kamrup (Assam) continued their sway. In 1226–27, Iwaz was defeated and killed in a battle with Iltutmish's son near Lakhnauti. Bengal and Bihar passed under the suzerainty of Delhi once again. But they were a difficult charge, and repeatedly challenged the authority of Delhi.

At about the same time, Iltutmish took steps to recover Gwaliyar and Bayana. Ajmer and Nagor remained under his control. He sent expeditions against Ranthambhor and Jalor to reassert his suzerainty. He also attacked Nagda, the capital of Mewar (about 22 km from Udaipur), but had to beat a retreat at the arrival of the Gujarat armies, which had come to aid the Rana. As a revenge, Iltutmish despatched an expedition against the Chalukyas of Gujarat, but it was repulsed with losses.

RAZIYA (1236–39)

During his last year, Iltutmish was worried over the problem of succession. He considered none of his surviving sons to be worthy of the throne. After anxious consideration, he finally decided to nominate his daughter, Raziya, to the throne, and induced the nobles and the theologians (*ulama*) to agree to the nomination. Although women had ruled as queens, both in ancient Iran and Egypt, and had acted as regents during the minority rule of princes, the nomination of a woman in preference to sons was a novel step. In order to assert her claim, Raziya had to contend against her brothers as well as against powerful Turkish nobles, and could rule only for three years. Though brief, her rule had a number of interesting features. It marked the beginning of a struggle for power between the monarchy and the Turkish chiefs, sometimes called 'the forty' or the *chahalgani*. Iltutmish had shown great deference to these Turkish chiefs. After his death, these chiefs, drunk with power and arrogance, wanted to install on the throne a puppet whom they could control. They soon discovered that though a woman, Raziya was not prepared

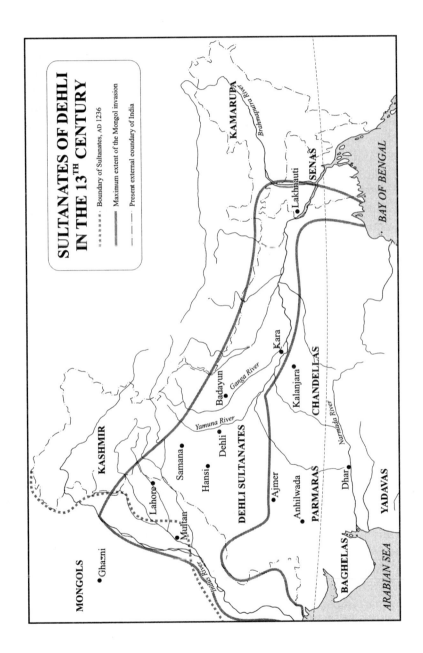

SULTANATES OF DEHLI IN THE 13ᵀᴴ CENTURY

Boundary of Sultanates, AD 1236

Maximum extent of the Mongol invasion

Present external eoundary of India

to play their game. She discarded the female apparel and started holding court with her face unveiled. She even hunted, and led the army in war. Iltutmish's *wazir*, Nizam-ul-Mulk Junaidi, who had opposed her elevation to the throne, and backed and supported a rebellion of nobles against her, was defeated and was forced to flee. She sent an expedition against Ranthambhor to control the Rajputs, and successfully established law and order in the length and breadth of her kingdom. But her attempt to create a party of nobles loyal to her and to raise a non-Turk to high office led to opposition. The Turkish nobles accused her of violating feminine modesty, and of being too friendly to an Abyssinian noble, Yaqut Khan. Yaqut Khan had been appointed Superintendent of the Royal Stable which implied closeness to the sovereign. But contemporary writers have not accused Raziya of any personal intimacy with him: the charge that he used to lift her from the arms-pit to her horse is wrong because Raziya always appeared in public on an elephant, not on horse-back. Rebellions broke out at Lahore and Sirhind. Razia personally led an expedition against Lahore, and compelled the governor to submit. On the way to Sirhind, an internal rebellion broke out in which Yaqut Khan was killed, and Raziya imprisoned at Tabarhinda. However, Raziya won over her captor, Altunia, and after marrying him made a renewed attempt on Delhi. Raziya fought valiantly, but was defeated and killed in a forest by bandits while she was in flight.

ERA OF BALBAN (1246–87)

The struggle between the monarchy and the Turkish chiefs continued, till one of the Turkish chiefs, Ulugh Khan, known in history by his later title of Balban, gradually arrogated all power to himself, and finally ascended the throne in 1265. During the earlier period, Balban held the position of *naib* or deputy to Nasiruddin Mahmud, a younger son of Iltutmish, whom Balban had helped in securing the throne in 1246. Balban further strengthened his position by marrying one of his daughters to the young sultan. The growing authority of Balban alienated many of the Turkish chiefs who had hoped to continue their former power and influence in the affairs of government, since Nasiruddin Mahmud was young and inexperienced. They, therefore, hatched a conspiracy (1253) and ousted Balban from his position. Balban was replaced by Imaduddin Raihan who was an Indian Muslim. Although the Turkish chiefs wanted that all power and authority should remain in their hands, they consented to the appointment of Raihan because they could not agree among themselves which one of them should succeed to Balban's post. Balban agreed to step aside, but carefully continued to build his own group. Within one and a half years of his dismissal, he managed to win over some of his opponents. Balban now made preparations for a military show-down. It seems that he had also established some contacts with the Mongols who had overrun a large part of the Punjab. Sultan Mahmud bowed to the superior strength of Balban's group and dismissed Raihan. After some time, Raihan was defeated and killed. Balban got rid of many of his other rivals by means fair or foul. He even went so far as to assume the royal insignia, the *chhatr*. But he did not assume the throne himself, probably due to the sentiments of the Turkish chiefs. In 1265, Sultan Mahmud died. Some historians are of the opinion that Balban poisoned the young king, and also did away with his sons, in order to clear his way to the throne. Balban's methods were often harsh and undesirable. But there is no doubt that with his accession to the throne there began an era of strong, centralised government.

Balban constantly sought to increase the prestige and power of the monarchy, because he was convinced that this was the only way to face the internal and external dangers facing him. It was an age in which authority and power was supposed to be the privilege of those born in noble houses or those who could boast of an ancient pedigree. Hence, Balban tried to strengthen his claim to the throne by declaring that he was the descendant of the legendary Iranian king Afrasiyab. In order to prove his claim to noble blood, Balban stood forth as the champion of the Turkish nobility. He refused to entertain for important government posts anyone who did not belong to a noble family. This virtually meant the exclusion of Indian Muslims from all positions of power and authority. He sometimes went to ridiculous lengths. For instance, he refused to grant audience to an important trader because he was not high born. The historian, Barani, who was himself a great champion of the Turkish nobles, put the following words in Balban's mouth: 'Whenever I see a base-born ignoble man, my eyes burn and I reach in anger for my sword (to kill him).' We do not know if Balban actually said these words, but they show his attitude towards the low born, whether Turk or non-Turk.

While claiming to act as a champion of the Turkish nobility, Balban was not prepared to share power with anyone, not even with members of his own family. His despotism was such that he was not prepared to hear any criticism even from his own supporters. Balban was determined to finally break the power of the *chahalgani*, i.e., the Turkish nobles, and to exalt the power and prestige of the monarchy. He did not hesitate even to poison his cousin, Sher Khan, to achieve this objective. At the same time, in order to win the confidence of the public, he administered justice with extreme impartiality. Not even the highest in the land were to be spared if they transgressed his authority. Thus, the father of the governor of Badaun as also the father of the governor of Awadh were given exemplary punishment for cruelty to their personal slaves. To keep himself well informed, Balban appointed spies in every department. He also organized a strong centralised army, both to deal with internal disturbances, and to repel the Mongols who had entrenched themselves in the Punjab and posed a serious danger to the Delhi Sultanat. For the purpose, he reorganized the military department (*diwan-i-arz*), and pensioned off those soldiers and troopers who were no longer fit for service. Since many of the troopers were Turks who had come to India in the time of Iltutmish, they raised a hue and cry against this decision, and Balban had to relent to some extend.

The law and order situation in the area around Delhi and in the doab had deteriorated. In the Ganga–Jamuna doab and Awadh, the roads were infested with robbers and dacoits, so much so that communication with the eastern areas had become difficult. Some of the Rajput zamindars had set up forts in the area, and defied the government. Near Delhi, the Mewatis had become so bold as to plunder people upto the outskirts of the city. To deal with these elements, Balban adopted a policy of 'blood and iron'. The Meos were ruthlessly hunted down and killed, the forests around Delhi cut down, and many military out-posts (*thanas*) established there. In the doab and in Katehar (modern Rohilkhand) Balban ordered forests to be cleared, rebellious villagers destroyed and the men, women and children enslaved. Colonies of Afghan soldiers were settled there to safeguard the roads, and to deal with the Rajput zamindars whenever they raised a disturbance against the government.

By these harsh methods, Balban controlled the situation. In order to impress the people with the strength of his government and to awe them, Balban maintained a magnificent court. Whenever he went out, he was surrounded by a large force of bodyguards with drawn swords. He refused to laugh and joke in the court, and even gave up drinking wine so that no one may see him in a non-serious mood. To emphasize that the nobles were not his equals, he insisted on the ceremony of *sijada* and *paibos* (prostration and kissing the monarch's feet). These and many other ceremonies which he copied were Iranian in origin and were considered un-Islamic. However, little objection could be raised because at the time when most Muslim states of Central and West Asia had disappeared in the face of the Mongol onslaught, Balban and the Sultanat of Delhi stood out almost alone as the champions of 'Islam'. Although Balban had a strong army, he did not lead any distant expeditions except the one to Bengal, or to expand the empire for fear of Mongol attack on Delhi. But he exercised his army by arranging elaborate hunting expeditions.

Balban died in 1286. He was undoubtedly one of the main architects of the Sultanat of Delhi, particularly of its form of government and institutions. By asserting the power of the monarchy, Balban strengthened the Delhi Sultanat. But even he could not fully defend northern India against the inroads of the Mongols. Moreover, by largely excluding non-Turks from positions of power and authority and by trying to base the government on a very narrow group, he made many people dissatisfied. This led to fresh disturbances and troubles after his death.

THE MONGOLS AND THE PROBLEM OF THE NORTHWEST FRONTIER

On account of its natural boundaries, India has been safeguarded during most of its history from external invasions. It was only in the northwest that India was vulnerable. As we have seen, it was through the mountain passes of this area that the Turks, like the earlier invaders such as the Huns, Scythians, etc., had been able to penetrate into India and establish an empire there. The configuration of these mountains was such that in order to prevent an invader from reaching the fertile valleys of the Punjab and Sind it was necessary to control the area extending from Kabul to Ghazni and Qandahar. The control of this area flanked by the Hindukush was important, for it was the main route for the arrival of reinforcements from Central Asia.

Due to the fluid situation in West Asia, the Delhi Sultanat was not able to attain these frontiers, posing a persistent danger to India.

With the rise of the Khwarizmi empire, the control of the Ghurids over Kabul, Qandahar and Ghazni had been lost, and the boundary of the Khwarizmi empire had reached the river Indus. It appeared that a struggle for the mastery of north India was about to begin between the Khwarizmi rulers and the successor of Qutbuddin Aibak. Just then an even bigger danger made its appearance. This was the arrival of Changez Khan, the Mongol leader, who prided in calling himself 'the scourge of God'. The Mongols attacked the Khwarizmi empire in 1218. They ruthlessly sacked flourishing cities from the Jaxartes to the Caspian Sea and from Ghazni to Iran, and ravaged the countryside. Many Turkish soldiers went over to the side of the Mongols. The Mongols deliberately used terror as an instrument of war. Whenever a city refused to surrender or was conquered after putting up resistance, all the soldiers and large number of their chiefs were slaughtered, their women and children sold into slavery. Nor were even the civilians spared. Craftsmen from among them were picked out for service with the Mongol army, while other able-bodied men were drafted into labour levies to be used against other towns. All this led to a serious setback to the economy and cultural life of the area. But in due course, the establishment of peace and law and order in the area by the Mongols, and the safeguarding of the trade routes from China to the shores of the Mediterranean Sea started a process of recovery. But several generations passed before Iran, Turan and Iraq were able to recover their previous prosperity. Meanwhile, the Mongol onslaught had serious repercussions on the Sultanat of Delhi. Many princes and large numbers of scholars, theologians, learned men and persons from leading families flocked to Delhi. As the only remaining Muslim state in the area, the Delhi Sultanat, thus, became the centre of Islam. Thus, there was emphasis on Islam as the only bond of unity among different sections of the new rulers. It also implied that the Turkish invaders, who were cut off from their homelands and deprived of reinforcements, were compelled to adapt themselves to the Indian situation as quickly as possible.

The Mongol threat to India appeared in 1221. After the defeat of the Khwarizmi ruler, the crown prince, Jalaluddin, fled and was pursued by Changez Khan. Jalaluddin fought a brave battle on the bank of the Indus, and after being defeated, he flung his horse into the river and crossed over to India. Although Changez loitered near the river Indus for three months, he decided not to cross into India, preferring to give his attention to conquering the remaining portions of the Khwarizmi empire. It is difficult to say what would have happened if Changez had decided to invade India. The Turkish state in India was still too feeble and disorganized. Possibly, India would have had to undergo death, destruction and devastation on a scale far exceeding what it had to endure at the hands of the Turks. Iltutmish, who was ruling at Delhi at the time, tried to appease the Mongols by politely refusing a request from Jalaluddin for asylum. Jalaluddin remained, for some time, in the area between Lahore and the river Sutlej, that is the Cis-Sutlej area. This resulted in a series of Mongol attacks. The river Indus ceased to be India's western boundary.

Lahore and Multan were a bone of contention between Iltutmish and his rivals, Yalduz and Qubacha. Yalduz and Qubacha exhausted themselves in the fight for Lahore. Ultimately, Iltutmish was able to conquer both Lahore and Multan and, thus, formed a fairly strong line of defence against the Mongols.

After the death of Changez Khan in 1227, the mighty Mongol empire was divided among his sons. During this period, the Mongols under Batu Khan overran Russia. However, till 1240 the Mongols desisted from making any encroachments in India beyond the river Indus. The major reason for this was the Mongol pre-occupation with Iraq and Syria. This gave breathing time to the Sultans of Delhi to organize a centralized state and a strong army in India.

In 1241, Tair Bahadur, the commander of the Mongol forces in Herat, Ghur, Ghazni and Turkhistan, appeared at Lahore. Despite urgent appeals to Delhi, no help was forthcoming, and the governor fled from the town. The Mongols sacked and almost depopulated the town. In 1245, the Mongols invested Multan, and only a speedy march by Balban saved the situation. When Balban was busy dealing with the threat to his position from his rivals led by Imaduddin Raihan, the Mongols found an opportunity to capture and hold Lahore. Even some Turkish nobles, including Sher Khan, the governor of Multan, threw in their lot with the Mongols. Although Balban fought against the Mongols stoutly, the frontiers of Delhi gradually receded from the river Jhelum to the Beas, which flowed between the rivers Ravi and the Sutlej. Multan was recovered by Balban, but it remained under heavy Mongol pressure.

It was this situation that Balban had to face as a ruler. Balban adopted a policy of both force and diplomacy. He repaired the forts of Tabarhinda, Sunam and Samana, and posted a strong force in order to prevent the Mongols from crossing the river Beas. He himself remained at Delhi, and never moved out to distant expeditions in order to maintain the utmost vigilance at the frontier. Simultaneously, he sent diplomatic feelers to Halaku, the Mongol Il-Khan of Iran and the neighbouring areas. Envoys from Halaku reached Delhi and were received with great honour by Balban. Balban tacitly agreed to leave the major portion of the Punjab under the Mongol control. The Mongols, on their part, did not make any attack on Delhi. The frontier, however, remained undefined and Balban had to conduct almost annual expeditions against the Mongols in order to keep them in check. He was successful in wresting Multan, and placed it as an independent charge under his eldest son, Prince Mahmud. It was in the effort at holding the Multan–Beas line that Prince Mahmud, the heir-apparent of Balban, was killed in an encounter.

Although Balban died in 1286, the strategic and diplomatic arrangements made by him continued to serve the Delhi Sultanat. In 1292, Abdullah, a grandson of Halaku, advanced on Delhi with 1,50,000 horses. He was defeated by Jalaluddin Khalji near Balban's frontier line of Tabarhinda, Sunam, etc. The demoralised Mongols asked for a truce, and 4000 Mongols, who had embraced Islam, came over to the side of the Indian rulers and settled down near Delhi.

The Mongol attempt to pass beyond the Punjab and to attack Delhi itself was due to a change in Central Asian politics. The Mongol Il-

Khan of Iran had, on the whole, maintained friendly relations with the sultans of Delhi. Their rivals in the East were the Chaghatai Mongols who ruled over Trans-Oxiana. The ruler of Trans-Oxiana, Dawa Khan, being unable to prevail against Il-Khan of Iran, made an attempt to conquer India. From 1297, he mounted a series of campaigns against the forts defending Delhi. In 1299, a Mongol force of 2,00,000 under his son, Qutlugh Khwaja, arrived to conquer Delhi. The Mongols cut off the communications of Delhi with the neighbouring areas, and even entered many streets in the city. This was the first time the Mongols had launched a serious campaign to establish their rule over Delhi. Alauddin Khalji, who was ruling over Delhi, decided to face the Mongols outside Delhi. In a number of actions, the Indian armies held their own, though in one isolated action the famous general, Zafar Khan, died. After some time, the Mongols withdrew without risking a full-scale battle. In 1303, the Mongols appeared again with a force of 1,20,000. Alauddin Khalji, who was campaigning in Rajputana against Chittor, rushed back and fortified himself at his new capital, Siri, near Delhi. The two armies camped facing each other for two months. During this period, the citizens of Delhi had to suffer many hardships. There were daily skirmishes. Finally, the Mongols retreated again, without having achieved anything.

These two invasions of Delhi showed that the sultans of Delhi could match themselves against the Mongols, something which the Central or West Asian rulers had not been able to do till then.[1] At the same time, it was a stern warning to the sultans of Delhi. Alauddin Khalji now took serious steps to raise a large, efficient army, and repaired the fortresses near the Beas. He was, thus, able to repel with great slaughter the Mongol invasions which took place in the following years. In 1306, Dawa Khan, the Mongol ruler of Trans-Oxiana, died and his death was followed by confusion and a civil war. The Mongols now ceased to be a threat to India, till a new conqueror, Timur, unified the Mongols. Taking advantage of the confusion among the Mongols, the rulers of Delhi were able to recover

1 The first defeat suffered by the Mongols in their career of conquest was at the hands of the Egyptians in 1260 near Jerusalem.

Lahore and, in course of time, extended their control up to the river Indus.

It will, thus, be seen that during the entire thirteenth century, the Sultanat of Delhi had to face a serious danger from the northwest. Although the Mongols were gradually able to bring almost the entire Punjab as well as Kashmir under their control, and to threaten Delhi, due to the firmness and vigour of the Turkish rulers, and their diplomacy, this threat was averted, and later the Punjab was recovered. However, the serious threat posed to the Sultanat of Delhi by the Mongols had a powerful effect on all the internal problems of the Sultanat.

Internal Rebellions and the Struggle for the Territorial Consolidation of the Delhi Sultanat

During the rule of the Ilbari Turks (sometimes called the Mameluk or Slave rulers), the Sultans of Delhi had to face not only internal dissensions and foreign invasions, but internal rebellions as well. Some of these rebellions were led by ambitious Muslim chiefs who wanted to become independent; others were led by Rajput rajas and zamindars who were eager to expel the Turkish invaders from their territories or to exploit the difficulties of the Turkish rulers and to aggrandize themselves at the expense of their weaker neighbours. Thus, these rajas and zamindars not only fought against the Turks, but against each other as well. The nature and objectives of the various internal rebellions differed. Hence, it is not correct to lump them together as 'Hindu resistance'. India was a big country, and due to the geographical factors it was difficult to rule the country effectively from one centre. Provincial governors had to be given a large amount of autonomy, and this, combined with local sentiments which were always strong, encouraged them to repudiate the control of Delhi and declare themselves independent. Local rulers could count on regional sentiments which had become stronger between the seventh and twelfth centuries, to rally opposition to the rule of Delhi.

It is not necessary to list all the rebellions against the sultans of Delhi. The eastern region of India which included Bengal and Bihar strove continuously to throw off the yoke of Delhi. It has been noted in an earlier chapter how the Khalji chief, Muhammad bin Bakhtiyar

Khalji, succeeded in expelling the Sena king, Lakshmana Sena, from Lakhnauti. After some confusion, a person called Iwaz who took the title of Ghiyasuddin Sultan began to function as an independent ruler there. Taking advantage of Iltutmish's preoccupations in the northwest, he extended his authority over Bihar and exacted tribute from the ruler of Jajnagar (Orissa), Tirhut (north Bengal), Bang (east Bengal) and Kamrup (Assam).

When Iltutmish was free from his preoccupations, in 1225 he marched against Iwaz. Iwaz submitted at first, then asserted his independence once Iltutmish had turned his back. A son of Iltutmish who was the governor of Awadh defeated and killed Iwaz in a battle. However, affairs continued to be confused till Iltutmish led a second expedition in 1230.

After the death of Iltutmish, the governors of Bengal sometimes asserted their independence and sometimes submitted to Delhi according to their convenience. During this period, Bihar generally remained under the control of Lakhnauti. The governors who acted as independent rulers tried, though without much success, to bring, the areas between Awadh and Bihar under their control. They also attempted to extend their rule over Radha (south Bengal), Orissa and Kamrup, (Assam). In this conflict, the rulers of Orissa and Assam more than held their own. In 1244 the ruler of Orissa badly defeated the Muslim forces near Lakhnauti. Subsequent efforts of the Muslims against Jajnagar, the capital of Orissa, also failed. This showed that the independent Muslim rulers of Lakhnauti were not strong enough to bring the neighbouring Hindu areas under their control.

With the emergence of a strong ruler in the person of Balban, Delhi was eager to reassert its control over Bihar and Bengal. A formal allegiance to Delhi was not enough any longer. Tughril, who had submitted to Balban and then asserted his independence, was hunted down by Balban (1280). Savage punishment was given by Balban to Tughril's family members and followers. This campaign which lasted three years was the only distant campaign undertaken by Balban.

However, Delhi could not keep control over Bengal for long. After Balban's death, his son, Bughra Khan, who had been appointed the governor of Bengal, preferred to rule over that part rather than stake his life for the throne of Delhi. He, therefore, assumed independence and set up a dynasty which ruled over Bengal for the next forty years.

Thus, Bengal and Bihar remained outside the control of Delhi during the greater part of the thirteenth century. The bulk of the Punjab, too had passed under the control of the Mongols. The Turkish rule was not fully secure even in the Ganga doab. The Katehariya Rajputs who had their capital at Ahichchatra across the Ganga were a force to be reckoned with. They frequently raided the district of Badaun. Finally, after his accession, Balban led a large force which resorted to large-scale massacre and wholesale plunder. The district was almost depopulated, jungles were cleared and roads built. Barani records that from that date the iqtas of Baran, Amroha, Sambhal and Katehar (in modern west U.P.) were rendered safe and permanently freed from any trouble.

The southern and western frontier of the Delhi Sultanat was also not fully secure. The problem here was two-fold. Under Aibak, the Turks had captured the chain of forts–Tijara (Alwar), Bayana, Gwaliyar, Kalinjar, etc. They had overrun parts of eastern Rajasthan extending up to Ranthambhor, Nagaur, Ajmer, and Nadol near Jalor. Most of these areas had at one time belonged to the Chauhan empire and were still being ruled by Chauhan families. Aibak's operations against them were, thus, a part of the campaign against the Chauhan empire. However, in the subsequent period, far from advancing into Malwa and Gujarat, the Turks were hard put to defend their gains in eastern Rajasthan and even to maintain their hold on the redoubts defending Delhi and the Gangetic region.

Taking advantage of Iltutmish's preoccupations with the northwest, the Rajput rajas had recovered Kalinjar, Gwaliyar and Bayana. Many other principalities, including Ranthambhor and Jalor, repudiated Turkish suzerainty. From 1226, Iltutmish commenced operations to recover his control over these areas. He first invested Ranthambhor and compelled the ruler to accept Turkish suzerainty. He also captured Jalor which was on the route to Gujarat. The efforts of Iltutmish to extend his control over Gujarat and Malwa, however, failed. The Chalukyas of Gujarat repulsed an attack by Iltutmish. The Paramaras of Malwa were also too strong for the Turks. Iltutmish, however, made a raid into Malwa and plundered Ujjain and Raisina. One of his general also raided Bundi. In the east, Iltutmish recovered Bayana and Gwaliyar, but was unable to make much headway against the Rajputs of Baghelkhand.

The Turkish control over eastern Rajputana was again shaken in the confusion following Iltutmish's death. Many Rajput rulers threw off Turkish suzerainty. The fort of Gwaliyar was also recovered by them. The Bhatti Rajputs, who were entrenched in the area of Mewat, isolated Bayana and extended their depredations up to the outskirts of Delhi.

Balban's attempt to conquer Ranthambhor and to recover Gwaliyar failed. However, he subdued Mewat ruthlessly so that Delhi remained secure from Mewati inroads for almost one hundred years. Ajmer and Nagaur continued to remain under the firm control of the Delhi Sultanat. Balban, thus, consolidated the Turkish rule in eastern Rajasthan, despite his other preoccupations. The continuous fighting among the Rajput rulers also aided the Turks, and made impossible any effective combination of the Rajputs against them.

The establishment of a strong monarchy, the repelling of the Mongol invaders, and the consolidation of the territory of the Delhi Sultanat in the Ganga doab and control over eastern Rajasthan paved the way for the next step in the history of the Delhi Sultanat, viz., its expansion into western India and the Deccan.

SEVEN

The Delhi Sultanat—II
(*Circa* 1200–1400)

THE KHALJIS AND THE TUGHLAQS

After the death of Balban in 1286, there was again confusion in Delhi for some time. Balban's chosen successor, Prince Mahmud, had died earlier in a battle with the Mongols. A second son, Bughra Khan, preferred to rule over Bengal and Bihar although he was invited by the nobles at Delhi to assume the throne. Hence, a grandson of Balban was installed in Delhi. But he was too young and inexperienced to cope with the situation. There had been a good deal of resentment and opposition at the attempt of the Turkish nobles to monopolize high offices. Many non-Turks, such as the Khaljis, had come to India at the time of the Ghurid invasion. They had never received sufficient recognition in Delhi, and had to move to Bengal and Bihar for an opportunity for advancement. They had also found employment as soldiers, many of them being posted in the northwest to meet the Mongol challenge. In course of time, many Indian Muslims had been admitted to the nobility. They also were dissatisfied at being denied high offices, as may be inferred from the manner in which Imaduddin Raihan was put up against Balban. Balban's own example of setting aside the sons of Nasiruddin Mahmud had demonstrated that a successful general could ascend the throne by ousting the scions of an established dynasty, provided he had sufficient support in the nobility and the army.

THE KHALJIS (1290–1320)

For these reasons, a group of Khalji nobles led by Jalaluddin Khalji, who had been the warden of the marches in the northwest and had fought many successful engagements against the Mongols, overthrew the incompetent successors of Balban in 1290. The Khalji rebellion was welcomed by the non-Turkish sections in the nobility. The Khaljis who were of a mixed Turkish–Afghan origin, did not exclude the Turks from high offices, but the rise of the Khaljis to power ended the Turkish monopoly of high offices.

Jalaluddin Khalji ruled only for a brief period of six years. He tried to mitigate some of the harsh aspects of Balban's rule. He was the first ruler of the Delhi Sultanat to clearly put forward the view that the state should be based on the willing support of the governed, and that since the large majority of the people in India were Hindus, the state in India could not be a truly Islamic state. He also tried to gain the goodwill of the nobility by a policy of tolerance and avoiding harsh punishments. However, many people, including his supporters, considered this to be a weak policy which was not suited to the times. The Delhi Sultanat faced numerous internal and external foes, and for this reason there was a sense of insecurity. Jalaluddin's policy was reversed by Alauddin who awarded drastic punishments to all those who dared to oppose him.

Alauddin Khalji (1296–1316) came to the throne by treacherously murdering his uncle and father-in-law, Jalaluddin Khalji. As the governor of Awadh, Alauddin had accumulated a vast treasure by invading Deogir in the Deccan. Jalaluddin had gone to visit his nephew at Kara in the hope of getting hold of this treasure. He had left most of his army behind and had crossed the river Ganges with only a few followers so that his nephew might not take fright and run away. After murdering his uncle, Alauddin won over most of the nobles and soldiers to his side by a lavish use of gold. But for some time, Alauddin had to face a series of rebellions—some by disgruntled nobles, and some by Alauddin's own relations. To overawe his opponents, Alauddin Khalji adopted methods of utmost severity and ruthlessness. Most of the nobles who had defected to him by the lure of gold were either killed or dismissed and their properties confiscated. Severe punishments were given to the rebellious members of his own family. He resorted to a wholesale massacre of the Mongols, a couple of thousands of them having settled down in Delhi after embracing Islam in the time of Jalaluddin. These new converts had rebelled, demanding a larger share in the loot in Gujarat having campaigned there. Alauddin gave harsh punishments even to the wives and children of these rebels, a practice which, according to the historian Barani, was a new one and was continued by his successors. Alauddin framed a series of regulations to prevent the nobles from conspiring against him. They were forbidden to hold banquets or festivities, or to form marriage alliances without the permission of the sultan. To discourage festive parties, he banned the use of wines and intoxicants. He also instituted a spy service to inform the sultan of all that the nobles said and did.

By these harsh methods, Alauddin Khalji cowed down the nobles, and made them completely subservient to the crown. No further rebellions took place during his lifetime. But, in the long run, his methods proved harmful to the dynasty. The old nobility was destroyed, and the new nobility was taught to accept anyone who could ascend the throne of Delhi. This became apparent after Alauddin Khalji's death in 1316. His favourite, Malik Kafur, raised a minor son of Alauddin to the throne and imprisoned or blinded his other sons, without encountering any opposition from the nobles. Soon after this, Kafur was killed by the palace guards, and a Hindu convert, Khusrau, ascended the throne. Although the historians of the time accuse Khusrau of violating Islam and of committing all types of crimes, the fact is that Khusrau was no worse than any of the preceding monarchs. Nor was any open resentment voiced against him by the Muslim nobles or by the population of Delhi. Even Nizamuddin Auliya, the famous Sufi saint of Delhi, acknowledged Khusrau by accepting his gifts. This had a positive aspect too. It showed that the Muslims of Delhi and the neighbouring areas were no longer swayed by racist considerations, and were prepared to obey anyone irrespective of his family or racial background. This helped in broadening the social base of the nobility still further. However, in 1320, a group of officers led by Ghiyasuddin Tughlaq raised the banner of revolt. They broke out into open rebellion, and in a hard fought battle outside the capital, Khusrau was defeated and killed.

THE TUGHLAQS (1320–1412)

Ghiyasuddin Tughlaq established a new dynasty which ruled till 1412. The Tughlaqs provided three competent rulers: Ghiyasuddin, his son Muhammad bin Tughlaq (1324–51), and his nephew Firuz Shah Tughlaq (1351–88). The first two of these sultans ruled over an empire which comprised almost the entire country. The empire of Firuz was smaller but even then it was almost as large as that ruled over by Alauddin Khalji. After the death of Firuz, the Delhi Sultanat disintegrated and north India was divided into a series of small states. Although the Tughlaqs continued to rule till 1412, the invasion of Delhi by Timur in 1398 may be said to mark the end of the Tughlaq empire.

We shall first examine the remarkable expansion of the Delhi Sultanat from the time of Alauddin Khalji, then the various internal reforms in the Sultanat during the period, and the factors which led to the disintegration of the Sultanat.

I. Expansion of the Delhi Sultanat

We have seen how eastern Rajasthan, including Ajmer and some of its neighbouring territories, had come under the control of the Delhi Sultanat, though from the time of Balban, Ranthambhor, which was the most powerful Rajput state, had gone out of its control. Jalaluddin had undertaken an invasion of Ranthambhor but found the task too difficult for him. Thus, southern and western Rajasthan had remained outside the control of the Sultanat. With the rise to power of Alauddin Khalji, a new situation developed. Within a space of twenty-five years, the armies of the Delhi Sultanat not only brought Gujarat and Malwa under their control and subdued most of the princes in Rajasthan, they also overran the Deccan and south India upto Madurai. In due course, an attempt was made to bring this vast area under the direct administrative control of Delhi. The new phase of expansion was initiated by Alauddin Khalji and was continued under his successors, the climax being reached during the reign of Muhammad bin Tughlaq.

We have already seen how the Delhi Sultanat was gradually geared up for this renewed phase of expansion. At this time, Malwa, Gujarat and Deogir were being ruled by Rajput dynasties, most of which had come into existence towards the end of the twelfth and the beginning of the thirteenth century. Despite the establishment of the Turkish rule in the Ganga valley, these dynasties had hardly changed their old ways. Moreover, each one of them was contending for mastery over the entire region. So much so, when under Iltutmish the Turks attacked Gujarat, the rulers of both Malwa and Deogir attacked it from the south. In the Maratha region the rulers of Deogir were constantly at war with Warangal in the Telengana region, and with the Hoysalas in the Karnataka area. The Hoysalas, in turn, were at war with their neighbours, the Pandyas in Mabar (Tamil area). These rivalries not only made the conquest of Malwa and Gujarat easier, but tended to draw an invader further and further into the south.

The Turkish rulers had strong reasons for coveting Malwa and Gujarat. Not only were these areas fertile and populous, they controlled the western sea-ports and the trade routes connecting them with the Ganga valley. The overseas trade from Gujarat ports brought in a lot of gold and silver which had been accumulated by the rulers of the area. Another reason for the sultans of Delhi to establish their rule over Gujarat was that it could secure them a better control over the supply of horses to their armies. With the rise of the Mongols in Central and West Asia and their struggle with the rulers of Delhi, the supply of horses of good quality to Delhi from this region had been beset with difficulties. The import of Arabi, Iraqi and Turki horses to India from the western sea-ports had been an important item of trade since the eighth century.

Early in 1299, an army under two of Alauddin Khalji's noted generals marched against Gujarat by way of Rajasthan. On their way, they raided and captured Jaisalmer also. The Gujarat ruler, Rai Karan, was taken by surprise, and fled without offering a fight. The chief cities of Gujarat, including Anhilwara where many beautiful buildings and temples had been built over generations, were sacked. The famous temple of Somnath which had been rebuilt in the twelfth century was also plundered and sacked. An enormous booty was collected. Nor were the wealthy Muslim merchants of Cambay spared. It was here that Malik Kafur, who later led the invasions of south India, was captured. He was presented to Alauddin, and soon rose in his estimation.

Gujarat now passed under the control of Delhi. The rapidity and ease with which Gujarat was conquered suggests that the Gujarat ruler was not popular among his subjects. It appears that one of his ministers, who had fallen out with him, had approached Alauddin to invade Gujarat, and had helped him. The Gujarat army may not have been well trained, and the administration was probably lax. With the help of Ramachandra, the ruler of Deogir, the ousted ruler Rai Karan, managed to hold on to a portion of south Gujarat. As we shall see, this provided an additional cause of war between Delhi and the Yadavas of Deogir.

Rajasthan

After the conquest of Gujarat, Alauddin turned his attention to the consolidation of his rule over Rajasthan. The first to invite his attention was Ranthambhor which was being ruled by the Chauhan successors of Prithviraj. Its ruler, Hamirdeva, had embarked on a series of war-like expeditions against his neighbours. He is credited with having won victories against Raja Bhoj of Dhar, and the Rana of Mewar. But it were these victories which proved to be his undoing. After the Gujarat campaign, on their way back to Delhi, the Mongol soldiers rebelled, following a dispute regarding the share of the booty. The rebellion was crushed and a wholesale massacre followed. Two of the Mongol nobles fled for refuge to Ranthambhor. Alauddin sent messages to Hamirdeva to kill or expel the Mongol nobles. But Hamir Deva, with a high sense of dignity and obligation to those who had sought refuge with him, and being confident of the strength of his fort and his armies, sent haughty replies. He was not far wrong in his estimation, for Ranthambhor was reputed to be the strongest fort in Rajasthan and had earlier defied Jalaluddin Khalji. Alauddin despatched an army commanded by one of his reputed generals but it was repulsed with losses by Hamirdeva. Finally, Alauddin himself had to march against Ranthambhor. The famous poet, Amir Khusrau, who went along with Alauddin, has given a graphic description of the fort and its investment. After three months of close siege, the fearful *jauhar* ceremony took place: the women mounted the funeral pyre, and all the men came out to fight to the last. This is the first description we have of the *jauhar* in Persian. All the Mongols, too, died fighting with the Rajputs. This event took place in 1301.

Alauddin, next, turned his attention towards Chittor which, after Ranthambhor, was the most powerful state in Rajasthan. It was, therefore, necessary for Alauddin to subdue it. Apart from this, its ruler Ratan Singh had annoyed him by refusing permission to his armies to march to Gujarat through Mewar territories. Chittor also dominated the route from Ajmer to Malwa. There is a popular legend that Alauddin attacked Chittor because he coveted Padmini, the beautiful queen of Ratan Singh. Many modern historians do not accept this legend because it is mentioned for the first time more than a hundred years later. It was embellished later by a Hindi poet, Malik Muhammad Jaisi. In this story, Padmini is the princess of Singhaldvipa and Ratan Singh crosses the seven seas to reach her and brings her back to Chittor after many adventures which appear improbable. The Padmini legend is a part of this account. That the sultan could have demanded to see the face of a queen who was the wife of another ruler is also as unthinkable as the idea that the proud Rana would have agreed to show her, even through a mirror. Such a suggestion would have been an insult to the Rajput sense of honour for which they willingly sacrificed their lives.

Alauddin closely invested Chittor. After a valiant resistance by the besieged for several months, Alauddin stormed the fort (1303). The Rajputs performed *jauhar* and most of the warriors died fighting. Padmini, and the other queens, also sacrificed their lives. But it seems that Ratan Singh was captured alive and kept a prisoner for some time. Chittor was assigned to Alauddin's minor son, Khizr Khan, and a Muslim garrison was posted in the fort. After some time, its charge was handed over to a cousin of Ratan Singh.

Alauddin also overran Jalor which lay on the route to Gujarat. Almost all the other major states in Rajasthan were forced to submit. However, it seems that Alauddin did not try to establish direct administration over the Rajput states. The Rajput rulers were allowed to rule but had to pay regular tribute, and to obey the orders of the sultan. Muslim garrisons were posted in some of the important towns, such as Ajmer, Nagaur, etc. Thus, Rajasthan was thoroughly subdued.

Deccan and South India

Even before completing the subjugation of Rajasthan, Alauddin had conquered Malwa which, says Amir Khusrau, was so extensive that even wise geographers were unable to delimit its frontiers. Unlike Rajasthan, Malwa was brought under direct administration, and a governor was appointed to look after it.

In 1306–07, Alauddin planned two campaigns. The first was against Rai Karan who after his expulsion from Gujarat, had been holding Baglana on the border of Malwa. Rai Karan fought bravely, but he could not resist for long. The second expedition was aimed against Rai Ramachandra, the ruler of Deogir, who had been in alliance with Rai Karan. In an earlier campaign, Rai Ramachandra had agreed to pay a yearly tribute to Delhi. This had fallen into arrears. The command of the second army was entrusted to Alauddin's slave, Malik Kafur. Rai Ramachandra who surrendered to Kafur, was honourably treated and carried to Delhi where, after some time, he was restored to his dominions with the title of Rai Rayan. A gift of one lakh *tankas* was given to him along with a golden coloured canopy which was a symbol of rulership. He was also given a district of Gujarat. One of his daughters was married to Alauddin. The alliance with Rai Ramachandra was to prove to be of great value to Alauddin in his further aggrandisement in the Deccan.

Between 1309 and 1311, Malik Kafur led two campaigns in south India—the first against Warangal in the Telengana area and the other against Dwar Samudra (modern Karnataka), Mabar and Madurai (Tamil Nadu). A great deal has been written about these expeditions partly because they struck the imagination of the contemporaries. The court poet, Amir Khusrau, made them the subject of a book. These campaigns reflected boldness, self-confidence and a high degree of a spirit of adventure on the part of the Delhi rulers. For the first time, Muslim armies penetrated as far south as Madurai, and brought back untold wealth. They provided first-hand information about conditions in the south though they hardly provided any fresh geographical knowledge. The trade routes to south India were well known, and when Kafur's armies reached Virachala in Mabar, they found a colony of Muslim merchants settled there. The ruler even had a contingent of Muslim troops in his army. These expeditions greatly raised Kafur in public estimation, and Alauddin appointed him *malik-naib* or vice-regent of the empire. Politically, however, the effects of these campaigns were limited. Kafur was able to force the rulers of Warangal and Dwar Samudra to sue for peace, to surrender all their treasures and elephants, and to promise an annual tribute. But it was well known that to secure these tributes an annual campaign would be needed. In the case of Mabar, even this formal agreement was not forthcoming. The rulers there had avoided a pitched battle. Kafur had plundered as much as he could including a number of wealthy temples, such as those at Chidambaram. But he had to return to Delhi without being able to defeat the Tamil armies.

Despite the troubles following the death of Alauddin, within a decade and a half of his death, all the southern kingdoms mentioned above were wiped out, and their territories brought under the direct administration of Delhi. Alauddin himself was not in favour of direct administration of the southern states. However, the change in this policy had begun in his own lifetime. In 1315, Rai Ramachandra, who had remained steadily loyal to Delhi, died and his sons threw off the yoke of Delhi. Malik Kafur quickly came and crushed the rebellion and assumed direct administration of the area. However, many outlying areas, declared themselves independent while a few remained under the control of the descendants of the rai.

On succeeding to the throne, Mubarak Shah a successor of Alauddin, subdued Deogir again, and installed a Muslim governor there. He also raided Warangal, and compelled the ruler to cede one of his districts, and pay an annual tribute of forty gold bricks. Khusrau Khan, a slave of the sultan, made a plundering raid into Mabar and sacked the rich city of Masulipatnam. No conquests were made in the area.

Following the accession of Ghiyasuddin Tughlaq in 1320, a sustained and vigorous forward policy was embarked upon. The sultan's son, Muhammad bin Tughlaq, was posted to Deogir for the purpose. On the excuse that the ruler of Warangal had not paid the stipulated tribute, Muhammad bin Tughlaq besieged Warangal again. At first, he suffered a reverse. Following a rumour of the sultan's death in Delhi, the Delhi armies were disorganized, and the defenders fell upon them inflicting heavy losses. Muhammad bin Tughlaq had to retreat to Deogir. After reorganizing his armies, he attacked again, and this time no quarter was given to the rai. This was followed by the conquest of Mabar which was also annexed. Muhammad bin Tughlaq then raided Orissa, and returned to Delhi with rich plunder. Next year, he subdued Bengal which had been independent since the death of Balban.

Thus, by 1324, the territories of the Delhi Sultanat reached up to Madurai. The last Hindu principality in the area, Kampili in south Karnataka, was annexed in 1328. A cousin of Muhammad bin Tughlaq, who had rebelled, had been given shelter there, thus providing a convenient excuse for attacking it.

The sudden expansion of the Delhi Sultanat to the far south and to the east, including Orissa, created tremendous administrative and financial problems which had to be faced by Muhammad bin Tughlaq. We shall now turn to a study of the manner in which he tried to cope with these problems, and the strains which it imposed on the Sultanat itself.

II. Internal Reforms and Experiments

By the time Alauddin Khalji came to the throne, the position of the Delhi Sultanat was fairly well consolidated in the central portion of the empire, i.e., the portion comprising the upper Ganga valley and eastern Rajasthan. This emboldened the sultans to undertake a series of internal reforms and experiments, aimed at improving the administration, strengthening the army, gearing up the machinery of land revenue administration, taking steps to expand and improve cultivation and providing for the welfare of the citizens in the rapidly expanding towns. Not all the measures were successful, but they mark important new departures. Some of the experiments failed on account of lack of experience, some because they were not well conceived, or on account of opposition of vested interests. They do, however, show that the Turkish state had now acquired a measure of stability, and that it was no longer concerned merely with warfare and law and order.

Market Control and Agrarian Policy of Alauddin

For contemporaries, Alauddin's measures to control the markets was one of the great wonders of the world. In a series of orders after his return from the Chittor campaign, Alauddin sought to fix the cost of all commodities from foodgrains, sugar and cooking oil to a needle, and from costly imported cloth to horses, cattle, and slave boys and girls. For the purpose, he set up three markets at Delhi—one market for foodgrains, the second for costly cloth, and the third for horses, slaves and cattle. Each market was under the control of a high officer called *shahna* who maintained a register of the merchants, and strictly controlled the shopkeepers and the prices. Regulation of prices, especially foodgrains, was a constant concern of medieval rulers, because without the supply of cheap foodgrains to the towns, they could not hope to enjoy the support of the citizens, and the army stationed there. But Alauddin had some additional reasons for controlling the market. The Mongol invasions of Delhi had pin-pointed the need to raise a large army to check them. But such an army would soon exhaust his treasures unless he could lower the prices, and hence lower their salaries. To realize his objectives, Alauddin proceeded in a characteristically thorough way. In order to ensure a regular supply of cheap foodgrains, he declared that the land revenue in the doab region, that is, the area extending from Meerut near the Yamuna to the border of Kara near Allahabad would be paid directly to the state, i.e., the villages in the area would not be assigned in *iqta* to anyone. Further, the land revenue was raised to half of the produce. This was a heavy charge and Alauddin adopted a number of measures, which we shall note later, to cope with the situation. By raising the state demand, and generally obliging the peasants to pay it in cash, the peasants were forced to sell their foodgrains at a low price to *banjaras* who were to carry them to the towns, and to sell them at prices fixed by the state. To ensure that there was no hoarding, all the *banjaras* were registered, and their agents and their family were held collectively responsible for any violations. As a further check, the state itself set up warehouses and stocked them with foodgrains which were released whenever there was a famine or a threat of a shortfall in supply. Alauddin kept himself constantly informed of everything and very harsh punishment was given if any shopkeeper charged a higher price, or tried to cheat by using false weights and measures. Barani tells us that prices were not allowed to be increased by a *dam* or a paisa even during the time of famine. Thus, wheat sold at 7½ *jitals* a *man*, barley at 4 *jitals*, good quality rice at 5 *jitals*.[1] Barani says: 'The permanence of prices in the grain market was a wonder of the age'.

Control of the prices of horses was important for the sultan because without the supply of good horses at reasonable prices to the army, the efficiency of the army could not be maintained. The position of the supply of horses had improved as a result of the conquest of Gujarat. Good quality horses could be sold only to the state. The price of a first grade horse fixed by Alauddin was 100 to 120 *tankas*, while a *tattu* (pony) not fit for the army cost 10 to 25 *tankas*. The prices of cattle as well as of slaves were strictly regulated, and Barani gives us their prices in detail. The prices of cattle and slaves are mentioned side by side by Barani. This shows that slavery was accepted in medieval India as a normal feature. Control of the prices of other goods, especially of costly cloth, perfumes, etc., was not vital for the sultan. However, their prices were also fixed, probably because it was felt that high prices in this sector would affect prices in general. Or, it might have been done in order to please the nobility. We are told that large sums of money were advanced to the Multani traders for bringing fine quality cloth to Delhi from various parts of the country. As a result, Delhi became the biggest market for fine cloth, the price of which was fixed and traders from all places flocked to Delhi in order to buy it and sell it at a higher price elsewhere.

Realization of land revenue in cash enabled Alauddin to pay his soldiers in cash. He was the first sultan in the Sultanat to do so. A *sawar* (cavalryman) in his time was paid 238 *tankas* a year, or about 20 *tankas* a month. It appears that he was expected to maintain himself and his horse and his equipment out of this amount. Even then, this was not a low salary, for during Akbar's time, when prices were far higher, a Mughal cavalryman received a salary of about 20 rupees a month. Actually, a Turkish cavalryman during the thirteenth and fourteenth centuries was almost a gentleman, and expected a salary which would enable him to live as such. In view of this, the salary fixed by Alauddin was low, and the control of the market was, therefore, necessary.

---

1 48 *jitals* made a *tanka*. Alauddin's *man* was about 15 kg of today. Thus, a citizen of Delhi could buy for a *tanka* (almost equivalent to a silver rupee) 96 kg wheat, 144 kg rice, and 180 kg barley.

The historian Barani thought that a major objective of Alauddin's control of markets was his desire to punish the Hindus since most of the traders were Hindus and it was they who resorted to profiteering in foodgrains and other goods. However, most of the overland trade to West and Central Asia was in the hands of Khurasanis who were Muslims, as also Multanis, many of whom were Muslims. Alauddin's measures, therefore, affected these sections also, a fact which Barani does not mention.

It is not clear whether the market regulations of Alauddin were applied only to Delhi, or also to other towns in the empire. Barani tells us that the regulations concerning Delhi always tended to be followed in other towns also. In any case, the army was stationed not only in Delhi but in other towns as well. However, we do not have sufficient information to be certain in the matter. It is clear that while the merchants—Hindus and Muslims—might have complained against the price control, not only the army but all citizens, irrespective of their religious beliefs, benefited from the cheapness of foodgrains and other articles.

Agrarian Reforms

Apart from the control of the market, Alauddin took important steps in the field of land revenue administration. He was the first monarch in the Sultanat who insisted that in the doab, land revenue would be assessed on the basis of measuring the land under cultivation. This implied that the rich and the powerful in the villages who had more land could not pass on their burden to the poor. Alauddin wanted that the landlords of the area—called *khuts* and *muqaddams*, should pay the same taxes as the others. Thus, they had to pay taxes on milch cattle and houses like the others, and forgo other illegal cesses which they were in the habit of realizing. In the picturesque language of Barani, 'the *khuts* and *muqaddams* could not afford to ride on rich caprisoned horses, or to chew betel leaves and they became so poor that their wives had to go and work in the houses of Muslims'.

The policy of direct collection of land revenue by the state, based on measurement could only succeed if the *amils* and other local officials were honest. Although Alauddin had given these elements sufficient salaries to enable them to live in comfort, he insisted that their accounts should be audited strictly. We are told that for small defaults, they would be beaten and sent to prison. Barani says that their life had become so insecure for them that no one was willing to marry their daughters to them! No doubt this is an exaggeration because, then as now, government service was considered to be prestigious and those who held government offices, whether they were Hindus or Muslims, were eagerly sought as marriage partners.

Although Barani writes as if all the measures mentioned above were directed solely against the Hindus, it is clear that they were, in the main, directed against the privileged sections in the countryside. But these can hardly be considered as socialistic measures. They were basically designed to meet an emergency situation, viz., the danger posed by the Mongols. Perhaps, it would have been better for Alauddin to have controlled only the price of essential commodities, such as food-grains, etc. But, as the contemporary writers, Barani, says, he tried to control the price of everything, from 'caps to socks, from combs to needles, vegetables, soups, sweetmeats to *chapatis.*' These led to vexatious laws which were sought to be violated and led to drastic punishments and resentment. Alauddin's agrarian policy was certainly harsh and must have affected the ordinary cultivators also. But it was not so burdensome as to drive them into rebellion, or flight.

The market regulations of Alauddin came to an end with his death, but it did achieve a number of gains. We are told by Barani that the regulations enabled Alauddin to raise a large and efficient cavalry which enabled him to defeat the subsequent Mongol onslaughts, with great slaughter, and to drive them beyond the Indus. The land revenue reforms of Alauddin marked an important step towards closer relationship with the rural areas. Some of his measures were continued by his successors, and later provided a basis for the agrarian reforms of Sher Shah and Akbar.

MUHAMMAD TUGHLAQ'S EXPERIMENTS

Next to Alauddin Khalji, Muhammad bin Tughlaq (1324–51) is best remembered as a ruler who undertook a number of bold experiments, and showed a keen interest in agriculture.

In some ways, Muhammad bin Tughlaq was one of the most remarkable rulers of his age. He was deeply read in religion and philosophy, and had a critical and open mind. He conversed not only with the Muslim mystics, but also with the Hindu yogis and Jain saints such as Jinaprabha Suri. This was not liked by many orthodox theologians who accused him of being a 'rationalist', that is, one who was not prepared to accept religious beliefs as a matter of faith. He was also prepared to give high offices to people on the basis of merit, irrespective of whether they belonged to noble families or not. Unfortunately, he was inclined to be hasty and impatient. That is why so many of this experiments failed, and he has been dubbed an 'ill starred idealist'.

Muhammad Tughlaq's reign started under inauspicious circumstances. Sultan Ghiyasuddin Tughlaq was returning to Delhi after a successful campaign against Bengal. A wooden pavilion was erected hastily at the orders of Muhammad Tughlaq to give a fitting reception to the sultan. When the captured elephants were being paraded, the hastily erected structure collapsed, and the Sultan was killed. This led to a number of rumours—that Muhammad Tughlaq had planned to kill his father, that this was a curse of the heavens and of the famous saint of Delhi, Shaikh Nizamuddin Auliya, whom the ruler had threatened to punish, etc.

The most controversial step which Muhammad Tughlaq undertook soon after his accession was the so-called transfer of the capital from Delhi to Deogir. As we have seen, Deogir had been a base for the expansion of Turkish rule in south India. Muhammad Tughlaq himself had spent a number of years there as a prince. The attempt to bring the entire south India under the direct control of Delhi had led to serious political difficulties. The people of the area were restive under what they felt was an alien rule. A number of Muslim nobles had tried to take advantage of this situation to proclaim their independence there. The most serious rebellion was that of a cousin of Muhammad Tughlaq, Gurshasp, against whom the sultan had to proceed personally. It appears that the sultan wanted to make Deogir a second capital so that he might be able to control south India better. For this purpose, he ordered many of the officers and their followers and leading men, including many Sufi saints, to shift

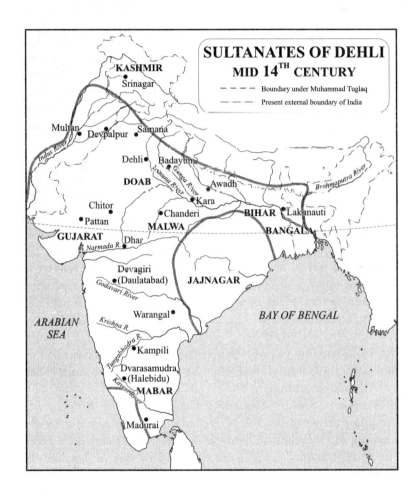

SULTANATES OF DEHLI
MID 14TH CENTURY

---- ---- ---- Boundary under Muhammad Tuglaq
— · — · — Present external boundary of India

KASHMIR
Srinagar

Multan
Devpalpur Samana

Dehli Badayuns

DOAB Awadh

Kara

Chitor Chanderi BIHAR Lakhnauti

Pattan MALWA BANGALA

GUJARAT Dhar
Narmada R.

Devagiri
(Daulatabad) JAJNAGAR
Godavari River

Warangal BAY OF BENGAL

ARABIAN
SEA Krishna R.

Kampili

Dvarasamudra
(Halebidu)
MABAR

Madurai

Indus River
Jumna River
Ganga River
Brahmaputra River
Tungabhadra R.
Kaveri River

to Deogir which was renamed Daulatabad. It seems that a good deal of official pressure was exerted on these sections to migrate. Liberal grants were also provided to them, and arrangements made for their stay at Daulatabad. No attempt was made to shift the rest of the population. Delhi remained a large and populous city in the absence of the sultan. Coins minted in Delhi, while the sultan was at Deogir, testify to this. Though Muhammad Tughlaq had built a road from Delhi to Daulatabad and set up rest houses on the way to help the travellers, Daulatabad was more than 1500 km away. Many people died due to the rigours of the journey and the heat, since this movement took place during the summer season. Many of those who reached Daulatabad felt homesick, for some of them had lived for several generations in Delhi and looked upon it as their home. Hence, there was a good deal of discontent. After a couple of years, Muhammad Tughlaq decided to abandon Daulatabad, largely because he soon found that just as he could not control the south from Delhi, he could not control north India from Daulatabad.

Though the attempt to make Deogir a second capital failed, the exodus did have a number of long-range benefits. It helped in bringing north and south India closer together by improving communications. Many people, including religious divines who had gone to Daulatabad, settled down there. They became the means of spreading in the Deccan the cultural, religious and social ideas which the Turks had brought with them to north India. This resulted in a new process of cultural interaction between north and south India, as well as in south India itself.

Another step which Muhammad Tughlaq took at this time was the introduction of the 'token currency'. Since money is merely a medium of exchange, all countries in the world today have token currencies—generally paper currency, so that they do not have to depend upon the supply of gold and silver. There was a shortage of silver in the world in the fourteenth century. Moreover, Qublai Khan of China had already successfully experimented with a token currency. A Mongol ruler of Iran, Ghazan Khan, had also experimented with it. Muhammad Tughlaq decided to introduce a bronze coin which was to have the same value as the silver *tanka*. Specimens of this coin have been found in different parts of India, and can be seen in museums. The idea of a token currency was a new one in India, and it was difficult to induce the traders as well as the common man to accept it. Muhammad Tughlaq might still have been successful if the government had been able to prevent people from forging the new coins. The government was not able to do so, and soon the new coins began to be greatly devalued in the markets. Finally Muhammad Tughlaq decided to withdraw the token currency. He promised to exchange silver pieces for bronze coins. In this way many people exchanged the new coins. But the forged coins which could be found out from tests were not exchanged. These coins were heaped up outside the fort and, Barani says, they remained lying there for many years.

The failure of these two experiments affected the prestige of the sovereign, and also meant wastage of money. However, the government quickly recovered. The Moroccan traveller, Ibn Battuta, who came to Delhi in 1333, could not see any harmful after-effects of these experiments. A far more serious problem with which Muhammad bin Tughlaq had to contend was that of the security of the frontiers. Administration, especially revenue administration, and his relations with the nobles also presented some serious problems.

We have seen in an earlier section the serious problems posed to the Delhi Sultanat by the steady expansion of the Mongol power into the Punjab, and their assaults on Delhi. Although the Mongols had by then become weak due to their internal dissensions, they were still strong enough to threaten the Punjab and the areas near Delhi. In the early years of Muhammad Tughlaq's reign, the Mongols under their leader Tarmashrin burst into Sind, and a force reached up to Meerut, about 65 km from Delhi. Muhammad Tughlaq not only defeated the Mongols in a battle near the Jhelum, but also occupied Kalanaur and for some time his power extended beyond the Indus upto Peshawar. This showed that the sultan of Delhi was now in a position to go over to the offensive against the Mongols. After coming back from Deogir, the sultan recruited a large army in order to occupy Ghazni and Afghanistan. Barani says that his object was to occupy Khurasan and Iraq. We have no means of finding out the true objective of Muhammad Tughlaq. Maybe his objective was to reestablish what has been called the 'scientific frontier', viz., the line formed by the Hindukush and Qandahar. Many of the princes and others who had fled from Central Asia and taken shelter at the court of Muhammad Tughlaq may have thought that it was a good opportunity to oust the Mongols from the area. After a year, and following the failure of the experiment of establishing a token currency, and improvement of relations with the Mongols, the army was disbanded. Meanwhile, the situation in Central Asia changed rapidly. In due course, Timur united the entire area under his control and posed a fresh threat to India.

The effects of the Khurasan project should not be exaggerated, or confused with the Qarachil expedition. This expedition was launched in the Kumaon hills in the Himalayas, though, according to a modern historian, the expedition was aimed at Kashmir in order to control the entry of horses from the Chinese side, i.e., Sinkiang. However, it never aimed at the conquest of China, as some later historians have suggested. After some success, the armies went too far into the inhospitable region of the Himalayas, and suffered a disaster. We are told that from an army of 10,000, only 10 persons returned. However, it seems that the hill rajas accepted the overlordship of Delhi. Subsequently Muhammad Tughlaq undertook an expedition in the Kangra hills also. Thus, the hill regions were fully secured.

Agrarian Reforms and Nobility

Muhammad Tughlaq undertook a number of measures to improve agriculture. Most of these were tried out in the doab region. Muhammad Tughlaq did not believe in Alauddin Khalji's policy of trying to reduce the *khuts* and *muqaddams* (headmen in the villages) to the position of ordinary cultivators. But he did want an adequate share of the land revenue for the state. The measures he advocated had a long term impact, but they failed disastrously during his reign. It is difficult to say whether the measures failed because of bad planning, or faulty implementation by officials who lacked experience.

Right at the beginning of Muhammad Tughlaq's reign, there was a serious peasant rebellion in the Gangetic doab. Peasants fled the villages and Muhammad Tughlaq took harsh measures to capture and punish them. Historians are of the opinion that the trouble started due to over-assessment. Although the share of state remained half as in the time of Alauddin, it was fixed arbitrarily, not on the basis of actual produce. Prices were also fixed artificially for converting the produce into money. A severe famine which ravaged the area for half a dozen years made the situation worse. Efforts at relief by giving advances for cattle and seeds, and for digging wells came too late. So many people died at Delhi that the air became pestilential. The sultan left Delhi and for two and half years lived in a camp called Swargadwari, 100 miles from Delhi on the banks of the Ganges near Kanauj.

After returning to Delhi, Muhammad Tughlaq launched a scheme to extend and improve cultivation in the doab. He set up a separate department called *diwan-i-amir-i-kohi*. The area was divided into development blocs headed by an official whose job was to extend cultivation by giving loans to the cultivators and to induce them to cultivate superior crops—wheat in place of barley, sugarcane in place of wheat, grapes and dates in place of sugarcane, etc. The scheme failed largely because the men chosen for the purpose proved to be inexperienced and dishonest, and misappropriated the money for their own use. The large sums of money advanced for the project could not be recovered. Fortunately for all concerned, Muhammad Tughlaq had died in the meantime, and Firuz wrote off the loans. But the policy advocated by Muhammad Tughlaq for extending and improving cultivation was not lost. It was taken up by Firuz, and even more vigorously later on by Akbar.

Another problem which Muhammad Tughlaq had to face was the problem of the nobility. With the downfall of the Chahalgani Turks, and the rise of the Khaljis, the nobility was drawn from Muslims belonging to different races, including Indian converts. Muhammad Tughlaq went a step further. He entertained people who did not belong to noble families, but belonged to castes such as barbers, cooks, weavers, wine-makers, etc. He even gave them important offices. Most of these were the descendants of the Muslim converts, though a few Hindus were also included. There is no reason to believe that these people were uneducated or were inefficient in their jobs. But the office-holders of the earlier period, who were the descendants of old noble families, deeply resented it. The historian, Barani, makes this a main point in his denunciation of Muhammad

Tughlaq. Muhammad Tughlaq also welcomed foreigners to the nobility, a large number of whom came to his court.

Thus, the nobility of Muhammad Tughlaq consisted of many divergent sections. No sense of cohesion could develop among them, nor any sense of loyalty towards the sultan. On the other hand, the vast extent of the empire provided favourable opportunities for rebellion, and for striving to carve out independent spheres of authority. The hot and hasty temperament of Muhammad Tughlaq and his tendency to give extreme punishments to those whom he suspected of opposition or disloyalty strengthened this trend.

Thus, the reign of Muhammad bin Tughlaq, while marking the zenith of the Delhi Sultanat, also saw the beginning of the process of its disintegration.

III. Decline and Disintegration of the Delhi Sultanat: Firuz and his Successors

During the latter half of Muhammad Tughlaq's reign, there were repeated rebellions in different parts of the empire. Rebellions by ambitious nobles, particularly in the outlying areas, were not a new feature. In most cases, the sultans had been able to suppress them with the help of the central army and a band of loyal nobles. Muhammad Tughlaq's difficulties were several. The rebellions took place one after another in different parts of the empire—in Bengal, in Mabar (Tamil Nadu), in Warangal, in Kampili (Karnataka), in West Bengal, in Awadh, and in Gujarat and Sindh. Muhammad Tughlaq did not trust any one, at least not sufficiently. So, he dashed from one part of the country to the other to suppress the rebellions and wore out his armies. The rebellions in south India were the most serious. At first, rebellions in these areas were organised by the local governors. The sultan hurried to south India. After some time, plague broke out in the army. We are told that two-thirds of the army perished in this plague. This was a blow from which Muhammad Tughlaq could never recover. Soon after the return of the sultan from south India, there was another rebellion there, led by two brothers, Harihara and Bukka. They set up a principality which gradually expanded. This was the Vijayanagara empire which soon embraced the entire south. Further north, in the Deccan, some foreign nobles set up a principality near Daulatabad which expanded into the Bahmani empire. We shall trace the achievements of these two remarkable empires in a subsequent chapter. Bengal also became independent. With a great effort, Muhammad Tughlaq was able to quell the rebellions in Awadh, Gujarat and Sind. While still in Sind, Muhammad Tughlaq died, and was succeeded by his cousin, Firuz Tughlaq.

Muhammad Tughlaq's policies had created deep discontent among the nobles as well as in the army. He had also clashed with Muslim theologians and the sufi saints who were very influential. But the unpopularity of Muhammad Tughlaq should not be exaggerated. Even when he was away from the capital for long periods, the administration in Delhi, the Punjab and other parts of the empire in north India continued to function normally.

After his accession, Firuz Tughlaq was faced with the problem of preventing the imminent break-up of the Delhi Sultanat. He adopted a policy of trying to appease the nobles, the army and the theologians, and of asserting his authority over only such areas which could be easily administrated from the centre. He, therefore, made no attempt to re-assert his authority over south India and the Deccan. He led two campaigns into Bengal, but was unsuccessful in both. Bengal was, thus, lost to the Sultanat. Even then, the Sultanat continued to be as large as it was during the early years of the reign of Alauddin Khalji. Firuz led a campaign against the ruler of Jajnagar (Orissa). He desecrated the temples there and gathered a rich plunder, but made no attempt to annex Orissa. He also led a campaign against Kangra in the Punjab hills. His longest campaigns were to deal with rebellions in Gujarat and Thatta. Although the rebellions were crushed, the army suffered great hardship due to losing its way in the Rann of Kutch.

Thus, Firuz was by no means a distinguished military leader. But his reign was a period of peace, and of quiet development. He decreed that whenever a noble died, his son should be allowed to succeed to his position, including his *iqta*, and if he had no son, his son-in-law and, in his absence, his slave. Firuz abolished the practice of torturing nobles and their officials if any balance was found against them at the time of auditing the accounts of their *iqta*. These steps pleased the nobles and was a major factor for the absence of rebellions by the nobles, with the minor exception of one in Gujarat and in Thatta. However, in the long run, the policy of making offices and *iqta* hereditary was bound to be harmful. It reduced the chance of competent men being recruited into the service outside a small circle, and made the sultan dependent on a narrow oligarchy.

Firuz extended the principle of heredity to the army as well. Old soldiers were allowed to rest in peace and to send, in their place, their sons or sons-in-law, and if they were not available, their slaves. The soldiers were not to be paid in cash, but by assignments on the land revenue of villages. This meant that a soldier either had to go to the villages to collect his salary and absent himself from service, or to give the assignment to some middleman who would give him half or one-third of its value. Thus, the soldier did not benefit in the long run. The entire military administration became lax, and soldiers were allowed to pass useless horses at the muster by bribing the clerks. In a mistaken view of generosity, the sultan himself once gave money to a soldier to bribe the clerk of the muster.

Firuz tried to win over the theologians by proclaiming that he was a true Muslim king, and that the state under him was a truly Islamic state. Actually, right from the time of Iltutmish's accession to the throne, there was a tussle between the orthodox theologians and the sultans regarding the nature of the state, and the policy to be adopted by the state towards the non-Muslims. As has been stated earlier, from the time of Iltutmish, and especially under Alauddin and Muhammad Tughlaq, the Turkish rulers did not allow the theologians to dictate the policy of the state. They waged *jihad* against the Hindu rulers, whenever it was convenient for them to do so. In order to keep the theologians satisfied, a number of them were appointed to high offices. The judiciary and the educational system, of course, remained in the hands of the theologians.

Despite outer trappings and appearances, Firuz followed the policy of his predecessors in essentials. There is no reason to believe that he allowed the theologians to dictate the state policy. But he gave a number of important concessions to the theologians. He tried to ban practices which the orthodox theologians considered un-Islamic. Thus, he prohibited the practice of Muslim women going out to worship at the graves of saints. He persecuted a number of Muslim sects which were considered heretical by the theologians. It was during the time of Firuz that *jizyah* became a separate tax. Earlier, it was a part of land revenue. Firuz refused to exempt the Brahmans from the payment of *jizyah* since this was not provided for in the *sharia*. Only women, children, the disabled and the indigent who had no means of livelihood were exempt from it. Worse, he publicly burnt a Brahman for preaching to the people, including Muslims, on the ground that it was against the *sharia*. On the same ground, he even ordered that the beautiful wall paintings in his palace be erased. However, he patronized music, and despite his orthodoxy, was fond of wine.

These narrow views of Firuz Tughlaq were certainly harmful. At the same time, Firuz Tughlaq was the first ruler who took steps to have Hindu religious works translated from Sanskrit into Persian, so that there may be a better understanding of Hindu ideas and practices. Many books on music, medicine and mathematics were also translated from Sanskrit into Persian during his reign.

Firuz also took a number of humanitarian measures. He banned inhuman punishments such as cutting of hands, feet, nose, etc., for theft and other offences. He set up hospitals for free treatment of the poor, and ordered the *kotwals* to make lists of unemployed persons. He provided dowries for the daughters of the poor. It is likely that these measures were basically designed to help Muslims of good families who had fallen into bad times. This, again, shows the limited nature of the state in India during the medieval times. However, Firuz did emphasize that the state was not meant merely for awarding punishments and collecting taxes, but was a benevolent institution as well. In the context of the medieval times, the assertion of this principle of benevolence was a valuable one, and Firuz deserves credit for it.

Firuz was keenly interested in the economic improvement of the country. He set up a large department of public works which looked after his building programme. Firuz repaired and dug a number of canals. The longest canal was about 200 kilometres which took off from the river Sutlej to Hansi; another canal took off from the Yamuna. These and other canals were meant for irrigation purposes, and also for providing water to some of the new towns which Firuz built. These towns, Hissar-Firuzah or Hissar (in modern Haryana) and Firuzabad (in modern Uttar Pradesh) exist even today.

Another step which Firuz took was both economic and political in nature. He ordered his officials that whenever they attacked a place, they should select handsome and well-born young boys and send them to the sultan as slaves. In this way, Firuz gradually gathered about 1,80,000 slaves. Some of these he trained for carrying on various handicrafts, and posted them in the royal workshops (*karkhanas*) all over the empire. From others he formed a corps of soldiers who would be directly dependent on the sultan and hence, he hoped, would be completely loyal to him. The policy was not a new one. As we have seen, the early Turkish sultans in India had followed the practice of recruiting slaves. But experience had shown that these slaves could not be depended on for their loyalty to the descendants of their master, and that they soon formed a separate interest group apart from the nobility. When Firuz died in 1388, the administrative and political problems which had to be faced after the death of every sultan came to the surface. The struggle for power between the sultan and the nobles started once again. The local zamindars and rajas took advantage of the situation to assume airs of independence. A new factor in this situation was the active intervention of the Firuzi slaves, and their attempt to put their own nominee on the throne. Sultan Muhammad, son of Firuz, was able to stabilize his position with their help. But one of his first steps was to break up the power of the slaves, killing and imprisoning many of them and scattering the rest. However, neither he nor his successor, Nasiruddin Mahmud, who ruled from 1394 to 1412, could control the ambitious nobles and the intransigent rajas. Perhaps, the major reason for this were the reforms of Firuz which had made the nobility too strong and the army inefficient. The governors of provinces became independent, and gradually the sultan of Delhi was confined virtually to a small area surrounding Delhi. As a wit said, 'The dominion of the Lord of the Universe (being the title of the sultans of Delhi) extends from Delhi to Palam.'[1]

The weakness of the Delhi Sultanat was made even worse by Timur's invasion of Delhi (1398), Timur, who was a Turk but could claim a blood relationship with Changez, had started his career of conquest in 1370, and gradually brought under his rule the entire

1 A village near the present airport of Delhi.

tract from Syria to Trans-Oxiana and from southern Russia to the Indus. The raid into India was a plundering raid, and its motive was to seize the wealth accumulated by the sultans of Delhi over the last 200 years. With the collapse of the Delhi Sultanat, there was no one to meet this incursion. Timur's army mercilessly sacked and plundered the various towns on the way to Delhi. Timur then entered Delhi and sacked it without mercy; large number of people, both Hindu and Muslim, as well as women and children lost their lives.

Timur's invasion once again showed the dangers facing weak government in the country. It resulted in the drain of large amount of wealth, gold, silver, jewellery, etc., from India. Timur also took with him a large number of Indian artisans, such as masons, stone cutters, carpenters, etc. Some of them helped him in putting up many fine building in his capital, Samarqand. He had adopted a similar policy in the case of many Iranian towns he had captured. But the direct political effect of Timur's invasion of India was small. The invasion of Timur may, however, be regarded as marking the end of the phase of strong rule by the Delhi sultans, although the Tughlaq dynasty itself lingered on till 1412.

The responsibility for the disintegration of the Delhi Sultanat cannot be ascribed to any one ruler. We have seen that there were some persistent problems during the medieval times, such as the relations between the monarch and the nobles, the conflict with local rulers and zamindars, the pull of regional and geographical factors, etc. Individual rulers tried to cope with these problems but none of them was in a position to effect fundamental changes in society to offset these perennial factors. Disintegration of the political fabric was, thus, just beneath the surface and any weakness in the central administration set off a chain of events leading to political disintegration. Firuz was able to contain the chain reactions which had set in due to the over-extension of the empire under Ghiyasuddin and Muhammad Tughlaq. He instituted a series of reforms aimed at appeasing the nobles and the soldiers which, however, weakened the central machinery of administration as we have seen.

The period from 1200 to 1400 saw many new features in Indian life, viz., the system of government, changes in the life and condition of the people, and the development of art and architecture. These will be the subject of another chapter.

EIGHT

Government, and Economic and Social Life under the Delhi Sultanat

The state set up by the Turks towards the end of the twelfth century in northern India gradually developed into a powerful and highly centralized state which, for some time, controlled almost the entire country extending as far south as Madurai. The Delhi Sultanat disintegrated towards the beginning of the fifteenth century, and a series of independent states were set up in different parts of the country. However, the administrative system of the Sultanat had a powerful effect on many of them, and also influenced the Mughal system of administration which developed in the sixteenth century.

THE SULTAN

Although many of the Turkish sultans in India declared themselves 'lieutenant of the faithful', i.e., of the Abbasid caliph at Baghdad, and included his name in the *khutba* in the Friday prayers, it did not mean that the caliph became the legal ruler. The caliph had only a moral position. By proclaiming his supreme position, the sultans at Delhi were only proclaiming that they were a part of the Islamic world.

The sultan's office was the most important in the Sultanat and supreme political, military, and even legal authority, was vested in him. He was responsible for the safety and security of the state. As such, he was responsible for administration and was also the commander-in-chief of the military forces. He was also responsible for the maintenance of law and justice. To discharge this function, he appointed judges but the sultan acted as a court of appeal from the judges. A direct appeal could be made to him against the high-handedness of any of his officials. The dispensation of justice was regarded as a very important function of any ruler. We have referred to the stern manner in which Balban dispensed justice, not sparing even his relations or high officers of state. Muhammad Tughlaq applied this even to the religious classes (*ulama*) who had previously been exempted from harsh punishments.

No clear law of succession developed among Muslim rulers. The Islamic theory adhered to the idea of the election of the ruler, but accepted in practice the succession of any son of a successful ruler. However, all the sons of a ruler were considered to have an equal claim to the throne. The idea of primogeniture was fully acceptable neither to the Muslims nor to the Hindus. Some rulers did try to nominate one of the sons, not necessarily the eldest, as the successor. Iltutmish even nominated a daughter in preference to his sons. But it was for the nobles to accept such a nomination. While the Muslim opinion generally adhered to the idea of legitimacy, there was no safeguard against the usurpation of the throne by a successful military leader, as happened more than once in the Delhi Sultanat. Thus, military strength was the main factor in succession to the throne. However, public opinion could not be ignored. For fear of public opinion, the Khaljis could not dare to enter Delhi for a long time after deposing the successors of Balban, but built a new town called Siri.

CENTRAL ADMINISTRATION

The sultan was assisted by a number of ministers who were chosen by him and remained in office at his pleasure. The number, powers and functions of the ministers varied from time to time. A definite system of administration developed towards the end of the thirteenth century. The key figure in administration was the *wazir*. In the earlier period, the *wazir* were primarily military leaders. In the fourteenth century, the *wazir* began to be considered more an expert in revenue affairs, and presided over a large department dealing both with income and expenditure. Muhammad Tughlaq paid close attention to the organisation of the revenue department. His *wazir*, Khwaja Jahan, was widely respected, and was left in charge of the capital when Muhammad Tughlaq went out to deal with rebellions. A separate Auditor General for scrutinizing expenditure, and an Accountant

General for inspecting income worked under the *wazir*. Although quarrels between different officers hampered the smooth functioning of the department, the revenue department under Muhammad Tughlaq was able to cope with the affairs of the largest empire that had come into existence in India since the break up of the Mauryan empire. Khan-i-Jahan, a converted Tailang Brahman who was deputy to the previous *wazir*, was chosen by Firuz Tughlaq as his *wazir*. He enjoyed full authority in the revenue department. His long spell of 18 years as *wazir* is generally considered to be the high watermark of the *wazir's* influence. Khan-i-Jahan was succeeded as *wazir* by his son, Khan-i-Jahan II. The attempt of Khan-i-Jahan II to play the king-maker after the death of Firuz and the failure of the attempt resulted in a setback to the *wazir's* position. The importance of the *wazir* could revive only under the Mughals.

The most important department of state, next to the *wazir's* was the *diwan-i-arz* or the military department. The head of this department was called the *ariz-i-mamalik*. The *ariz* was not the commander-in-chief of the army, since the sultan himself commanded all the armed forces. In those days, no king could have survived on the throne if he entrusted the chief command of the armed forces to someone else. The special responsibility of the *ariz's* department was to recruit, equip and pay the army. The office of the *ariz* was an important one under the Seljukids, but we hear of it in India for the first time under Balban as a separate department. He, and later Alauddin Khalji, paid close attention to its working. Alauddin insisted upon a regular muster of the armed forces. He also introduced the branding system (*dagh*) of the horses so that the soldiers may not bring horses of poor quality to the muster. A descriptive roll of each soldier was also maintained. The army was posted in different parts of the country, a strong contingent remaining with the ruler in the capital. Balban kept his army in good trim by making it march over long distances on the pretext of undertaking hunting excursions. Of all the Delhi rulers, Alauddin Khalji had the largest standing army. The strength of his army is placed at 3,00,000 by Barani which appears to be an exaggeration. Alauddin was also the first sultan who paid his soldiers fully in cash. Earlier, the Turkish soldiers had been assigned a number of villages in the doab for the payment of their salaries. These soldiers had begun to look upon these assignments as hereditary, and were not prepared to give up their posts though many of them had become too old and feeble to serve. Balban tried to resume these holdings, but modified his order due to the agitation created by these soldiers and the pleading of his old friend, the Kotwal of Delhi. But Alauddin abolished these holdings by a stroke of the pen. He paid 238 *tankas* to a trooper and 78 *tankas* more to one who maintained two horses. The efficiency of Alauddin's army was the main factor in his ability to contain the Mongol invasions while at the same time conquering the Deccan.

The Turks also maintained a large number of elephants which were trained for war purposes. A corps of sappers and miners was attached to the army for clearing the roads and removing the obstacles for the march of the army. The Turks and Afghans predominated in the cavalry which was considered prestigious. The Hindus were employed both in the cavalry and the infantry at the time of the Ghaznavids. They continued to be employed but largely in the infantry in the subsequent period.

There were two other important departments of state: the *diwan-i-risalat* and the *diwan-i-insha*. The former dealt with religious matters, pious foundations and stipends to deserving scholars and men of piety. It was presided over by the chief *sadr*, who was generally a leading *qazi*. He was generally also the chief *qazi*. The chief *qazi* was the head of the department of justice. *Qazis* were appointed in various parts of the empire, particularly in those places where there was a sizeable Muslim population. The *qazis* dispensed civil law based on the Muslim law (*sharia*). The Hindus were governed by their own personal laws which were dispensed by *panchayats* in the villages, and by the leaders of the various castes in the cities. Criminal law was based on regulations framed for the purpose by the rulers.

The *diwan-i-insha* dealt with state correspondence. All the correspondence, formal or confidential, between the ruler and the sovereigns of other states, and with his subordinate officials was dealt with by this department.

There were a number of other departments in addition to these. The rulers posted intelligence agents called *barids* in different parts of the empire to keep them informed of what was going on. Only a nobleman who enjoyed the fullest confidence of the ruler was appointed the chief *barid*. The ruler's household was another important department of state. It looked after the personal comforts of the sultan and the requirements of the large numbers of women in the royal household. It also looked after a large number of *karkhanas* or departments in which goods and articles needed by the king and the royal household were stored. Sometimes, these articles were manufactured under royal supervision. Firuz Tughlaq had set up a separate department of slaves, many of whom were employed in these royal 'workshops'. The officer in charge of all these activities was called *wakil-i-dar*. He was also responsible for the maintenance of proper decorum at the court, and placing nobles in their proper order of precedence at formal receptions. Firuz also set up a separate department of public works which built canals and many of his public buildings.

LOCAL ADMINISTRATION

When the Turks conquered the country, they divided it into a number of tracts called *iqtas* which were parcelled out among the leading Turkish nobles. The holders of these offices were called *muqtis* or *walis*. It were these tracts which later became provinces or *subas*. We are told that under Muhammad Tughlaq there were twenty-four provinces stretching upto Mabar in the south. At first, the *muqtis* were almost independent; they were expected to maintain law and order in their tracts, and collect the land revenue due to the government. Out of the money they collected they were expected to meet the salaries due to the soldiers and keep the balance. As the central government became stronger and gained experience, it began to control the *muqtis* more closely. It began to try to ascertain the actual income, and to fix the salaries of the soldiers and the *muqti* in cash. The *muqti* was now required to remit to the centre the balance of the income after meeting the expenditure. The auditing of the accounts, which took place after a couple of years was often accompanied by harshness, including torture and imprisonment of the *muqti*. These were relaxed by Firuz Tughlaq towards the end of the Sultanat.

Below the provinces were the *shiqs* and below them the *pargana*. We do not know much about the administration of these units. We are told that the villagers were grouped into units of 100 to 84 (traditionally called *chaurasi*). This must have been the basis of the *parganas*. The pargana was headed by the *amil*. The most important persons in the village were the *khut* (landowners) and *muqaddam* or headman. We also hear of the village accountant or *patwari*. We do not know how exactly the village was administered—it was perhaps not interfered with as long as it paid the land revenue due from it.

In the initial stage, hardly any change was made in the working of the administration at the local level. Land revenue continued to be collected in the same manner, more or less by the same set of people. This must have been a major factor in the Turks establishing their authority in the countryside quickly. The changes we have mentioned began from the time of Alauddin Khalji at the beginning of the fourteenth century, and they led to conflicts, including peasant rebellions.

ECONOMIC AND SOCIAL LIFE

We have very little information about the economic condition of the people under the Delhi Sultanat. The historians of the period were more interested in the events at the court than in the lives of ordinary people. However, they do sometimes tell us the prices of commodities. Ibn Battutah, a resident of Tangier in North Africa, visited India in the fourteenth century and lived at the court of Muhammad Tughlaq for eight years. He travelled widely all over India and has left a very interesting account of the products of the country, including fruits, flowers, herbs, etc., the condition of the roads, and the life of the people. We have some other accounts also. The foodgrains and other crops, the fruits, and the flowers mentioned by these travellers are familiar to us. Rice and sugarcane were produced in the east and south, and wheat, oil-seeds, etc., in the north. Ibn Battutah says that the soil was so fertile that it could produce two crops every year, rice being sown three times a year. Sesame, indigo and cotton were also grown. They formed the basis of many village industries, such as oil pressing, making of jaggery, weaving, and dyeing of cloth, etc.

Peasants and Rural Gentry

As before, peasants formed the overwhelming majority of the population. The peasant continued to work hard and to eke out bare subsistence. There were recurring famines and wars in different parts of the country, and these added to the hardships of the peasant.

All the peasants did not live at the level of subsistence. Apart from the village artisans and share-croppers, there was a more prosperous section of people who were owner cultivators of their lands. They were considered the original settlers of the village, and dominated the village *panchayat*. The village headmen (*muqaddams*) and smaller landlords (*khuts*) enjoyed a higher standard of life. In addition to their own holdings, they held lands for which they paid revenue at concessional rates. Sometimes, they misused their offices to force the ordinary peasants to pay their share of the land revenue also. These people were prosperous enough to ride on costly Arabi and Iraqi horses, wear fine clothes, and behave like members of the upper classes. As we have seen, Alauddin Khalji took stern action against them and curtailed many of their privileges. Even then they continued to enjoy a standard of life higher than that of the ordinary peasants. It seems that after the death of Alauddin, they were able to resume their own ways.

A section which enjoyed a high standard of life were the Hindu *rais* or autonomous rajas, many of whom continued to hold their previous estates. There are a number of references to the visits of the Hindu *rais* to the court of Balban. There is little doubt that these Hindu *rais* continued to be powerful even in the area under the direct control of the sultans of Delhi.

Trade, Industry and the Merchants

With the consolidation of the Delhi Sultanat and the improvement of communications, and the establishment of a sound currency system based on the silver *tanka* and the copper *dirham*, there was a definite growth of trade in the country. This was marked by the growth of towns and town life. Ibn Battutah calls Delhi the largest city in the eastern part of the Islamic world. He says that Daulatabad (Deogir) equalled Delhi in size—an index of the growth of trade between the north and the south. The other important cities of the times were Lahore and Multan in the northwest, Kara and Lakhnauti in the east, and Anhilwara (Patan) and Cambay (Khambayat) in the west. A modern historian says that on the whole 'the Sultanat presents the picture of a flourishing urban economy. Such an economy must have necessitated commerce on a large scale.' Bengal and the towns in Gujarat were famous for their fine quality fabrics. Cloth of fine quality was produced in other towns as well. Cambay in Gujarat was famous for textiles and for gold and silver work. Sonargaon in Bengal was famous for raw silk and fine cotton cloth (called muslin later on). There were many other handicrafts as well, such as leather work, metal work, carpet weaving, wood-work including furniture, stone-cutting, etc., for which India was famous. Some of the new crafts introduced by the Turks included the manufacturer of paper. The art of manufacturing paper had been discovered by the Chinese in the second century. It was known in the Arab world in the eighth century, and travelled to Europe only during the fourteenth century.

The production of textiles was also improved by the introduction of the spinning-wheel. Cotton could be cleaned faster and better by wider use of the cotton carder's bow (*dhunia*). But there is little doubt that most important was the skill of the Indian craftsmen. Indian textiles had already established their position in the trade to countries on the Red Sea and the Persian Gulf. During this period, fine Indian textiles were introduced to China as well where it was valued more than silk. India imported from West Asia high grade textiles (satin, etc.) glassware and, of course, horses. From China it imported raw silk and porcelain. Ivory was imported from Africa and spices from Southeast Asia, in return for Indian textiles. Since India had a favourable trade balance, gold and silver came to India from these countries.

India's foreign trade both overland and overseas was truly an international enterprise. Although the Arabs were the dominant partners in the India Ocean trade, they had by no means ousted the Indian traders, viz., the Tamils, Kalingas and Gujaratis, both Hindu and Muslim. The coastal trade and trade between the coastal ports and north India was in the hands of Marwaris and Gujaratis, many of whom were Jains. The Muslim Bohra merchants also participated in this trade. The overland trade with Central and West Asia was in the hands of Multanis, who were mostly Hindus but included Muslims, who were Khurasanis, Afghans, Iranians, etc. Many of these merchants had settled down in Delhi. The Gujarati and Marwari merchants were extremely wealthy and some of them, particularly the Jains, spent large sums for the construction of temples. Cambay was a great city in which many wealthy merchants lived. They had lofty houses built in fine stone and mortar, with tiled roofs. Their houses were surrounded by orchards and fruit-gardens which had many tanks. These wealthy merchants and the skilled craftsmen lived a luxurious life, and were accustomed to good food and clothing. The merchants, Hindu and Muslim, and foreigners were attended by pages bearing swords with silver and gold work. In Delhi, the Hindu merchants rode horses with costly trappings, lived in fine houses, and celebrated their festivals with great pomp and show. Barani tells us that the Multani merchants were so rich that gold and silver were to be found in abundance in their houses alone. The nobles were so extravagent that every time they wanted to hold a feast or a celebration, they had to run to the houses of the Multanis in order to borrow money.

In those days, travel was always risky due to robbers and dacoits and various marauding tribes. However, the royal roads were kept in good shape and there were many *sarais* on the way for the comfort and safety of the travellers. In addition to the royal road from Peshawar to Sonargaon, Muhammad Tughlaq built a road to Daulatabad. There were arrangements for the post being carried quickly from one part of the country to another. This was done by relays of horses or even more efficiently and quickly by runners who were posted every few kilometres in towers which were built for the purpose. The runner continually clanged a bell as he ran so that the man on the next relay may be able to see him from the tower and get ready to take his burden. We are told that by means of these relays, fresh fruits were obtained for the sultan from Khurasan. When Muhammad Tughlaq was at Daulatabad, which was 40 days' journey from Delhi, he regularly used to receive the Ganga water for drinking purposes by means of these relays.

Economic life was quickened in the period by the improvement of communications and the growth of trade, both overland and by sea. The Turks introduced or popularized a number of new crafts and techniques. We have already referred to the use of the iron stirrup, and a large-scale use of armour, both for the horse and the rider for heavy and light cavalry preferred by the new rulers. This led to the growth of the metallurgical industry, and metal crafts.

An even more important development was the improvement of the *rahat* (miscalled the Persian wheel) so that water could be lifted from a deeper level for irrigation. The other crafts included paper-making, glass-making, the spinning wheel and an improved loom for weaving.

Mention may also be made of the introduction of a superior mortar which enabled the Turks to erect magnificent buildings based on the arch and the dome. Not all these crafts were new, but their expansion and improvement, and agricultural growth were two of the most important factors which made the second half of the fourteenth century a period of growth and relative affluence.

THE SULTAN AND THE NOBLES

The Sultan and his chief nobles enjoyed a standard of living which was comparable to the highest standard in the world at that time, viz., to the standards of the ruling class in the Islamic world in West and Central Asia. While Europe was still trying to overcome its backwardness, the opulence and wealth of the ruling classes in the Islamic world was dazzling, and set a standard which the ruling classes in every country tried to emulate. Like the Hindu rulers, almost every sultan in India built his own palace. Balban had a dazzling court which was designed to impress and strike a sense of awe in the hearts of the visitors. Alauddin Khalji and his successors followed the same tradition. The palace of Muhammad Tughlaq has been described by Ibn Battutah. A person who wanted to visit the sultan had to pass through three lofty gates which were heavily guarded. He then entered the 'court of thousand pillars' which was a huge hall supported by polished wooden pillars and was decorated with all kinds of costly materials and furnishings. This was the place where the sultan held his public court.

Muhammad Tughlaq used to present two robes of honour, one in the cold and the other in the hot season, to each of his nobles. It has been estimated that he presented 2,00,000 robes every year. These robes, woven in the royal workshops, generally consisted of imported cloth—velvet, damask or wool on which brocade and costly materials were used. They must have cost an enormous sum. Numerous gifts used to be bestowed on the nobles and others on festive occasions such as the sultan's birthday, the *nauroz* (the Persian new year), and the annual coronation day.

The royal *karkhanas* which we have referred to earlier catered to all the needs of the sultan. They manufactured costly articles made of silk, gold and silver ware, etc. They were also stores of choice and rare goods. The superintendents of the stores were instructed by Firuz Tughlaq to buy finely finished articles wherever and at whatever price they were available. It is said that on one occasion a single pair of shoes for the sultan cost 70,000 *tankas*. Most of the articles of royal use were worked in gold and silver, embroidery and jewels. The stores also catered to the women in the *haram*.

Almost every sultan had a *haram* containing queens and a large number of slaves from various countries. A large number of servants and slaves, men and women, were employed to safeguard them, and to look after their comforts. All the women relations of the sultan, including his mother, aunts, etc., also lived in the *haram*. Separate accommodation had to be provided to each of them.

The nobles tried to ape the sultans in ostentatious living. They had magnificent palaces to live in, they used costly articles of apparel, and were surrounded by a large number of servants, slaves and retainers. They vied with each other in holding lavish feasts and festivals. However, some of the nobles also patronised men of arts and letters.

Alauddin sternly repressed the nobles, but the ostentatious mode of life revived under his successors. The nobility came into its own under the Tughlaqs. Due to the rapid expansion of the empire, large salaries and allowances were given to the nobles by Muhammad Tughlaq. We are told that his *wazir* enjoyed an income as large as that of the province of Iraq. The other leading ministers got 20,000 to 40,000 tankas a year, the chief *sadr* getting 60,000 tankas a year.

Khan-i-Jahan, the *wazir* of Firuz Tughlaq, used to get 15 lakhs. His sons and sons-in-law who were very numerous got separate allowances.

During the Tughlaq period, a number of nobles were able to acquire large fortunes. Thus, Bashir, who was Firuz's *ariz-i-mamalik*, left 13 crores at his death. On the ground that Bashir had been originally his slave, Firuz confiscated most of his wealth and distributed the rest among his sons. This may be regarded more or less as an exception. The property of a noble was generally safe, and was allowed to pass on to his sons. It was this section which bought lands on which they built gardens, orchards, markets, etc. The sultan and his nobles took keen interest in improving the quality of fruits in India, especially melons and grapes. Firuz Tughlaq is said to have built 1200 orchards in the neighbourhood of Delhi.

In this way, a new type of landed gentry began to develop. The break up of the Delhi Sultanat towards the beginning of the fifteenth century halted this trend.

TOWN LIFE: SLAVES, ARTISANS AND OTHERS

We have already referred to the revival of towns and town life under the Sultanat. The Turkish ruling class was essentially an urban ruling class with a taste for town life. Many of the towns grew around military garrisons as providers of food, goods and services to them. In due course, many of them emerged as cultural centres as well.

The medieval towns had a miscellaneous population, including many nobles and a large class of clerks for running government offices, shopkeepers, artisans, beggars, etc. The posts of clerks and lower government officials had, obviously, to be given to the people who could read and write. Since the work of teaching was largely in the hands of the Muslim theologians (*ulama*), the *ulama* and the lower officials tended to think and behave alike. Most of the historians were drawn from this section, and their writings reflect the opinions and prejudices of this section. Beggars, who generally wore arms like the ordinary citizens, formed a large mass and could sometimes create a problem of law and order.

Another large section in the town consisted of slaves and domestic servants. Slavery had existed in India as well as in West Asia and

Europe for a long time. The position of different types of slaves—one born in the household, one purchased, one acquired and one inherited is discussed in the Hindu *shastras*. Slavery had been adopted by the Arabs and, later, by the Turks also. The most usual method of acquiring a slave was capture in war. Even the *Mahabharata* considered it normal to enslave a prisoner of war. The Turks practised this on a large scale in their wars, in and outside India. Slave markets for men and women existed in West Asia as well as in India. The Turkish, Caucasian, Greek and Indian slaves were valued and were sought after. A small number of slaves were also imported from Africa, mainly Abyssinia. Slaves were generally bought for domestic service, for company, or for their special skills. Skilled slaves or comely boys and handsome girls sometimes fetched a high price. Skilled slaves were valued and some of them rose to high offices as in the case of the slaves of Qutbuddin Aibak. Firuz Tughlaq also prized slaves and collected about 1,80,000 of them. Many of them mere employed in handicrafts, while others formed the sultan's personal bodyguard. The largest number of slaves were, however, used for personal service. Such slaves were sometimes treated harshly. It can be argued that the condition of slave was better than that of a domestic servant because the master of the former was obliged to provide him food and shelter, while a free person may starve to death. Slaves were allowed to marry, and to own some personal property. However, it was widely accepted that slavery was degrading. Giving a slave his or her liberty was considered a meritorious act both among the Hindus and the Muslims.

In general, food-grains were cheap for the townsfolk during the Sultanat period. We have mentioned the price of food-grains under Alauddin Khalji. In his reign, a *man* (about 15 kg) of wheat was sold for 7½ *jitals*, barley for 4 and rice for 5 *jitals*, with 48 *jitals* being equal to a silver *tanka*. Prices rose sharply under Muhammad Tughlaq but declined almost to Alauddin's level under Firuz. It is possible that this was due to the extension of cultivation during his reign.

It is difficult to compute the cost of living in towns. A modern historian has estimated that during Firuz's reign, a family consisting of a man, his wife, a servant and one or two children could live on five *tankas* for a whole month. Thus, for a lower government official or a soldier, living was cheap. But this did not apply to the artisan and workers in the same way. In Alauddin Khalji's reign, the wages of an artisan amounted to 2 or 3 jitals per day or about 1½ to 2 tankas per month. Household servants were paid even less. Even under Akbar, an unskilled labourer earned 2½ to 3 rupees a month, or even less. In terms of their income, the living conditions of artisans and workers in towns appear to have been hard.

Thus, medieval society was a society of great inequalities. This was reflected in the Muslim society even more than in the Hindu, the latter being predominantly rural where inequalities were less marked. In towns, the Muslim nobility led a life of great ostentation. Some of the wealthy merchants, Hindu and Muslim, also led lives of ostentation. The great mass of people, in towns as well as in the countryside, lived a simple life, and often had to face many hardships. It was, however, not a life without joy, as numerous festivals, fairs, etc., relieved, to some extent, the monotony of their lives.

CASTE, SOCIAL MANNERS AND CUSTOMS

There were hardly any changes in the structure of the Hindu society during the period. The *smriti* writers of the time continued to assign a high place to the Brahmans, while strongly denouncing the unworthy members of the order. According to one school of thinking, the Brahmans were permitted to engage in agriculture not only in times of distress, but also in normal times since officiating at sacrifices, etc., did not furnish means of subsistence in the *Kali* Age.

The *smriti* texts continue to emphasize that punishing the wicked and cherishing the good was the duty of the Kshatriya and that the right to wield weapons for the purpose of protecting the people likewise belonged to him alone. The duties and occupations of Shudras were more or less repeated. While the highest duty of the shudra was the service of the other castes, he was allowed to engage in all occupations, except to deal in liquor and meat. The ban on the study and recitation of the Vedas by shudras was repeated, but not on hearing the recitation of the Puranas. Some writers go as far as to say that not only eating a shudra's food but also living in the same house with him, sitting in the same cot and receiving religious instructions from a learned shudra were to be avoided. This may be regarded as an extreme view. However, the severest restrictions were placed on mingling with the Chandalas and other 'outcastes'.

There was little change in the position of women in the Hindu society. The old rules enjoining early marriage for girls, and the wife's obligation of service and devotion to the husband continued. Annulment of the marriage was allowed in special circumstances, such as desertion, loathsome disease, etc. But not all writers agree with this. Widow remarriage was among the practices prohibited in the *Kali* Age. But this apparently applied to the three upper castes only. Regarding the practice of sati, some writers approve it emphatically, while others allow it with some conditions. A number of travellers mention its prevalence in different regions of the country. Ibn Battutah mentions with horror the scene of a woman burning herself in the funeral pyre of her husband with great beating of drums. According to him, permission from the sultan had to be taken for the performance of *sati*.

Regarding property, the commentators uphold the widow's right to the property of a sonless husband, provided the property was not joint, i.e., had been divided. The widow was not merely the guardian of this property, but had the full right to dispose of it. Thus, it would appear that the property rights of women improved in the Hindu law.

During this period, the practice of keeping women in seclusion and asking them to veil their faces in the presence of outsiders, that is, the practice of *purdah* became widespread among the upper class women. The practice of secluding women from the vulgar gaze was practised among the upper class Hindus, and was also in vogue in ancient Iran, Greece, etc. The Arabs and the Turks adopted this custom and brought it to India with them. Due to their example, it became widespread in India, particularly in north India. The growth of *purdah* has been attributed to the fear of the Hindu women being captured by the invaders. In an age of violence, women were liable to be treated as prizes of war. Perhaps, the most important factor for the growth of *purdah* was social—it became a symbol of the higher classes in society and all those who wanted to be considered respectable tried to copy it. Also religious justification was found for it. Whatever the reason, it affected women adversely, and made them even more dependent on men.

During the Sultanat period, the Muslim society remained divided into ethnic and racial groups. We have already noticed the deep economic disparities within it. The Turks, Iranians, Afghans and Indian Muslims rarely married each other. In fact, these sections developed some of the caste exclusiveness of the Hindus. Converts from lower sections of the Hindus were also discriminated against.

The Hindu and Muslim upper classes did not have much social intercourse between them during this period, partly due to the superiority complex of the latter, and partly due to the religious restrictions on the part of the Hindus of inter-marriage and inter-dining with them. The Hindu upper castes applied to the Muslims the restrictions they applied to the shudras. But it should be borne in mind that caste restrictions did not close social intercourse between the Muslims and the upper caste Hindus and the shudras. At various times, Hindu soldiers were enrolled in Muslim armies. Most of the nobles had Hindus as their personal managers. The local machinery of administration remained almost entirely in the hand of the Hindus. Thus, occasions for mutual intercourse were manifold. The picture of the two communities being confined within themselves and having little to do with each other is, thus, neither real nor one which could be practised. Nor it is borne out by the evidence available to us. Conflict of interests as well as differences in social and cultural ideas, practices and beliefs did, however, create tensions, and slowed down the processes of mutual understanding and cultural assimilation. These will be dealt with in a subsequent chapter.

NATURE OF THE STATE

The Turkish state in India was militaristic and aristocratic. The Turkish nobles tried, at first, to monopolize the high offices of state, denying a share to the Tajiks, Afghans and other non-Turkish immigrants. The nobility acquired a broader base only under the Tughlaqs. However, a noble birth still remained a very important qualification for high office. The vast majority of the Muslims as well as the Hindus had, therefore, little opportunity for occupying high offices of state. Of course, the Muslims in the towns had a better chance of being enrolled in the armies and of getting state employment. The Hindus dominated trade and constituted the rural aristocracy, and the lower administrative wing without whose cooperation the state could not function. A kind of tacit sharing of power between the rural Hindu aristocracy and the city-based administrators was, thus, a factor of capital importance for the Delhi Sultanat, though there were frequent fights between these two sections. Often given a religious colour, the basic causes for the struggle between them were secular, such as fight for power and land, or rather, for the share of the surplus produced by land since land was not generally sold in those times. The Muslims also fought among themselves for the attainment of these objectives.

In a formal sense, the state was Islamic. The Sultans were keen to emphasize the Muslim character of the state, and to follow the Holy Law (*sharia*) as far as possible. This also meant not allowing any open violation of the Islamic law. They appointed Muslim divines to profitable offices of state and granted revenue-free lands to many of them. However, the sultans did not allow the Muslim divines to dictate the policy of the state. We are told that during the reign of Iltutmish, a part of Muslim divines approached the sultan, and asked him to enforce the Muslim law strictly, giving the Hindus the option of only Islam or death. On behalf of the sultan, his *wazir* told the theologians that this was impractical and impolitic since the Muslims were so little (in number) as salt in a dish of food.

The sultans had to supplement the Muslim law by framing their own regulations (*zawabit*). Alauddin Khalji told the leading *qazi* of the city that he did not know what was lawful or unlawful but framed laws according to the needs of the state. This is why the historian Barani refused to consider the state in India as truly Islamic, but one based on worldly or secular considerations (*jahandari*).

As for the Hindu subjects, from the time of the Arab invasion of Sind, they had been given the status of *zimmis* or protected people i.e., those who accepted the Muslim rule and agreed to pay tax called *jizyah*. This was really a tax in lieu of military service, and was paid on a graduated scale according to means. Women, children and the indigent, who had insufficient means, were exempted from it. The

Brahmans also remained exempt, though this was not provided for in the Muslim law. At first, *jizyah* was collected along with land revenue. In fact it was difficult to distinguish *jizyah* from land revenue since all the cultivators were Hindus. Later, Firuz while abolishing many illegal cesses, made *jizyah* a separate tax. He levied it on the Brahman also. Sometimes, the theologians who were in charge of collecting the tax tried to use it to humiliate and harass the Hindus. However, *jizyah* by itself could not be a means to force the Hindus to convert to Islam. In general, it might be said that medieval states were not based on the idea of equality, but on the notion of privileges. Before the Turks, the Rajputs and, to some extent, the Brahmans formed the privileged sections. They were replaced by the Turks. Later, the Turks and others, including the Iranians, the Afghans, and a narrow group of Indian Muslims, formed the privileged sections. The Muslim theologians were also a part of this privileged group. For the large bulk of the Hindus who were not included in the privileged group earlier, this change did not affect their daily lives which continued in the same manner as before.

Thus, while claiming to be Islamic, the state was militaristic and aristocratic in character, being dominated by a narrow clique of military leaders, headed by and under the control of the sultan.

RELIGIOUS FREEDOM UNDER THE SULTANAT

The extent of religious freedom accorded to the non-Muslims under the Delhi Sultanat may be seen in this context. In the early phase of the conquest many cities were sacked, temples being a special target partly to justify the conquest and partly to seize the fabulous treasures they were supposed to contain. During this period, a number of Hindu temples were converted into mosques. The most notable example of this is the Quwwat-ul-Islam mosque near the Qutab Minar in Delhi. Formerly, it had been a Vishnu temple. In order to convert it into a mosque, the inner sanctum which contained the deity was pulled down, and in front of it a screen of arches containing inscribed verses from the Quran was put up. Pillars from many temples were used to put a cloister around the courtyard. The courtyard has remained more or less intact. This was done in a number of other places, such as Ajmer. But as soon as the Turks were settled, they started building their own mosques. Their policy towards temples and places of worship of the Hindus, Jains, etc., rested on the Muslim law (*sharia*) which forbade new places of worship being built 'in opposition to Islam'. But it allowed the repair of old temples 'since buildings cannot last for ever'. This meant that there was no ban on erecting temples in the villages, since there were no practices of Islam there. Similarly temples could be built within the privacy of homes. But this policy of limited toleration was not followed in times of war. Then the enemies of Islam, whether human beings or gods, were to be fought and destroyed.

In times of peace, however, within the Turkish territories and in those areas where the rajas had submitted to the Muslim rule, the Hindus practised their religion, even openly and ostentatiously. According to Barani, Jalaluddin Khalji observed that even in the capital and provincial centres, the idols were publicly worshipped and the texts of Hinduism publicly preached. 'The Hindus pass beneath the wall of the royal palace in processions, singing, dancing and beating drums to immerse the idols in the Yamuna, and I am helpless,' he said.

Despite the pressure of a section of the orthodox theologians, and the narrow approach of some of the sultans and their supporters, this policy of 'toleration within limits' was maintained during the Sultanat, though with occasional lapses. Sometimes, prisoners of war were converted, or criminals exempted from punishment if they accepted Islam. Firuz executed a Brahman on a charge of abusing the Prophet of Islam.

On the whole, conversions to Islam were not effected with the strength of the sword. If that was so, the Hindu population of the Delhi region would have been the first to be converted. The Muslim rulers had realised that the Hindu faith was too strong to be destroyed by force. Shaikh Nizamuddin Auliya, the famous Sufi saint of Delhi, observed, 'Some Hindus know that Islam is a true religion but they do not embrace Islam'. Barani also says that attempt to use force had no effect on the Hindus.[1]

---

1 He uses a very picturesque simile. He says that though cowed down, 'They have plucked Islam from their hearts as a hair is discarded while kneading flour.'

Conversions to Islam were due to hopes of political gain or economic advantage, or to improve one's social position. Sometimes when an important ruler or a tribal chief converted, his example was followed by his subject. In some areas, such as west Punjab, the valley of Kashmir, east Bengal, etc., where tribal peoples were induced to become cultivators, they changed their earlier beliefs, and accepted the faith of the ruling elements, in this case, Islam. In the towns, many artisans, following the new crafts introduced by the Turks, or depending on the patronage of the ruling class, such as weavers, iron-workers, paper-makers etc., converted to Islam. The Sufi saints too played a role, though they were generally unconcerned with conversions, and welcomed both the Hindus and the Muslims to their discourses. The saintly character of some of the Sufi saints created a receptive climate for Islam. There is no evidence, however, that large numbers of persons belonging to the lower castes embraced Islam due to the discrimination against them in the Hindu society or due to the influence of the Sufi saints. Conversions were, thus, due to personal, political and, in some cases, regional factors (as in the Punjab, east Bengal, etc.).

Following the Mongol invasion of West Asia, many persons belonging to prominent Muslim families fled to India. There was also a steady influx of the Afghans into India. Many of them enrolled themselves in the Turkish armies or were engaged in trade. A further influx of the Afghans took place in the fifteenth century under the Lodi rule. Despite this, the number of Muslims in India remained comparatively small. The nature of the Hindu–Muslim relations and the cultural attitudes of the two, which will be examined in a subsequent chapter, were conditioned by this situation.

NINE

The Age of Vijayanagara and the Bahmanids, and the Coming of the Portuguese (*Circa 1350–1565*)

The Vijayanagara and Bahmani kingdoms dominated India south of the Vindhyas, for more than 200 years. They not only built magnificent capitals and cities, and beautified them with many splendid buildings and promoted arts and letters, but also provided for law and order and the development of commerce and handicrafts. Thus, while the forces of disintegration gradually triumphed in north India, south India and the Deccan had a long spell of stable governments. This ended with the disintegration of the Bahmani empire towards the end of the fifteenth century, and of the Vijayanagara empire more than fifty years later, after its defeat in 1565 in the battle of Bannihatti. Meanwhile, the Indian scene was transformed, first with the arrival of the Portuguese in southern India and their attempt to dominate the Indian seas, and second, with the advent of the Mughals in north India. The coming of the Mughals paved the way for another spell of integration in north India. The coming of the Portuguese marked the long era of confrontation between the land-based Asian powers and the European powers which dominated the seas.

THE VIJAYANAGARA EMPIRE—ITS FOUNDATION AND CONFLICT WITH THE BAHMANI KINGDOM

The Vijayanagara kingdom was founded by Harihara and Bukka who belonged to a family of five brothers. According to a legend, they had been the feudatories of the Kakatiyas of Warangal and later became ministers in the kingdom of Kampili in modern Karnataka.

When Kampili was overrun by Muhammad Tughlaq for giving refuge to a Muslim rebel, the two brothers were imprisoned, converted to Islam, and appointed to deal with the rebellions there. The Muslim governor of Madurai had already declared himself independent, and the Hoysala ruler of Mysore and the ruler of Warangal were also trying to assert their independence. After a short time, Harihara and Bukka forsook their new master and their new faith. At the instance of their guru, Vidyaranya, they were re-admitted to Hinduism and established their capital at Vijayanagar. Some modern scholars do not accept the tradition of their conversion to Islam, but consider them to be among the nayaks of Karnataka who had rebelled against Turkish rule.

The date of Harihara's coronation is placed at 1336. At first, the young king had to contend both with the Hoysala ruler of Mysore and the sultan of Madurai. The sultan of Madurai was ambitious. He had defeated the Hoysala ruler, and executed him in a barbarous manner. The dissolution of the Hoysala kingdom enabled Harihara and Bukka to expand their tiny principality. By 1346, the whole of the Hoysala kingdom had passed into the hands of the Vijayanagara rulers. In this struggle, Harihara and Bukka were aided by their brothers and by their relations who took up the administration of the areas conquered by their efforts. The Vijayanagara kingdom was, thus, a kind of a cooperative commonwealth at first. Bukka succeeded his brother to the throne of Vijayanagara in 1356, and ruled till 1377.

The rising power of the Vijayanagara empire brought it into clash with many powers both in the south and to the north. In the south, its main rivals were the sultans of Madurai. The struggle between Vijayanagara and the sultans of Madurai lasted for about four decades. By 1377, the Sultanat of Madurai had been wiped out. The Vijayanagara empire then comprised the whole of south India upto Rameshwaram, including the Tamil country as well as that of the Cheras (Kerala). To the north, however, Vijayanagara faced a powerful enemy in the shape of the Bahmani kingdom. The Bahmani kingdom had come into existence in 1347. Its founder was Alauddin Hasan, an Afghan adventurer. He had risen in the service of a Brahman, named Gangu, and is, therefore, known as Hasan Gangu. After his coronation, he assumed the title of Alauddin Hasan Bahman

Shah. He is said to have traced his descent from a half-mythical hero of Iran, Bahman Shah. But according to a popular legend mentioned by Ferishta, the word Bahman Shah was meant to be a tribute to his Brahman patron. In any case, it is from this title that the kingdom was called the Bahmani kingdom.

The interests of the Vijayanagara rulers and the Bahmani sultans clashed in three separate and distinct areas: in the Tungabhadra doab, in the Krishna–Godavari delta, and in the Marathwada country. The Tungabhadra doab was the region between the rivers Krishna and Tungabhadra and consisted of 30,000 square miles. On account of its wealth and economic resources, it had been the bone of contention between the western Chalukyas and the Cholas in the earlier period, and between the Yadavas and the Hoysalas later on. The struggle for the mastery of the Krishna–Godavari basin which was very fertile and which, with its numerous ports, controlled the foreign trade of the region was often linked up with the struggle for the Tungabhadra doab. In the Maratha country, the main contention was for the control of the Konkan and the areas which gave access to it. The Konkan was a narrow strip of land between the Western Ghats and the sea. It was extremely fertile, and included within it the port of Goa which was an important outlet for the products of the region, as well as for the import of horses from Iran and Iraq. As has been noted earlier, good quality horses were not bred in India. The import of horses from Goa was, thus, of great importance to the southern states.

Military conflicts between the Vijayanagara and the Bahmani kingdom were almost a regular feature and lasted as long as these kingdoms continued. These military conflicts resulted in widespread devastation of the contested areas and the neighbouring territories, and a considerable loss of life and property. Both sides sacked and burnt towns and villages, imprisoned and sold into slavery men, women and children, and committed various other barbarities. Thus in 1367, when Bukka I assaulted the fortress of Mudkal in the disputed Tungabhadra doab, he slaughtered the entire garrison, except one man. When this news reached the Bahmani sultan, he was enraged and, on the march, vowed that he would not sheath his sword till he had slaughtered one hundred thousand Hindus in revenge. In spite of the rainy season and the opposition of the

Vijayanagara forces, he crossed the Tungabhadra, the first time a Bahmani sultan had in person entered the Vijayanagara territories. The Vijayanagara king was defeated in the battle and retreated into the jungle. We hear, for the first time, of the use of artillery by both sides during this battle. The victory of the Bahmani sultan was due to his superior artillery and more efficient cavalry. The war dragged on for several months, but the Bahmani sultan could neither capture the raja nor his capital. In the meanwhile, wholesale slaughter of men, women and children went on. Finally, both the side were exhausted, and decided to conclude a treaty. This treaty restored the old position whereby the doab was shared between the two. Even more important, it was agreed that since the two kingdoms would remain neighbours for a long time, it was advisable to avoid cruelty in war. It was, therefore, stipulated that in future wars, helpless and unarmed inhabitants should not be slaughtered. Although this accord was not fully implemented, it helped to make warfare in south India more humane.

Having strengthened its position in south India by eliminating the Sultanat of Madurai, the Vijayanagara empire embarked upon a policy of expansion towards the eastern sea coast under Harihara II (1377–1404). There were a series of Hindu principalities in the region, the most notable being the Reddis on the upper reaches of the delta, and the rulers of Warangal in the lower reaches of the Krishna–Godavari delta. The rulers of Orissa to the north, as well as the Bahmani sultans were also interested in this area. Although the ruler of Warangal had helped Hasan Gangu in his struggle against Delhi, his successor had invaded Warangal and seized the stronghold of Kaulas and the hill fort of Golconda. Vijayanagara had been too busy in the south to intervene. The Bahmani sultan fixed Golconda as the boundary of his kingdom and promised that neither he nor his successors would encroach against Warangal any further. To seal this agreement, the ruler of Warangal presented to the Bahmani sultan a throne set with valuable jewels. It is said that it had been originally prepared as a present to Muhammad Tughlaq. The alliance of the Bahmani kingdom and Warangal lasted for over 50 years, and was a major factor in the inability of Vijayanagara to overrun the Tungabhadra doab, or to stem the Bahmani offensive in the area.

The battles between Vijayanagara and the Bahmanis are described in great detail by medieval writers. However, they are not of much historical importance to us, the position of the two sides remaining more or less the same, with the fortune of war swinging sometimes to one side, and sometimes to the other. Harihara II was able to maintain his position in the face of the Bahmani–Warangal combine. His greatest success was in wresting Belgaum and Goa in the west from the Bahmani kingdom. He also sent an expedition to north Sri Lanka.

After a period of confusion, Harihara II was succeeded by Deva Raya II (1404–1422). Early in his reign, there was a renewed fight for the Tungabhadra doab. He was defeated by the Bahmani ruler Firuz Shah, and he had to pay ten lakhs of *huns* and pearls and elephants as an indemnity. He also agreed to marry his daughter to the sultan, ceding to him in dowry Bankapur in the doab in order to obviate all future dispute. The marriage was celebrated with great pomp and show. When Firuz Shah Bahmani arrived near Vijayanagara for the marriage, Deva Raya came out of the city and met him with a show of great splendour. From the gate of the city to the palace, which was a distance of ten km, the road was spread with cloths of gold, velvet, satin and other rich stuffs. The two monarchs rode on horseback together from the centre of the city square. The relations of Deva Raya joined the cavalcade, marching on foot before the two kings. The festivities lasted three days.

This was not the first political marriage of its type in south India. Earlier, the ruler of Kherla in Gondwana had married his daughter to Firuz Shah Bahmani in order to effect peace. It is said that this princess was the favourite queen of Firuz. However, these marriages could not by themselves bring about peace. The question of the Krishna–Godavari basin led to a renewed conflict between Vijayanagara, the Bahmani kingdom and Orissa. Following a confusion in the Reddi kingdom, Deva Raya entered into an alliance with Warangal for partitioning the kingdom between them. Warangal's defection from the side of the Bahmani kingdom changed the balance of power in the Deccan. Deva Raya was able to inflict a shattering defeat on Firuz Shah Bahmani and annexed the entire Reddi territory up to the mouth of the Krishna river.

Deva Raya I did not neglect the arts of peace. He constructed a dam across the Tungabhadra so that he could bring the canals into the city to relieve the shortage of water. It irrigated the neighbouring fields also, for we are told that the canals increased his revenues by 350,000 *pardaos*. He also built a dam on the river Haridra for irrigation purposes.

After some confusion, Deva Raya II (1425–1446), who is considered the greatest ruler of the dynasty, ascended the throne at Vijayanagara. In order to strengthen his army, he reorganized his army, incorporating in it many features of the armies of the Delhi Sultanat. According to Ferishta, Deva Raya II felt that the superiority of the Bahmani army was due to their sturdier horses and their large body of mounted archers. He, therefore, enlisted 2000 Muslim cavalrymen, gave them *jagirs,* and commended all his Hindu soldiers and officers to learn the art of archery from them. The employment of Muslims in the Vijayanagara army was not new, for Deva Raya I is said to have kept 10,000 Muslims in his army. Ferishta tells us that Deva Raya II assembled 60,000 Hindus well skilled in archery, besides 80,000 cavalry, and 2,00,000 infantry. These figures may be exaggerated. However, the collection of a large cavalry force and standing army made the Vijayanagara empire a more centralized polity than any of the earlier Hindu kingdoms in the south, even though it must have put a strain on the resources of the state since most of the good mounts had to be imported, and the Arabs, who controlled the trade, charged high prices for them.

With his new army, Deva Raya II crossed the Tungabhadra river in 1443 and tried to recover Mudkal, Bankapur, etc., which were south of the Krishna river and had been lost to the Bahmani sultans earlier. Three hard battles were fought, but in the end the two sides had to agree to the existing frontiers.

Nuniz, a Portuguese writer of the sixteenth century, tells us that the kings of Quilon, Sri Lanka, Pulicat, Pegu and Tenasserim (in Burma and Malaya) paid tribute to Deva Raya II. It is doubtful whether the Vijayanagara rulers were powerful enough on the sea to extract regular tribute from Pegu and Tenasserim. Perhaps, what was meant was that the rulers of these countries were in contact with Vijayanagara, and had sent presents and embassies to secure its goodwill. Sri Lanka, however, had been invaded a number of times. This could not have been attained without a strong navy.

Under a series of capable rulers, Vijayanagara emerged as the most powerful and wealthy state in the south during the first half of the fifteenth century. The Italian traveller Nicolo Conti who visited Vijayanagara in 1420 had left us a graphic account of it. He says: 'The circumference of the city is sixty miles, its walls carried up to the mountains, and enclose the valleys at their foot.... In this city there are estimated to be ninety thousand men fit to bear arms. Their king is more powerful than all the other kings in India.' Ferishta also says: 'The princes of the house of Bahmani maintained their superiority by valour only; for in power, wealth and the extent of the country, the rayas of Beejanagar (Vijayanagara) greatly exceeded them.'

The Persian traveller Abdur Razzaq, who had travelled widely in and outside India, visited Vijayanagara in the reign of Deva Raya II. He gives a glowing account of the country, saying: 'This latter prince has in his dominions three hundred ports, each of which is equal to Calicut, and on *terra firma* his territories comprise a space of three months journey'. All travellers agree that the country was thickly populated, with numerous towns and villages. Abdur Razzaq says: 'The country is for the most part well cultivated, very fertile. The troops amount in number to eleven lakhs.'

Abdur Razzaq considers Vijayanagara to be one of the most splendid cities anywhere in the world which he had seen or heard of. Describing the city, he says: 'It is built in such a manner that seven citadels and the same number of walls enclose each other. The seventh fortress, which is placed in the centre of the others, occupies an area ten times larger than the market place of the city of Herat.' Starting from the palace, there were four bazars 'which were extremely long and broad.' As was the Indian custom, people belonging to one caste or profession lived in one quarter of the town. The Muslims appear to have lived in separate quarters provided for them. In the bazars as well as in the king's palace, 'one sees numerous running streams and canals formed of chiselled stone, polished and smooth.' Another later traveller says that the city was larger than Rome, one of the biggest towns in the western world at that time.

The kings of Vijayanagara were reputed to be very wealthy. Abdur Razzaq mentions the tradition that 'in the king's palace are several cell-like basins filled with bullion, forming one mass.' The hoarding of wealth by a ruler was an ancient tradition. However, such hoarded wealth remained out of circulation, and sometimes invited foreign attack.

THE BAHMANI KINGDOM—ITS EXPANSION AND DISINTEGRATION

The history of the rise of the Bahmani kingdom and its conflict with the Vijayanagara empire till the death of Deva Raya II (1446) has already been traced. The most remarkable figure in the Bahmani kingdom during the period was Firuz Shah Bahmani (1397–1422). He was well-acquainted with the religious sciences, that is, commentaries on the *Quran*, jurisprudence, etc., and was particularly fond of the natural sciences such as botany, geometry, logic, etc. He was a good calligraphist and a poet and often composed extempore verses. According to Ferishta, he was well versed not only in Persian, Arabic and Turkish, but also in Telugu, Kannada and Marathi. He had a large number of wives in his *haram* from various countries and regions, including many Hindu wives, and we are told that he used to converse with each of them in their own language.

Firuz Shah Bahmani was determined to make the Deccan the cultural centre of India. The decline of the Delhi Sultanat helped him, for many learned people migrated from Delhi to the Deccan. The king also encouraged learned men from Iran and Iraq. He used to say that kings should draw around them the learned and meritorious persons of all nations, so that from their society they might obtain information and thus acquire some of the advantages acquired by travelling into different regions of the globe. He generally spent his time till midnight in the company of divines, poets, reciters of history, and the most learned and witty among his courtiers. He had read the Old and New Testaments and respected the tenets of all religions. Ferishta calls him an orthodox Muslim, his only weakness being his fondness for drinking wine and listening to music.

The most remarkable step taken by Firuz Shah Bahmani was the induction of Hindus in the administration on a large scale. It is said that from his time the Deccani Brahmans became dominant in the administration, particularly in the revenue administration. The Deccani Hindus also provided a balance against the influx of foreigners. Firuz Shah Bahmani encouraged the pursuit of astronomy and built an observatory near Daulatabad. He paid much attention to the principal ports of his kingdom, Chaul and Dabhol, which attracted trading ships from the Persian Gulf and the Red Sea, and brought in luxury goods from all parts of the world.

Firuz Bahmani started the Bahmani expansion towards Berar by defeating the Gond raja, Narsing Rai of Kherla. The rai made a present of 40 elephants, 5 maunds of gold and 50 maunds of silver. A daughter of the rai was also married to Firuz. Kherla was restored to Narsing who was made an *amir* of the kingdom and given robes of state, including an embroidered cap.

Firuz Shah Bahmani's marriage with a daughter of Deva Raya I and his subsequent battles against Vijayanagara have been mentioned already. The struggle for the domination of the Krishna–Godavari basin, however, continued. In 1419, the Bahmani kingdom received a setback when Firuz Shah Bahmani was defeated by Deva Raya I. This defeat weakened the position of Firuz. He was compelled to abdicate in favour of his brother, Ahmad Shah I, who is called a saint (*wali*) on account of his association with the famous sufi saint, Gesu Daraz. Ahmad Shah continued the struggle for the domination of the eastern seaboard in south India. He could not forget that in the last two battles in which the Bahmani sultan had been defeated, the ruler of Warangal had sided with Vijayanagara. In order to wreak vengeance, he invaded Warangal, defeated and killed the ruler in a battle, and annexed most of its territories. In order to consolidate his rule over the newly acquired territories, he shifted the capital from Gulbarga to Bidar. After this, he turned his attention towards Malwa, Gondwana and the Konkan.

Mahmud Gawan

The loss of Warangal to the Bahmani kingdom changed the balance of power in south India. The Bahmani kingdom gradually expanded, and reached its height of power and territorial limits during the prime ministership of Mahmud Gawan. The early life of Mahmud Gawan is obscure. He was an Iranian by birth and was at first a trader. He was introduced to the sultan and soon became a favourite, and was granted the title of *Malik-ut-Tujjar*. Soon, he became prime minister or Peshwa. For almost 20 years, Mahmud Gawan dominated the affairs of the state. He extended the Bahmani kingdom by making further annexations in the east. A deep raid in the Vijayanagara territories up to Kanchi demonstrated the strength of the Bahmani army. Mahmud Gawan's major military contribution, however, was the over-running of the western coastal areas, including Dabhol and Goa. The loss of these ports was a heavy blow to Vijayanagara. Control of Goa and Dabhol led to further expansion of the Bahmani overseas trade with Iran, Iraq, etc. Internal trade and manufacture also grew.

Mahmud Gawan also tried to settle the northern frontiers of the kingdom. Since the time of Ahmad Shah I, the kingdom of Malwa ruled by the Khalji rulers had been contending for the mastery of Gondwana, Berar and the Konkan. In this struggle, the Bahmani sultans had sought and secured the help of the rulers of Gujarat. After a good deal of conflict, it had been agreed that Kherla in Gondwana would go to Malwa, and Berar to the Bahmani sultan. However, the rulers of Malwa were always on the lookout for seizing Berar. Mahmud Gawan had to wage a series of bitter battles against Mahmud Khalji of Malwa over Berar. He was able to prevail due to the active help given to him by the ruler of Gujarat.

It would, thus, be seen that the pattern of struggle in the south did not allow divisions along religious lines: political and strategic considerations and control over trade and commerce being more important causes of the conflict. Secondly, the struggle between the various states in north India and in south India did not proceed completely in isolation from each other. In the west, Malwa and Gujarat were drawn into the affairs of the Deccan; in the east, Orissa was involved in a struggle with Bengal and also cast covetous eyes on the commercially rich Coromandel coast. The Orissa rulers made deep raids into south India after 1450, their armies reaching as far south as Madurai and the territories of Orissa extended upto the river Krishna. Their activities further weakened the Vijayanagara empire which was passing through a phase of internal discord following the death of Deva Raya II.

Mahmud Gawan carried out many internal reforms also. He divided the kingdom into eight provinces or *tarafs*. Each *taraf* was governed by a *tarafdar*. The salaries and obligations of each noble were fixed. For maintaining a contingent of 500 horses, a noble received a salary of 1,00,000 *huns* per year. The salary could be paid in cash or by assigning a *jagir*. Those who were paid by means of a *jagir* were allowed expenses for the collection of land revenue. In every province, a tract of land (*khalisa*) was set apart for the expenses of the sultan. Efforts were made to measure the land and to fix the amount to be paid by the cultivator to the state.

Mahmud Gawan was a great patron of arts. He built a magnificent *madarasa* or college in the capital, Bidar. This fine building, which was decorated with coloured tiles, was three storeys high, and had accommodation for one thousand teachers and students who were given clothes and food free. Some of the most famous scholars of the time belonging to Iran and Iraq came to the *madarasa* at the instance of Mahmud Gawan.

One of the most difficult problem which faced the Bahmani kingdom was strife among the nobles. The nobles were divided into the long-established Deccanis and the new-comers who were foreigners (*afaqis,* also called *gharibs*). As a newcomer, Mahmud Gawan was hard put to win the confidence of the Deccanis. Though he adopted a broad policy of conciliation, the party strife could not be stopped. His opponents managed to poison the ears of the young sultan who had him executed in 1482. Mahmud Gawan was over 70 years old at the time. The party strife now became even more intense. The various governors became independent. Soon, the Bahmani kingdom was divided into five principalities: Golconda, Bijapur, Ahmadnagar, Berar and Bidar. Of these, the kingdoms of Ahmadnagar, Bijapur and Golconda played a leading role in the Deccan politics till their absorption in the Mughal empire during the seventeenth century.

The Bahmani kingdom acted as a cultural bridge between the north and the south. The culture which developed as a result had its own specific features which were distinct from north India. These cultural traditions were continued by the successor states and also influenced the development of Mughal culture during the period.

CLIMAX OF THE VIJAYANAGARA EMPIRE AND ITS DISINTEGRATION

As mentioned earlier, there was confusion in the Vijayanagara empire after the death of Deva Raya II (1446). Since the rule of primogeniture was not established in Vijayanagara, there were a series of civil wars among the various contenders to the throne. Many feudatories assumed independence in the process. The ministers became very powerful, and began to exact presents and heavy taxes from the people, causing considerable distress to them. The authority of the Raya shrunk to Karnataka and to some portions of the western Andhra region. The rulers were sunk in pleasures and neglected the affairs of the state. After some time, the throne was usurped by the king's minister, Saluva. The earlier dynasty, thus, came to an end. Saluva restored internal law and order, and founded a new dynasty. This dynasty too soon came to an end. Ultimately, a new dynasty (called the Tuluva dynasty) was founded by Krishna Deva. Krishna Deva Raya (1509–30) was the greatest figure of this dynasty. Some historians consider him to be the greatest of all the Vijayanagara rulers. Krishna Deva had not only to re-establish internal law and order, he had also to deal with the old rivals of Vijayanagara, viz., the successor states of the Bahmani kingdom and the state of Orissa which had usurped many Vijayanagara territories. In addition, he had to contend with the Portuguese whose power was slowly growing. They were using their control over the seas to browbeat the smaller vassal states of Vijayanagara in the coastal areas in order to gain economic and political concessions. They had even offered to buy the neutrality of the Raya by promising him assistance in recovering Goa from Bijapur and giving him a monopoly in the supply of horses.

In a series of battles lasting seven years, Krishna Deva first compelled the ruler of Orissa to restore to Vijayanagara all the territories up to the river Krishna. Having thus strengthened himself, Krishna Deva renewed the old struggle for the control of the Tungabhadra doab. This led to a hostile alliance between his two main opponents, Bijapur and Orissa. Krishna Deva made grand preparations for the conflict. He opened the hostilities by overrunning Raichur and Mudkal. In the battle which followed, the Bijapur ruler was completely defeated (1520). He was pushed across the river Krishna, barely escaping with his life. In the west, the Vijayanagara armies reached Belgaum, occupied and sacked Bijapur for a number of days and destroyed Gulbarga before a truce was made.

Thus, under Krishna Deva, Vijayanagara emerged as the strongest military power in the south. However, in their eagerness to renew the old feuds, the southern powers largely ignored the danger posed to them and to their commerce by the rise of the Portuguese. Unlike the Cholas and some of the early Vijayanagara rulers, Krishna Deva seems to have paid scant attention to the development of a navy.

The conditions in Vijayanagara during this period are described by a number of foreign travellers. Paes, an Italian who spent a number of years at Krishna Deva's court, has given a glowing account of his personality. But he remarks: 'He is a great ruler and a man of much justice, but subject to sudden fits of rage.' He cherished his subjects, and his solicitude for their welfare became proverbial. He also tried to create a more centralized administration by ousting all the *nayaks* from the Tungbhadra doab, and bringing it under direct administration.

Krishna Deva was also a great builder. He built a new town near Vijayanagara and dug an enormous tank which was also used for irrigation purposes. He was a gifted scholar of Telugu and Sanskrit. Of his many works, only one in Telugu on polity and a drama in Sanskrit are available today. His reign marked a new era in Telugu literature when imitation of Sanskrit works gave place to independent works. He extended his patronage to Telugu, Kannada and Tamil poets alike. Foreign travellers like Barbosa, Paes and Nuniz speak of his efficient administration and the prosperity of the empire under his sway.

The Vijayanagara rulers are considered great protectors of Hinduism. Under their patronage a large number of temples, schools and *maths* were built. In this period, temples became very elaborate in structure and organization; even old temples were amplified by the addition of pillared halls, pavilions and other subordinate structures. However, speaking of the broad toleration that prevailed in the empire of Krishna Deva, Barbosa says: 'The king allows such freedom that every man may come and go and live according to his own creed, without suffering any annoyance, and without enquiry whether he is a Christian, Jew, Moor or heathen.' Barbosa also pays tribute to Krishna Deva for the justice and equity prevailing in his empire.

After the death of Krishna Deva (1530), there was a struggle for succession among his relations since his sons were all minors. Ultimately, in 1543, Sadashiva Raya ascended the throne and reigned till 1567. But the real power lay in the hands of a triumvirate in which the leading person was Rama Raja. Rama Raja was able to play off the various Muslim powers against one another. He entered into a commercial treaty with the Portuguese whereby the supply of horses to the Bijapur ruler was stopped. In a series of wars he completely defeated the Bijapur ruler, and also inflicted humiliating defeats on Golconda and Ahmadnagar. It seems that Rama Raja had no larger purpose than to maintain a balance of power favourable to Vijayanagara between these three powers. At length, they combined to inflict a crushing defeat on Vijayanagara at Bannihatti, near Talikota, in 1565. This is also called the battle of Talikota or the battle of Rakshasa-Tangadi. Rama Raja was surrounded, taken prisoner and immediately executed. It is said that 1,00,000 Hindus were slain during the battle. Vijayanagara was thoroughly looted and left in ruins.

The battle of Bannihatti is generally considered to mark the end of the great age of Vijayanagara. Although the kingdom lingered on for almost one hundred more years, its territories decreased continually and the raya no longer counted in the political affairs of south India.

State and Economy under Vijayanagara

The concept of kingship among the Vijayanagara rulers was high. In his book on polity, Krishna Deva Raya advises the king that 'with great care and according to your power you should attend to the work of protecting (the good) and punishing (the wicked) without neglecting anything that you see or hear.' He also enjoined upon the king to 'levy taxes from his people moderately.'

In the Vijayanagara kingdom the king was advised by a council of ministers which consisted of the great nobles of the kingdom. The kingdom was divided into *rajyas* or *mandalam* (provinces) below which were *nadu* (district), *sthala* (sub-district) and *grama* (village).

The Chola traditions of village self-government were considerably weakened under Vijayanagara rule. The growth of hereditary nayakships tended to curb their freedom and initiative. The governors of the provinces were royal princes at first. Later, persons belonging to vassal ruling families and nobles were also appointed as governors. The provincial governors had a large measure of autonomy. They held their own courts, appointed their own officers, and maintained their own armies. They were allowed to issue their own coins, though of small denominations only. There was no regular term for a provincial governor, his term depending on his ability and his strength. The governor had the right to impose new taxes or remit old ones. Each governor paid a fixed contribution in men and money to the central government. It had been estimated that while the income of the kingdom was 12,000,000 *parados*, the central government got only half the amount.

There were many areas in the empire which were under the control of subordinate rulers, i.e., those who had been defeated in war, but whose kingdoms had been restored to them. In the large centrally controlled area, the king granted *amaram* or territory with a fixed revenue to military chiefs. These chiefs, who were called *palaiyagar* (*palegar*) or *nayaks*, had to maintain a fixed number of foot, soldiers, horses and elephants for the service of the state. The *nayaks* or *palegars* also had to pay a sum of money to the central exchequer. They formed a very powerful section and sometimes it was difficult for the government to control them. These internal weaknesses of the Vijayanagara empire contributed to its defeat in the battle of Bannihatti and its subsequent disintegration. Many of the *nayaks*, such as those of Tanjore and Madurai, became independent from that time.

Historians are not agreed about the economic condition of the peasantry under the Vijayanagara rule, because most of the travellers had little knowledge about village life and, thus, spoke of it in very general terms. In general, it may be presumed that the economic life of the people remained more or less the same; their houses were mostly thatched with a small door; they generally went about barefooted and wore little above the waist. People of the upper classes sometimes wore costly shoes and a silk turban on their heads, but did not cover themselves above the waist. All classes of people were fond of ornaments, and wore them 'in their ears, on their necks, on their arms, etc.'

We have very little idea about the share of the produce the peasants were required to pay. According to an inscription, the rates of taxes were as follows:

One-third of the produce of *kuruvai* (a type of rice) during winter
One-fourth of sesame, ragi, horsegram, etc
One-sixth of millet and other crops cultivated on dry land

Thus, the rate varied according to the type of crops, soil, method of irrigation, etc.

In addition to the land tax, there were various other taxes, such as property tax, tax on sale of produce, profession taxes, military contribution (in times of distress), tax on marriage, etc. The sixteenth-century traveller, Nikitin, says: 'The land is overstocked with people, but those in the country are very miserable while the nobles are extremely affluent and delight in luxury.'

Urban life grew under the Vijayanagara empire and trade flourished. Towns grew, many of them around temples. The temples were very large and needed supply of food stuffs and commodities for distribution of *prasadam* to the pilgrims, service of the god, the priests, etc. The temples were rich and also took active part in trade, both internal and overseas. There was considerable growth of towns and urbanization under Vijayanagara rule. It is in this sense that many historians consider the period of Vijayanagara rule to be a period of transition from the old to the new economy.

THE ADVENT OF THE PORTUGUESE

The landing of Vasco da Gama at Calicut in 1498 with two ships, with Gujarati pilots aboard who had guided the ships from the African coast to Calicut, has often been considered the beginning of a new phase during which the control of the Ocean passed into the hands of the Europeans. Indian trade and traders received a setback and ultimately the Europeans were able to establish their colonial rule and domination over India and most of the neighbouring countries. This picture has been called into question by both western and Indian historians, especially after World War II and the end of European political rule over the countries of the region.

Before we assess the impact of the Portuguese on Indian society, economy and politics, let us first examine the factors which brought the Portuguese to India. Very broadly, the Portuguese came to India at a time when European economy was growing rapidly, thanks to the expansion of land under cultivation on account of the drainage of marshes and cutting of forests, the introduction of a improved plough, and a more scientific rotation of crops which also led to an increase in the growth of cattle, and supply of meat. The growth was reflected in the rise of towns, and increase of trade, both internal and external. Since Roman times, there had been a steady demand for oriental goods. These included silk from China, and spices and drugs from India and Southeast Asia. With economic revival, this demand increased, especially the demand for pepper and spices which were needed to make meat palatable since due to shortage of fodder many cattle were slaughtered during winter and the meat salted up.

Pepper was brought to the Levant, Egypt and the Black Sea ports overland and partly by sea from India and Southeast Asia. With the rise of the power of the Ottoman Turks from the early part of the 15th century, all these areas came under the control of the Turks. Thus, they captured Constantinople in 1453, and Syria and Egypt later. The Turks were not opposed to trade, but the virtual monopoly over pepper established by them was bound to work against the Europeans. The expansion of Turkish power towards eastern Europe and the growth of the Turkish navy which made the eastern Mediterranean a Turkish lake also alarmed the Europeans. Venice and Genoa which had been the most active in the trade of oriental goods were too small to stand up to the Turks. Venice, in particular quickly came to terms with the Turks. The banner of struggle against the Turkish danger was, therefore, taken up by the powers in the western part of the Mediterranean, Spain and Portugal. They were aided with money and men by the North Europeans and by ships and technical knowledge by the Genoese, who were the rivals of Venice. It was not the Portuguese alone, but all these elements which started the search for a direct sea route to India, and hence started the era of naval discoveries, including the 'discovery' of America by the Genoese, Christopher Columbus (or rediscovery, because Norsemen from the North had reached America earlier as also the Red Indians across the Bering Straits). The work of the Portuguese ruler Dom Henrique, generally called Henry the Navigator, should be seen in this context.

From 1418, Prince Henry sent two or three ships every year to explore the western coast of Africa, and to search out a sea-route to India. His objects were two fold: first, to oust the Arabs as well as his European rivals, the Venetians, from the rich eastern trade, and second, to counterpoise the growing power of the Turks and Arabs by converting the 'heathens' of Africa and Asia to Christianity. Both objectives were steadily pursued. In fact, they justified and supported each other. The Pope lent his support by issuing a Bull in 1453 by which he granted to Portugal 'in perpetuity' whatever lands it 'discovered' beyond Cape Nor in Africa up to India on the condition of converting to Christianity the peoples of those lands.

In 1488, Bartholomew Diaz rounded the Cape of Good Hope and laid the basis of direct trade links between Europe and India. Such long sea-voyages were made possible by a number of remarkable inventions, notably the mariner's compass and the astrolabe for fixing the height of heavenly bodies for purposes of navigation. The former was known to the Chinese several centuries earlier, but was not widely used. The astrolabe was, however, widely used by the Arabs, Indians and others. Nor were the European ships superior in construction to the ships, such as the Chinese junks, used in Asian waters at the time. The spirit of daring and enterprise displayed by the Europeans was certainly new. This spirit has been traced back to the revival and growth of trade and commerce from the 13th century onwards, leading to intense rivalry among the European states. As important was the new intellectual stirring called the Renaissance. The Renaissance signified, above all, a spirit of independent investigation

rather than basing oneself either on the revealed word, or on wisdom
enshrined in the Church. These developments led to the rapid
assimilation, dispersal and improvement of other foreign (Arab and
Chinese) inventions such as the gun-powder, printing, telescope, etc.
Developments in metallurgy led to the production of better quality
guns.

Vasco da Gama landed at Calicut in 1498, with Gujarati pilots on
board. The strong colony of the Arab merchants settled there was
hostile, but the Zamorin welcomed the Portuguese and allowed them
to take pepper, drugs, etc., on board. In Portugal, the goods brought
by Gama were computed at sixty times the cost of the entire
expedition. Despite this, direct trade between India and Europe grew
slowly. One reason for this was the monopoly exercised by the
Portuguese government. From the beginning, the Portuguese rulers
were determined to treat the eastern trade as a royal monopoly,
excluding not only rival nations in Europe and Asia, but also private
Portuguese traders.

Alarmed at the growing power of the Portuguese, the sultan of
Egypt fitted a fleet and sent it towards India. The fleet was joined by
a contingent of ships belonging to the ruler of Gujarat. After an initial
victory in which the son of the Portuguese governor, Don Almaida,
was killed, this combined fleet was routed by the Portuguese in 1509.
This made the Portuguese navy supreme in the Indian Ocean, and
enabled the Portuguese to extend their operations towards the Persian
Gulf and the Red Sea.

Shortly afterwards, Albuquerque succeeded as the governor of the
Portuguese possession in the east. He advocated and embarked upon
a policy of dominating the entire oriental commerce by setting up
forts at various strategic places in Asia and Africa. This was to be
supplemented by a strong navy. Defending his philosophy, he wrote:
'A dominion founded on a navy alone cannot last.' Lacking forts, he
argued, 'neither will they (the rulers) trade or be on friendly terms
with you.'

Albuquerque initiated his new policy by capturing Goa from
Bijapur in 1510. The island of Goa was an excellent natural harbour
and fort. It was strategically located, and from it the Portuguese could
command the Malabar trade and watch the policies of the rulers in

the Deccan. It was also near enough to the Gujarat sea-ports for the Portuguese to make their presence felt there. Goa was, thus, suited to be the principal centre of Portuguese commercial and political activity in the east. The Portuguese were also able to extend their possession on the mainland opposite Goa, and to blockade and sack the Bijapuri ports of Danda-Rajouri and Dabhol, thus paralysing Bijapur's sea-trade.

From their base at Goa, the Portuguese further strengthened their position by establishing forts at Colombo in Sri Lanka, at Achin in Sumatra, and at the Malacca port which controlled the exit and entry to the narrow gulf between the Malay peninsula and Sumatra. The Portuguese also established a station at the island of Socotra at the mouth of the Red Sea. They failed to capture Aden, and the Red Sea remained outside their control. But they forced the ruler of Ormuz which controlled entry into the Persian Gulf to permit them to establish a fort there.

The success of the Portuguese was, however, more apparent than real. From the beginning they had to face a number of challenges, both external and internal. The external challenge was the one posed by the Turks who were sometimes joined by the Arabs and some Indian powers. After conquering Syria, Egypt and Arabia, the Turks had gone on to conquer Eastern Europe, and in 1529 threatening Vienna, the capital of Central Europe and the key to its defence. The growth of Turkish power on the coast of the Red Sea and the Persian Gulf seemed to presage a conflict between the Turks and the Portuguese for dominating the western part of the Indian Ocean. The Ottoman grand *wazir*, Lutfi Pasha, writing after 1541, told the Turkish sultan, Sulaiman the Magnificent, 'Under the previous sultans there were many who ruled the land, but few who ruled the sea. In the conduct of naval warfare, the infidels are ahead of us. We must overcome them'.

In view of the growing Portuguese threat to the Gujarat trade and coastal areas, the sultan of Gujarat sent an embassy to the Ottoman ruler, congratulating him on his victories, and seeking his support. In return, the Ottoman ruler expressed a desire to combat the infidels, that is, the Portuguese, who had disturbed the shores of Arabia. From this time onwards, the there was a continuous exchange of embassies and letters between the two countries. The Turks ousted the Portuguese from the Red Sea, and in 1529 a strong fleet under Sulaiman Rais was despatched to aid Bahadur Shah, the ruler of Gujarat. Bahadur Shah received it well, and two of the Turkish officials, who were given Indian names, were appointed governors of Surat and Diu, respectively. Of these two, Rumi Khan was later to earn a great name for himself as a master-gunner.

In 1531, after intriguing with local officials, the Portuguese attacked Daman and Diu but the Ottoman commander, Rumi Khan, repulsed the attack. However, the Portuguese built a fort at Chaul lower down the coast.

Before the Gujarat–Turkish alliance could be consolidated, a bigger threat to Gujarat appeared from the side of the Mughals. Humayun attacked Gujarat. In order to meet this threat, Bahadur Shah granted the island of Bassein to the Portuguese. A defensive-offensive alliance against the Mughals was also concluded, and the Portuguese were allowed to build a fort at Diu. Thus were the Portuguese able to establish their foothold in Gujarat.

Bahadur Shah soon repented his concessions to the Portuguese. Following the expulsion of the Mughals from Gujarat, he once again appealed to the Ottoman sultan for help, and tried to limit the Portuguese encroachments at Diu. During the negotiations, Bahadur Shah who was abroad one of the ships of the governor of the fort suspected treachery. In the scuffle which ensued, the Portuguese governor was killed and Bahadur Shah drowned while swimming ashore. This was in 1536.

Although the Ottoman sultans claimed to be champions of Islam and hence opponents of the Portuguese, they did not, in practice, seriously contest the position of the Portuguese in the Persian Gulf or beyond. This despite the fact that the Turks had broadly kept pace with the growth of artillery and, to a lesser extent, with the naval sciences in the west. The Turkish navy dominated the eastern Mediterranean and even made raids beyond Gibraltar.

The Turks made their biggest naval demonstration against the Portuguese in Indian waters in 1536. Their fleet consisted of 45 galleons carrying 20,000 men, including 7000 land soldiers or *janissaries*. Many of the sailors had been pressed into service from the

Venetian galleys at Alexandria. The fleet commanded by Sulaiman Pasha, an old man of 82, who was the most trusted man of the sultan and had been appointed the governor of Cairo, appeared before Diu in 1538 and besieged it. Unfortunately, the Turkish admiral behaved in an arrogant manner and the sultan of Gujarat withdrew his support. After a siege of two months, the Turkish fleet retired, following news of the arrival of a formidable Portuguese armada to relieve Diu.

The Turkish threat to the Portuguese persisted for another two decades. In 1551, Peri Rais, who was assisted by the Zamorin of Calicut, attacked the Portuguese forts at Muscat and Ormuz. Meanwhile, the Portuguese strengthened their position by securing Daman from its ruler. A final Ottoman expedition was sent under Ali Rais in 1554. The failure of these expeditions resulted in a final change in the Turkish attitude. In 1566, the Portuguese and the Ottomans came to an agreement to share the spice and the Indian trade and not to clash in the Arab seas. The Ottomans shifted their interest once again to Europe, and came to an agreement with the Portuguese for dividing the oriental trade between them. This precluded their alliance with the rising Mughal power against the Portuguese. But it also had economic consequences, as we shall see.

Portuguese Impact on the Indian Trade, Society and Politics

From the beginning, the Portuguese could neither adequately police the vast expanse of the Indian Ocean, nor control the trade or the traders there. All that they could try to do was to monopolize certain goods, and tax the others. Thus, trade in pepper, arms and ammunition, and war horses was declared a royal monopoly. No nation, not even Portuguese private traders, were allowed to engage in the trade of these goods. Ships engaged in the trade of other commodities had to take a permit from the Portuguese officials. The Portuguese also attempted to force all ships going to the east or to Africa to pass by Goa, and pay customs duty there.

To enforce these rules, the Portuguese arrogated to themselves the right to search any ship suspected of engaging in 'contraband' trade. Ships which refused to be searched could be treated as prizes of war and sunk or captured, and the men and women aboard treated as slaves. This led to continuous friction. The Portuguese soon found that they stood more to lose on land than they gained on sea by such practices which were quite contrary to the practice and tradition of open trade in Asian waters. True, many Arab and Indian ships began to carry cannons and soldiers, but it was more a safeguard against sea pirates which infested the Malabar and Arab coast.

The Portuguese were hardly able to change the established pattern of Asian trade networks. The Gujarati and Arab traders continued to dominate some of the most lucrative Asian trade, i.e., the trade in Indian textiles, supplemented by rice and sugar, against which they obtained spices from the Southeast, gold and horses from West Asia, and silk and porcelain from China. The Portuguese were not even able to monopolize the pepper and spice trade to Europe, except for a couple of decades at the outset. By the end of the sixteenth century, the supply of pepper to the Levant and Egyptian markets, both overland and by the Red Sea, was as large as it had been earlier. This was because the great Asian empires, the Mughal and the Safavid, were able to promote and safeguard overland trade, and also because the Gujaratis were able to arrange a new supply route from Achin in Sumatra to Egypt via Lakshadweep and the Red Sea where the Portuguese navy could not operate.

Nor were the Portuguese able to develop Goa as the dominant centre of the Asian trade, eclipsing Cambay and later Surat in Gujarat. However, they adversely affected the Malabar trade, and the sea trade from Bengal which they preyed upon from Chittagong.

The Portuguese, however, opened up India's trade with Japan from which copper and silver were obtained. They also opened up India's trade with the Philipplines. From the Philippines, the Portuguese carried Indian textiles to South America and brought back silver in exchange. They demonstrated how naval power could be used to harass and hamper the trade even of such a well developed country as India, as also to open new lines of trade.

The Portuguese could not act as a bridge for transmitting to India the science and technology which had grown in Europe since the Renaissance. This was partly because the Portuguese were themselves not as deeply affected by the Renaissance as Italy and North Europe. Later, with the growth of a Catholic religious reaction led by the

Jesuits, they even set their face against the new science. They did, however, help to transmit a number of agricultural products from Central America, such as potato, tobacco, maize, peanut, etc. These became widespread only gradually.

The defeat of Vijayanagara at Banihatti in 1565 emboldened the Deccani states to make a concerted effort to dislodge the Portuguese from the Deccan coast. So long as Vijayanagara had threatened Bijapur in the south, peace with the Portuguese was essential since they controlled the horse-trade and hostilities with them would have meant a diversion of the trade in favour of Vijayanagara. In 1570, Ali Adil Shah, the sultan of Bijapur, entered into an agreement with the sultan of Ahmadnagar. The Zamorin of Calicut was also drawn into the alliance. The allies decided to attack the Portuguese positions in their own dominions. Adil Shah personally led the attack against Goa, while Nizam Shah besieged Chaul. But, once again, the Portuguese defence, backed up by their navy, proved to be too strong. Thus, the Portuguese remained masters of the Indian seas and of the Deccan coast.

Struggle for Empire in North India—I
(*Circa* 1400–1525)

The growing weakness of the Delhi Sultanat, and the attack of Timur on Delhi in 1398, followed by the flight of the Tughlaq king from his capital, emboldened a number of provincial governors and autonomous rulers to declare their independence. Apart from the Deccan states, Bengal in the east, and Sindh and Multan in the west were among the first to break away from Delhi. Soon, the governors of Gujarat, Malwa and Jaunpur (in eastern Uttar Pradesh) also declared themselves independent. With the expulsion of the Muslim governor from Ajmer, the various states of Rajputana asserted their independence.

Gradually, a definite pattern of balance of power emerged between the states belonging to the various regions. In the west, Gujarat, Malwa and Mewar balanced and checked the growth of each other's power. Bengal was checked by the Gajapati rulers of Orissa, as well as by Jaunpur. The rise of the power of the Lodis in Delhi from about the middle of the fifteenth century resulted in a long drawn-out tussle between them and the rulers of Jaunpur for the mastery of the Ganga-Yamuna valley. The situation began to change with the absorption of Jaunpur by the Lodis towards the end of the fifteenth century. Following this victory, the Lodis began to expand their power in eastern Rajasthan and Malwa. Malwa started disintegrating at this time due to internal factors, thereby sharpening the rivalry between Gujarat, Mewar and the Lodis. It appeared that the victor in this contest would dominate the entire north India. Thus, the struggle for the domination of Malwa was the cockpit for the struggle for the mastery of north India. It was this heightened rivalry which perhaps prompted Rana Sanga to invite Babur in the hope that the destruction of the power of the Lodis would leave Mewar as the strongest power in the field.

EASTERN INDIA—BENGAL, ASSAM AND ORISSA

As we have seen above, Bengal had frequently become independent of the control of Delhi due to its distance, climate, and the fact that much of its communication depended upon waterways with which the Turkish rulers were unfamiliar. Due to the preoccupation of Muhammad Tughlaq with rebellions in various quarters, Bengal again broke away from Delhi in 1338. Four year later, one of the nobles, Ilyas Khan, captured Lakhnauti and Sonargaon, and ascended the throne under the title Sultan Shamsuddin Ilyas Khan. He extended his dominions in the west, from Tirhut to Champaran and Gorakhpur, and finally up to Banaras. This forced Firuz Tughlaq to undertake a campaign against him. Marching through Champaran and Gorakhpur, the territories newly acquired by Ilyas, Firuz Tughlaq occupied the Bengali capital Pandua, and forced Ilyas to seek shelter in the strong fort of Ekdala. After a siege of two months, Firuz tempted Ilyas out of the fort by feigning flight. The Bengali forces were defeated, but Ilyas once again retreated into Ekdala. Finally, a treaty of friendship was concluded by which the river Kosi in Bihar was fixed as the boundary between the two kingdoms. Though Ilyas exchanged regular gifts with Firuz, he was in no way subordinate to him. Friendly relations with Delhi enabled Ilyas to extend his control over the kingdom of Kamrup (in modern Assam).

Ilyas Shah was a popular ruler and had many achievements to his credit. When Firuz was at Pandua, he tried to win over the inhabitants of the city to his side by giving liberal grants of land to the nobles, the clergy and other deserving people. His attempts failed. The popularity of Ilyas might have been one of the reasons for the failure of Firuz against him.

Firuz Tughlaq invaded Bengal a second time when Ilyas died and his son, Sikandar, succeeded to the throne. Sikandar followed the tactics of his father, and retreated to Ekdala. Firuz failed, once again, to capture it, and had to beat a retreat. After this, Bengal was left alone for about 200 years and was not invaded again till after the Mughals had established their power at Delhi. It was overrun by Sher Shah in 1538. During this period, a number of dynasties flourished in Bengal. The frequent changes of dynasties did not, however, disturb the even tenor of the lives of the common people.

The most famous sultan in the dynasty of Ilyas Shah was Ghiyasuddin Azam Shah (1389–1409). He was known for his love of justice. It is said that he once accidentally killed the son of a widow who complained to the *qazi*. The sultan, when summoned to the court, humbly appeared and paid the fine imposed by the *qazi*. At the end of the trial, the sultan told the *qazi* that if he had failed to do his duty, he would have had him beheaded.

Azam Shah had close relations with the famous learned men of his times, including the famous Persian poet, Hafiz of Shiraz. He re-established friendly relations with the Chinese. The Chinese emperor received his envoy cordially and, in 1409, sent his own envoy with presents to the sultan and his wife, and a request to send Buddhist monks to China. This was accordingly done. Incidentally, this shows that Buddhism had not died completely in Bengal till then.

The revival of contact with China helped in the growth of the overseas trade of Bengal. The Chittagong port became a flourishing port for trade with China, and for the re-export of Chinese goods to other parts of the world.

During this period, there was a brief spell of Hindu rule under Raja Ganesh. However, his sons preferred to rule as Muslims.

The sultans of Bengal adorned their capitals, Pandua and Gaur, with magnificent buildings. These had a style of their own, distinct from the style which had developed in Delhi. The materials used were both stone and brick. The sultans also patronised the Bengali language. The celebrated poet Maladhar Basu, compiler of *Sri-Krishna-Vijaya*, was patronised by the sultans and was granted the title of Gunaraja Khan. His son was honoured with the title of Satyaraja Khan. But the most significant period for the growth of the Bengali language was the rule of Alauddin Hussain (1493–1519). Some of the famous Bengali writers of the time flourished under his rule.

A brilliant period began under the enlightened rule of Alauddin Hussain. The sultan restored law and order, and adopted a liberal policy by offering high offices to the Hindus. Thus, his *wazir* was a talented Hindu. The chief physician, the chief of the bodyguard, the master of the mint were also Hindus. The two famous brothers who were celebrated as pious Vaishnavas, Rupa and Sanatan, held high posts, one of them being the sultan's private secretary. The sultan is also said to have shown great respect to the famous Vaishnavite saint, Chaitanya.

Since the time of Muhammad bin Bakhtiyar Khalji, the Muslim rulers of Bengal had tried to bring the Brahmaputra valley in modern Assam under their control, but had to suffer a series of disastrous defeats in this region which was little known to them. The independent sultans of Bengal tried to follow in the footsteps of their predecessors. There were two warring kingdoms in north Bengal and Assam at that time. Kamata (called Kamrup by the writers of the time) was in the west, and the Ahom kingdom was in the east. The Ahoms, a Mongoloid tribe from north Burma, had succeeded in establishing a powerful kingdom in the thirteenth century, and had become Hinduized in course of time. The name Assam is derived from them.

Ilyas Shah invaded Kamta and, it seems, penetrated up to Gauhati. However, he could not hold the area, and the river Karatoya was accepted as the northeast boundary of Bengal. Plundering raids into Kamta by some of the successors of Ilyas Shah did not change the situation. The rulers of Kamta were gradually able to recover many of the areas on the eastern bank of the Karatoya. They also fought against the Ahoms. By alienating both their neighbours they sealed their doom. An attack by Alauddin Hussain Shah which was supported by the Ahoms led to the destruction of the city of Kamtapur (in modern Cooch Bihar), and the annexation of the kingdom to Bengal. The sultan appointed one of his sons as governor of the area. A colony of Afghans was planted in the area. A subsequent attack on the Ahom kingdom, probably by Nusrat Shah, the son of Alauddin Hussain, was unsuccessful and was repulsed with considerable losses. The eastern Brahmaputra valley was at this time under Suhungmung who is considered the greatest of the Ahom rulers. He changed his name to Svarga Narayana. This was an index of the rapid Hinduization of the Ahoms. He not only repulsed the Muslim attack, but also extended his kingdom in all directions. The Vaishnavite reformer, Shankaradeva, belonged to his time and played an important role in the spread of Vaishnavism in the area.

The sultans of Bengal also tried to bring Chittagong and a part of Arakan under their control. Sultan Hussain Shah not only wrested Chittagong from the Arakan king, but also conquered Tipperah from its ruler.

The rulers of Bengal had also to contend with Orissa. During the period of the Sultanat rule over Bengal, the Ganga rulers of Orissa had aided Radha (south Bengal), and even made an attempt at the conquest of Lakhnauti. These attacks had been repulsed but the rulers of Orissa were powerful enough not to allow the governor of Bengal to penetrate into Orissa. It were the rulers of the Ganga dynasty who built the famous Puri temple, and the Sun temple (Konark). It was only after 1338 that the independent ruler of Bengal, Ilyas Shah, raided Jajnagar (Orissa). It is said that overcoming all opposition, he advanced up to the Chilka Lake and returned with a rich booty, including a number of elephants. A couple of years later, in 1360, while returning from his Bengal campaign, Firuz Tughlaq also raided Orissa. He occupied the capital city, massacred a large number of people, and desecrated the Jagannatha temple of Puri. These two raids destroyed the prestige of the Ganga dynasty. In due course, a new dynasty, called the Gajapati dynasty, came to the fore. The Gajapati rule marks a brilliant phase in Orissa history. The rulers were great builders and warriors. The Gajapati rulers were mainly instrumental in extending their rule in the south towards Karnataka. As we have seen, this brought them into conflict with Vijayanagara, the Reddis and the Bahmani sultans. Perhaps, one reason why the Gajapati rulers preferred aggrandizement in the south was their feeling that the sultans of Bengal were too strong to be easily dislodged from the Bengal-Orissa border. But the Orissa rulers could not hold on to their southern conquests for any length of time, due to the power and capabilities of the Vijayanagara and Bahmani rulers.

In Bengal, the Orissa frontier at this time was the river Saraswati which then carried much of the waters of the Ganga. Thus, a large part of Midnapore district and part of the Hugli district were included in Orissa territories. There is some evidence that the Orissa rulers tried to extend their control up to Bhagirathi, but were compelled to retreat. Some of the sultans of Bengal, including Alauddin Hussain Shah, made raids into Orissa which extended up to Puri and Cuttack.

Intermittent fighting also went on the frontier. However, the rulers of Bengal were not able to dislodge the Orissan rulers from their frontiers, or to gain any territory beyond the river Saraswati. That the Orissan rulers were able to engage successfully in battles at the same time in such far-flung areas as Bengal and Karnataka testifies to their strength and prowess.

Western India—Gujarat, Malwa and Mewar

On account of the excellence of its handicrafts and its flourishing seaports, as well as the richness of its soil, Gujarat was one of the richest provinces of the Delhi Sultanat. Under Firuz Tughlaq, Gujarat had a benign governor who, according to Ferishta, 'encouraged the Hindu religion and thus promoted rather than suppressed the worship of idols'. He was succeeded by Zafar Khan whose father, Sadharan, was a Rajput who had converted to Islam, and given his sister in marriage to Firuz Tughlaq. After Timur's invasion of Delhi, both Gujarat and Malwa became independent in all but name. However, it was not till 1407 that Zafar Khan formally proclaimed himself the ruler, with the title Muzaffar Shah.

The real founder of the kingdom of Gujarat was, however, Ahmad Shah I (1411–43), the grandson of Muzaffar Shah. During his long reign, he brought the nobility under control, settled the administration, and expanded and consolidated the kingdom. He shifted the capital from Patan to the new city of Ahmedabad, the foundation of which he laid in 1413. He was a great builder, and beautified the town with many magnificent palaces and bazars, mosques and *madarsas*. He drew on the rich architectural traditions of the Jains of Gujarat to devise a style of building which was markedly different from Delhi. Some of its features are: slender turrets, exquisite stone-carving, and highly ornate brackets. The Jama Masjid in Ahmedabad and the Tin Darwaza are fine examples of the style of architecture during his time.

Ahmad Shah tried to extend his control over the Rajput states in the Saurashtra region, as well as those located on the Gujarat-Rajasthan border. In Saurashtra, he defeated and captured the strong fort of Girnar, but restored it to the raja on his promise to pay tribute.

He then attacked Sidhpur, the famous Hindu pilgrim centre, and levelled to the ground many of the beautiful temples there. He imposed *jizyah* on the Hindus in Gujarat which had not been imposed on them earlier. All these have led many medieval historians to hail Ahmad Shah as a great enemy of the infidels, while many modern historians have called him a bigot. The truth, however, appears to be more complex. While Ahmad Shah acted as a bigot in ordering the destruction of Hindu temples, he did not hesitate to induct Hindus in his government. Manik Chand and Motichand, belonging to the Bania or trader community, were ministers under him. He was so strict in his justice that he had his own son-in-law executed in the market-place for a murder he had committed. Although he fought the Hindu rulers, he fought no less the Muslim rulers of the time, particularly the Muslim rulers of Malwa. He subordinated the powerful fort of Idar, and brought the Rajput states of Jhalawar, Bundi, Dungarpur, etc., under his control.

From the beginning, the kingdoms of Gujarat and Malwa were bitter rivals and were generally found in opposite camps on almost every occasion. Muzaffar Shah had defeated and imprisoned Hushang Shah, the ruler of Malwa. Finding it difficult to control Malwa, he had, however, released Hushang Shah after a few years and reinstated him. Far from healing the breach, it had made the rulers of Malwa even more apprehensive of Gujarat power. They were always on the lookout for weakening Gujarat by giving help and encouragement to disaffected elements there, be they rebel nobles, or Hindu rajas at war with the Gujarat ruler. The rulers of Gujarat tried to counter this by trying to install their own nominee on the throne of Malwa. This bitter rivalry weakened the two kingdoms, and made it impossible for them to play a larger role in the politics of north India.

MAHMUD BEGARHA

The successors of Ahmad Shah continued his policy of expansion and consolidation. The most famous sultan of Gujarat was Mahmud Begarha. Mahmud Begarha ruled over Gujarat for more than 50 years (from 1459 to 1511). He was called Begarha because he captured two of the most powerful forts (*garhs*), Girnar in Saurashtra (now called Junagarh), and Champaner in south Gujarat.[1] The ruler of Girnar had paid tribute regularly, but Mahmud Begarha decided to annex his kingdom as part of his policy of bringing Saurashtra under full control. Saurashtra was a rich and prosperous region and had many fertile tracts and flourishing ports. Unfortunately, the Saurashtra region was also infested by robbers and sea pirates who preyed on trade and shipping. The powerful fort of Girnar was considered suitable not only for administering Saurashtra, but also as a base of operations against Sindh.

Mahmud Begarha besieged Girnar with a large force. Though the raja had only a few guns in the fort, he resisted gallantly, but to no avail. It is said that the conquest of this inaccessible fort was due to treason. The ruler of Girnar had forcibly taken the wife of his *kamdar* (minister agent) who schemed in secret for the downfall of his master. After the fall of the fort, the raja embraced Islam and was enrolled in the service of the sultan. The sultan founded at the foot of the hill a new town called Mustafabad. He built many lofty buildings there and asked all his nobles to do the same. Thus, it became the second capital of Gujarat.

Later in his reign, Mahmud sacked Dwarka, on the ground it harboured pirates who preyed on the pilgrim traffic to Mecca. The campaign was however, also used to raze the famous Hindu temples there.

The fort of Champaner was strategically located for the sultan's plans of bringing Khandesh and Malwa under his control. The ruler, though a feudatory of Gujarat, had close relations with the sultan of Malwa. Champaner fell in 1454 after the gallant raja and his followers, despairing of help from any quarter, performed the *jauhar* ceremony and fought to the last man. Mahmud constructed a new town called Muhammadabad near Champaner. He laid out many fine gardens there and made it his principal place of residence.

Champaner is now in ruins. But the building which still attracts attention is the Jama Masjid. It has a covered courtyard, and many

---

1 According to another version, he was called Begarha because his moustaches resembled the horns of a cow (begarha).

Jain principles of architecture have been used in it. The stone work in the other buildings constructed during this period is so fine that it can only be compared to the work of goldsmiths.

Mahmud Begarha also had to deal with the Portuguese who were interfering with Gujarat's trade with the countries of West Asia. He joined hands with the ruler of Egypt to check the Portuguese naval power, but he was not successful.

During the long and peaceful reign of Mahmud Begarha, trade and commerce prospered. He constructed many caravan-sarais and inns for the comfort of the travellers. The merchants were happy because roads were safe for traffic.

Though Mahmud Begarha had never received a systematic education, he had gained considerable knowledge by his constant association with the learned men. Many works were translated from Arabic into Persian during his reign. His court poet was Udayaraja who composed in Sanskrit.

Mahmud Begarha had a striking appearance. He had a flowing beard which reached up to his waist, and his moustache was so long that he tied it over the head. According to a traveller, Barbosa, Mahmud, from his childhood, had been nourished on some poison so that if a fly settled on his hand, it swelled and immediately lay dead.

Mahmud was also famous for his voracious appetite. It is said that for breakfast he ate a cup of honey, a cup of butter and one hundred to one hundred and fifty plantains. He ate 10 to 15 kilos of food a day and we are told that plates of meat patties (*samosas*) were placed on both sides of his pillow at night in case he felt hungry!

Under Mahmud Begarha the Gujarat kingdom reached its maximum limit, and emerged as one of the most powerful and well-administered states in the country. Later on, it was powerful enough to pose a serious challenge to the Mughal ruler, Humayun.

MALWA

The state of Malwa was situated on the high plateau between the rivers Narmada and Tapti. It commanded the trunk routes between Gujarat and northern India, as also between north and south India.

As long as Malwa continued to be strong, it acted as a barrier to the ambitions of Gujarat, Mewar, the Bahmanis and the Lodi sultans of Delhi. The geopolitical situation in northern India was such that if any of the powerful state of the region could extend its control over Malwa, it would be well on its way to make a bid for the domination of the entire north India.

During the fifteenth century, the kingdom of Malwa remained at the height of its glory. The capital was shifted from Dhar to Mandu, a place which was highly defensible and which had a great deal of natural beauty. Here the rulers of Malwa constructed a large number of buildings, the ruins of which are still impressive. Unlike the Gujarat style of architecture, the Mandu architecture was massive and was made to look even more so by using a very lofty plinth for the buildings. The large-scale use of coloured and glazed tiles provided variety to the buildings. The best known among them are Jama Masjid, the Hindola Mahal and the Jahaz Mahal.

From the beginning, the kingdom of Malwa was torn by internal dissensions. The struggle for succession between different contenders to the throne was accompanied by fighting between different groups of nobles for power and profit. The neighbouring states of Gujarat and Mewar were always ready to take advantage of this factionalism for their own purposes.

One of the early rulers of Malwa, Hushang Shah, adopted a broad policy of religious toleration. Many Rajputs were encouraged to settle in Malwa. Thus, two of the elder brothers of Rana Mokal of Mewar were granted jagirs in Malwa. From the inscription of the Lalitpur temple which was built during this period, it appears that no restrictions were placed on the construction of temples. Hushang Shah extended his patronage to the Jains who were the principal merchants and bankers of the area. Thus, Nardeva Soni, a successful merchant, was the treasurer of Hushang Shah, and was one of his advisers.

However, all the rulers of Malwa were not equally tolerant. Mahmud Khalji (1436–69), who is considered the most powerful of the Malwa rulers, destroyed many temples during his struggle with Rana Kumbha of Mewar, and with the neighbouring Hindu rajas. This was reprehensible, and a setback from the policy of broad toleration which had gradually developed under the Delhi Sultanat. However, it was not part of any policy of general destruction of Hindu temples.

Mahmud Khalji was a restless and ambitious monarch. He fought with almost all his neighbours—the ruler of Gujarat, the rajas of Gondwana and Orissa, the Bahmani sultans, and even the sultan of Delhi. However, his energies were principally devoted to overrunning south Rajputana and trying to subdue Mewar.

MEWAR

The rise of Mewar during the fifteenth century was an important factor in the political life of north India. We have seen how, after being ousted from Ajmer, the Chauhans had shifted to Ranthambhor, and set up a powerful state. With the conquest of Ranthambhor by Alauddin Khalji, the power of the Chauhans in Rajputana had finally come to an end. From its ruins a number of new states arose. The state of Marwar with its capital at Jodhpur (founded 1465) was one of these. Another state of consequence in the area was the Muslim principality of Nagaur. Ajmer which had been the seat of power of the Muslim governors changed hands several times, and was a bone of contention among the rising Rajput states. The mastery of eastern Rajputana was also in dispute, the ruler of Delhi being deeply interested in this area.

The early history of the state of Mewar is obscure. The virtual founder of Mewar is supposed to be Bapa Rawal of the Guihlot clan who it is said migrated from Gujarat in the seventh century, and dominated the southwestern part of Rajasthan. The Guihils ruled from Chittor to the time of Ratan Singh who was ousted by Alauddin Khalji. Chittor then passed into the hands of the Sishodias who had been feudatories of the Guihils. During the last quarter of the fourteenth century and the first quarter of the fifteenth century, Rao Lakha and Mokal made Mewar the most powerful state in Rajasthan. The ruler who raised it to the status of a power to be reckoned with was Rana Kumbha (1433–68). After cautiously consolidating his position by defeating his internal rivals, Kumbha renewed efforts for the conquest of Bundi, Kotah and Daungarpur on the Gujarat border. Kotah had earlier been paying allegiance to Malwa and Dungarpur to Gujarat. This brought him into direct conflict with both these kingdoms. There were other reasons for the conflict, too. The Khan of Nagaur who had been attacked by Rana Kumbha had appealed for help to the ruler of Gujarat. The rana had also given shelter at his court to a rival of Mahmud Khalji, and even attempted to install him on the Malwa throne. In retaliation, Mahmud Khalji had given shelter and active encouragement to some of the rivals of the rana, such as his brother Mokal.

The conflict with Gujarat and Malwa occupied Kumbha throughout his reign. During most of the time, the Rana also had to contend with the Rathors of Marwar. Marwar was under Mewar occupation, but soon it became independent after a successful struggle waged under the leadership of Rao Jodha.

Although sorely pressed from all sides, Rana Kumbha was largely able to maintain his position in Mewar. Kumbhalgarh was besieged a couple of times by Gujarat forces, while Mahmud Khalji was able to raid as far inland as Ajmer and install his own governor there. The rana was able to repulse these attacks and retain possession of most of his conquests, with the exception of some of the outlying areas such as Ranthambhor. Rana Kumbha's achievement in facing two such powerful states against all odds was no small achievement.

Kumbha was a patron of learned men, and was himself a learned man. He composed a number of books, some of which can still be read. The ruins of his palace and the Victory Tower (*Kirti Stambha*) which he built at Chittor show that he was an enthusiastic builder as well. He dug several lakes and reservoirs for irrigation purposes. Some of the temples built during his period show that the art of stone-cutting, sculpture, etc., were still at a high level.

Kumbha was murdered by his son, Uda, in order to gain the throne. Though Uda was soon ousted, he left a bitter trail. After a long fratricidal conflict with his brothers, Rana Sanga, a grandson of Kumbha, ascended the *gaddi* of Mewar in 1508. The most important development between the death of Kumbha and the rise of Sanga was the rapid internal disintegration of Malwa. The ruler, Mahmud II, had fallen out with Medini Rai, the powerful Rajput leader of eastern Malwa who had helped him to gain the throne. The Malwa ruler appealed for help to Gujarat, while Medini Rai

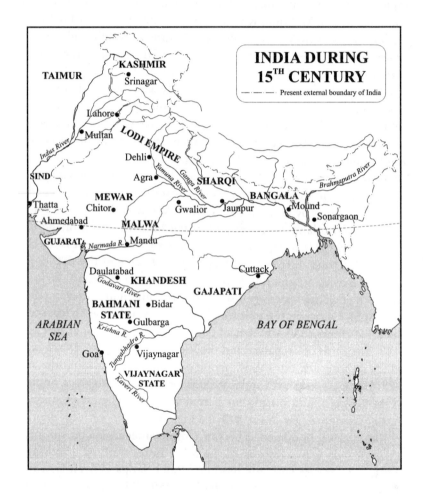

INDIA DURING
15TH CENTURY
————— Present external boundary of India

repaired to the court of Rana Sanga for help. In a battle in 1517, the Rana defeated Mahmud II and carried him a prisoner to Chittor. It is claimed that he released him after six months, keeping one of his sons as a hostage. Eastern Malwa, including Chanderi, passed under the overlordship of Rana Sanga.

The developments in Malwa alarmed the Lodi rulers of Delhi who were keenly watching the situation. The Lodi ruler, Ibrahim Lodi, invaded Mewar, but suffered a sharp reverse at the hands of Rana Sanga at Khatoli. Ibrahim Lodi withdrew in order to consolidate his internal position. Meanwhile, Babur was knocking at the gates of India.

Thus, by 1525, the political situation in north India was changing rapidly, and a decisive conflict for supremacy in north India seemed to be inevitable.

Northwest and North India—The Sharqis, the Lodi Sultans and Kashmir

As we have seen, after the invasion of Timur, Sultan Mahmud Tughlaq fled from Delhi and took shelter first in Gujarat and then in Malwa. By the time he decided to return, the prestige of the throne of Delhi had been shattered; in the neighbourhood of Delhi itself ambitious nobles and zamindars asserted their independence.

Amongst the first to assert independence in the Ganga valley was Malik Sarwar, a prominent noble of the time of Firuz Tughlaq. Malik Sarwar had been the *wazir* for some time, and then had been nominated to the eastern areas with the title *Malik-us-Sharq* (Lord of the East). His successors came to be called the Sharqis after his title. The Sharqi sultans fixed their capital at Jaunpur (in eastern Uttar Pradesh) which they beautified with magnificent palaces, mosques and mausoleums. Only a few of these mosques and mausoleums survive now. They show that the Sharqi sultans did not just copy the Delhi style of architecture: they created a magnificent style of their own marked by lofty gates and huge arches.

The Sharqi sultans were great patrons of learning and culture. Poets and men of letters, scholars and saints assembled at Jaunpur and shed lustre on it. In course of time, Jaunpur came to be known as the 'Shiraz of the East'. Malik Muhammad Jaisi, the author of the well known Hindi work *Padmavat*, lived at Jaunpur.

The Sharqi Sultanat lasted for less than a century. At its height, it extended from Aligarh in western Uttar Pradesh to Darbhanga in north Bihar, and from the boundary of Nepal in the north to Bundelkhand in the south. The Sharqi rulers were eager to conquer Delhi but they were not successful in doing so. With the establishment of the Lodis in Delhi towards the middle of the fifteenth century, the Sharqi rulers were gradually put on the defensive. They lost most of the areas in western Uttar Pradesh and exhausted themselves in a series of bitter but futile assaults on Delhi. At length, in 1484, Bahlul Lodi, the ruler of Delhi, occupied Jaunpur and annexed the Sharqi kingdom. The Sharqi king lived on as an exile at Chunar for some time, and died broken-hearted after repeated failures in regaining his kingdom.

The Sharqi rulers maintained law and order over a large tract following the collapse of the government in Delhi. They successfully prevented the rulers of Bengal in extending their control over eastern Uttar Pradesh. Above all, they established a cultural tradition which continued long after the downfall of the Sharqis.

After the Timurid invasion, a new dynasty, called the Saiyid dynasty, arose in Delhi. A number of Afghan sardars established themselves in the Punjab. The most important of these was Bahlul Lodi who had been granted the *iqta* of Sirhind. Bahlul Lodi checked the growing power of the Khokhars, a fierce warlike tribe which lived in the Salt Ranges. Soon, he dominated the entire Punjab. Called in to help the ruler of Delhi against an impending attack by the ruler of Malwa, Bahlul stayed on. Before long, his men took over the control of Delhi. Bahlul formally crowned himself (1451) when the ruler of Delhi died in exile. Thus ended the Saiyid dynasty.

The Lodis dominated the upper Ganga valley and the Punjab from the middle of the fifteenth century. As distinct from the earlier Delhi rulers who were Turks, the Lodis were Afghans. Although the Afghans formed a large group in the army of the Delhi Sultanat, very few Afghan nobles had been accorded important positions. The growing importance of the Afghan in north India was shown by the rise of the Afghan rule in Malwa. In the south, they held important positions in the Bahmani kingdom.

Bahlul Lodi's energies were occupied mainly in his contest against the Sharqi rulers. Finding himself in a weak position, Bahlul invited the Afghans of Roh to come to India so that 'they will get rid of the ignominy of poverty and I shall gain ascendancy.' The Afghan historian, Abbas Sarwani, adds: 'On receipt of these *farmans*, the Afghans of Roh came like locusts to join the service of Sultan Bahlul.'

This may be an exaggeration. But the incursion of a large number of Afghans not only enabled Bahlul to defeat the Sharqis, it changed the complexion of the Muslim society in India, making the Afghans a very numerous and important element in it, both in south and north India.

The most important Lodi sultan was Sikandar Lodi (1489–1517). A contemporary of Mahmud Begarha of Gujarat and of Rana Sanga of Mewar, Sikandar Lodi geared the kingdom of Delhi for the coming struggle for power with these states. He tried to subdue the Afghan sardars who had a sturdy sense of tribal independence, and were not accustomed to look upon the sultan as more than a first among equals. Sikandar made the nobles stand before him in order to impress them with his superior status. When a royal order was sent, all the nobles had to come out of the town to receive it with due honour. All those who held *jagirs* had to submit accounts regularly. Drastic punishments were given to those who embezzled money or were corrupt. Sikandar Lodi had only limited success in his efforts to control the nobles. At his death, Bahlul Lodi had divided the kingdom among his sons and relations. Though Sikandar had been able to undo this after a hard struggle, the idea of a partition of the empire among the sons of the ruler persisted among the Afghans.

Sikandar Lodi was able to establish efficient administration in his kingdom. He laid great emphasis on justice, and all the highways of the empire were made safe from robbers and bandits. The prices of all essential commodities were remarkably cheap. The sultan took keen interest in agriculture. He abolished the octroi duty on grains, and established a new measurement of the yard, called the *gazz-i-Sikandari*, which continued to prevail till the Mughal times. The rent rolls prepared in his time formed the basis of the rent rolls of Sher Shah later on.

Sikandar Lodi is regarded as an orthodox, even a bigoted king. He sternly forbade the Muslims from following practices which were against the *sharia* (Islamic law), such as women visiting the graves of saints or processions being taken out in the memory of saints. He re-imposed the *jizyah* on the Hindus, and executed a Brahman for holding that the Hindu and Muslim scriptures were equally sacred. He also demolished a few well known Hindu temples during his campaigns, such as the temple at Nagarkot.

Sikandar Lodi gave magnificent grants to scholars, philosophers, and men of letters so that cultured people of all climes and countries, including Arabia and Iran, flocked to his court. Due to the sultan's efforts, a number of Sanskrit works were translated into Persian. He was also interested in music and had a number of rare Sanskrit works on music translated into Persian. During his time, a large number of Hindus took to learning Persian and were recruited to various administrative posts.

Thus, the process of cultural rapprochement between the Hindus and the Muslims continued apace during his reign. Sikandar Lodi also extended his dominions by conquering Dholpur and Gwaliyar. It was during these operations that after careful survey and deliberations, Sikandar Lodi selected the site for the city of Agra (1506). The town was meant to command the area of eastern Rajasthan and the route to Malwa and Gujarat. In course of time, Agra became a large town and the second capital of the Lodis.

The growing interest of Sikandar in eastern Rajasthan and Malwa was shown by his taking the Khan of Nagaur under his protection, and by trying to make Ranthambhor transfer its allegiance from Malwa to Delhi. His successor, Ibrahim Lodi, even led a campaign against Mewar which, as has been noted earlier, was repulsed. The growing power of the rana in Malwa, and the extension of his power towards Agra and Bayana, presaged a conflict between Mewar and the Lodis. It is difficult to say what the outcome of this conflict would have been if Babur had not intervened.

KASHMIR

An account of north India in the fifteenth century would be incomplete without mentioning the Kingdom of Kashmir. The beautiful valley of Kashmir was for long a forbidden land for all outsiders. According to al-Biruni, entry into Kashmir was not allowed even to the Hindus who were not known personally to the nobles there. During the period, Kashmir was known to be a centre of Saivism. However, the situation changed with the ending of Hindu rule around the middle of the fourteenth century. The devastating attack on Kashmir in 1320 by the Mongol leader, Dalucha, was a prelude to it. It is said that Dalucha ordered a wholesale massacre of men, while women and children were enslaved and sold to the merchants of Central Asia. The towns and villages were ravaged and plundered and set on fire. The hapless Kashmir government could offer no opposition to these doings, thereby losing all public sympathy and support.

One hundred years after the Mongol invasion, Zainul Abidin, considered the greatest of the Muslim monarchs of Kashmir, ascended the throne. Kashmir society had profoundly changed during this period. There had been a continuous incursion of Muslim saints and refugees from Central Asia into Kashmir, the Baramulla route providing an easy access. Another development was the rise of a series of remarkable Sufi saints called Rishis, who combined some features of Hinduism and Islam. Partly by the preaching of the saints and partly by force, the lower class population had been converted to Islam. To complete the process, a vehement persecution of the Brahmans began in the reign of Sikandar Shah (1389–1413). The sultan ordered that all Brahmans and learned Hindus should become Muslims or leave the valley. Their temples were to be destroyed and the idols of gold and silver were to be melted down in order to be used for currency. It is said that these orders were issued at the instance of the king's minister, Suha Bhatt, who had converted to Islam, and was bent on harassing his former co-religionists.

This situation changed with the accession of Zainul Abidin (1420–70) who had all these orders cancelled. He conciliated and brought back to Kashmir all the non-Muslims who had fled. Those who wanted to revert to Hinduism, or had pretended to be Muslims in order to save their lives, were given freedom to do as they pleased. He even restored the libraries and the land grants which the Hindus had enjoyed. The temples were also restored. More than one hundred years later, Abul Fazl noted that Kashmir had one hundred and fifty majestic temples. It is likely that most of them had been restored under Zainul Abidin.

Zainul Abidin continued the policy of broad toleration in other spheres as well. He abolished *jizyah* and cow slaughter, and to respect the wishes of the Hindus, withdrew the ban on sati. The Hindus occupied many high offices in his government. Thus, Sriya Bhatt was minister of justice and was appointed court physician. His first two queens were Hindus, being the daughters of the Raja of Jammu. They were the mothers of all his four sons. He married a third wife after the death of his first two wives.

The sultan was himself a learned man, and composed poetry. He was well versed in Persian, Kashmiri, Sanskrit and Tibetan languages. He gave patronage to Sanskrit and Persian scholars and, at his instance, many Sanskrit works such as the *Mahabharata* and Kalhana's history of Kashmir, *Rajatarangini*, were translated into Persian and brought up-to-date. He was fond of music, and hearing of this, the Raja of Gwalior sent him two rare Sanskrit works on music.

The sultan also looked after the economic development of Kashmir. He sent two persons to Samarqand to learn the arts of paper-making and book-binding. He fostered many crafts in Kashmir, such as stone-cutting and polishing, bottle-making, gold-beating, etc. He also encouraged the art of shawl-making, for which Kashmir is so famous. Musket-making and the art of manufacturing fireworks had also developed in Kashmir. The sultan developed agriculture by making large numbers of dams, canals and bridges. He was an enthusiastic builder, his greatest engineering achievement being Zaina Lanka—the artificial island in the Woolur Lake on which he built his palace and a mosque.

Zainul Abidin is still called Bud Shah (the Great Sultan) by the Kashmiris. Though not a great warrior, he defeated the Mongol invasion of Ladakh, conquered the Baltistan area (called Tibbat-i-buzarg) and kept control over Jammu, Rajauri, etc. He, thus, unified the Kashmiri kingdom.

The fame of Zainul Abidin had spread far and wide. He was in touch with the leading rulers in the other parts of India, as also the leading rulers of Asia.

A quick survey of the developments during the fifteenth century shows that regional balance of power·could give neither peace nor stability. The regional kingdoms had, however, many cultural contributions to their credit. In these kingdoms, local styles of architecture were developed, often using local traditions. Local languages were also patronised. While some of the rulers did carry out a large scale destruction of temples, and tried to present themselves as orthodox Muslim kings, overall in these kingdoms the forces of mutual accommodation and cultural integration remained active, some of the rulers anticipating Akbar in a number of fields.

Cultural Development in India
(1300–1500)

The establishment of the Delhi Sultanat towards the beginning of the thirteenth century may be said to mark a new phase in the cultural development of the country. The Turkish invaders who came to India were by no means rude barbarians. Coming to West Asia during the ninth and tenth centuries from their Central Asian homelands, they had accepted Islam, just as the earlier invaders from Central Asia had accepted Buddhism and Hinduism. They had also assimilated rapidly the culture of the area. The Arabo-Persian culture, which had embraced the Islamic lands from Morocco and Spain to Iran and its adjacent area, was at its height at the time. The people of the region had made many important contributions in the field of science, navigation and literature, etc. When the Turks came to India, they not only had a well-defined faith in Islam to which they were deeply attached, they also had definite ideas of government, art, architecture, etc. The interaction of the Turks with the Indians who held strong religious beliefs and had well-developed ideas of art, architecture and literature resulted, in the long run, in the development of a new enriched culture. But the process was a long one, of destruction followed or accompanied by periods of construction. Mutual misunderstanding and strife is always present when the two sides have strongly-held views. More significant, however, were the efforts at mutual understanding which ultimately led to a process of assimilation in many fields, such as art and architecture, music, literature, and even in the fields of customs and ceremonies, rituals and religious beliefs, science and technology. However, the elements of confrontation and conflict remained strongly entrenched in both the communities. The process of assimilation and convergence, therefore, had many ups and downs, and varied from region to region, from field to field and from period to period.

ARCHITECTURE

One of the first requirements of the new rulers was houses to live in, and to have places of worship. They at first converted some temples and other existing buildings into mosques while destroying many others, and using their material for building mosques. Examples of this are the Quwwat-ul-Islam mosque near the Qutab Minar in Delhi, and the building at Ajmer called Arhai Din ka Jhonpra. The former had been a temple, the latter had been a monastery. The only new construction at Delhi was a facade of three elaborately carved arches in front of the *garbhagriha* which was demolished. The style of decoration used on these arches is very interesting: no human or animal figures were used since it was considered to be un-Islamic to do so. Instead, they used scrolls of flowers and verses of the *Quran* which were intertwined in a very artistic manner. Soon, the Turks started constructing their own buildings. For this purpose they mostly used the indigenous craftsmen, such as stone-cutters, masons, etc., who were famous for their skills. Later, some master architects came to India from West Asia. In their buildings, the Turks used the arch and the dome on a wide scale. Neither the arch nor the dome was a Turkish or Muslim invention. The Arabs borrowed them from Rome through the Byzantine empire, developed them and made them their own.

The use of the arch and the dome had a number of advantages. The dome provided a pleasing skyline and, as the architects gained more experience and confidence, the dome rose higher. Many experiments were made in putting a round dome on a square building, and in raising the dome higher and higher. In this way, many lofty and impressive buildings were constructed. The arch and the dome dispensed with the need for a large number of pillars to support the roof, and enabled the construction of large halls with a clear view. Such places of assembly were useful in mosques as well as in palaces. However, the arch and the dome needed a strong cement, otherwise the stones could not be held in place. The Turks used fine quality light mortar in their buildings. Thus, new architectural forms and mortar of a superior kind became widespread in north India, with the arrival of the Turks.

The arch and the dome were known to the Indians earlier, but they were not used on a large scale. Moreover, the correct scientific method of constructing the arch was rarely employed. The architectural device generally used by the Indians consisted of putting one stone over another, narrowing the gap till it could be covered by a coping-stone or by putting a beam over a slab of stones. The Turkish rulers used both the dome and arch method as well as the slab and beam method in their buildings.

In the sphere of decoration, the Turks eschewed representation of human and animal figures in their buildings. Instead, they used geometrical and floral designs, combining them with panels of inscriptions containing verses from the *Quran*. Thus, the Arabic script itself became a work of art. The combination of these decorative devices was called arabesque. They also freely borrowed Hindu motifs such as the bell motif, the *bel* motif, *swastika*, lotus, etc. Thus, like the Indians, the Turks were intensely fond of decoration. The skill of the Indian stone-cutters was fully used for the purpose. The walls of the small tomb of Iltutmish (near the Qutab Minar, Delhi) were so intricately carved that hardly a square inch is left vacant. The Turks also added colour to their buildings by using red sandstone. Yellow sandstone, or marble was used in these buildings for decoration and to show off the colour of red sandstone.

The most magnificent building constructed by the Turks in the thirteenth century was the Qutab Minar. This tapering tower, originally 71.4 metre high, was begun by Aibak, and completed by Iltutmish. It is wrong to think that it was dedicated to the Sufi saint, Qutab-ud-Din Bakhtiyar Kaki, the venerated saint of Delhi, since it was not called at the time as Qutab Minar but the Quwwat-ul-Islam mosque. Although traditions of building towers are to be found both in India and West Asia, the Qutab Minar is unique in many ways. It derives its effect mainly from the skilful manner in which the balconies have been projected yet linked with the main tower, the use of red and white sandstone and marble in panels and in the top stages, and the ribbed effect.

The Khalji period saw a lot of building activity. Alauddin built his capital at Siri, a few kilometres away from the site around the Qutab. Unfortunately, hardly anything of this city survives now. Alauddin planned a tower twice the height of the Qutab, but did not live to complete it. But he added an entrance door to the Qutab. This door, which is called the Alai Darwaza, has arches of very pleasing proportions. It also contains a dome which, for the first time, was built on correct scientific lines. Thus, the art of building the arch and the dome on scientific lines had been mastered by the Indian craftsmen by this time.

There was great building activity in the Tughlaq period which marked the climax of the Delhi Sultanat as well as the beginning of its decline. Ghiyasuddin and Muhammad Tughlaq built the huge palace-fortress complex called Tughlaqabad. By blocking the passage of the Yamuna, a huge artificial lake was created around it. The tomb of Ghiyasuddin marks a new trend in architecture. To have a good skyline, the building was put upon a high platform. Its beauty was heightened by a marble dome.

A striking feature of the Tughlaq architecture was the sloping walls. This is called 'batter' and gives the effect of strength and solidity to the building. However, we do not find any 'batter' in the buildings of Firuz Tughlaq. A second feature of the Tughlaq architecture was the deliberate attempt to combine the principles of the arch, and the lintel and beam in their buildings. This is found in a marked manner in the buildings of Firuz Tughlaq. The Hauz Khas was a pleasure resort and had a huge lake around it. It also had a *Madarsa*. The same is to be found in some buildings of Firuz Shah's new fort which is now called the Kotla. The Tughlaqs did not generally use the costly red sandstone in their buildings but the cheaper and more easily available greystone. Since it was not easy to carve this type of stone, the Tughlaq buildings have a minimum of decoration. But the decorative device found in all the buildings of Firuz is the lotus.

Many grand mosques were also built in this period. It is not possible to describe all of them here. What is worth noting is that, by this time, an independent style of architecture had emerged in India, combining many of the new devices brought by the Turks with the indigenous forms. The Lodis developed this tradition further. Both the arch, and the lintel and beam are used in their buildings. Balconies, kiosks and eaves of the Rajasthani-Gujarati style are also used. Another device used by the Lodis was placing their buildings, especially tombs, on a high platform, thus giving the building a feeling of size as well as a better skyline. Some of the tombs were placed in the midst of gardens. The Lodi Garden in Delhi is a fine example of this. Some of the tombs were of an octagonal shape. Many of these features were adopted by the Mughals later on, and their culmination is to be found in the Taj Mahal built by Shah Jahan.

By the time of the break up of the Delhi Sultanat, individual styles of architecture had also developed in the various kingdoms in different parts of India. Many of these, again, were powerfully influenced by the local traditions of architecture. This, as we have seen, happened in Bengal, Gujarat, Malwa, the Deccan, etc. During the fourteenth and fifteenth centuries, the style of architecture evolved in Delhi under the Tughlaqs was carried forward and modified in the various regional kingdoms.

Thus, there was an outburst of building activity, marked by the growth of many styles of architecture in different parts of the country.

RELIGIOUS IDEAS AND BELIEFS

Islam was not a stranger in India when the Turks established their empire in north India. Islam had been established in Sindh from the eighth century, and the Punjab from the tenth century, Arab travellers had settled in Kerala between the eighth and tenth centuries. During this period, Arab travellers and Sufi saints travelled in different parts of India. Al-biruni's book *Kitab-ul-Hind* and other writings had familiarized the learned sections in West Asia about Hindu ideas and beliefs. As has been noted earlier, Buddhist lores, Indian fables and books on astronomy and medicine had been translated into Arabic. Visits of Indian yogis to the region were not unknown. The influence of Buddhism and Vedantic ideas on Islamic thinking has been a subject of considerable debate among scholars. Remnants of Buddhist monasteries, stupas and images of the Buddha found in Afghanistan and parts of Central Asia, particularly along old trade routes, show the extent of Buddhist influence in these areas at one time. While it is difficult to determine the precise extent of the influence of Indian philosophic ideas, it is hardly disputable that both Greek and Indian ideas, in different proportions, made a definite contribution to the development of Islamic philosophy in its formative phase. These ideas provided the background to the rise of the Sufi movement which, after its establishment in India after the twelfth century, influenced both the Muslims and the Hindus and, thus, provided a common platform for the two. However, scholars believe that while various rituals and practices, including yogic practices, were freely drawn upon from Hinduism by the early Sufis and assimilated into their system, their basic ideological structure remained Islamic.

THE SUFI MOVEMENT

The tenth century is important in Islamic history for a variety of reasons: it marks the rise of the Turks on the ruins of the Abbasid Caliphate, as well as important changes in the realm of ideas and beliefs. In the realm of ideas, it marks the end of the domination of the *Mutazila* or rationalist philosophy, and the rise of orthodox schools based on the *Quran* and *Hadis* (traditions of the Prophet and his companions) and of the Sufi mystic orders. The 'rationalists' had been accused of spreading scepticism and atheism. In particular, it was argued that their philosophy of monism which held that God and the created world were fundamentally one was heretical on the ground that it abolished the difference between the creator and the created.

The works of the 'traditionalists' crystallized in four schools of the Islamic Law. Of these, the Hanafi school, which was the most liberal, was adopted by the eastern Turks who later came to India.

Mystics, who are called Sufis, had risen in Islam at a very early stage. Most of them were persons of deep devotion who were disgusted by the vulgar display of wealth and degeneration of morals following the establishment of the Islamic empire. Hence, these saints wanted to have nothing to do with the state—a tradition which continued later on. Some of the early Sufis, such as the woman mystic Rabia (d. eighth century) and Mansur bin Hallaj (d. tenth century), laid great emphasis on love as the bond between God and the individual soul. But their pantheistic approach led them into conflict with the orthodox elements who had Mansur executed for heresy. Despite this setback, mystic ideas continued to spread among the Muslim masses.

Al-Ghazzali (d. 1112), who is venerated both by the orthodox elements and the Sufis, tried to reconcile mysticism with Islamic orthodoxy. This he was able to do in a large measure. He gave a further blow to the 'rationalist' philosophy by arguing that positive knowledge of God and his qualities cannot be gained by reason, but only by revelation. Thus, the revealed book, *Quran*, was vital for a mystic.

Around this time, the Sufis were organized in 12 orders or *silsilahs*. A *silsilah* was generally led by a prominent mystic who lived in a *khanqah* or hospice along with his disciples. The link between the teacher or *pir* and his disciples or *murids* was a vital part of the Sufi system. Every *pir* nominated a successor or *wali* to carry on his work.

The monastic organisation of the Sufis, and some of their practices such as penance, fasting and holding the breath are sometimes traced to the Buddhist and Hindu yogic influence. Buddhism was widely prevalent in Central Asia before the advent of Islam, and the legend of the Buddha as a saintly man had passed into the Islamic legend. Yogis continued to visit West Asia even after the advent of Islam and the yogic book, *Amrit-kund*, had been translated into Persian from Sanskrit. Thus, Hindu and Buddhist practices and rituals seem to have been absorbed and assimilated by the Sufis even before they came to India. Whether, Buddhist philosophic ideas and Vedantist ideas had, in a significant manner, influenced Sufism is a matter of controversy. The origin of ideas is difficult to trace. The Sufi saints and many modern thinkers trace the Sufi ideas to the *Quran*. What is important to note here is that, irrespective of origin, there were many similarities in the ideas of the Sufis and the Hindu yogis and mystics about the nature of God, and His relationship with the soul, and the material world. This provided a basis for mutual toleration and understanding. The humane spirit of Sufism is well expressed by Sanai, a leading Persian poet of the time:

'Faith and Infidelity, both are galloping on the way towards Him;
And are exclaiming (together): He is one and none share His kingdom.'

The Sufi orders are broadly divided into two: *Ba-shara*, that is, those which followed the Islamic Law (*shara*) and *be-shara*, that is, those which were not bound by it. Both types of orders prevailed in

India, the latter being followed more by wandering saints. Although these saints did not establish an order, some of them became figures of popular veneration, often for the Muslims and Hindus alike.

THE CHISHTI AND SUHARWARDI SILSILAHS

Of the *ba-shara* movements, only two acquired significant influence and following in north India during the thirteenth and fourteenth centuries. These were the Chishti and Suharwardi *silsilahs*. The Chishti order was established in India by Khwaja Muinuddin Chishti who came to India around 1192, shortly after the defeat and death of Prithvi Raj Chauhan. After staying for some time in Lahore and Delhi he finally shifted to Ajmer which was an important political centre and already had a sizable Muslim population. No authentic record of his activities is available; he did not write any book, but his fame rose, it seems, along with that of his successors. Among the disciples of Shaikh Muinuddin (d. 1235) were Bakhtiyar Kaki and his disciple Farid-ud-Din Ganj-i-Shakar. Farid-ud-Din confined his activities to Hansi and Ajodhan (in modern Haryana and the Punjab, respectively). He was deeply respected in Delhi, so much so that streams of people would throng around him whenever he visited Delhi. His outlook was so broad and humane that some of his verses are later found quoted in the *Adi-Granth* of the Sikhs.

The most famous of the Chishti saints, however, were Nizamuddin Auliya and Nasiruddin Chiragh-i-Delhi. These early Sufis mingled freely with people of the lower classes, including the Hindus. They led a simple, austere life, and conversed with people in Hindawi, their local dialect. They were hardly interested in effecting conversions, though later on, many families and groups, attributed their conversion to the 'good wishes' of these saints. These Sufi saints made themselves popular by adopting musical recitations called *sama*, to create a mood of nearness to God. Moreover, they often chose Hindi verses for the purpose, since they could make a greater impact on their listeners. Nizamuddin Auliya adopted yogic breathing exercises, so much so that the yogis called him a *sidh* or 'perfect'.

After the death of Nasiruddin Chiragh-i-Delhi in the middle of the fourteenth century, the Chishtis did not have a commanding figure at Delhi. As a result, the Chishti saints dispersed, and extended their message to the eastern and southern parts of India.

The Suharwardi order entered India at about the same time as the Chishtis, but its activities were confined largely to the Punjab and Multan. The most well-known saints of the order were Shaikh Shihabuddin Suharwardi and Hamid-ud-Din Nagori. Unlike the Chishtis, the Suharwardi saints did not believe in leading a life of poverty. They accepted the service of the state, and some of them held important posts in the ecclesiastical department. The Chishtis, on the other hand, preferred to keep aloof from state politics and shunned the company of rulers and nobles. Nevertheless, both helped the rulers in their own way by creating a climate of opinion in which people belonging to different sects and religions could live in peace and harmony. While Mecca remained the holy of holies, the rise of popular saints provided a useful point of veneration and devotion to the mass of Muslims within the country.

THE BHAKTI MOVEMENT

The Bhakti movement which stressed mystical union of the individual with God had been at work in India long before the arrival of the Turks. Although the seeds of Bhakti can be found in the Vedas, it was not emphasized during the early period. The idea of the adoration of a personal God seems to have developed with the growing popularity of Buddhism. During the early centuries of the Christian era, under Mahayana Buddhism, the Buddha began to be worshipped in his 'gracious' (*avalokita*) form. The worship of Vishnu developed more or less at the same time. When many of the holy books, such as the *Ramayana* and the *Mahabharata*, were re-written during the Gupta times, Bhakti was accepted, along with *jnana* and *karma*, as one of the recognized roads to salvation.

However, the development of popular Bhakti took place in south India between the seventh and the twelfth century. As has been noticed earlier, the Saiva *nayanars* and the Vaishnavite *alvars* disregarded the austerities preached by the Jains and the Buddhists and preached personal devotion to God as a means of salvation. They disregarded the rigidities of the caste system and carried their message of love and personal devotion to God to various parts of south India by using the local languages.

Although there were many points of contact between south and north India, the transmission of the ideas of the Bhakti saints from south to north India was a slow and long drawn-out process. Oddly enough, the very reasons which made the *nayanars* and *alvars* popular in the south limited their appeal outside the area, yiz., the fact that they preached and composed in the local languages. Sanskrit was still the vehicle of thought in the country. The ideas of Bhakti were carried to the north by scholars as well as by saints. Among these, mention may be made of the Maharashtrian saint, Namadeva, who flourished in the first part of the fourteenth century, and Ramananda who is placed in the second half of the fourteenth and the first quarter of the fifteenth century. Namadeva was a tailor who it is said had taken to banditry before he became a saint. His poetry which was written in Marathi breathes a spirit of intense love and devotion to God. Namadeva is said to have travelled far and wide and engaged in discussions with the Sufi saints at Delhi. Ramananda, who was a follower of Ramanuja, was born at Prayag (Allahabad) and lived there and at Banaras. He substituted the worship of Rama in place of Vishnu. What is more, he taught his doctrine of Bhakti to all the four varnas, and disregarded the ban on people of different castes cooking together and sharing their meals. He enrolled disciples from all castes, including the low castes. Thus among his disciples was Ravidas, who was a cobbler by caste; Kabir, who was a weaver; Sena, who was a barber; and Sadhana, who was a butcher. Namadeva was equally broad-minded in enrolling his disciples.

The seeds scattered by these saints fell on fertile soil. The Brahmans had lost both in prestige and power following the defeat of the Rajput rulers and the establishment of the Turkish Sultanat. As a result, movements, such as the Nath Panthi movement challenging the caste system and the superiority of the Brahmans, had gained popularity.

These coincided with the Islamic ideas of equality and brotherhood which had been preached by the Sufi saints. People were no longer satisfied with a religion which only emphasized ceremonies and forms. They wanted a religion which could satisfy both their reason and emotions. It was due to these factors that the Bhakti movement became a popular movement in north India during the fifteenth and sixteenth centuries.

Among those who were most critical of the existing social order and made a strong plea for Hindu-Muslim unity, the names of Kabir and Nanak stand out. There is a good deal of uncertainty about the dates and early life of Kabir. Legend has it that he was the son of a Brahman widow who abandoned him after his birth and that he was brought up in the house of a Muslim weaver. He learned the profession of his adopted father, but while living at Kashi, he came in contact with both the Hindu and Muslim saints. Kabir, who is generally placed in the fifteenth century, emphasised the unity of God whom he calls by several names, such as Rama, Hari, Govinda, Allah, Sain, Sahib, etc. He strongly denounced idol-worship, pilgrimages, bathing in holy rivers or taking part in formal worship, including *namaz*. Nor did he consider it necessary to abandon the life of a householder for the sake of a saintly life. Though familiar with yogic practices, he considered neither asceticism nor book knowledge important for true knowledge. As a modern historian, Dr Tara Chand, says: 'The mission of Kabir was to preach a religion of love which would unite all castes and creeds. He rejected those features of Hinduism and Islam which were against this spirit and which were of no importance for the real spiritual welfare of the individual.' Kabir strongly denounced the caste system, especially the practice of untouchability, and emphasized the fundamental unity of man. He was opposed to all kinds of discrimination between human beings, whether on the basis of castes, or religion, race, family or wealth. His sympathies were decidedly with the poor with whom he identified himself. However, he was not a social reformer, his emphasis being reform of the individual under the guidance of a true guru or teacher.

Guru Nanak, from whose teaching the Sikh religion was derived, was born in a Khatri family in the village of Talwandi (now called Nankana) on the bank of the river Ravi in 1469. Although married early and trained in Persian to take his father's profession of accountancy, Nanak showed a mystic contemplative bent of mind, and preferred the company of saints and sadhus. Sometime later, he had a mystic vision and forsook the world. He composed hymns and sang them to the accompaniment of the *rabab*, a stringed instrument played by his faithful attendant, Mardana. It is said that Nanak undertook wide tours all over India and, even beyond it, to Sri Lanka in the south and Mecca and Medina in the West. He attracted a large number of people towards him and his name and fame had spread far and wide before his death in 1538.

Like Kabir, Nanak laid emphasis on the one God, by repeating whose name and dwelling on it with love and devotion one could get salvation without distinction of caste, creed or sect. However, Nanak laid great emphasis on the purity of character and conduct as the first condition of approaching God, and the need of a guru for guidance. Like Kabir, he strongly denounced idol-worship, pilgrimages and other formal observances of the various faiths. He advocated a middle path in which spiritual life could be combined with the duties of the householder.

Nanak had no intention of founding a new religion. His catholic approach aimed at bridging distinctions between the Hindus and the Muslims, in order to create an atmosphere of peace, goodwill and mutual give and take. This was also the aim of Kabir. Different opinions have been expressed by scholars about the impact of their ideas on the large mass of Hindus and Muslims. It has been argued that the old forms of religion continued almost unchanged. Nor was it possible to effect any major breach in the caste system. In course of time, the ideas of Nanak gave birth to a new creed, Sikhism, while the followers of Kabir shrank into a sect, the *Kabir Panthis*. The importance of the mission of Kabir and Nanak should, however, be assessed from a broader point of view. They created a climate of opinion which continued to work through the succeeding centuries. It is well known that the religious ideas and policies of Akbar reflected in a remarkable manner the fundamental teachings of these two great saints. Nor was Akbar alone in pursuing such policies, as we have seen in the earlier chapter.

However, it was hardly to be expected that the orthodox elements in the two main religions, Hinduism and Islam, would surrender without a fight. As we shall see, the orthodox elements mustered behind the defence of the old faith which was redefined to meet the new challenge. The struggle between these two broad trends, one liberal and non-sectarian, the other orthodox and traditional, was at the heart of the intellectual and religious controversies during the sixteenth, seventeenth and eighteenth centuries. It is this continuing struggle which shows that the impact of the ideas and concepts put forward by Kabir, Nanak and others of the same way of thinking was by no means insignificant.

THE VAISHNAVITE MOVEMENT

Apart from the non-sectarian movement led by Kabir and Nanak, the Bhakti movement in north India developed around the worship of Rama and Krishna, two of the incarnations of the god Vishnu. The childhood escapades of the boy Krishna and his dalliance with the milk-maids of Gokul, especially with Radha, became the themes of a remarkable series of saint-poets who lived and preached during the fifteenth and early sixteenth centuries. They used the love between Radha and Krishna in an allegorical manner to depict the relationship of love, in its various aspects, between the individual soul and the supreme soul. Like the early Sufis, Chaitanya popularised musical gathering or *kirtan* as a special form of mystic experience in which the outside world disappeared by dwelling on God's name. According to Chaitanya, worship consisted of love and devotion and song and dance which produced a state of ecstasy in which the presence of God, whom he called Hari, could be realised. Such a worship could be carried out by all, irrespective of caste or creed.

The writings of Narsinha Mehta in Gujarat, of Meera in Rajasthan, of Surdas in western Uttar Pradesh and of Chaitanya in Bengal and Orissa reached extraordinary heights of lyrical fervour and of love which transcended all boundaries, including those of caste and creed. These saints were prepared to welcome into their fold everyone, irrespective of caste or creed. This is seen most clearly in the life of Chaitanya. Born and schooled in Nadia which was the centre of Vedantic rationalism, Chaitanya's tenor of life was changed when he visited Gaya at the age of twenty-two and was initiated into the Krishna cult by a recluse. He became a god-intoxicated devotee who incessantly uttered the name of Krishna. Chaitanya is said to have travelled all over India, including Vrindavan, where he revived the Krishna cult. But most of his time was spent at Gaya. He exerted an extraordinary influence, particularly in the eastern parts of India, and attracted a wide following, including some Muslims and people from the low castes. He did not reject the scriptures or idol-worship, though he cannot be classified as a traditionalist.

All the saint-poets mentioned above remained within the broad framework of Hinduism. Their philosophic beliefs were a brand of Vedantic monism which emphasized the fundamental unity of God and the created world. The Vedantist philosophy had been propounded by a number of thinkers, but the one who probably influenced the saint-poets the most was Vallabha, a Tailang Brahman, who lived in the last part of the fifteenth and the early part of the sixteenth century.

The approach of these saint-poets was broadly humanistic. They emphasized the broadest human sentiments—the sentiments of love and beauty in all their forms. Like the other non- sectarians, they were not able to make an effective breach in the caste system. However, they softened its rigour and built a platform for unity which could be apprehended by wider sections.

The basic concepts of the saint-poets were reciprocated to a remarkable degree by the Sufi poets and saints of the period. During the fifteenth century, the monistic ideas of the great Arab philosopher, Ibn-i-Arabi, became popular among broad sections in India. Arabi had been vehemently denounced by the orthodox elements, and his followers persecuted because he held that all beings are essentially one, and everything is a manifestation of the divine substance. Thus, in his opinion, the different religions were identical. Arabi's doctrine of Unity of Being is known as *Tauhid-i-Wajudi* (unity of being). This doctrine kept gaining popularity in India and became the main basis of the Sufi thought before the time of Akbar. Contact with yogis and Hindu saints went a long way in popularising the concept of pantheism. The Indian Sufis started taking more interest in Sanskrit and Hindi and a few of them, including Malik Muhammad Jaisi, composed their works in Hindi. The Bhakti songs of the Vaishnavite saints written in Hindi and other languages touched the hearts of the Sufis more than Persian poetry did. The use of Hindi songs became so popular that an eminent Sufi, Abdul Wahid Bilgrami, wrote a treatise *Haqaiq-i-Hindi* in which he tried to explain such words as 'Krishna', 'Murli', 'Gopis', 'Radha', 'Yamuna', etc., in Sufi mystic terms.

Thus, during the fifteenth and the early part of the sixteenth century, the Bhakti and the Sufi saints had worked out in a remarkable manner a common platform on which people belonging to various sects and creeds could meet and understand each other.

This was the essential background to the ideas of Akbar and his concept of *tauhid* or unity of all religions.

LITERATURE AND FINE ARTS

Sanskrit Literature

Sanskrit continued to be a vehicle for higher thought and a medium for literature during the period under review. In fact, the production of works in Sanskrit in different branches was immense and perhaps greater than in the preceding period. Following the great Sankara, works in the field of philosophy by Ramanuja, Madhava, Vallabha, etc., continued to be written in Sanskrit. The speed with which their ideas were widely disseminated and discussed in different parts of the country showed the important role which Sanskrit continued to play during the period. There was a network of specialised schools and academies in different parts of the country, including areas under Muslim domination. These schools and academies were not interfered with and continued to flourish. In fact, many of them took advantage of the introduction of paper to reproduce and disseminate older texts. Thus, some of the oldest available texts of the *Ramayana* and the *Mahabharata* written on paper belong to the period between the eleventh and twelfth century.

Besides philosophy, works in the field of *kavya* (poetical narrative), drama, fiction, medicine, astronomy, music, etc., continued to be written in sanskrit. A large number of commentaries and digests on the Hindu law *(Dharmashastras)* were prepared between the twelfth and the sixteenth century. The great *Mitakshara* of Vijnaneshwar, which forms one of the two principal Hindu schools of law, cannot be placed earlier than the twelfth century. Another famous commentator was Chandeshwar of Bihar who lived in the fourteenth century. Most of the other works were produced in the south, followed by Bengal, Mithila and western India under the patronage of Hindu rulers. The Jains, too, contributed to the growth of Sanskrit. Hemachandra Suri was the most eminent of these. Oddly enough, these works largely ignored the presence of the Muslims in the country. Little attempt was made to translate Islamic works or Persian literature into Sanskrit. Possibly, the only exception was the translation of the love story of Yusuf and Zulaikha written by the famous Persian poet, Jami and translation of works on the astrolabe, used in navigation and astrology.

Arabic and Persian Literature

Although the greatest amount of literature and scientific works produced by the Muslims was in Arabic which was the language of the Prophet and was used as the language of literature and science from Spain to Baghdad, the Turks who came to India were deeply influenced by the Persian language which had become the literary and administrative language of Central Asia from the tenth century onwards. In India, the use of Arabic remained largely confined to a narrow circle of Islamic scholars and philosophers, most of the original literature on the subject being written in Arabic. A few works on science and astronomy were also translated from Arabic. In course of time, digests of the Islamic law were prepared in Persian with the help of Indian scholars. The most well-known of these were prepared in the reign of Firuz Tughlaq. But Arabic digests continued to be prepared, the most famous of these being the *Fatawa-i-Alamgiri*, or the Digest of Laws prepared by a group of jurists in the reign of Aurangzeb.

With the arrival of the Turks in India during the tenth century, a new language, Persian, was introduced in the country. There was a resurgence of the Persian language in Iran and Central Asia from the tenth century onwards and some of the greatest poets of the Persian language, such as Firdausi and Sadi, lived and composed their works between the tenth and fourteenth centuries. From the beginning, the Turks adopted Persian as the language of literature and administration in the country. Thus, Lahore emerged as the first centre for the cultivation of the Persian language. Although the works of only a few of these early writers of Persian in India have survived, we find in the writings of some of them, such as Masud Sad Salman, a sense of attachment and love for Lahore. However, the most notable Persian writer of the period was Amir Khusrau. Born in 1252 at Patiali (near Badayun in western Uttar Pradesh), Amir Khusrau took pride in being an Indian. He says: 'I have praised India for two reasons. First, because India is the land of my birth and our country. Love of the country is an important obligation... Hindustan is like heaven. Its climate is better than that of Khurasan...it is green and full of flowers all the year round...The Brahmans here are as learned as Aristotle and there are many scholars in various fields...'

Khusrau's love for India shows that the Turkish ruling class was no longer prepared to behave as a foreign ruling class, and that the ground had been prepared for a cultural rapproachement between them and the Indians.

Khusrau wrote a large number of poetical works, including historical romances. He experimented with all the poetical forms and created a new style of Persian which came to be called the *sabaq-i-hindi* or the style of India.

Khusrau has praised the Indian languages, including Hindi (which he calls Hindavi). Some of his scattered Hindi verses are found, though the Hindi work, *Khaliq Bari*, often attributed to Khusrau, was in all probability the work of a later poet of the same name. He was also an accomplished musician and took part in religious musical gatherings (*sama*) organised by the famous Sufi saint, Nizamuddin Auliya. Khusrau, it is said, gave up his life the day after he learnt of the death of his *pir*, Nizamuddin Auliya (1325). He was buried in the same compound.

Apart from poetry, a strong school of history writing in Persian developed in India during the period. The most famous historians of this period were Ziauddin Barani, Afif and Isami.

Through the Persian language, India was able to develop close cultural relations with Central Asia and Iran. In course of time, Persian became not only the language of administration and diplomacy, but also the language of the upper classes and their dependents, at first in north India and later of the entire country with the expansion of the Delhi Sultanat to the south and the establishment of Muslim kingdoms in different parts of the country.

Thus, Sanskrit and Persian, in the main, functioned as link languages in the country in politics, religion and philosophy, as well as being means of literary productions. At first, there was little interchange between the two. Zia Nakhshabi (d. 1350) was the first to translate into Persian Sanskrit stories which were related by a parrot to a woman whose husband had gone on a journey. This book *Tuti Nama* (Book of the Parrot), written in the time of Muhammad Tughlaq, proved very popular and was translated from Persian into Turkish and into many European languages as well. He also translated the old Indian treatise on sexology, the *Kok Shastra*, into Persian. Later, in the time of Firuz Shah, Sanskrit books on medicine and music were translated into Persian. Sultan Zain-ul-Abidin of Kashmir had the famous historical work *Rajatarangini* and the *Mahabharata* translated into Persian. At his instance, Sanskrit works on medicine and music were also translated into Persian. Recent research shows that some works on mathematics, astonomy and medicine were translated into Sanskrit during the period.

Regional Languages

During this period, literary works of high quality were produced in many of the regional languages as well. Many of these languages, such as Hindi, Bengali and Marathi, trace their origin back to the eighth century or so. Some others, such as Tamil, were much older. Written in the beginning of the fourteenth century, Amir Khusrau had noted the existence of regional languages and remarked: 'These languages have from ancient times applied in every way to the common purposes of life.' The rise to maturity of many of these languages and their use as means for literary works may be considered a striking feature of the medieval period. There were many reasons for this. Perhaps, with the loss of prestige by the Brahmans, Sanskrit also lost some of its prestige. The use of the common language by the Bhakti saints was, undoubtedly, an important factor in the rise of these languages. In fact, in many parts of the country, the early saints fashioned these languages for literary purposes. It seems that in many regional kingdoms of the pre-Turkish period, regional languages, such as Tamil, Kannada, Marathi, etc., were used for administrative purposes, in addition to Sanskrit. This must have continued under the Turkish rule, for we hear of Hindi-knowing revenue accountants appointed in the Delhi Sultanat. Later, when, the Delhi Sultanat broke up, local languages, in addition to Persian, continued to be used for administrative purpose in many of the regional kingdoms. Thus, literature in Telugu developed in south India under the patronage of the Vijayanagara rulers. Marathi was one of the administrative languages in the Bahmani kingdom, and later, at the court of Bijapur. In course of time, when these languages had reached a certain stage of development, some of the Muslim kings gave them patronage for literary purposes also. For example, Nusrat Shah of Bengal had the *Mahabharata* and the *Ramayana* translated into Bengali. Maladhar Basu also translated the *Bhagavata* into Bengali under his patronage. His patronage of Bengali poets has been mentioned earlier.

The use of Bhakti poems in Hindi by the Sufi saints in their musical gatherings has been mentioned before. In Jaunpur, the Sufi saints, such as Malik Muhammad Jaisi, wrote in Hindi and put forward Sufi concepts in a form which could be easily understood by the common man. They popularised many Persian forms, such as the *masnavi*.

FINE ARTS

Trends towards mutual understanding and integration are to be found not only in the fields of religious beliefs and rituals, architecture and literature, but also in the fields of fine arts, particularly music. When the Turks came to India, they inherited the rich Arab tradition of music which had been further developed in Iran and Central Asia. They brought with them a number of new musical instruments, such as the *rabab* and *sarangi*, and new musical modes and regulations. Indian music and Indian musicians at the court of the caliphs at Baghdad had possibly influenced the development of music there. However, systematic contact between the two began in India under the Sultanat. We have already referred to Amir Khusrau. Khusrau, who was given the title of *nayak* or master of both the theory and practice of music, introduced many Perso-Arabic airs (*ragas*), such as *aiman, ghora, sanam*, etc. He is credited with having invented the sitar, though we have no evidence of it. The tabla which is also attributed to him seems, however, to have developed during the late seventeenth or early eighteenth century.

The process of integration in the field of music continued under Firuz who used to listen to music every Friday after *namaz*. The Indian classical work *Ragadarpan* was translated into Persian during this reign. Musical gatherings spread from the abodes of the Sufis to the palaces of the nobles. Sultan Husain Sharqi, the ruler of Jaunpur, was a great patron of music. The Sufi saint, Pir Bodhan, is supposed to have been the second great musician of the age. Another regional kingdom where music was highly cultivated was the kingdom of Gwaliyar. Raja Man Singh of Gwaliyar was a great music lover. The work *Man Kautuhal* in which all the new musical modes introduced by the Muslims were included was prepared under his aegis. We do not know at what time the musical modes in north India began to differ from those in the south. But there is little doubt that the differentiation was largely due to the incorporation of Perso-Arabic modes, airs and scales. A distinctive style of music, influenced in considerable measure by Persian music, developed in the kingdom of Kashmir.

After the conquest of Jaunpur, Sikandar Lodi followed its tradition of patronising music on a lavish scale—a tradition which was adopted by the Mughal rulers later on.

TWELVE

Struggle for Empire in North India—II
Mughals and Afghans (1525–1555)

CENTRAL ASIA AND BABUR

Important changes took place in Central and West Asia during the fifteenth century. After the disintegration of the Mongol empire in the fourteenth century, Timur united Iran and Turan under one rule once again. Timur's empire extended from the lower Volga to the river Indus, and included Asia Minor (modern Turkey), Iran, Trans-Oxiana, Afghanistan and a part of the Punjab. Timur died in 1405, but his grandson, Shahrukh Mirza (d. 1448), was able to keep intact a large part of his empire. He gave patronage to arts and letters, and in his time, Samarqand and Herat became the cultural centres of West Asia. The ruler of Samarqand had great prestige in the entire Islamic world.

The power of the Timurids declined rapidly during the second half of the fifteenth century, largely owing to the Timurid tradition of partitioning the empire. The various Timurid principalities which arose always fought and wrangled among themselves. This provided an opportunity to two new elements to come to the forefront. From the north, a Turko-Mongol tribe, the Uzbeks, thrust into Trans-Oxiana. The Uzbeks had become Muslims, but were looked down upon by the Timurids who considered them to be uncultured barbarians. Further to the west, a new dynasty, the Safavid dynasty, began to dominate Iran. The Safavids were descended from an order of saints who traced their ancestry to the Prophet. They supported the Shiite sect among the Muslims, and persecuted those who were not prepared to accept the Shiite tenets. The Uzbeks, on the other hand, were Sunnis. Thus, political conflict between these two elements was embittered by sectarian strife. Further to the west of Iran, the power of the Ottoman Turks was growing. They wanted to dominate eastern Europe as well as Iraq and Iran. (See Map A, Appendix)

Thus the scene was set for the conflict of three mighty empires in Asia during the sixteenth century.

In 1494, at the young age of twelve, Babur succeeded to Farghana, a small state in Trans-Oxiana. Oblivious of the Uzbek danger, the Timurid princes were busy fighting one another. Babur, too, made a bid to conquer Samarqand from his uncle. He won the city twice but lost it in no time on both the occasions. The second time the Uzbek chief, Shaibani Khan, was called in to help oust Babur. Shaibani defeated Babur and conquered Samarqand. Soon, he overran the rest of the Timurid kingdoms in the area. This forced Babur to move towards Kabul which he conquered in 1504. For the next fourteen years, Babur kept biding his time for the re-conquest of his homeland from the Uzbeks. He tried to enlist the help of his uncle, the ruler of Herat, in the enterprise but to no avail. Ultimately, Herat, too, was overrun by Shaibani Khan. This led to a direct conflict between the Uzbeks and the Safavids since the latter also laid claim to Herat and the surrounding area which is called Khurasan by contemporary writers. In a famous battle in 1510, near Merv, Shah Ismail, the shah of Iran, defeated and killed Shaibani Khan. Babur now made another attempt to recover Samarqand, this time with the help of the Iranian forces. He was duly installed at Samarqand, but chafed under the control of the Iranian generals who wanted to treat Babur as the governor of an Iranian province rather than as an independent prince. Meanwhile, the Uzbeks recovered rapidly from their defeat. Once again Babur was ousted from Samarqand and had to return to Kabul. Finally, Shah Ismail himself was defeated by the Ottoman sultan in 1514, thus leaving the Uzbeks masters of Trans-Oxiana.

These developments finally forced Babur to look towards India.

CONQUEST OF INDIA

Babur says that from the time he obtained Kabul (1504), to his victory at Panipat, 'I had never ceased to think of the conquest of Hindustan.' But he had never found a suitable opportunity for undertaking it, 'hindered as I was sometimes by the apprehensions of my *begs*, sometimes by the disagreement between my brothers and myself.' Like countless earlier invaders from Central Asia, Babur was drawn

to India by the lure of its fabulous wealth. India was the land of gold
and riches. Babur's ancestor, Timur, had not only carried away a vast
treasure and many skillful artisans who helped him to consolidate
his Asian empire and beautify his capital, but also annexed some
areas in the Punjab. These areas remained in the possession of
Timur's successors for several generations. When Babur conquered
Afghanistan, he felt that he had a legitimate right to these areas.

Another reason why Babur coveted the Punjab *parganas* was the
meagre income of Kabul. The historian Abul Fazl remarks: 'He
(Babur) ruled over Badakhshan, Qandhar and Kabul which did not
yield sufficient income for the requirements of the army; in fact, in
some of the border territories the expense on controlling the armies
and administration was greater than the income.' With these meagre
resources Babur could not provide well for his *begs* and kinsmen. He
was also apprehensive of an Uzbek attack on Kabul and considered
India to be a good place of refuge, and a suitable base for operations
against the Uzbeks.

The political situation in northwest India was suitable for Babur's
entry into India. Sikandar Lodi had died in 1517, and Ibrahim Lodi
had succeeded him. Ibrahim's efforts to create a strong, centralised
empire had alarmed the Afghan chiefs as well as the Rajputs. One of
the most powerful of the Afghan chiefs was Daulat Khan Lodi, the
governor of the Punjab, who was almost an independent ruler. Daulat
Khan attempted to conciliate Ibrahim Lodi by sending his son to his
court to pay homage. At the same time, he wanted to strengthen his
position by annexing the frontier tracts of Bhira, etc.

In 1518–19, Babur conquered the powerful fort of Bhira. He then
sent letters and verbal messages to Daulat Khan and Ibrahim Lodi,
asking for the cession of the areas which had belonged to the Turks.
But Daulat Khan detained Babur's envoy at Lahore, neither granting
him audience nor allowing him to go to Ibrahim Lodi. When Babur
returned to Kabul, Daulat Khan occupied Bhira, and expelled Babur's
agents posted there.

In 1520–21, Babur once again crossed the Indus, and easily
captured Bhira and Sialkot, the twin gateways to Hindustan. Lahore
also capitulated to him. He might have proceeded further but for the
news of a revolt at Qandhar. He retraced his steps, and after a siege

of a year and a half recaptured Qandhar. Thus reassured, Bahur was once again able to turn his attention towards India.

It was about this time that Babur received an embassy from Daulat Khan Lodi, led by his son, Dilawar Khan. They invited Babur to India, and suggested that he should displace Ibrahim Lodi since he was a tyrant and enjoyed no support from his nobles. It is probable that a messenger from Rana Sanga arrived at the same time, inviting Babur to invade India. These embassies convinced Babur that the time was ripe for his conquest of the whole of the Punjab if not of India itself.

In 1525, while Babur was at Peshawar, he received the news that Daulat Khan Lodi had changed sides again. He had collected an army of 30,000–40,000 men, ousted Babur's men from Sialkot and was marching to Lahore. At Babur's approach, the army of Daulat Khan melted away. Daulat Khan submitted and was pardoned. Thus, within three weeks of crossing the Indus, Babur became the master of the Punjab.

THE BATTLE OF PANIPAT (20 APRIL 1526)

A conflict with Ibrahim Lodi, the ruler of Delhi, was inevitable, and Babur prepared for it by marching towards Delhi. Ibrahim Lodi met Babur at Panipat with a force estimated at 100,000 men and 1000 elephants. Since the Indian armies generally contained large hordes of servants, the fighting men on Ibrahim Lodi's side must have been far less than this figure. Babur had crossed the Indus with a force of 12,000, but this had been swelled by his army in India, and the large number of Hindustani nobles and soldiers who joined Babur in the Punjab. Even then, Babur's army was numerically inferior. Babur strengthened his position by resting one wing of his army on the city of Panipat which had a large number of houses, and protected the other by means of a ditch filled with branches of trees. In front, he lashed together a large number of carts, to act as a defending wall. Between two carts, breastworks were erected on which soldiers could rest their guns and fire. Babur calls his device an Ottoman (Rumi) device, for it had been used by the Ottomans in their famous battle against Shah Ismail of Iran. Babur had also secured the services of two Ottoman master-gunners, Ustad Ali and Mustafa. The use of gunpowder had been gradually developing in India. Babur says that he used it for the first time in his attacks on the fortress of Bhira. Apparently, gunpowder was known in India but its use for artillery became common in north India with the advent of Babur.

Ibrahim Lodi had no idea of the strongly defended position of Babur. He had apparently expected Babur to fight a mobile mode of warfare which was usual with the Central Asians, making rapid advance or retreat as the need arose. After skirmishing for seven or eight days, Ibrahim Lodi's forces came out for the fateful battle. Seeing the strength of Babur's position, they hesitated. While Ibrahim was still reorganising his forces, the two extreme wings of Babur's army wheeled round and attacked Ibrahim's forces from the side and rear. Babur's gunners used their guns with good effect from the front. But Babur gives a large part of the credit of his victory to his bowmen. Curiously, he makes little reference to Ibrahim's elephants. Apparently, Ibrahim had little time to use them.

Despite these early setbacks, Ibrahim Lodi's army fought valiantly. The battle raged for two or three hours. Ibrahim Lodi fought to the last, with a group of 5000–6000 people around him. It is estimated that besides him, more than 15,000 of his men were killed in the battle.

The battle of Panipat is regarded as one of the decisive battles of Indian history. It broke the back of Lodi power, and brought under Babur's control the entire area upto Delhi and Agra. The treasures stored up by Ibrahim Lodi at Agra relieved Babur from his financial difficulties. The rich territory up to Jaunpur also lay open to Babur. However, Babur had to wage two hard-fought battles, one against Rana Sanga of Mewar, and the other against the eastern Afghans, before he could consolidate his hold on this area. Viewed from this angle, the battle of Panipat was not as decisive in the political field as has been made out. Its real importance lies in the fact that it opened a new phase in the struggle for domination in north India.

The difficulties of Babur after his victory at Panipat were manifold. Many of his *begs* were not prepared for a long campaign in India. With the onset of the hot weather, their misgivings had increased. They were far away from home in a strange and hostile land. Babur tells us that the people of India displayed 'remarkable hostility', abandoning their villages at the approach of the Mughal armies. Obviously, the memories of Timur's sacking and plundering of the towns and villages were still fresh in their minds.

Babur knew that the resources in India alone would enable him to found a strong empire and satisfy his *begs*. 'Not for us the poverty of Kabul again', he records in his diary. He thus took a firm stand, proclaiming his intention to stay on in India, and granting leave to a number of his *begs* who wanted to go back to Kabul. This immediately cleared the air. But it also invited the hostility of Rana Sanga who began his preparations for a showdown with Babur.

The Battle of Khanwa

The growing conflict between Rana Sanga and Ibrahim Lodi for the domination of eastern Rajasthan and Malwa has already been mentioned. After defeating Mahmud Khalji of Malwa, the influence of the rana had gradually extended up to Piliya Khar—a small river in the neighbourhood of Agra. The establishment of an empire in the Indo-Gangetic valley by Babur was a threat to Rana Sanga. Sanga set afoot preparations to expel Babur or, at any rate, to confine him to the Punjab.

Babur accuses Rana Sanga of breach of agreement. He says that Sanga had invited him to India, and promised to join him against Ibrahim Lodi, but made no move while he (Babur) conquered Delhi and Agra. We do not know what precise promises Sanga had made. He might have hoped for a long-drawn-out warfare during which he (Sanga) would have been able to seize the areas he coveted. Or, he might have hoped that like Timur, Babur would withdraw after sacking Delhi and weakening the Lodis. Babur's decision to stay on in India completely changed the situation.

Many Afghans, including Mahmud Lodi, a younger brother of Ibrahim Lodi, rallied to Rana Sanga, in the hope of regaining the throne of Delhi in case Sanga won. Hasan Khan Mewati, the ruler of Mewat, also cast in his lot with Sanga. Almost all the Rajput rulers of note sent contingents to serve under Rana Sanga.

The reputation of Rana Sanga, and his early success against some of the outlying Mughal posts such as Bayana, demoralised Babur's soldiers. To rally them, Babur solemnly declared the war against Sanga to be a *jihad*. On the eve of the battle, he emptied all the wine jars and broke the wine flasks to demonstrate what a staunch Muslim he was. He also banned the sale and purchase of wine throughout his dominions and abolished customs taxes for Muslims.

Having carefully selected a site, Babur entrenched himself at Khanwa about 40 km from Agra. As at Panipat, he lashed together a number of wagons as an outer bastion and dug a trench in front for double protection. Gaps were left in the defences for his musketeers to fire and advance behind wheeled tripods.

The battle of Khanwa (1527) was fiercely contested. According to Babur, Sanga's forces exceeded 200,000 including 10,000 Afghan cavalrymen, and an equal force fielded by Hasan Khan Mewati. As usual, these figures may be greatly exaggerated, though Babur's forces were undoubtedly inferior in number. Sanga made fierce attacks on Babur's right and almost breached it. However, the Mughal artillery took a heavy toll of life, and slowly, Sanga's forces were pushed back. At this juncture, Babur ordered his soldiers in the centre, who had been sheltering behind their tripods, to launch an attack. The artillery also advanced behind the chained wagons. As at Panipat, Babur's flanking parties which attacked from the side and rear also came into play. Sanga's forces were thus hemmed in, and were defeated after a great slaughter. Rana Sanga escaped and wanted to renew the conflict with Babur. But he was poisoned by his own nobles who considered such a course to be dangerous and suicidal.

Thus died one of the most valiant warriors produced by Rajasthan. With Sanga's death, the dream of a united Rajasthan extending up to Agra received a serious setback.

The battle of Khanwa secured Babur's position in the Delhi-Agra region. Babur strengthened his position further by conquering the chain of forts—Gwaliyar, Dholpur, etc., east of Agra. He also annexed large parts of Alwar from Hasan Khan Mewati. He then led a campaign against Medini Rai of Chanderi in Malwa. Chanderi was captured after the Rajput defenders had died fighting to the last man and their women performed *jauhar*. Babur had to cut short his plan of further campaigns in the area on hearing of the growing activities of the Afghans in eastern Uttar Pradesh.

THE AFGHANS

Although the Afghans had been defeated, they had not been reconciled to the Mughal rule. Eastern Uttar Pradesh was still under the domination of the Afghan chiefs who had tendered their allegiance to Babur but were prepared to throw it off at any time. The Afghan sardars were being backed by Nusrat Shah, the ruler of Bengal, who had married a daughter of Ibrahim Lodi. Earlier, the Afghans had ousted the Mughal officials in eastern Uttar Pradesh and reached up to Kanauj. But their greatest weakness was the lack of a popular leader. After some time, Mahmud Lodi, a brother of Ibrahim Lodi, who had fought against Babur at Khanwa, reached Bihar. The Afghans hailed him as their ruler, and mustered strong under him.

This was a threat which Babur could not ignore. Hence, at the beginning of 1529, he left Agra for the east. Crossing the Ganga near Banaras, he faced the combined forces of the Afghans and Nusrat Shah of Bengal at the crossing of the river Ghagra. Although Babur crossed the river, and compelled the Bengal and the Afghan armies to retreat, he could not win a decisive victory. Being ill, and anxious about the situation in Central Asia, Babur decided to patch up an agreement with the Afghans. He put forward a vague claim for suzerainty over Bihar, but left most of it in the hands of the Afghan chiefs. He also patched up a treaty with Nusrat Shah of Bengal. He then returned to Agra. Shortly afterwards, Babur died near Lahore while on his way to Kabul.

SIGNIFICANCE OF BABUR'S ADVENT INTO INDIA

Babur's advent into India was significant from many points of view. For the first time since the downfall of the Kushan empire, Kabul and Qandhar became integral parts of an empire comprising north India. Since these areas had always acted as staging places for an invasion of India, by dominating them Babur and his successors were able to give to India security from external invasions for almost 200 years. Economically also, the control of Kabul and Qandhar strengthened India's foreign trade since these two towns were the starting points for caravans meant for China in the east, and the Mediterranean seaports in the west. Thus, India could take a greater share in the great trans-Asian trade.

In north India, Babur smashed the power of the Lodis and the Rajput confederacy led by Rana Sanga. Thereby, he destroyed the balance of power in the area. This was a long step towards the establishment of an all-India empire. However, a number of conditions had still to be fulfilled before this could be achieved.

Babur introduced a new mode of warfare in India. Although gunpowder was known in India earlier, Babur showed what a skilled combination of artillery and cavalry could achieve. His victories led to rapid popularisation of gunpowder and artillery in India. Since artillery was expensive, it favoured those rulers who had large resources at their command. Hence the era of small kingdoms ended.

By his new military methods as well as by his personal conduct, Babur re-established the prestige of the Crown which had been eroded since the death of Firuz Tughlaq. Although Sikandar Lodi and Ibrahim Lodi had tried to re-establish the prestige of the Crown, Afghan ideas of tribal independence and equality had resulted only in a partial success. Babur had the prestige of being a descendant of two of the most famous warriors of Asia, Changez and Timur. None of his nobles could, therefore, claim a status of equality with him, or aspire to his throne. The challenge to his position, if any, could come only from a Timurid prince.

Babur endeared himself to his *begs* by his personal qualities. He was always prepared to share the hardships with his soldiers. Once, at the height of winter, Babur was returning to Kabul. The snow was so deep that horses would sink into it and parties of soldiers had to trample the snow so that the horses could pass. Without hesitation, Babur joined in the back-breaking task. Following Babur's example, his *begs* also joined in the task.

Babur was fond of wine and good company and was a good and merry companion. At the same time, he was a stern disciplinarian and a hard taskmaster. He took good care of his *begs*, and was prepared to excuse many of their faults as long as they were not disloyal. He was prepared to adopt the same attitude towards his Afghan and Indian nobles. However, he did have a streak of cruelty, probably inherited from his ancestors, for he made towers of skulls from the heads of his opponents on a number of occasions. These, and other instances of personal cruelty, have to be seen in the context of the harsh time in which Babur lived.

An orthodox Sunni, Babur was not bigoted or led by the religious divines. At a time when there was a bitter sectarian feud between the Shias and the Sunnis in Iran and Turan, his court was free from theological and sectarian conflicts. He declared the battle against Sanga a *jihad* and assumed the title of *ghazi* after the victory, but the reasons were clearly political. Though his reign was a period of war, only a few instances can be found of destruction of temples. There is no evidence that the mosques built at Sambhal and Ayodhya by the local governors were built by breaking the Hindu temples there. Perhaps, they only repaired existing mosques, and put in an inscription in honour of Babur.

Babur was deeply learned in Persian and Arabic, and is regarded as one of the two most famous writers in the Turkish language which was his mother tongue. As a prose writer, he had no equal, and his famous memoirs, the *Tuzuk-i-Baburi*, is considered one of the classics of world literature. His other works include a *masnavi* and the Turkish translation of a well-known Sufi work. He was in touch with the famous poets and artists of the time and describes their works in his memoirs. He was a keen naturalist, and has described the flora and fauna of India in considerable detail. He laid out a number of formal gardens with running water thereby establishing a tradition of building gardens.

Babur introduced a new concept of the state which was to be based on the strength and prestige of the Crown, absence of religious and sectarian bigotry, and the careful fostering of culture and the fine arts. He thus provided a precedent and a direction for his successors.

HUMAYUN'S CONQUEST OF GUJARAT AND HIS
TUSSLE WITH SHER SHAH

Humayun succeeded Babur in December 1530 at the young age of 23. He had to grapple with a number of problems left behind by Babur. The administration had not yet been consolidated, and the finances were precarious. The Afghans had not been subdued, and were nursing the hope of expelling the Mughals from India. Finally, there was the Timurid legacy of partitioning the empire among all the brothers. Babur had counselled Humayun to deal kindly with his brothers, but had not favoured the partitioning of the infant Mughal empire, which would have been disastrous.

When Humayun ascended the throne at Agra, the empire included Kabul and Qandhar, while there was loose control over Badakhshan beyond the Hindukush mountains. Kabul and Qandhar were under the charge of Humayun's younger brother, Kamran. It was only natural that they should remain in his charge. However, Kamran was not satisfied with these poverty-stricken areas. He marched on Lahore and Multan, and occupied them. Humayun, who was busy elsewhere, and did not want to start a civil war, had little option but to agree. Kamran accepted the suzerainty of Humayun, and promised to help him whenever necessary. Kamran's action created the apprehension that the other brothers of Humayun might also follow the same path whenever an opportunity arose. However, by formally granting the Punjab and Multan to Kamran, Humayun had the immediate advantage that he was free to devote his attention to the eastern parts without having to bother about his western frontier.

Apart from these, Humayun had to deal with the rapid growth of the power of the Afghans in the east, and the growing power and sweep of Bahadur Shah, the ruler of Gujarat. At the outset, Humayun was inclined to consider the Afghan danger to be the more serious of the two. In 1532, at a place called Dadrah, he defeated the Afghan forces which had conquered Bihar and overrun Jaunpur in eastern Uttar Pradesh. After this success, Humayun besieged Chunar. This powerful fort commanded the land and the river route between Agra and the east, and was known as the gateway of eastern India. It had recently come in the possession of an Afghan sardar, Sher Khan, who had become the most powerful of the Afghan sardars.

After the siege of Chunar had gone on for four months, Sher Khan persuaded Humayun to allow him to retain possession of the fort. In return, he promised to be loyal to the Mughals, and sent one of his sons to Humayun as a hostage. Humayun accepted the offer because he was anxious to return to Agra. The rapid increase in the power of Bahadur Shah of Gujarat, and his activities in the areas bordering Agra, had alarmed him. He was not prepared to continue the siege of Chunar under the command of a noble since that would have meant dividing his forces.

Bahadur Shah, who was of almost the same age as Humayun, was an able and ambitious ruler. Ascending the throne in 1526, he first overran and conquered Malwa. He then turned to Rajasthan and besieged Chittor. Soon he reduced the Rajput defenders to sore straits. According to some later legends, Rani Karnavati, the widow of Rana Sanga, sent a *rakhi* to Humayun seeking his help, and Humayun gallantly responded. No contemporary writer has mentioned the story, and it may not be true. However, it is a fact that Humayun moved from Agra to Gwaliyar, and due to fear of Mughal intervention, Bahadur Shah patched up a treaty with the rana, leaving the fort in his hands after extracting a large indemnity in cash and kind.

During the next year and a half, Humayun spent his time in building a new city at Delhi, which he named Dinpanah. He organised many grand feasts and festivities during the period. Humayun has been blamed for wasting valuable time in these activities, while Sher Khan was steadily augmenting his power in the east. It has also been said that Humayun's inactivity was due to his habit of taking opium. Neither of these charges is fully true. Babur had continued to use opium, after he gave up wine. Humayun took opium occasionally in place of or in addition to wine, as did many of his nobles. But neither Babur nor Humayun was an opium addict. The building of Dinpanah was meant to impress friends and foes alike. It could also serve as a second capital in case Agra was threatened by Bahadur Shah who, in the meantime, had conquered Ajmer and overrun eastern Rajasthan.

Bahadur Shah offered a still greater challenge to Humayun. He had made his court the refuge of all those who feared or hated the

Mughals. He again invested Chittor and, simultaneously, supplied arms and men to Tatar Khan, a cousin of Ibrahim Lodi. Tatar Khan was to invade Agra with a force of 40,000 while diversions were to be made in the north and the east.

Humayun easily defeated the challenge posed by Tatar Khan. The Afghan forces melted away at the approach of the Mughals, and Tatar Khan was defeated and killed. Determined to end the threat from Bahadur Shah's side once for all, Humayun now invaded Malwa.

In the struggle which followed, Humayun showed considerable military skill, and remarkable personal valour. Bahadur Shah did not dare face the Mughals. He abandoned Chittor which he had captured, and fortified himself at a camp at Mandsor. But Humayun's cautious tactics forced him to flee to Mandu after spiking his guns, but leaving behind all his rich equipage. Humayun was hot on his heels. He invested the fortress of Mandu and captured it without much opposition. Bahadur Shah fled from Mandu to Champaner. A small party scaled the fort of Champaner by a path considered inaccessible. Humayun was the 41st man to scale the walls. Bahadur Shah now fled to Ahmedabad and finally to Kathiawar. Thus, the rich provinces of Malwa and Gujarat, as well as the large treasures hoarded by the Gujarat rulers at Mandu and Champaner, fell into the hands of Humayun.

Both Gujarat and Malwa were lost as quickly as they had been gained. After the victory, Humayun placed Gujarat under the command of his younger brother, Askari, and then retired to Mandu which was centrally located and enjoyed a fine climate. The major problem was the deep attachment of the people to the Gujarati rule. Askari was inexperienced, and the Mughal nobles were divided. A series of popular uprisings, military actions by Bahadur Shah's nobles, and the rapid revival of Bahadur Shah's power, unnerved Askari. He fell back upon Champaner, but received no help from the commander of the fort who doubted his intentions. Hence, Askari decided to return to Agra. This immediately raised the fear that he might try to displace Humayun from Agra, or attempt to carve out a separate empire for himself. Deciding to take no chances, Humayun abandoned Malwa and moved after Askari by forced marches. He overtook Askari in Rajasthan, the two brothers were reconciled, and returned to Agra. Meanwhile, both Gujarat and Malwa were lost.

The Gujarat campaign was not a complete failure. While it did not add to the Mughal territories, it destroyed forever the threat posed to the Mughals by Bahadur Shah: Humayun was now in a position to concentrate all his resources in the struggle against Sher Khan and the Afghans. Soon after, Bahadur Shah drowned in a scuffle with the Portuguese on board one of their ships. This ended whatever danger remained from the side of Gujarat.

SHER KHAN

During Humayun's Malwa campaign (February 1535 to February 1537), Sher Khan had further strengthened his position. He had made himself the unquestioned master of Bihar. The Afghans from far and near had rallied round him. Though he continued to profess loyalty to the Mughals, he systematically planned to expel the Mughals from India. He was in close touch with Bahadur Shah who had helped him with heavy subsidies. These resources enabled him to recruit and maintain a large and efficient army which included 1200 elephants. Shortly after Humayun's return to Agra, he had used this army to defeat the Bengal king, and compel him to pay an indemnity of 13,00,000 *dinars* (gold coins).

After equipping a new army, Humayun marched against Sher Khan and besieged Chunar towards the end of the year. Humayun felt it would be dangerous to leave such a powerful fort behind, threatening his line of communications. However, the fort was strongly defended by the Afghans. Despite the best efforts by the master-gunner, Rumi Khan, it took six months for Humayun to capture it. Meanwhile, Sher Khan captured by treachery the powerful fort of Rohtas where he could leave his family in safety. He then invaded Bengal for a second time, and captured Gaur, its capital.

Thus, Sher Khan completely outmanoeuvred Humayun. Humayun should have realised that he was in no position to offer a military challenge to Sher Khan without more careful preparations. However, he was unable to grasp the political and military situation facing him. After his victory over Gaur, Sher Khan made an offer to Humayun that he would surrender Bihar and pay an annual tribute of ten lakhs of *dinars* if he was allowed to retain Bengal. It is not clear how far Sher Khan was sincere in making this offer. But Humayun was not prepared to leave Bengal to Sher Khan. Bengal was the land of gold, rich in manufactures, and a centre for foreign trade. Moreover, the king of Bengal who had reached Humayun's camp in a wounded condition, urged that resistance to Sher Khan was still continuing. All these factors led Humayun to reject Sher Khan's offer and decide upon a campaign to Bengal. Soon after, the Bengal king succumbed to his wounds. Humayun had, thus, to undertake the campaign to Bengal all alone.

Humayun's march to Bengal, was the prelude to the disaster which overtook his army at Chausa almost a year later. Sher Khan had left Bengal and was in south Bihar. He let Humayun advance into Bengal without opposition so that he might disrupt Humayun's communications and bottle him up in Bengal. Arriving at Gaur, Humayun quickly took steps to establish law and order. But this did not solve any of his problems. His situation was made worse by the attempt of his younger brother, Hindal, to assume the Crown himself at Agra. Due to this and Sher Khan's activities, Humayun was totally cut off from all news and supplies from Agra.

After a stay of three to four months at Gaur, Humayun started back for Agra, leaving a small garrison behind. Despite the rumblings of discontent in the nobility, the rainy season, and the constant harrying attacks of the Afghans, Humayun managed to get his army back to Chausa near Buxar, without any serious loss. This was a big achievement for which Humayun deserves credit. Meanwhile, Kamran had advanced from Lahore to Agra to quell Hindal's rebellion. Though not disloyal, Kamran made no attempt to send reinforcements to Humayun which might have swung the military balance in favour of the Mughals.

Despite these setbacks, Humayun was still confident of success against Sher Khan. He forgot that he was facing an Afghan army which was very different from the one a year before. It had gained battle experience and confidence under the leadership of the most skilful general the Afghans ever produced. Misled by an offer of peace from Sher Khan, Humayun crossed to the eastern bank of the Karmnasa river, giving full scope to the Afghan horsemen encamped there to attack. Humayun showed not only bad political sense, but bad generalship as well. He chose his ground badly, and allowed himself to be taken unawares.

Humayun barely escaped with his life from the battle field, swimming across the river with the help of a water-carrier. Immense booty fell in Sher Khan's hands. About 7000 Mughal soldiers and many prominent nobles were killed.

After the defeat at Chausa (March 1539), only the fullest unity among the Timurid princes and the nobles could have saved the Mughals. Kamran had a battle-hardened force of 10,000 troops under his command at Agra. But he was not prepared to loan them to Humayun as he had lost confidence in Humayun's generalship. On the other hand, Humayun was not prepared to entrust the command of the armies to Kamran, lest the latter use it to assume power himself. The suspicions between the brothers grew till Kamran decided to return to Lahore with the bulk of his army.

The army hastily assembled by Humayun at Agra was no match against Sher Khan. However, the battle of Kanauj (May 1540) was bitterly contested. Both the younger brothers of Humayun, Askari and Hindal, fought valiantly but to no avail.

The battle of Kanauj decided the issue between Sher Khan and the Mughals. Humayun, now, became a prince without a kingdom, Kabul and Qandhar remaining under Kamran. He wandered about in Sindh and its neighbouring regions for the next two and a half years, hatching various schemes to regain his kingdom. But neither the rulers of Sindh nor Maldeo, the powerful ruler of Marwar, were prepared to help him in this enterprise. Worse, his own brothers turned against him, and tried to have him killed or imprisoned. Humayun faced all these trials and tribulations with fortitude and courage. It was during this period that Humayun's character showed itself at its best. Ultimately, Humayun took shelter at the court of the Iranian king, and with his help recaptured Qandhar and Kabul in 1545.

It is clear that the major cause of Humayun's failure against Sher Khan was his inability to understand the nature of the Afghan power. Due to the existence of large numbers of Afghan tribes scattered over north India, the Afghans could always reunite under a capable leader and pose a challenge. Without winning over the local rulers and zamindars to their side, the Mughals were bound to remain numerically inferior. In the beginning, Humayun was, on the whole, loyally served by his brothers. Real differences among them arose only after Sher Khan's victories. Some historians have unduly exaggerated the early differences of Humayun with his brothers, and his alleged faults of character. Though not as vigorous as Babur, Humayun showed himself to be a competent general and politician, till his ill-conceived Bengal campaign. In both the battles with Sher Khan, the latter showed himself to be a superior general.

Humayun's life was a romantic one. He went from riches to rags, and again from rags to riches. In 1555, following the breakup of the Sur empire, he was able to recover Delhi. But he did not live long to enjoy the fruits of the victory. He died from a fall from the first floor of the library building in his fort at Delhi. His favourite wife built a magnificent mausoleum for him near the fort. This building marks a new phase in the style of architecture in north India, its most remarkable feature being the magnificent dome of marble.

SHER SHAH AND THE SUR EMPIRE (1540–55)

Sher Shah ascended the throne of Delhi at the age of 54 or so. We do not know much about his early life. His original name was Farid and his father was a small *jagirdar* at Jaunpur. Farid acquired sound administrative experience by looking after the affairs of his father's *jagir*. Following the defeat and death of Ibrahim Lodi and the confusion in Afghan affairs, he emerged as one of the most important Afghan sardar. The title of Sher Khan was given to him by his patron for killing a tiger (*sher*) or, for services rendered. Soon, Sher Khan emerged as the right-hand of the ruler of Bihar, and its master in all but name. This was before the death of Babur. The rise of Sher Khan to prominence was, thus, not a sudden one.

As a ruler, Sher Shah ruled the mightiest empire which had come into existence in north India since the time of Muhammad bin Tughlaq. His empire extended from Bengal to the Indus, excluding Kashmir. In the west, he conquered Malwa, and almost the entire Rajasthan. Malwa was then in a weak and distracted condition and in no position to offer any resistance. It was during the Malwa campaign that an episode took place which is a blot on the memory of Sher Shah. Puran Mal, the possessor of the powerful fort of Chanderi, had vacated the fort on a binding oath of safe conduct. However, he and his party of 1000 Rajputs, along with their families, were treacherously attacked, and killed outside the fort. The theologians ruled that no faith need be kept with an infidel, and that Puran Mal deserved punishment because he had oppressed Muslims, and kept Muslim women in his house. The situation in Rajasthan was different. Maldeo, the ruler of Marwar who had ascended the *gaddi* in 1532, had rapidly brought the whole of western and northern Rajasthan under his control. He further expanded his territories during Humayun's conflict with Sher Shah. With the help of the Bhatis of Jaisalmer, he conquered Ajmer. In his career of conquest he came into conflict with the rulers of the area, including Mewar. His latest act had been the conquest of Bikaner. In the course of the conflict, the Bikaner ruler was killed after a gallant resistance. His sons, Kalyan Das and Bhim, sought shelter at the court of Sher Shah. Many others, including his relation, Biram Deo of Merta, whom Maldeo had dispossessed from his holding, also repaired to Sher Shah's court.

Maldeo's attempt to create a large centralised state in Rajasthan under his aegis was bound to be regarded as a threat by the ruler of Delhi and Agra. It was believed that Maldeo had an army of 50,000. However, there is no evidence that Maldeo coveted Delhi or Agra. Now, as before, the bone of contention between the two was the domination of the strategically important eastern Rajasthan.

The Rajput and Afghan forces clashed at Samel (1544) between Ajmer and Jodhpur. After waiting for about a month, Maldeo, considering it suicidal to attack the strongly fortified Afghan camp in the absence of a strong artillery, and wanted to retreat to Jodhpur and Siwana where he could prepare a better defence. Divided counsel, with some of the Rajput sardars considering any retreat to be dishonourable, or suspicion sown in the minds of Maldeo about the loyalty of some of his sardars on account of Sher Shah's ruse of dropping some letters addressed to Rajput commanders near Maldeo's camp, resulted in Maldeo withdrawing the bulk of his forces towards Jodhpur. Some Rajput sardars refused to retreat. With a small force of about, 10,000 they vigorously attacked Sher Shah's centre and created confusion in his army. Soon, superior number and Afghan gunfire halted the Rajput charge, and led to their defeat.

The battle of Samel sealed the fate of Rajasthan. Sher Shah now besieged and conquered Ajmer and Jodhpur, forcing Maldeo to take shelter in the fort of Siwana where he died soon afterwards. Sher Shah then turned towards Mewar. The rana was in no position to resist, and sent the keys of Chittor to Sher Shah who set up his outposts up to Mount Abu.

Thus, in a brief period of ten months, Sher Shah overran almost the entire Rajasthan. His last campaign was against Kalinjar, a strong fort that was the key to Bundelkhand. During the siege, a gun burst and severely injured Sher Shah. He died (1545) after he heard that the fort had been captured.

Sher Shah was succeeded by his second son, Islam Shah, who ruled till 1553. Islam Shah was a capable ruler and general, but most of his energies were occupied with the rebellions raised by his brothers, and with tribal feuds among the Afghans. These and the ever-present fear of a renewed Mughal invasion prevented Islam Shah from attempting to expand his empire. His death at a young age led to a civil war among his successors. This provided Humayun the opportunity he had been seeking for recovering his empire in India. In two hotly contested battles in 1555, he defeated the Afghans, and recovered Delhi and Agra.

CONTRIBUTION OF SHER SHAH

The Sur empire may be considered in many ways as a continuation and culmination of the Delhi Sultanat, the advent of Babur and Humayun being in the nature of an interregnum. Amongst the foremost contributions of Sher Shah was his re-establishment of law and order across the length and breadth of his empire. He dealt sternly with robbers and dacoits, and with zamindars who refused to pay land revenue or disobeyed the orders of the government. We are told by Abbas Khan Sarwani, the historian of Sher Shah, that the zamindars were so cowed down that none of them dared to raise the banner of rebellion against him, or to molest the travellers passing through their territories.

Sher Shah paid great attention to the fostering of trade and commerce and the improvement of communications in his kingdom. Sher Shah restored the old imperial road called the Grand Trunk Road, from the river Indus in the west to Sonargaon in Bengal. He also built a road from Agra to Jodhpur and Chittor, evidently linking up with the road to the Gujarat seaports. He built a third road from Lahore to Multan. Multan was at that time the staging point for caravans going to West and Central Asia. For the convenience of travellers, Sher Shah built a sarai at a distance of every two *kos* (about eight km) on these roads. The sarai was a fortified lodging or inn where travellers could pass the night and also keep their goods in safe custody. Separate lodgings for Hindus and Muslims were provided in these sarais. Brahmans were appointed for providing bed and food to the Hindu travellers, and grain for their horses. Abbas Khan says, 'It was a rule in these sarais that whoever entered them received provision suitable to his rank, and food and litter for his cattle, from government.' Efforts were made to settle villages around the sarais, and land was set apart in these villages for the expenses of the sarais. Every sarai had several watchmen under the control of a *shahna* (custodian).

We are told that Sher Shah built 1700 sarais in all. Some of these are still existing, which shows how strong they were. His roads and sarais have been called 'the arteries of the empire'. They helped in quickening trade and commerce in the country. Many of the sarais developed into market-towns (*qasbas*) to which peasants flocked to sell their produce. The sarais were also used as stages for the news service or *dak-chowki*. The organisation of these *dak-chowkis* has been described in an earlier chapter. By means of these, Sher Shah kept himself informed of the developments in his vast empire.

Sher Shah also introduced other reforms to promote the growth of trade and commerce. In his entire empire, customs duty for goods were paid only at two places: goods produced in Bengal or imported from outside paid customs duty at the border of Bengal and Bihar at Sikrigali, and goods coming from West and Central Asia paid customs duty at the Indus. No one was allowed to levy customs at roads, ferries or towns anywhere else. Duty was paid a second time at the time of sale of goods.

Sher Shah directed his governors and *amils* to treat merchants and travellers well in every way, and not to harm them at all. If a merchant died, they were not to seize his goods as if they were unowned. Sher Shah enjoined upon them the dictum of Shaikh Nizami: 'If a merchant should die in your country it is a perfidy to lay hands on his property.' Sher Shah made the local village headmen (*muqaddams*) and zamindars responsible for any loss that a merchant suffered on the roads. If the goods were stolen, the *muqaddams* and the zamindars had to produce them, or point out the haunts of the thieves or highway robbers, failing which they had to undergo the punishment meant for thieves and robbers. The same law was applied in cases of murders on the roads. It was a barbarous law to make the innocent responsible for the wicked but it seems to have been effective. In the picturesque language of Abbas Sarwani, 'a decrepit old woman might place a basketful of gold ornaments on her head and go on a journey, and no thief or robber would come near her for fear of the punishment which Sher Shah inflicted.'

The currency reforms of Sher Shah also helped in the growth of commerce and handicrafts. He struck fine coins of gold, silver and copper of uniform standard in place of the earlier debased coins of mixed metal. His silver rupee was so well executed that it remained a standard coin for centuries after him. His attempt to fix standard weights and measures all over the empire were also helpful for trade and commerce.

Sher Shah did not make many changes in the administrative divisions prevailing since the Sultanat period. A number of villages comprised a *pargana*. The *pargana* was under the charge of the *shiqdar*, who looked after law and order and general administration, and the *munsif* or *amil* who looked after the collection of land revenue. Accounts were maintained both in Persian and the local languages (Hindavi). Above the *pargana* was the *shiq* or *sarkar* under the charge of the *shiqdar-i-shqdaran* or *faujdar* and a *munsif-i-munsifan*. It seems that only the designations of these officers were new since both *pargana* and *sarkar* were units of administration in the earlier period also.

A number of *sarkars* were sometimes grouped into provinces, but we do not know how many of such provinces existed and the pattern of provincial administration. It seems that the provincial governors were all-powerful in some areas. In some areas such as Bengal, real power remained in the hands of tribal chiefs and the governor exercised only a loose control over them.

Sher Shah apparently continued the central machinery of administration which had been developed during the Sultanat period. However, we do not have much information about it. Sher Shah did not favour leaving too much authority in the hands of ministers. He worked exceedingly hard, devoting himself to the affairs of the state from early morning to late at night. He also toured the country constantly to know the condition of the people. But no single individual, however hardworking, could look after all the affairs of a vast country like India. Sher Shah's excessive centralisation of authority in his hands was a source of weakness, and its harmful effects became apparent when a masterful sovereign like him ceased to sit on the throne.

Sher Shah paid special attention to the land revenue system, the army, and justice. Having administered his father's jagir for a number of years, and then as the virtual ruler of Bihar, Sher Shah knew the working of the land revenue system at all levels. With the help of a capable team of administrators, he toned up the entire system. The produce of land was no longer to be based on guess work, or by dividing the crops in the fields or on the threshing floor. Sher Shah insisted on measurement of the sown land. A crop rate (called *ray*) was drawn up, laying down the state's share of the different types of crops. This could then be converted into cash on the basis of the prevailing market rates in different areas. The share of the state was one-third of the produce. The lands were divided into good, bad and middling. Their average produce was computed, and one-third of it became the share of the state. The peasants were given the option of paying in cash or kind, though the state preferred cash.

The areas sown, the type of crops cultivated, and the amount each peasant had to pay was written down on a paper called *patta* and each peasant was informed of it. No one was allowed to charge from the peasants anything extra. Even the rates which the members of the measuring party were to get for their work were laid down. In order to guard against famine and other natural calamities, a cess at the rate of two and a half *seers* per *bigha* was also levied.

Sher Shah was very solicitous for the welfare of the peasantry. He used to say, 'The cultivators are blameless, they submit to those in power, and if I oppress them they will abandon their villages, and the country will be ruined and deserted, and it will be a long time before it again becomes prosperous.' Since there was plenty of land available for cultivation in those days, the desertion of villages by the peasants in case of oppression was a real threat and helped in putting a limit on the exploitation of the peasants by the rulers.

Sher Shah set up a strong army in order to administer his vast empire. He dispensed with tribal levies under tribal chiefs, and recruited soldiers directly, after verifying their character. Every soldier had his descriptive roll (*chehra*) recorded, and his horse branded with the imperial sign so that horses of inferior quality may not be substituted. Sher Shah seems to have borrowed this system, known as the *dagh* (branding) system, from the military reforms of Alauddin Khalji. The strength of Sher Shah's personal army is put at 1,50,000 cavalry and 25,000 infantry armed with matchlocks or bows, 5,000 elephants and a park of artillery. He set up cantonments in different parts of the empire and a strong garrison was posted in each of them.

Sher Shah placed considerable emphasis on justice. He used to say, 'Justice is the most excellent of religious rites, and it is approved alike by the king of infidels and of the faithful'. He did not spare oppressors whether they were high nobles, men of his own tribe or near relations. *Qazis* were appointed at different places for justice but, as before, the village panchayats and zamindars also dealt with civil and criminal cases at the local level.

A big step forward in the dispensation of justice was, however, taken by Sher Shah's son and successor, Islam Shah. Islam Shah codified the laws, thus doing away with the necessity of depending on a special set of people who could interpret the Islamic law. Islam Shah also tried to curb the powers and privileges of the nobles, and to pay cash salaries to soldiers. But most of the regulations disappeared with his death.

There is no doubt that Sher Shah was a remarkable figure. He established a sound system of administration in his brief reign of five years. He was also a great builder. The tomb which he built for himself at Sasaram during his lifetime is regarded as one of the masterpieces of architecture. It is considered as a culmination of the earlier style of architecture and a starting point for the new style which developed later.

Sher Shah also built a new city on the bank of the Yamuna near Delhi. The only survivor of this is the Old Fort (Purana Qila) and the fine mosque within it.

Sher Shah also patronized the learned men. Some of the finest works in Hindi, such as the *Padmavat* of Malik Muhammad Jaisi, were completed during his reign.

Sher Shah was not a bigot in the religious sphere, as is evident from his social and economic policy. Neither Islam Shah nor he depended on the *ulama*, though they respected them a great deal. Religious slogans were sometimes used to justify political actions. The treacherous murder of Puran Mal and his associates after he had vacated the fort of Raisen in Malwa on the basis of a binding oath is one such example. Sher Shah did not, however, initiate any new liberal policies. *Jizyah* continued to be collected from the Hindus, while his nobility was drawn almost exclusively from the Afghans.

Thus, the state under the Surs remained an Afghan institution based on race and tribe. A fundamental change came about only with the emergence of Akbar.

THIRTEEN

Consolidation of the Mughal Empire
Age of Akbar

When Humayun was retreating from Bikaner, he was gallantly offered shelter and help by the rana of Amarkot. It was at Amarkot, in 1542, that Akbar, the greatest of the Mughal rulers, was born. When Humayun fled to Iran, young Akbar was captured by his uncle, Kamran. He treated the child well on the whole. Akbar was re-united with his parents after the capture of Qandhar. When Humayun died, Akbar was at Kalanaur in the Punjab, commanding operations against the Afghan rebels there. He was crowned at Kalanaur in 1556 at the young age of thirteen years and four months.

Akbar succeeded to a difficult position. The Afghans were still strong beyond Agra, and were regrouping their forces under the leadership of Hemu for a final showdown. Kabul had been attacked and besieged. Sikandar Sur, the defeated Afghan ruler, was loitering in the Siwalik Hills. However, Bairam Khan, the tutor of the prince and a loyal and favourite officer of Humayun, rose to the occasion. He became the *wakil* of the kingdom, with the title of *Khan-i-Khanan*, and rallied the Mughal forces. The threat from the side of Hemu was considered the most serious. The area from Chunar to the border of Bengal was under the domination of Adil Shah, a nephew of Sher Shah. Hemu, who had started life as a superintendent of the markets under Islam Shah, had rapidly risen under Adil Shah. He had not lost a single one of the twenty-two battles in which he had fought. Adil Shah had appointed him the *wazir* with the title of Vikramajit, and entrusted him with the task of expelling the Mughals. Hemu captured Agra, and with an army of 50,000 cavalry, 500 elephants and a strong artillery, he marched upon Delhi.

In a well-contested battle, Hemu defeated the Mughals near Delhi and occupied the city. However, Bairam Khan took energetic steps to meet the situation. His bold stand put heart into his army, and it marched on Delhi before Hemu could have time to consolidate his position. The battle between the Mughals and the Afghan forces led by Hemu, took place once again at Panipat (5 November 1556). Although Hemu's artillery had been captured earlier by a Mughal detachment, the tide of battle was in favour of Hemu when an arrow hit him in the eye and he fainted. The leaderless Afghan army was defeated, Hemu was captured and executed. Thus, Akbar had virtually to reconquer his empire.

EARLY PHASE—CONTEST WITH THE NOBILITY (1556–67)

Bairam Khan remained at the helm of affairs of the empire for almost four years. During the period, he kept the nobility fully under control The danger to Kabul was averted, and the territories of the empire were extended from Kabul up to Jaunpur in the east, and Ajmer in the west. Gwaliyar was captured, and forces were sent to conquer Ranthambhor and Malwa.

Meanwhile, Akbar was approaching the age of maturity. Bairam Khan had offended many powerful persons while he held supreme power. They complained that Bairam Khan was a Shia, and that he was appointing his own supporters and Shias to high offices while neglecting the old nobles. These charges were not very serious in themselves because Bairam was known for his liberal religious views. But Bairam Khan had become arrogant, and failed to realise that Akbar was growing up. There was friction on small points which made Akbar realise that he could not leave the affairs of the state in someone else's hands for any length of time.

Akbar played his cards deftly. He left Agra on the pretext of hunting, and reached Delhi. From Delhi he issued a *farman* dismissing Bairam Khan from his office, and calling upon all the nobles to come and submit to him personally. Once Bairam Khan realised that Akbar wanted to take power in his own hands, he was prepared to submit, but his opponents were keen to ruin him. They heaped humiliation upon him till he was goaded to rebel. The rebellion distracted the empire for almost six months. Finally, Bairam Khan was forced to submit. Akbar received him cordially, and gave him the option of serving at the court or anywhere outside it, or retiring to Mecca. Bairam Khan chose to go to Mecca. However, on his way, he was assassinated at Patan near Ahmedabad by an Afghan who bore him a personal grudge. Bairam's wife and a young child were brought to Akbar at Agra. Akbar married Bairam Khan's young wife who was his cousin. He brought up Bairam's child as his own son. This child later became famous as Abdur Rahim Khan-i-Khanan and held some of the most important offices and commands in the empire.[1]

Akbar's confrontation with Bairam Khan and the kind of treatment accorded to his family subsequently show some typical traits of Akbar's character. He was unrelenting once he had made up his mind about a course of action, but was prepared to go out of his way in being generous to an opponent who had submitted to him.

During Bairam Khan's rebellion, groups and individuals in the nobility had become politically active. They included Akbar's foster-mother, Maham Anaga, and her relations. Though Maham Anaga soon withdrew from politics, her son, Adham Khan was an impetuous young man who assumed independent airs when sent to command an expedition against Malwa. Removed from the command, he laid claim to the post of the *wazir*, and when this was not conceded, he stabbed the acting *wazir* in his office. Akbar was enraged and had him thrown down to his death from the parapet of the fort (1561). However, it was many years before Akbar was to establish his authority fully. The Uzbeks formed a powerful group in the nobility. They held important positions in eastern Uttar Pradesh, Bihar and Malwa. Although they had served the empire well by subduing the powerful Afghan groups in those areas, they had become arrogant and were defying the young ruler. Between 1561 and 1567 they broke out in rebellion several times, forcing Akbar to take the field against them. Each time Akbar was induced to pardon them. When they again rebelled in 1565, Akbar was so exasperated that he vowed to make Jaunpur his capital till he had routed them out. Meanwhile, a rebellion by the Mirzas, who were Timurids and were related to Akbar by marriage, threw the areas west of modern Uttar Pradesh into confusion. Encouraged by these rebellions, Akbar's half-brother,

1 He was the son of Jamal Khan Mewati's daughter.

Mirza Hakim, who had seized control of Kabul, advanced into the Punjab, and besieged Lahore. The Uzbek rebel nobles formally proclaimed him their ruler.

This was the most serious crisis Akbar had to face since Hemu's capture of Delhi. However, Akbar's grit and a certain amount of luck enabled him to triumph. From Jaunpur he marched to Lahore, forcing Mirza Hakim to retire. Meanwhile, the rebellion of the Mirzas was crushed, with the Mirzas fleeing to Malwa and thence to Gujarat. Akbar marched back from Lahore to Jaunpur. Crossing the river Yamuna near Allahabad at the height of the rainy season, he surprised the rebels led by the Uzbek nobles and completely routed them (1567). The Uzbek leaders were killed in the battle, thus bringing their protracted rebellion to an end. All the rebellious nobles, including those among them who had been dreaming of independence, were cowed down. Akbar was now free to concentrate on the expansion of the empire.

EARLY EXPANSION OF THE EMPIRE (1560–76)

During Bairam Khan's regency, the territories of the Mughal empire had been expanded rapidly. Apart from Ajmer, an important conquest during this period was that of Malwa. Malwa was being ruled, at that time, by a young prince, Baz Bahadur. His accomplishments included a mastery of music and poetry. Stories about the romance of Baz Bahadur and Rupmati, who was famous for her beauty as well as for music and poetry are well known. During his time, Mandu had become a celebrated centre for music. The army, however, had been neglected by Baz Bahadur. The expedition against Malwa was led by Adham Khan, son of Akbar's foster-mother, Maham Anaga. Baz Bahadur was badly defeated (1561) and the Mughals took valuable spoils, including Rupmati. However, she preferred to commit suicide to being dragged to Adham Khan's *haram*. Due to the senseless cruelties of Adham Khan and his successor, there was a reaction against the Mughals which enabled Baz Bahadur to recover Malwa.

After dealing with Bairam Khan's rebellion Akbar sent another expedition to Malwa. Baz Bahadur had to flee, and for some time he took shelter with the rana of Mewar. After wandering about from one area to another, he finally repaired to Akbar's court and was enrolled as a Mughal *mansabdar*.[1] The extensive country of Malwa thus came under Mughal rule.

At about the same time, Mughal arms overran the kingdom of Garh-Katanga. The kingdom of Garh-Katanga included the Narmada valley and the northern portions of present Madhya Pradesh. It had been welded together by Aman Das who flourished in the second half of the fifteenth century. Aman Das had helped Bahadur Shah of Gujarat in the conquest of Raisen and had received from him the title of Sangram Shah.

The kingdom of Garh-Katanga included a number of Gond and Rajput principalities. It was the most powerful kingdom set up by the Gonds. It is said that the ruler commanded 20,000 cavalry, a large infantry and 1000 elephants. We do not know, however, to what extent these figures are dependable. Sangram Shah had further strengthened his position by marrying his son to a princess of the famous Chandel rulers of Mahoba. This princess, who is famous as Durgavati, became a widow soon afterwards. But she installed her minor son on the throne and ruled the country with great vigour and courage. She was a good marksman, both with guns and bow and arrow. She was fond of hunting and, according to a contemporary, 'it was her custom that whenever she heard that a tiger had appeared she did not drink water till she had shot it.' She fought many successful battles against her neighbours, including Baz Bahadur of Malwa. These border conflicts apparently continued even after Malwa had been conquered by the Mughals. Meanwhile, the cupidity of Asaf Khan, the Mughal governor of Allahabad, was roused by the stories of the fabulous wealth and the beauty of the rani. Asaf Khan advanced with 10,000 cavalry from the side of Bundelkhand. Some of the semi-independent rulers of Garha found it a convenient moment to throw off the Gond yoke. The rani was thus left with a small force. Though wounded, she fought on gallantly. Finding that the battle was lost and that she was in danger of being captured, she stabbed herself to death. Asaf Khan then stormed the capital, Chauragarh, near modern Jabalpur.

---

1 H   rose to the rank of 2000. According to tradition, he was buried near a tank at Ujjain where his favourite consort, Rupmati, was also buried.

'So much plunder in jewels, gold, silver and other things were taken that it is impossible to compute even a fraction of it,' says Abul Fazl. 'Out of all the plunder Asaf Khan sent only two hundred elephants to the court, and retained all the rest for himself.' Kamaladevi, the younger sister of the rani, was sent to the court.

When Akbar had dealt with the rebellion of the Uzbek nobles he forced Asaf Khan to disgorge his illegal gains. He restored the kingdom of Garh-Katanga to Chandra Shah, the younger son of Sangram Shah, after taking ten forts to round off the kingdom of Malwa.

Rajasthan and Gujarat

During the next ten years, Akbar brought the major part of Rajasthan under his control and also conquered Gujarat and Bengal. A major step in his campaign against the Rajput states was the siege of Chittor. This redoubtable fortress, which had faced a number of sieges in its history, was considered a key to central Rajasthan. It commanded the shortest route from Agra to Gujarat. Above all, it was a symbol of the Rajput spirit of resistance. Akbar realised that without conquering Chittor, he could not induce the other Rajput rulers to accept his suzerainty. Chittor fell (1568) after a gallant siege of six months. At the advice of his nobles, Rana Udai Singh had retired to the hills, leaving the famous warriors, Jaimal and Patta, in charge of the fort. Many peasants from the surrounding area had also taken shelter within the fort, and actively aided the defenders. When the Mughals stormed the fort, these peasants and many of the Rajput warriors amounting to 30,000 were massacred—the first and the last time Akbar indulged in such a carnage. The Rajput warriors died after extracting as much vengeance as possible. In honour of the gallant Jaimal and Patta, Akbar ordered that two stone statues of these warriors, seated on elephants, be erected outside the chief gate of the fort at Agra.

The fall of Chittor was followed by the conquest of Ranthambhor reputed to be the most powerful fortress in Rajasthan. Jodhpur had been conquered earlier. As a result of these victories, most of the Rajput rajas, including those of Bikaner and Jaisalmer, submitted to Akbar. Only Mewar continued to resist.

Gujarat had been in a sorry state of affairs since the death of Bahadur Shah. The fertility of its soil, its highly developed crafts, and its importance as the centre of the import-export trade with the outside world had made it a prize worth fighting for. Akbar also laid claim to it because Humayun had ruled over it for some time. An additional reason was that the Mirzas who had failed in their rebellion near Delhi had taken shelter in Gujarat. Akbar was not prepared for such a rich province to become a rival centre of power. In 1572, Akbar advanced on Ahmedabad via Ajmer. Ahmedabad surrendered without a fight. Akbar then turned his attention to the Mirzas who held Broach, Baroda and Surat. At Cambay, Akbar saw the sea for the first time, and rode on it in a boat. A group of Portuguese merchants also came and met him for the first time. The Portuguese dominated the Indian seas by this time, and had ambition of establishing an empire in India. Akbar's conquest of Gujarat frustrated these designs.

While Akbar's armies were besieging Surat, Akbar crossed the river Mahi and assaulted the Mirzas with a small body of 200 men which included Man Singh and Bhagwant Das of Amber. For some time, Akbar's life was in danger. But the impetuosity of his charge routed the Mirzas. Thus, Gujarat came under Mughal control. However, as soon as Akbar had turned his back, rebellions broke out all over Gujarat. Hearing the news, Akbar marched out of Agra and traversed across Rajasthan in nine days by means of camels, horses and carts. On the eleventh day, he reached Ahmedabad. In this journey, which normally took six weeks, only 3000 soldiers were able to keep up with Akbar. With these he defeated an enemy force of 20,000 (1573).

After this, Akbar turned his attention to Bengal. The Afghans had continued to dominate Bengal and Bihar. They had also overrun Orissa and killed its ruler. However, in order not to give offence to the Mughals, the Afghan ruler had not formally declared himself king, but read the *khuba* in Akbar's name. Internal fights among the Afghans, and the declaration of independence by the new ruler, Daud Khan, gave Akbar the excuse he was seeking. Akbar advanced with a strong flotilla of boats accompanying him. The Afghan king was believed to possess a large army consisting of 40,000 well-mounted cavalry, an infantry of about 1,50,000, several thousand guns and elephants, and a strong flotilla of war boats. If Akbar had not been as careful, and the Afghans had a better leader, the contest between Humayun and Sher Shah might well have been repeated. Akbar first captured Patna, thus securing Mughal communications in Bihar. He then returned to Agra, leaving Khan-i-Khanan Munaim Khan, an experienced officer, in charge of the campaign. The Mughal armies invaded Bengal and, after hard campaigning, Daud was forced to sue for peace. He rose in rebellion soon afterwards. Though the Mughal position in Bengal and Bihar was still weak, the Mughal armies were better organised and led. In a stiff battle in Bihar in 1576, Daud Khan was defeated and executed on the spot.

Thus ended the last Afghan kingdom in northern India. It also brought to an end the first phase of Akbar's expansion of the empire.

ADMINISTRATION

During the decade following the conquest of Gujarat, Akbar found time to look at the administrative problems of the empire. The system of administration elaborated by Sher Shah had fallen into confusion after the death of Islam Shah. Akbar, therefore, had to start afresh.

One of the most important problems facing Akbar was the system of land revenue administration. Sher Shah had instituted a system by which the cultivated area was measured and a crop rate (*ray*) was drawn up, fixing the dues of the peasant crop-wise on the basis of the productivity of land. This schedule was converted every year into a central schedule of prices. Akbar adopted Sher Shah's system. But it was soon found that the fixing of a central schedule of prices often led to considerable delays, and resulted in great hardships to the peasantry since the prices fixed were generally those prevailing at the imperial court, and were higher than those in the countryside. The peasants, therefore, had to part with a larger share of their produce.

At first, Akbar reverted to a system of annual assessment. The *qanungos*, who were hereditary holders of land as well as local officials conversant with local conditions, were ordered to report on the actual produce, state of cultivation, local prices, etc. But in many areas the *qanungos* were dishonest and concealed the real produce. Annual assessments also resulted in great difficulty for the peasants and for the state. After returning from Gujarat (1573), Akbar paid personal attention to the land revenue system. Officials called *karoris* were appointed all over north India. They were responsible for the collection of a crore of *dams* (Rs 2,50,000), and also checked the facts and figures supplied by the *qanungos*. On the basis of the information provided by them regarding the actual produce, local prices, productivity, etc., in 1580, Akbar instituted a new system called the *dahsala*. Under this system, the average produce of different crops as well as the average prices prevailing over the last ten (*dah*) years were calculated. One-third of the average produce was the state share. The state demand was, however, stated in cash. This was done by converting the state share into money on the basis of a schedule of average prices over the past ten years. Thus, the produce of a *bigha* of land under share was given in *maunds*. But on the basis of average princes, the state demand was fixed in rupees per *bigha*.

Later, a further improvement was made. Not only were local prices taken into account, *parganas* having the same type of productivity were grouped into separate assessment circles. Thus, the peasant was required to pay on the basis of local productivity as well as local prices.

There were a number of advantages of this system. As soon as the area sown by the peasant had been measured by means of the bamboos linked with iron rings, the peasants as well as the state knew what the dues were. The peasant was given remission in the land revenue if crops failed on account of drought, floods, etc. The system of measurement and the assessment based upon it is called the *zabti* system. Akbar introduced this system in the area from Lahore to Allahabad, and in Malwa and Gujarat. The *dahsala* system was a further development of the *zabti* system.

A number of other systems of assessment were also followed under Akbar. The most common and, perhaps, the oldest was called *batai* or *ghalla-bakhshi*. In this system, the produce was divided between the peasants and the state in fixed proportion. The crop was divided after it had been thrashed, or when it had been cut and tied in stacks, or while it was standing in the field. This system was considered a very fair one, but it needed an army of honest officials to be present at the time of the ripening or the reaping of the crops.

The peasants were allowed to choose between *zabti* and *batai* under certain conditions. Thus, such a choice was given when the crops had been ruined. Under *batai*, the peasants were given the choice of paying in cash or in kind, though the state preferred cash. In case of crops such as cotton, indigo, oil seeds, sugarcane, etc., the state demand was invariably in cash. Hence, these were called cash crops.

A third system which was widely used in Akbar's time was *nasaq*. It was a rough calculation of the amount payable by the peasant on the basis of what he had been paying in the past. Hence, some modern historians think that it was merely a system of computing the peasant's past dues, not a different system of assessment. Others think that it meant rough appraisement both on the basis of the inspection of the crops and past experience, and thereby fixing the amount to be paid by the village as a whole. It is also called *kankut*, or estimation.

Other local methods of assessment also continued in some areas.

In fixing the land revenue, continuity of cultivation was taken into account. Land which remained under cultivation almost every year was called *polaj*. When it remained uncultivated it was called *parati* (fallow). *Parati* land paid at the full (*polaj*) rate when it was cultivated. Land which had been fallow for two to three years was called *chachar*, and *banjar* if longer than that. These were assessed at concessional rates, the revenue demand gradually rising till the full or *polaj* rate was paid in the fifth or the eighth year. In this way, the state helped in bringing virgin and uncultivated wasteland under cultivation. Land was classified further into good, middling and bad. One-third of the average produce was the state demand, but it varied according to the productivity of the land, the method of assessment, etc.

Akbar was deeply interested in the improvement and extension of cultivation. He asked the *amil* to act like a father to the peasants. He was to advance money by way of loans (*taccavi*) to the peasants for seeds, implements, animals, etc., in times of need, and to recover them in easy instalments. He was to try and induce the peasants to plough as much land as possible and to sow superior quality crops. The zamindars of the area were also enjoined to cooperate in the task. The zamindar had a hereditary right to take a share of the produce. The peasants, too, had a hereditary right to cultivate their land and could not be ejected as long as they paid the land revenue.

The *dahsala* was not a ten-year settlement. Nor was it a permanent one, the state retaining the right to modify it. However, with some changes, Akbar's settlement remained the basis of the land revenue system of the Mughal empire till the end of the seventeenth century. The *zabti* system is associated with Raja Todar Mal, and is sometimes called Todar Mal's *bandobast*. Todar Mal was a brilliant revenue officer who had first served under Sher Shah. But he was only one of a team of brilliant revenue officials who came to the forefront under Akbar. The *dahsala* system was the result of their combined labours.

MANSABDARI SYSTEM AND THE ARMY

Akbar would not have been able to expand his empire and maintain his hold over it without a strong army. For this purpose, it was necessary for him to organise the nobility as well as his army. Akbar realised both these objectives by means of the *mansabdari* system. Under this system, every officer was assigned a rank (*mansab*). The lowest rank was 10, and the highest was 5000 for the nobles. Princes of the blood received higher *mansabs*. Towards the end of Akbar's reign, the highest rank a noble could attain was raised from 5000 to 7000, and two premier nobles of the empire, Mirza Aziz Koka and Raja Man Singh, were honoured with the rank of 7000 each. This limit was retained basically till the end of Aurangzeb's reign. The mansab system under Akbar developed gradually. At first there was only one rank (*mansab*). From the fortieth year (1594–95), the ranks were divided into two—*zat* and *sawar*. The word *zat* means personal. It fixed the personal status of a person, and also the salary due to him. The *sawar* rank indicated the number of cavalrymen (*sawars*) a person was required to maintain. A person who was required to maintain as many *sawars* as his *zat* rank was placed in the first category of that rank; if he maintained half or more, then in the second category and if he maintained less than half then in the third category. Thus, there were three categories in every rank (*mansab*).

Great care was taken to ensure that the *sawars* recruited by the nobles were experienced and well-mounted. For this purpose, a descriptive roll (*chehra*) of the soldier was maintained, and his horse was branded with the imperial marks. This was called the *dagh* system. Every noble had to bring his contingent for periodic inspection before persons appointed by the emperor for the purpose.

The horses were carefully inspected and only good quality horses of Arabic and Iraqi breed were employed. Ideally, for every ten cavalrymen, the *mansabdar* had to maintain twenty horses. This was so, because horses had to be rested while on march, and replacements were necessary in time of war. A *sawar* with only one horse was considered to be only half a *sawar*. The Mughal cavalry force remained an efficient one as long as the 10–20 rule was adhered to.

Provision was made that the contingents of the nobles should be mixed ones, that is drawn from all the group—Mughal, Pathan, Hindustani and Rajput. Thus, Akbar tried to weaken the forces of tribalism and parochialism. Only the Mughal and Rajput nobles were allowed to have contingents exclusively of Mughals or Rajputs, but in course of time, mixed contingents became the general rule.

Apart from cavalrymen, bowmen, musketeers (*bandukchi*), sappers and miners were also recruited in the contingents. The salaries varied, the average salary of a *sawar* was Rs 20 per month. Iranis and Turanis received a higher salary than Rajputs and Hindustanis (Indian Muslims). An infantryman received about Rs 3 per month. The salary due to the soldiers was added to the salary of the *mansabdar*, who was paid by assigning to him a *jagir*. Sometimes, the *mansabdars* were paid in cash. It is wrong to think that Akbar did not like the jagir system and tried to do away with it, but failed as it was too deeply entrenched. A *jagir* did not confer any hereditary rights on the holder, or disturb any of the existing rights in the area. It only meant that the land revenue due to the state was to be paid to the *jagirdar*.

The *mansabdari* system, as it developed under the Mughals, was a distinctive and unique system which did not have any exact parallel outside India. The origins of the *mansabdari* system can, perhaps, be traced back to Changez Khan who organised his army on a decimal basis, the lowest unit of command being ten, and the highest ten thousand (*toman*) whose commander was called *khun*. The Mongol system influenced, to some extent, the military system of the Delhi Sultanat, for we hear of commanders of hundred (*sadis*) and one thousand (*hazaras*). Under the Surs, we have nobles who were designated commanders of 20,000, or 10,000 or 5,000 *sawars*. But we do not quite know the system which was prevalent under Babur and Humayun.

Persons holding ranks below 500 *zat* were called *mansabdars*, those from 500 to below 2500 were called *amirs*, and those holding ranks of 2500 and above were called *amir-i-umda* or *umda-i-azam*. However, the word *mansabdar* is sometimes used for all the three categories. Apart from status, this classification had a significance: an *amir* or an *amir-i-umda* could have another *amir* or *mansabdar* serve under him, but a *mansabdar* could not do so. Thus, a person with a rank of 5000 could have under him a *mansabdar* up to a rank of 500 *zat*, and one with a rank of 4000 could have a *mansabdar* up to a rank of 400 *zat*, and so on.

The categories were not rigid. Persons were generally appointed at a low *mansab* and gradually promoted, depending upon their merits and the favour of the emperor. A person could also be demoted as a mark of punishment. Thus, there was only one service including both armymen and civilians. People who entered service at the lower rung of the ladder, could hope to rise to the position of an *amir* or even *amir-i-umda*. To that extent, careers were thrown open to talent.

In addition of meeting his personal expenses, the *mansabdar* had to maintain out of his salary a stipulated quota of horses, elephants, beasts of burden (camels and mules) and carts. Thus a *mansabdar* holding a *zat* rank of 5000 had to maintain 340 horses, 100 elephants, 400 camels, 100 mules and 160 carts. Later, these were maintained centrally, but the *mansabdar* had to pay for them out of his salary. The horses were classified into six categories, and the elephants into five according to quality, the number and quality of horses and elephants being carefully prescribed. This was so because horses and elephants of high breed were greatly prized and were considered indispensable for an efficient military machine. Cavalry and elephants, in fact, formed the main basis of the army in those days, though the artillery was rapidly becoming more important. The transport corps was vital for making the army more mobile.

For meeting these expenses, the Mughal *mansabdars* were paid handsomely. A *mansabdar* with a rank of 5000 could get a salary of Rs 30,000 per month, a *mansabdar* of 3000, Rs 17,000 and of 1000, Rs 8,200 per month. Even a humble *sadi* holding a rank of 100, could get Rs 7000 per year. Roughly, a quarter of these salaries were spent on meeting the cost of the transport corps. Even then, the Mughal *mansabdars* formed the highest paid service in the world.

Akbar kept a large body of cavalrymen as his bodyguards. He kept a big stable of horses. He also maintained a body of gentleman troopers (*ahadis*). These were persons of noble lineage who did not have the means of raising a contingent or were persons who had impressed the emperor. They were allowed to keep eight to ten horses, and received a high salary of about Rs 800 a month. They were answerable only to the emperor, and had a separate muster-master. These people could be compared to the knights of medieval Europe.

Akbar was very fond of horses and elephants. He also maintained a strong park of artillery. Akbar was specially interested in guns. He devised detachable guns which could be carried on an elephant or a camel. There were also heavy siege guns for breaching forts; some of these were so heavy that 100 or 200 oxen and several elephants were needed to pull them. A strong park of light artillery accompanied the emperor whenever he moved out of the capital.

We do not know whether Akbar ever had any plans of building a navy. The lack of a strong navy remained a key weakness of the Mughal empire. If Akbar had the time, he might have paid attention to it. He did build an efficient flotilla of war boats which he used in his eastern campaigns. Some of the boats were over 30 metres long and displaced over 350 tons.

ORGANIZATION OF GOVERNMENT

Hardly any changes were made by Akbar in the organisation of local government. The *pargana* and the *sarkar* continued as before. The chief officers of the *sarkar* were the *faujdar* and the *amalguzar*, the former being in charge of law and order, and the latter responsible for the assessment and collection of the land revenue. The territories of the empire were divided into *jagir*, *khalisa* and *inam*. Income from *khalisa* villages went directly to the royal exchequer. The *inam* lands were those which were allotted to learned and religious men. *Jagirs* were allotted to nobles and members of the royal family including the queens. The *amalguzar* was required to exercise a general supervision over all types of holdings so that the imperial rules and regulations for the assessment and collection of land revenue were followed uniformly. Only autonomous rajas were left free to continue their traditional land revenue system in their territories. Even there, Akbar encouraged them to follow the imperial system.

Akbar paid great attention to the organisation of the central and provincial governments. His system of central government was based on the structure of government which had evolved under the Delhi Sultanat, but the functions of the various departments were carefully reorganised, and meticulous rules and regulations were laid down for the conduct of affairs. Thus, he gave a new shape to the system and breathed new life into it.

The Central Asian and Timurid tradition was of having an all-powerful *wazir* under whom various heads of departments functioned. He was the principal link between the ruler and the administration. In course of time, a separate department, the military department, had come into being. The judiciary had always been separate. Thus, in practice, the concept of an all-powerful *wazir* had been given up. However, in his capacity as *wakil*, Bairam Khan had exercised the powers of an all-powerful *wazir*.

Akbar reorganised the central machinery of administration on the basis of the division of power between various departments, and of checks and balances. While the post of *wakil* was not abolished, it was stripped of all power and became largely decorative. The post was given to important nobles from time to time, but they played little part in administration. The head of the revenue department continued to be the *wazir*. Under Akbar, generally the wazir did not hold a high *mansab*. Many nobles held *mansabs* which were higher than his. Thus, he was no longer the principal adviser to the ruler, but one who was an expert in revenue affairs. To emphasize this point, Akbar generally used the title of *diwan* or *diwan-i-ala* in preference to the word *wazir*. Sometimes, several persons were asked to discharge the duties of *diwan* jointly. The *diwan* was responsible for all income and expenditure, and held control over *khalisa*, *jagir* and *inam* lands.

The head of the military department was called the *mir bakhshi*. It was the *mir bakhshi* and not the *diwan* who was considered the head of the nobility. Therefore, only the leading grandees were appointed to this post. Recommendations for appointment to *mansabs* or for promotions etc., were made to the emperor through the *mir bakhshi*. Once the emperor had accepted a recommendation, it was sent to the *diwan* for confirmation and for assigning a *jagir* to the appointee. The same procedure was followed in case of promotions.

The *mir bakhshi* was also the head of the intelligence and information agencies of the empire. Intelligence officers (*barids*) and news reporters (*waqia-navis*) were posted to all parts of the empire. Their reports were presented to the emperor at the court through the *mir bakhshi*.

It will thus be seen that the *diwan* and the *mir bakhshi* were almost on par, and supported and checked each other.

The third important officer was the *mir saman*. He was in charge of the imperial household, including the supply of all the provisions and articles for the use of the inmates of the *haram* or the female apartments. Many of these articles were manufactured under supervision in royal workshops called *karkhanas*. Only nobles who enjoyed the complete confidence of the emperor were appointed to this office. The maintenance of etiquette at the court, the control of the royal bodyguard, etc., were all under the overall supervision of this officer.

The fourth important department was the judicial department headed by the chief *qazi*. This post was sometimes combined with that of the chief *sadr* who was responsible for all charitable and religious endowments. Thus, it was a post which carried considerable power and patronage. It fell into bad odour due to the corruption and venality of Akbar's chief *qazi*, Abdun Nabi.

After instituting a careful scrutiny of the grants held by various persons, Akbar separated the *inam* lands from the *jagir* and *khalisa* lands, and divided the empire into six circles for purposes of grant of *inam* lands and their administration. Two features of the *inam* grants are noteworthy. First, Akbar made it a deliberate part of his policy to grant *inam* lands to all persons, irrespective of their religious faith and beliefs. *Sanads* of grant to various Hindu *maths* made by Akbar are still preserved. Second, Akbar made it a rule that half of the *inam* land should consist of cultivable wasteland. Thus, the *inam* holders were encouraged to extend cultivation.

In order to make himself accessible to the people as well as to the ministers, Akbar carefully divided his time. The day started with the emperor's appearance at the *jharoka* of the palace. Large number of people assembled daily to have a glimpse of the ruler, and to present petitions to him, if necessary. These petitions were attended to immediately, or in the open darbar (*diwan-i-am*) which followed, and lasted till midday. The emperor then retired to his apartments for meals and rest.

Separate time was allotted to the ministers. For confidential consultations, the ministers were generally called to a chamber which was situated near Akbar's bathing apartment (*ghusal khana*). In course of time, this private consultation chamber came to be called *ghusal khana*.

Akbar divided the empire into twelve subas in 1580. These were Bengal, Bihar, Allahabad, Awadh, Agra, Delhi, Lahore, Multan, Kabul, Ajmer, Malwa and Gujarat. A governor (*subedar*), a *diwan*, a *bakhshi*, a *sadr*, a *qazi*, and a *waqia-navis* were appointed to each of the provinces. Thus, orderly government based on the principle of checks and balances was extended to the provinces.

RELATIONS WITH THE RAJPUTS

Akbar's relations with the Rajputs have to be seen against the wider background of Mughal policy towards the powerful rajas and zamindars of the country. When Humayun came back to India, he embarked upon a deliberate policy of trying to win over these elements. Abul Fazl says that in order 'to soothe the minds of the zamindars, he entered into matrimonial relations with them.' Thus when Jamal Khan Mewati, who was the cousin of Hasan Khan Mewati, 'one of the great zamindars of India', submitted to Humayun, he married one of his beautiful daughters himself and married the younger sister to Bairam Khan. In course of time, Akbar expanded and elaborated this policy.

Bhara Mal, the ruler of Amber, had come to Akbar's court at Agra immediately after his accession. He had made a favourable impression on the young king, for when people were running helter-skelter from a maddened elephant, the Rajputs under Bhara Mal had stood firm. In 1562, when Akbar was going to Ajmer, he learnt that Bhara Mal was being harassed by the local Mughal governor. Bhara Mal paid personal homage to Akbar, and cemented the alliance by marrying his younger daughter, Harkha Bai, to Akbar.

Marriages between Muslim rulers and the daughters of Hindu potentates were not unusual. Many cases of such alliances in various parts of the country during the fourteenth and fifteenth centuries have been cited earlier. Maldeo, the powerful ruler of Jodhpur, had married his daughter, Bai Kanaka, to Sultan Mahmud of Gujarat and another, Lal Bai, to the Sur ruler, probably Islam Shah Sur. Bhara Mal himself had married his elder daughter to Haji Khan Pathan who had been the virtual ruler of Alwar after the death of Islam Shah Sur. Most of these marriages had not led to the establishment of any stable personal relations between the concerned families. The girls were generally lost to their families and never came back after marriage. Akbar followed a different policy. He gave complete religious freedom to his Hindu wives, and gave an honoured place to their parents and relations in the nobility. Bhara Mal was made a high grandee. His son, Bhagwant Das, rose to the rank of 5000 and his grandson, Man Singh, to the rank of 7000. This rank was accorded by Akbar to only one other noble, Aziz Khan Koka, his foster-brother. Akbar emphasised his special relationship with the Kachhawaha ruler in other ways as well. The infant prince, Danyal, was sent to Amber to be brought up by Bhara Mal's wives. In 1572, when Akbar dashed to Gujarat, Bhara Mal was placed in charge of Agra where all the royal ladies were residing, a signal honour, given only to nobles who were either relations or close confidants of the emperor.

But Akbar did not insist upon matrimonial relations as a precondition. No matrimonial relations were entered into with the Hadas of Ranthambhor, yet they remained high in Akbar's favour. Rao Surjan Hada was placed in charge of Garh-Katanga, and rose to the rank of 2000. Similarly no matrimonial relations were entered into with the rulers of Sirohi and Banswara when they submitted to Akbar later on.

Akbar's Rajput policy was combined with a policy of broad religious toleration. In 1564, he abolished the *jizyah* which was sometimes used by the *ulama* to humiliate non-Muslims and was often considered a symbol of Muslim domination and superiority. He had earlier abolished the pilgrim tax, and the practice of forcible conversion of prisoners of war.

Following the conquest of Chittor, most of the leading Rajput rulers had accepted Akbar's suzerainty and paid personal homage to him. The rulers of Jaisalmer and Bikaner had also entered into matrimonial relations with Akbar. The only state which had steadfastly refused to accept Mughal suzerainty was Mewar.

Although Chittor and the plain area around it had come under Mughal domination, Udaipur and the hilly area which formed the larger part of Mewar had remained under the control of the rana. In 1572, Rana Pratap succeeded Rana Udai Singh to the *gaddi*. A series of embassies were sent by Akbar to Rana Pratap to persuade him to accept Mughal suzerainty and to do personal homage. These embassies, including the one led by Man Singh, were courteously received by the rana. The story that he insulted Man Singh is not a historical fact, and is uncharacteristic of the rana who always behaved in a chivalrous and courteous manner, even towards his opponents. Man Singh's embassy was followed by one under Bhagwant Das, and another under Raja Todar Mal. At one time, it seems that the rana was prepared for a compromise. He put on the imperial robe sent by Akbar, and sent his son, Amar Singh, to the court with Bhagwant Das to pay homage to Akbar and accept his service. But no final agreement could be reached as the proud rana was not prepared to accept Akbar's demand for tendering personal homage. Also, it seems that the Mughals wanted to keep hold of Chittor which was not acceptable to the rana.

Early in 1576, Akbar moved to Ajmer, and deputed Raja Man Singh with a force of 5000 to lead a campaign against the rana. In anticipation of this move, the Rana had devastated the entire territory up to Chittor so that the Mughal forces might get no food or fodder. He had also fortified all the passes in the hills. A furious battle between the two sides was waged at Haldighati below a narrow defile leading to Kumbhalgarh, which was then the rana's capital. Apart from select Rajput forces, the rana's van consisted of the Afghan contingent led by Hakim Khan Sur. Thus the battle of Haldighati was not a struggle between the Hindus and the Muslims, or between the Indians and the foreigners. A small force of the Bhils whom the rana had befriended was also present. The rana's forces are put at 3000. The onslaught by the Rajputs and the Afghans threw the Mughal forces into disarray. But the rumours that Akbar had arrived in person rallied them. With fresh Mughal reinforcements, the tide of battle began to turn against the Rajputs. Seeing this, the rana escaped. The Mughal forces were too tired to pursue him but, after some time, they advanced through the pass and occupied Gogunda, a strong point which had been evacuated by the rana earlier.

This was the last time the rana engaged in a pitched battle with the Mughals. Henceforth he resorted to methods of guerilla warfare. The defeat at Haldighati did not weaken Rana Pratap's resolve to fight on for independence. However, the cause for which he stood had already been lost; most of the Rajput states had accepted Mughal suzerainty. By his policy of inducting the Rajput rajas into Mughal service and treating them on par with the Mughal grandees, according broad religious toleration to his subjects, and his courteous behaviour to his former opponents, Akbar succeeded in cementing his alliance with the Rajput rulers. Therefore, Rana Pratap's refusal to bow before the Mughals had little effect on most of the other Rajput states which realised that in the existing situation, it was impossible for small states to stand out for long in favour of complete independence. Moreover, by allowing a large measure of autonomy to the Rajput rajas, Akbar established an empire which those Rajput rajas did not consider harmful to their best interests.

Rana Pratap's defiance of the mighty Mughal empire, almost alone and unaided by the other Rajput states, constitutes a glorious saga of Rajput valour and the spirit of sacrifice for cherished principles. Rana Pratap's method of sporadic warfare was later elaborated further by Malik Ambar, the Deccani general, and by Shivaji.

It is not necessary to discuss in detail the struggle between Akbar and Rana Pratap. For some time, Akbar exerted relentless pressure on the raja. The Mughals overran the states of Dungarpur, Banswara, Sirohi, etc., which were dependent allies of Mewar and had supported Rana Pratap. Akbar concluded separate treaties with these states, thus further isolating Mewar. The rana was hunted from forest to forest and from valley to valley. Both Kumbhalgarh and Udaipur were occupied by the Mughals. The raja underwent great hardships, but thanks to the support of the Bhil chiefs, he continued his defiance. The Mughal pressure relaxed after 1579 due to a serious revolt in

Bihar and Bengal, in protest against some reforms effected by Akbar. Akbar's half- brother, Mirza Hakim, made an incursion into the Punjab in order to fish in troubled waters. Thus, Akbar had to face a most serious internal crisis. In 1585, Akbar moved to Lahore to watch the situation in the north-west which had become dangerous. He remained there for the next 12 years. No Mughal expedition was sent against Rana Pratap after 1585.

Taking advantage of the situation, Rana Pratap recovered many of his territories, including Kumbhalgarh and the areas near Chittor. But he could not recover Chittor itself. During this period, he built a new capital, Chavand, near modern Dungarpur. He died in 1597 at the young age of 51, due to an internal injury incurred by him while trying to draw a stiff bow.

Apart from Mewar, Akbar had to face opposition in Marwar as well. Following the death of Maldeo (1562), there was a dispute for succession between his sons. The younger son of Maldeo, Chandrasen, who was the son of the favourite queen of Maldeo, succeeded to the *gaddi*. Due to the pressure of the Mughals, he had to give parts of his country in *patta* to his elder brothers. But Chandrasen did not like this arrangement and after some time, rose in rebellion. Akbar now took Marwar under direct Mughal administration. Possibly, one reason for this was his desire to safeguard the Mughal supply route to Gujarat which passed through Jodhpur. After its conquest, Akbar appointed Rai Singh Bikaneri to look after Jodhpur. Chandrasen resisted valiantly and waged a guerilla warfare. But after some time he had to seek refuge in Mewar. Even there he was hunted from place to place by the Mughals. He died in 1581. A couple of years later, Akbar conferred Jodhpur upon Udai Singh, the elder brother of Chandrasen. To strengthen his position, Udai Singh married his daughter, Jagat Gosain or Jodha Bai as she came to be called, to Akbar's eldest son Salim. Unlike the *dola* form of earlier marriages, the bridegroom's party went to the raja's house in *barat*, and a number of Hindu practices were followed. This happened when Akbar was residing at Lahore.

Akbar also had close personal relations with the rulers of Bikaner and Bundi who served in various campaigns with distinction. In 1593, when the son-in-law of Rai Singh of Bikaner died due to a fall from his *palki*, Akbar went personally to the raja's house to console him, and dissuaded his daughter from performing *sati*, as her children were young.

The Rajput policy of Akbar proved beneficial to the Mughal state as well as to the Rajputs. The alliance secured to the Mughal empire the services of the bravest warriors in India. The steadfast loyalty of the Rajputs became an important factor in the consolidation and expansion of the empire. The alliance ensured peace in Rajasthan, and enabled the Rajputs to serve in far-flung parts of the empire without worrying about the safety of their homelands. By being enrolled into the imperial service, important positions in the empire were open to the Rajput rajas. Thus, Bhagwant Das of Amber was appointed joint governor of Lahore, while his son, Man Singh was appointed the governor of Bihar and Bengal. Other Rajput rajas were placed in charge of strategic provinces, such as Agra, Ajmer and Gujarat, at various times. As high grandees of the empire, they were granted *jagirs* in addition to their hereditary kingdoms, thus augmenting their resources.

Akbar's Rajput policy was continued by his successors, Jahangir and Shah Jahan. Jahangir, whose mother was a Rajput princess, had himself married a Kacchawaha princess as well as a Jodhpur princess. Princesses of the houses of Jaisalmer and Bikaner were also married to him. Jahangir gave positions of honour to the rulers of all these houses.

The main achievement of Jahangir, however, was the settlement of the outstanding dispute with Mewar. Rana Pratap had been succeeded by his son, Amar Singh. Akbar had sent a series of expeditions against Amar Singh in order to force him to accept his conditions. Jahangir himself was sent against him twice, but could achieve little. After his accession in 1605, Jahangir took up the matter energetically. Three successive campaigns were launched, but they could not break the rana's will. In 1613, Jahangir himself reached Ajmer to direct the campaign. Prince Khurram (later Shah Jahan) was deputed with a large army to invade the mountainous parts of Mewar. The heavy pressure of the Mughal army, the depopulation of the country, and ruination of agriculture, at last produced their effect. Some sardars defected to the Mughals, many others pressed the rana for peace. The rana's son, Karan Singh, who was deputed to proceed to Jahangir's court was graciously received. Jahangir got up from the throne, embraced him in darbar and loaded him with gifts. To save the rana's prestige, Jahangir did not insist upon the rana paying personal homage to him, or entering the royal service. Prince Karan was accorded the rank of 5000, which had been earlier accorded to the rulers of Jodhpur, Bikaner and Amber. He was to serve the Mughal emperor with a contingent of 1500 *sawars*. All the territories of Mewar, including Chittor, were restored. But in view of the strategic importance of Chittor, it was stipulated that its fortifications would not be repaired.

Thus, Jahangir completed the task begun by Akbar, and further strengthened the alliance with the Rajputs.

REBELLIONS AND FURTHER EXPANSION OF THE MUGHAL EMPIRE

The new system of administration introduced by Akbar, as described above, implied tightening of the administrative machinery, greater control over the nobles, and more attention to the interests of the people. It was, therefore, not to the liking of many nobles. Sentiments of regional independence were still strong, particularly in areas such as Gujarat, Bengal and Bihar, all of which had a long tradition of forming separate kingdoms. In Rajasthan, Rana Pratap's struggle for freedom was continuing apace. In this situation, Akbar had to deal with a series of rebellions. Gujarat remained in a state of unrest for two years due to a bid for freedom by a representative of the old ruling dynasty. The most serious rebellion during the period was in Bengal and Bihar which extended to Jaunpur. The main cause of the rebellion was the strict enforcement of the *dagh* system or branding of the horses of the jagirdars, and strict accounting of their income. The discontent was fanned by some religious divines who were unhappy at Akbar's liberal views, and at his policy of resuming the large revenue-free grants of land which had been obtained by them, sometimes illegally. Akbar's half-brother, Mirza Hakim, the ruler of Kabul, also abetted the rebellion and held out the hope of invading the Punjab at a suitable time in order to help. A large number of Afghans in the eastern parts were sullen at the loss of the Afghan power and were ever ready to join a rebellion.

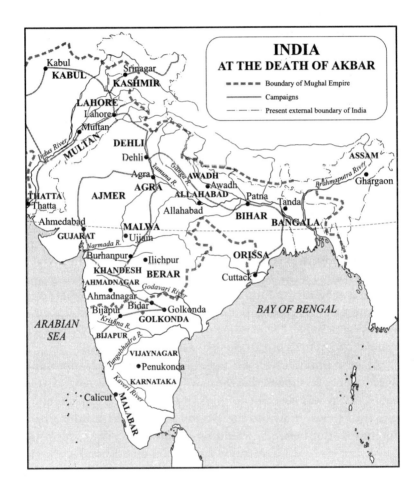

The rebellion kept the empire distracted for almost two years (1580–81), and Akbar was faced with a very difficult and delicate situation. Due to the mishandling of the situation by local officials, Bengal and almost the whole of Bihar passed into the hands of the rebels who proclaimed Mirza Hakim as their ruler. They even got a religious divine to issue a *fatwa*, calling on the faithful to take the field against Akbar.

Akbar did not lose his nerve. He despatched a force under Todar Mal against Bihar and Bengal, and another under Raja Man Singh to check the expected attack by Mirza Hakim. Todar Mal proceeded with great vigour and tact, and brought the situation in the east under control before Mirza Hakim's invasion took place. Mirza Hakim advanced on Lahore with 15,000 horses, but could not take the city due to the stout defence by Raja Man Singh and Bhagwant Das. His hopes that large number of nobles in the Punjab would rebel and join him were also belied. Meanwhile, Akbar marched on Lahore with a well-disciplined force of 50,000 horses. Mirza Hakim had no option but to beat a hasty retreat.

Akbar crowned his success by marching to Kabul (1581). Since Mirza Hakim refused to accept Akbar's suzerainty, or to come to pay personal allegiance to him, and the Indian nobles and soldiers were becoming restive, Akbar handed over Kabul to his sister, before returning to India. The handing over of a kingdom to a woman was symbolic of Akbar's broad-mindedness and liberalism.

Akbar's triumph over his opponents was not only a personal success, but also showed that the new system was beginning to strike roots. Akbar was now free to think of the further expansion of his empire. He was drawn to the Deccan in which he had long been interested. But before he could do anything, the situation in the northwest claimed his attention again. Abdullah Khan Uzbek, the hereditary enemy of the Mughals, had been gradually gathering strength in Central Asia. In 1584, he overran Badakhshan which had been ruled by the Timurids. Kabul appeared to be next on the list. Both Mirza Hakim and the Timurid princes ousted from Badakhashan now appealed to Akbar for help. But before he could act, Mirza Hakim died due to excessive drinking, leaving Kabul in a state of disturbance.

Akbar now ordered Man Singh to march to Kabul, and himself moved to Attok on the river Indus. In order to block all roads to the Uzbeks, he sent expeditions against Kashmir (1586), and against Baluchistan. The whole of Kashmir, including Ladakh and Baltistan (called Tibet Khurd and Tibet Buzurg), came under Mughal domination, and a daughter of the chief of Baltistan was married to young Salim. Expeditions were also sent to clear the Khyber Pass which had been blocked by rebellious tribesmen. In an expedition against them, Raja Birbal, the favourite of Akbar, lost his life. But the Afghan tribesmen were gradually forced to submit.

The consolidation of the northwest, and fixing a scientific frontier of the empire were two of the major contributions of Akbar. His conquest of Sindh (1590) also opened the trade down the river Indus for Punjab. Akbar stayed at Lahore till 1598 when the death of Abdullah Uzbek finally removed the threat from the side of the Uzbeks.

After settling the affairs of the northwest, Akbar turned his attention towards the affairs of eastern and western India and the Deccan. Orissa, which was at the time under the domination of Afghan chiefs, was conquered by Raja Man Singh who was the Mughal governor of Bengal. Man Singh also conquered Cooch-Bihar and parts of east Bengal, including Dacca. Mirza Aziz Koka, the foster-brother of Akbar, conquered Kathiawar in the west. Khan-i-Khanan Munim Khan was deputed to the Deccan along with prince Murad. The developments in the Deccan would be dealt with in a separate chapter. Suffice it to say here that by the turn of the century, Mughal control had been extended up to Ahmadnagar, bringing the Mughals into direct contact with the Marathas for the first time.

Thus, the political integration of north India had been achieved by the turn of the century, and the Mughals had started the penetration of the Deccan. But what was even more important, the cultural and emotional integration of the people within this vast empire had developed apace.

Towards Integration: State, Religion and Social Reforms

We have seen how, during the fifteenth century, a number of rulers in different parts of the country had tried to promote greater understanding between the Hindus and the Muslims by having secular and religious literature in Sanskrit translated into Persian, by giving patronage to local languages and literature, by adopting a more liberal policy of religious toleration and, in some cases, by giving important jobs, including service at the court, and in the army, to the Hindus. We have also seen how a remarkable series of popular saints, such as Kabir, Chaitanya and Nanak, in different parts of the country emphasised the essential unity of Islam and Hinduism, and laid stress on a religion based on love and devotion rather than one based on rituals or a literal interpretation of revealed books. They thus created the atmosphere in which liberal sentiments and views could grow and religious narrowness began to be looked down upon. This was the atmosphere in which Akbar was born and reared.

One of the first actions which Akbar took, after he had taken power in his own hands, was to abolish the poll tax or *jizyah* which the non-Muslims were required to pay in a Muslim state. Although it was not a heavy tax, it was disliked because it made a distinction between subject and subject. At the same time, Akbar abolished the pilgrim tax on bathing at holy places such as Prayag, Banaras, etc. He also abolished the practice of forcibly converting prisoners of war to Islam. This laid the essential foundation of an empire based on equal rights to all citizens, irrespective of their religious beliefs.

The liberal principles of the empire were strengthened by bringing able Hindus into the nobility. While most of these were Rajput rajas, many of whom entered into matrimonial relations with Akbar, and with whom he had established a personal relationship, *mansabs* were given to others also on the basis of their competence. Among the latter, the ablest and the most well- known were Todar Mal, an expert in revenue affairs, who rose to the post of *diwan*, and Birbal, who was a personal favourite of the emperor. There were others, such as Rai Patr Das, entitled as Rai Bikramajit.

Akbar's attitude towards his Hindu subjects is closely linked with his views of how a sovereign should behave towards his subjects. These views which have been carefully explained by Akbar's biographer, Abul Fazl, were an amalgam of Timurid, Persian and Indian ideas of sovereignty. According to Abul Fazl, the office of a true ruler was a very responsible one which depended on divine illumination (*farr-i-izadi*). Hence, no one could stand between God and a true ruler. A true ruler was distinguished by a paternal love towards his subjects without distinction of sect or creed, a large heart so that the wishes of great and small are attended to, and prayer and devotion and a daily increasing trust in God who is considered as the real ruler. It was also the duty of the ruler to maintain equilibrium in society by not allowing people of one rank of profession to interfere in the duties and obligations of another. Above all he was not to allow the dust of sectarian strife to rise. All these together constituted what has been called the policy of *sulh-kul* or 'peace to all'.

Akbar was deeply interested in religion and philosophy. At the outset, Akbar was an orthodox Muslim. He paid great deference to the leading *qazi* of the state, Abdun Nabi Khan, who held the post of *sadr-us-sadur*. On one occasion, Akbar even carried his slippers for him. But by the time Akbar reached adulthood, mysticism which was being preached in the length and breadth of the country, began to influence him. We are told that he spent whole nights in thoughts of God, continually pronounced his name, and for a feeling of thankfulness for his success, he would sit many a morning alone, in prayer and contemplation, on a large flat stone of an old building near his palace in Agra. Gradually, he turned away from the path of narrow orthodoxy. He had already abolished the *jizyah* and pilgrim tax, as we have seen. He gathered at the court a band of talented people with liberal ideas. The most noted among these were Abul Fazl and his brother Faizi who, along with their father who was a noted scholar, had been persecuted by the *mullahs* for having sympathy with Mahdawi ideas to which the orthodox elements were strongly opposed. Another was a Brahman, Mahesh Das, who was given the title of Raja Birbal, and was a constant companion of Akbar.

In 1575, Akbar built a hall called Ibadat Khana or the Hall of Prayer at his new capital, Fatehpur Sikri. To this he called selected theologians, mystics and those of his courtiers and nobles who were known for their scholarship and intellectual attainments. Akbar discussed religious and spiritual topics with them. He frequently said, 'My sole object, oh wise *mullahs*, is to ascertain truth, to find out and disclose the principles of genuine religion...' The proceedings, at first, were confined to the Muslims. They were hardly orderly. The *mullahs* wrangled, shouted, and abused each other even in the presence of the emperor. The behaviour of the *mullahs*, their pride and conceit in their learning disgusted Akbar, and further alienated him from the *mullahs*.

At this stage, Akbar opened the Ibadat Khana to people of all religions—Christians, Zoroastrians, Hindus, Jains, even atheists. This broadened the discussions, and debates began even on issues on which all Muslims were agreed, such as whether the *Quran* was the last revealed book and Muhammad its prophet, resurrection, nature of God, etc. This horrified the theologians, and all kinds of rumours began to circulate about Akbar's desire to forsake Islam. As a modern historian of repute, R.P. Tripathi says, 'The patience and open-mindedness of Akbar was construed in a variety of way by persons of different faiths. Instead of bringing credit, the Ibadat Khana brought growing discredit.'

At this time, an enquiry was conducted into the affairs of the Chief *Sadr*, Abdun Nabi, who was found to be extremely corrupt and tyrannical in his dealings in the distribution of charitable lands (*madad-i-maash*). He had amassed wealth in other corrupt ways as well. He was a bigot and had inflicted the punishment of death on the Shias, and on a Brahman of Mathura for their beliefs. At first, Abdun Nabi was sheared of his power, and *sadrs* were appointed in every province for distributing charitable lands. Soon he was dismissed and ordered to proceed to Mecca for *haj*. At about the same time, in 1580 a rebellion broke out in the east. A number of *fatwas* were given by the *qazis*, declaring Akbar to be a heretic. Akbar suppressed the rebellion and gave drastic punishment to the *qazis*.

To further strengthen his position in dealing with the *mullahs*, Akbar also issued a declaration or *mahzar* which asserted that if there were conflicting views among those who were considered fit to interpret the *Quran*, that is *mujtaddids*, Akbar, by virtue of being 'a most just and wise king', and his rank being higher in the eyes of God than of the *mujtaddids*, was entitled to choose any one of the interpretations, which would be of 'benefit to the nation and in the interests of good order.' Further, if Akbar issued a new order 'in conformity with the *Quran* and calculated to benefit the nation', all should be bound by it.

The declaration which was signed by the leading *ulamas* had been wrongly called a 'Decree of Infallibility'. Akbar claimed the right to choose only when there was a difference of opinion among those qualified to interpret the *Quran*. At a time when there were bloody conflicts between the Shias, the Sunnis and the Mahdawis in different parts of the country, Akbar wanted the widest toleration. There is little doubt that the *mahzar* had a salutary effect in stabilising the religious situation in the empire.

But Akbar was less successful in his effort to find a meeting ground between the votaries of different religions in the country. The debates in the Ibadat Khana had not led to a better understanding between different religions, but to greater bitterness, as the representatives of each religion denounced the others and tried to prove that their religion was superior to others. Hence, in 1582, Akbar discontinued the debates in the Ibadat Khana. But he did not give up his quest for truth. Even his bitter critic, Badayuni, says: 'Night and day people did nothing but inquire and investigate.' Akbar invited Purushottam and Devi to expound the doctrines of Hinduism, and Maharji Rana to explain the doctrines of Zoroastrianism. He met some Portuguese priests and in order to understand the Christian doctrines better, he sent an embassy to Goa, requesting them to send two learned missionaries to his court. The Portuguese sent Aquaviva and Monserrate who remained at Akbar's court for almost three years and have left a valuable account. But their hope of converting Akbar to Christianity never had any basis. Akbar came into touch with the Jains also and, at his instance, the leading Jain saint of Kathiawar, Hira Vijaya Suri, spent a couple of years at Akbar's court.

Contacts with leaders of various religions, listening to their learned works, meetings with the Sufi saints and yogis gradually convinced Akbar that while there were differences of sect and creed, all religions had a number of good points which were obscured in the heat of controversy. He felt that if the good points of various religions were emphasised, an atmosphere of harmony and amity would prevail which would be for the good of the country. Further, he felt that behind all the multiplicity of names and forms, there was but one God. As Badayuni observed, as a result of all the influences which were brought to bear on His Majesty, 'there grew gradually as the outline of a stone, the conviction in his heart that there were some sensible men in all religions. If some true knowledge was thus everywhere to be found, why should truth be confined to one religion?'

Badayuni asserts that as a result, Akbar gradually turned away from Islam and set up a new religion which was compounded of many existing religions—Hinduism, Christianity, Zoroastrianism, etc. However, modern historians are not inclined to accept this view, and think that Badayuni has exaggerated. There is little evidence to prove that Akbar intended or actually promulgated a new religion. The word used by Abul Fazl and Badayuni for the so-called new path was *tauhid-i-Ilahi* which literally means 'Divine Monotheism'. The *tauhid-i-Ilahi* was really an order of the Sufistic type. Those who were willing to join, and whom the emperor approved, were allowed to become members. Sunday was fixed as the day for initiation. The novice placed his head at the feet of the emperor who raised him up, and gave him the formula, called *shast* in the Sufi terminology, which he was to repeat and concentrate upon. This contained Akbar's favourite motto 'Allah-o-Akbar' or God is great. The initiates were to abstain from meat as far as possible, at least in the month of their birth, give a sumptuous feast and alms on their birthday. There were no sacred books or scriptures, no priestly class, no place of worship or rituals and ceremonies, except the initiation.

Tauhid-i-Ilahi should not be confused with Akbar selecting a small group of trusted nobles who were totally devoted to him. According to Badayuni, those selected were to promise sacrifice of property, life, honour and religion. Giving up religion, apparently meant giving up attachment to the narrow concepts and observances which, again, was in keeping with Sufi ideas. However, many leading nobles, including all the great Hindu nobles, except Birbal, declined to join. The number of this group, as far as we know, amounted to about eighteen only, while those who were enrolled as disciples of Akbar amounted to thousands. Akbar did not, use force, nor was money used for enrolling disciples or *murids*.

In enrolling *murids*, Akbar evidently had some political purpose also. He wanted a band of nobles and others who would be personally loyal to him, and support him in his concept of a state based on *sulh-i-kul*, i.e. equal toleration of and respect to all sections, irrespective of their religious beliefs. Orthodox elements, such as Badayuni, neither sympathized with or supported such a state. Badayuni ascribes this move of Akbar, to enroll disciples, to his head being turned by many unworthy flatterers and panegyrists who suggested to him that he was the *insdan-i-kamil* or the 'Perfect Man' of the age. It was at their instance that Akbar initiated the ceremony of *pabos* or kissing the floor before the sovereign, a ceremony which was previously reserved for God.

There were many precedents of rulers trying to combine temporal and spiritual powers in their person. Abul Fazl says that it was natural for people to turn to their ruler for spiritual guidance and that Akbar was well qualified to lead the people to spiritual bliss and to establish harmony among warring creeds.

The *tauhid-i-Ilahi* virtually died with Akbar though the practice of enrolling *murids* and giving them a *shast* was continued for some time by Jahangir. However, Akbar's attempt of tying the nobles to the emperor by personal bonds succeeded, many nobles continuing to pride themselves as being the *banda* or slaves, or *murids* of the emperor. Also, by and large, the nobles did not support elements propagating religious orthodoxy in social and political matters. However, the belief of looking upon the king as someone having miraculous powers, so that people could be cured by the king's touch, or by his breathing upon a pot of water, continued. Even an orthodox ruler such as Aurangzeb could not shake off this belief.

Akbar tried to emphasise the concept of *sulh-i-kul* or peace and harmony among religions in other ways as well. He set up a big translation department for translating works in Sanskrit, Arabic, Greek, etc., into Persian. Thus, the *Singhasan Battisi*, the *Atharva Veda* and the *Bible* were taken up first for translation. These were followed by the *Mahabharata*, the *Gita* and the *Ramayana*. Many others, including the *Panchatantra* and works of geography, were also translated. The *Quran* was also translated into Persian, perhaps for the first time.

Akbar also introduced a number of social and educational reforms. He stopped *sati*, the burning of a widow, unless she herself, of her own free will, persistently desired it. Widows of tender age who had not shared the bed with their husbands were not to be burnt at all. Widow remarriage was also legalised. Akbar was against anyone having more than one wife unless the first wife was barren. The age of marriage was raised to 14 for girls and 16 for boys. The sale of wines and spirits was restricted. Not all these steps were, however, successful. As we know, the success of social legislation depends largely on the willing cooperation of the people. Akbar was living in an age of superstition and it seems that his social reforms had only limited success.

Akbar also revised the educational syllabus, laying more emphasis on moral education and mathematics, and on secular subjects such as agriculture, geometry, astronomy, rules of government, logic, history, etc. He also gave patronage to artists, poets, painters and musicians, so much so that his court became famous for the galaxy of renowned people known as the *navaratna*.

Thus, under Akbar, the state became essentially secular, liberal and enlightened in social matters, and a promoter of cultural integration.

FOURTEEN

The Deccan and South India
(*Up to 1656*)

We have mentioned in an earlier chapter that following the break up of the Bahmani kingdom, three powerful states, Ahmadnagar, Bijapur and Golconda emerged on the scene, and that they combined to crush Vijayanagara at the battle of Bannihatti, near Talikota, in 1565. After the victory, the Deccani states resumed their old ways. Both Ahmadnagar and Bijapur claimed Sholapur which was a rich and fertile tract. Neither wars nor marriage alliances between the two could resolve the issue. Both the states had the ambition of conquering Bidar. Ahmadnagar also wanted to annex Berar in the north. In fact, as the descendants of the old Bahmani rulers, the Nizam Shahis claimed a superior, if not a hegemonistic position in the Deccan. Their territorial claims were contested not only by Bijapur, but also by the rulers of Gujarat who had their eyes on the rich Konkan area, in addition to Berar. The Gujarat rulers actively aided Berar against Ahmadnagar, and even engaged in war against Ahmadnagar in order that the existing balance of power in the Deccan was not upset. Bijapur and Golconda clashed over the possession of Naldurg.

The Mughal conquest of Gujarat in 1572 created a new situation. The conquest of Gujarat could have been a prelude to the Mughal conquest of the Deccan. But Akbar was busy elsewhere and did not want, at that stage, to interfere in the Deccan affairs. Ahmadnagar took advantage of the situation to annex Berar. In fact, Ahmadnagar and Bijapur came to an agreement whereby Bijapur was left free to expand its dominions in the south at the expense of Vijayanagara, while Ahmadnagar overran Berar. Golconda, too, was interested in extending its territories at the cost of Vijayanagara which was divided into small nayakhoods. All the Deccani states were, thus, expansionists.

Another feature of the situation was the growing importance of the Marathas in the affairs of the Deccan. As we have seen, the

Maratha troops had always been employed as loose auxiliaries or *bargirs* (usually called *bargis*) in the Bahmani kingdom. The revenue affairs at the local level were in the hands of the Deccani Brahmans. Some of the old Maratha families which rose in the service of the Bahmani rulers and held *mansabs* and *jagirs* from them were the More, Nimbalkar, Ghatge, etc. Most of them were powerful zamindars, or *deshmukhs* as they were called in the Deccan. However, unlike the Rajputs, none of them was an independent ruler, or ruled over a large kingdom. Secondly, they were not the leaders of clans on whose backing and support they could depend. Hence, many of the Maratha sardars appear to be military adventurers who were prepared to shift their loyalty according to the prevailing wind. Nevertheless, the Marathas formed the backbone of the landed aristocracy of the Deccan and had a position similar to the one held by the Rajputs in large parts of north India. During the middle of the sixteenth century, the rulers of the Deccan states embarked upon a definite policy of winning over the Marathas to their side. The Maratha chiefs were accorded service and positions in all the three leading states of the Deccan. Ibrahim Adil Shah of Bijapur who ascended the throne in 1535 was the leading advocate of this policy. It is said that he entertained 30,000 Maratha auxiliaries (*bargis*) in his army, and showed great favour to the Marathas in the revenue system. He is supposed to have introduced Marathi in revenue accounts at all levels. Apart from increasing his favours to old families, a few other families such as the Bhonsales who had the family name of Ghorpade, the Dafles (or Chavans), etc., also rose to prominence in Bijapur as a result of this policy. Maharashtrian Brahmans were regularly used for diplomatic negotiations as well. Thus the title of Peshwa was accorded to a Brahman, Kankoji Narsi, by the rulers of Ahmadnagar. Marathas played an important role in the states of Ahmadnagar and Golconda as well.

It will thus be seen that the policy of allying with local landed classes which were military-minded had been initiated by the Deccani rulers even before such a policy was implemented by the Mughals under Akbar.

MUGHAL ADVANCE TOWARDS THE DECCAN

It was logical to expect a Mughal advance towards the Deccan after the consolidation of the empire in north India. Although the Vindhyas divided the north and the south, they were not an insurmountable barrier. Travellers, merchandise, pilgrims and wandering saints had always passed between the north and the south, making the two culturally one, though each had its own distinctive cultural features. The conquest of the Deccan by the Tughlaqs and the improved communications between the north and the south had let to a strengthening of the commercial and cultural relations between the two. After the decline of the Delhi Sultanat, many Sufi saints and persons in search of employment had migrated to the court of the Bahmani rulers. Politically also, the north and south were not isolated. As we have seen, the rulers of Gujarat and Malwa in the west, and Orissa in the east had been continually involved in the politics of south India. Hence, after the conquest of Malwa and Gujarat in the 1560s and early 1570s, the Mughals could hardly have kept themselves aloof from Deccan politics. In 1576, a Mughal army invaded Khandesh, and compelled the ruler to submit. However, urgent matters called Akbar elsewhere. For twelve years, between 1586 and 1598, Akbar lived at Lahore, watching the northwestern situation. In the interval, affairs in the Deccan deteriorated.

The Deccan was a seething cauldron of politics. War between the various Deccani states was a frequent occurrence. The death of a ruler often led to factional fights among the nobles, with each party trying to act as king-maker. In this, hostility between the Deccanis and the newcomers (*afaqis* or *gharibs*) found free play. Among the Deccanis, too, the Habshis (Abyssinians or Africans) and Afghans formed separate groups. These groups and factions had little contact with the life and culture of the people of the region. The process of the assimilation of the Marathas into the military and political system of the Deccani states which had started earlier did not make much headway. The rulers and the nobles, therefore, commanded little loyalty from the people.

The situation was worsened by sectarian conflicts and controversies. Towards the beginning of the century, Shiism became the state religion of Iran under a new dynasty called the Safavid dynasty. Shiism had been a suppressed sect for a long time, and in the first flush of enthusiasm, the votaries of the new sect indulged in a good deal of persecution of their erstwhile opponents. As a result, members of many eminent families fled to India and sought shelter at the court of Akbar who made no distinction between Shias and Sunnis. Some of the Deccani states, notably Golconda, adopted Shiism as a state creed. At the courts of Bijapur and Ahmadnagar, too, the Shiite party was strong, but was able to prevail only from time to time. This resulted in heightened party strife.

Mahdawi ideas had also spread widely in the Deccan. The Muslims believed that in every epoch a man from the family of the Prophet will make an appearance and will strengthen the religion, and make justice triumph. Such a person was called the Mahdi. Although many Mahdis had appeared in different countries at different times, the end of the first millennium of Islam, which was due towards the end of the sixteenth century, had raised expectations throughout the Islamic world. In India, one Saiyid Muhammad, who was born at Jaunpur in the first half of the fifteenth century, proclaimed himself to be the Mahdi. Saiyid Muhammad travelled widely all over India and in the Islamic world, and created great enthusiasm. He established his *dairas* (circles) in different parts of the country, including the Deccan where his ideas found a fertile soil. The orthodox elements were as bitterly opposed to Mahdawism as to Shiism, though there was no love lost between the two. It was in this context that Akbar had put forward the concept of *sulh-kul*. He was afraid that the bitter sectarian rivalries prevailing in the Deccani states would spill over into the Mughal empire.

Akbar was also apprehensive of the growing power of the Portuguese. The Portuguese had been interfering in pilgrim traffic to Mecca, not sparing even the royal ladies. In their territories, they carried out proselytizing activities which Akbar disliked. They were constantly trying to expand their positions on the mainland, and had even tried to lay their hand on Surat which was saved by the timely arrival of a Mughal commander. Akbar apparently felt that the coordination and pooling of the resources of the Deccani states under Mughal supervision would check, if not eliminate, the Portuguese danger.

These were some of the factors which impelled Akbar to involve himself in the Deccani affairs.

CONQUEST OF BERAR, AHMADNAGAR AND KHANDESH

Akbar claimed suzerainty over the entire country. He was, therefore, keen that like the Rajputs, the rulers of the Deccani states should acknowledge his suzerainty. Embassies sent by him earlier suggesting that the Deccani states recognise his over-lordship and be friends with him, did not, however, produce any positive results. It was obvious that the Deccani states would not accept Mughal suzerainty till the Mughals were in a position to exert military pressure on them.

In 1591, Akbar launched a diplomatic offensive. He sent embassies to all the Deccani states 'inviting' them to accept Mughal suzerainty. As might have been expected, none of the states accepted this demand, the only exception being Khandesh which was too near and exposed to the Mughals to resist. Burhan Nizam Shah, the ruler of Ahmadnagar, was rude to the Mughal envoy; the others only made promises of friendship. It seemed that Akbar was on the verge of making a definite move in the Deccan. The necessary opportunity was provided to him when factional fighting broke out among the Nizam Shahi nobles following the death of Burhan in 1595. There were four candidates for the throne, backed by different parties. The strongest claim was that of Bahadur, son of the deceased ruler. Ibrahim Adil Shah II, the ruler of Bijapur, was inclined to support Bahadur's claim. Chand Bibi was the sister of Burhan, and the widow of the former ruler of Bijapur who was Ibrahim Adil Shah's uncle. She was a remarkable woman and had virtually ruled Bijapur for almost ten years when Ibrahim Adil Shah was a minor. She had gone to Ahmadnagar to condole the death of her brother Burhan, but she stayed on to take up with vigour the cause of her nephew, Bahadur, who was a minor. It was against this background that the leaders of the rival party, the Deccanis, invited the Mughals to intervene. The struggle which now began was really a struggle between Bijapur and the Mughals for the domination of Ahmadnagar state.

The Mughal invasion was led by prince Murad, who was the governor of Gujarat, and by Abdur Rahim Khan-i-Khanan. The ruler of Khandesh was asked to cooperate. Due to factional fights among the Ahmadnagar nobles, the Mughals encountered little opposition till they reached the capital, Ahmadnagar. Chand Bibi shut herself up in the fort with the boy king, Bahadur. After a close siege of four months in which Chand Bibi played a valiant role, the two sides came to an agreement. They agreed to cede Berar to the Mughals in return for their recognition of the claim of Bahadur. Mughal suzerainty was also recognised. This was in 1596.

The Mughal annexation of Berar alarmed the Deccani states. They felt, not without reason, that Berar would give the Mughals a permanent foothold in the Deccan which could be enlarged upon at any time. Hence, they sided with Ahmadnagar and created obstacles in the Mughals taking possession of Berar. Soon, a combined force of Bijapur, Golconda and Ahmadnagar led by a Bijapur commander invaded Berar in strength. In a hard-fought battle in 1597, the Mughals defeated a Deccani force three times their number. The Bijapuri and Golconda forces now withdrew, leaving Chand Bibi alone to face the situation. Although Chand Bibi was in favour of observing the treaty of 1596, she could not stop the harassing attacks on the Mughals in Berar by her nobles. This resulted in a second Mughal siege of Ahmadnagar. In the absence of any help from any quarter, Chand Bibi opened negotiations with the Mughals. She was, however, accused of treachery by a hostile faction and murdered. Thus ended the life of one of the most romantic figures in Deccani politics. The Mughals now assaulted and captured Ahmadnagar. The boy-king, Bahadur, was sent to the fortress of Gwaliyar. Balaghat, too, was added to the empire and a Mughal garrison was stationed at Ahmadnagar. This was in 1600.

The fall of Ahmadnagar fort and city, and the capture of Bahadur Nizam Shah did not solve Akbar's problems in the Deccan. There was now no Nizam Shahi prince or noble with sufficient standing to negotiate with. At the same time, the Mughals were not inclined to advance beyond Ahmadnagar, or try to seize all the remaining territories of the state. The situation became further confused due to constant wrangling among the Mughal commanders.

To study the situation on the spot, Akbar advanced into Malwa and then into Khandesh. There he was told that the new ruler of

Khandesh had not shown due respect to prince Daniyal when he had passed through his territory on his way to Ahmadnagar. Akbar was also keen to secure the fort of Asirgarh in Khandesh which was reputed to be the strongest fort in the Deccan. After a tight siege, and when a pestilence had broken out in the fort, the ruler came out and surrendered (1601). Khandesh was incorporated to the Mughal empire.

Meanwhile, prince Daniyal, the youngest son of Akbar, who had been placed in command of Mughal armies in the Deccan, concluded a peace with Murtaza Nizam Shah II who after the fall of Ahmadnagar had been proclaimed ruler, by a group of Nizam Shahi nobles. According to the agreement, Ahmadnagar, Balaghat and parts of Telengana were surrendered to the Mughals, and the remaining portions of the kingdom confirmed to Murtaza Nizam Shah on condition of loyalty, and the promise that he would never rebel. This was in 1601. After the capture of Asirgarh, Akbar returned to the north to deal with the rebellion of his son, Salim.

Although the conquest of Khandesh, Berar and Balaghat, and Mughal control over the fort of Ahmadnagar were substantial achievements, the Mughals had yet to consolidate their position in the Deccan. Akbar was conscious that no lasting solution to the Deccan problem could be arrived at without an agreement with Bijapur. He had, therefore, sent messages of assurances to Ibrahim Adil Shah II who offered to marry his daughter to prince Daniyal. But soon after the marriage (1602), the prince died of excessive drinking. Thus the situation in the Deccan remained nebulous, and had to be tackled afresh by Akbar's successor, Jahangir.

RISE OF MALIK AMBAR AND FRUSTRATION OF MUGHAL ATTEMPT AT CONSOLIDATION

After the fall of Ahmadnagar and capture of Bahadur Nizam Shah by the Mughals, the state of Ahmadnagar would have disintegrated and different parts of it would have, in all probability, been swallowed up by the neighbouring states but for the rise of a remarkable man, Malik Ambar. Malik Ambar was an Abyssinian, born in Ethiopia. We do not know much about his early life and career. It seems that

his poor parents sold him at the slave market of Baghdad. In course
of time, he was purchased by a merchant who treated him well and
brought him to the Deccan which was a land of promise. Malik Ambar
rose in the service of Changez Khan, a famous and influential Habshi
noble of Murtaza Nizam Shah. When the Mughals invaded
Ahmadnagar, Ambar at first went to Bijapur to try his luck there.
But he soon came back and enrolled himself in the powerful Habshi
(Abyssinian) party which was opposed to Chand Bibi. After the fall
of Ahmadnagar, Malik Ambar found a Nizam Shahi prince and with
the tacit support of the ruler of Bijapur, set him up as Murtaza Nizam
Shah II, with himself as the Peshwa—a title which had been
common in Ahmadnagar much earlier. Malik Ambar gathered
around him a large band of Maratha troopers or *bargis*. The Marathas
were adept in rapid movements, and in plundering and cutting off
the supplies of the enemy troops. Although this guerilla mode of
warfare was traditional with the Marathas in the Deccan, the Mughals
were not used to it. With the help of the Marathas, Ambar made it
difficult for the Mughals to consolidate their position in Berar,
Ahmadnagar and Balaghat.

The Mughal commander in the Deccan at the time was Abdur
Rahim Khan-i-Khanan, a shrewd and wily politician and an able
soldier. He inflicted a crushing defeat on Ambar in 1601 in Telengana
at a place called Nander. However, he decided to make friends with
Ambar since he considered it desirable that there should be some
stability in the remaining Nizam Shahi kingdom. In his turn, Ambar
also found it useful to cultivate the friendship of the Khan-i-Khanan
since it enabled him to deal with his internal rivals. However, after
the death of Akbar, when the position of the Mughals in the Deccan
became weak due to differences among the Mughal commanders,
Ambar unleashed a fierce campaign to expel the Mughals from Berar,
Balaghat and Ahmadnagar. In this enterprise he was helped by
Ibrahim Adil Shah, the ruler of Bijapur, who considered it necessary
that the Nizam Shah state should continue as a buffer between
Bijapur and the Mughals. He gave Ambar the powerful fort of
Qandahar in Telengana for the residence of his family, and for storing
treasures, provisions, etc. He also lent him 10,000 horsemen for whose
support a definite tract of territory was to be set apart. The treaty was

cemented by a marriage alliance between the daughter of one of the leading Ethiopian nobles of Bijapur with Malik Ambar's son. The marriage was celebrated in 1609 with great rejoicing, with Adil Shah giving a handsome dowry to the bride, and spending about Rs 80,000 on fireworks alone.

Fortified with the support of Bijapur, and with the active aid of the Marathas, Ambar soon forced Khan-i-Khanan to retreat to Burhanpur. Thus, by 1610, all the gains in the Deccan made by Akbar were lost. Although Jahangir sent prince Parvez to the Deccan with a large army, he could not meet the challenge posed by Malik Ambar. Even Ahmadnagar was lost, and Parvez had to conclude a disgraceful peace with Ambar.

The affairs of Malik Ambar continued to prosper and the Mughals were not able to re-assert themselves as long as he had the solid support of the Marathas and other elements in the Deccan. But in course of time, Malik Ambar became arrogant and alienated his allies. The Khan-i-Khanan, who had again been posted as the Mughal viceroy of the Deccan, took advantage of the situation and won over to his side a number of Habshi and Maratha nobles, such as Jagdev Rai, Babaji Kate, Udaji Ram, etc. Jahangir himself was well aware of the value of the Marathas, for he observed in his *Memoirs* that the Marathas 'are a hardy lot and are the centre of resistance in that country.' With the help of the Maratha sardars, Khan-i-Khanan inflicted a crushing defeat on the combined forces of Ahmadnagar, Bijapur and Golconda in 1616. The Mughals occupied the new Nizam Shahi capital, Khirki, and burnt all its buildings before they left. This defeat shook the Deccani alliance against the Mughals. However, Ambar continued his resistance.

To carry forward Khan-i-Khanan's victory, Jahangir sent a grand army under his son, prince Khurram (later Shah Jahan), and himself moved to Mandu to support the prince (1618). Faced with this threat, Ambar had no option but to submit. It is significant, however, that in the treaty Jahangir did not try to enlarge the conquests made by Akbar in the Deccan. This was not due to any military weakness on the part of Jahangir, as has been sometimes imagined, but due to deliberate policy. Apparently, Jahangir did not want to extend Mughal commitments in the Deccan, or become too deeply embroiled in its affairs. Moreover, he was still hopeful that his moderation would enable the Deccani states to settle down, and live in peace with the Mughals. As a part of this policy, Jahangir tried to win over Bijapur to his side, and sent a gracious *farman* to Adil Shah, calling him 'son'.

Despite these reverses, Ambar continued to lead the Deccani struggle against the Mughals and there was no peace in the Deccan. However, two years later, the combined Deccani forces again suffered a severe defeat at the hands of the Mughals. Ambar had to restore all the Mughal territories, and another 14 kos of adjoining territory. The Deccani states had to pay an indemnity of Rs 5,00,000. The credit for these victories was given to prince Khurram.

This second defeat, coming so soon after the first, finally shattered the united front of the Deccani states against the Mughals. The old rivalries among the Deccani states now came to the surface. Ambar conducted a series of campaigns against Bijapur for the recovery of Sholapur which was a bone of contention between the two states. By a rapid movement Ambar reached the Bijapur capital, burnt the new capital of Nauraspur built by Ibrahim Adil Shah, and forced him to flee for shelter to the fort. This might be regarded the climax of Ambar's power.

Although Ambar showed remarkable military skill, energy and determination, his achievements were short-lived due to his inability or unwillingness to come to terms with the Mughals. The chief significance of the rise of Ambar, however, is that it represented a clear recognition of the importance of the Marathas in Deccani affairs. The success of the Marathas under the leadership of Malik Ambar gave them confidence which enabled them to play an independent role later on.

Malik Ambar tried to improve the administration of the Nizam Shahi state by introducing Todar Mal's system of land revenue. He abolished the old system of giving land on contract (*ijara*) which was ruinous for the peasants, and adopted the *zabti* system.

After 1622, when the Deccan was in turmoil due to the rebellion of prince Khurram against Jahangir, Malik Ambar was able to recover once again many of the old territories which had been ceded to the Mughals. Jahangir's attempt at consolidating the Mughal position in the Deccan was, thus, frustrated. However, the long-range benefits to Ahmadnagar for reopening the dispute with the Mughals may be considered doubtful. It led to the situation in which Shah Jahan decided that he had no alternative but to extinguish Ahmadnagar as an independent state. Malik Ambar breathed his last in 1626 at the ripe age of 80. But the bitter fruits of his legacy had to be reaped by his successors.

EXTINCTION OF AHMADNAGAR, AND ACCEPTANCE OF MUGHAL SUZERAINTY BY BIJAPUR AND GOLCONDA

Shah Jahan ascended the throne in 1628. Having commanded two expeditions to the Deccan as a prince and spent a considerable period in the Deccan during his rebellion against his father. Shah Jahan had a great deal of experience and personal knowledge of the Deccan and its politics.

Shah Jahan's first concern as a ruler was to recover the territories in the Deccan which had been lost to the Nizam Shahi ruler. For the purpose, he deputed an old and experienced noble, Khan-i-Jahan Lodi. However, Khan-i-Jahan Lodi failed in the enterprise, and was recalled to the court. Shortly afterwards, he rebelled and joined the Nizam Shah who deputed him to expel the Mughals from the remaining portions of Berar and Balaghat. Giving asylum to a leading Mughal noble in this manner was a challenge which Shah Jahan could not ignore. It was clear that even after Malik Ambar's death, his policy of refusing to recognise the Mughal position in Berar and Balaghat was being continued by the Nizam Shahi ruler. Shah Jahan, therefore, came to the conclusion that there could be no peace for the Mughals in the Deccan as long as Ahmadnagar continued as an independent state. This was a major departure from the policy which had been followed by Akbar and Jahangir. However, Shah Jahan was not keen to extend Mughal territories in the Deccan beyond what was absolutely necessary. He, therefore, wrote to the Bijapur ruler offering to cede to him roughly one-third of the Ahmadnagar state if he would cooperate with the Mughals in the projected campaign against Ahmadnagar. This was a shrewd move on the part of Shah

Jahan to isolate Ahmadnagar diplomatically and militarily. He also sent feelers to the various Maratha sardars to join Mughal service.

At first, Shah Jahan was successful in his overtures. Malik Ambar had defeated and killed some prominent Bijapuri nobles during his campaigns. The Adil Shah also was smarting at the humiliation of the burning of Nauraspur and the annexation of Sholapur by Malik Ambar. He, therefore, accepted Shah Jahan's proposal, and posted an army at the Nizam Shahi border to cooperate with the Mughals. Around this time, Jadhav Rao, a prominent Maratha noble who had defected to the side of the Mughals during the reign of Jahangir but had gone back to the service of the Nizam Shah, was treacherously murdered on a charge of conspiring with the Mughals. As a result Shahji Bhonsale, who was his son-in-law (and the father of Shivaji), defected to the Mughal side along with his relations. Shah Jahan accorded him a *mansab* of 5000, and gave him *jagirs* in the Poona reg on. A number of other prominent Maratha sardars also joined Shah Jahan.

In 1629, Shah Jahan deputed large armies against Ahmadnagar, one of them to operate in the west in the Balaghat region, and other in the east in the Telengana region. The emperor himself moved to Burhanpur to coordinate their movements. Under relentless pressure, large parts of the Ahmadnagar state were brought under Mughal occupation. Parenda, one of the last outposts of the kingdom, was besieged. The Nizam Shah now sent a piteous appeal to the Adil Shah, stating that most of the kingdom was under Mughal occupation, and if Parenda fell it would mean the end of the Nizam Shahi dynasty, after which, he warned, would come the turn of Bijapur. A strong group at the Bijapur court had been uneasy at the steady Mughal advance in Ahmadnagar. In fact, the Bijapuri forces at the border had merely watched the situation, taking no active part in the Mughal operations. The Mughals, on their part, had refused to hand over to the Adil Shah the areas allotted to him under the agreement. As a result, the Adil Shah made a somersault and decided to help the Nizam Shah who agreed to return Sholapur to him. This turn in the political situation compelled the Mughals to raise the siege of Parenda, and to retreat. However, the internal situation in Ahmadnagar now turned in favour of the Mughals. Fath Khan, the son of Malik Ambar, had recently been appointed Peshwa by the Nizam Shah in the hope that he would be able to induce Shah Jahan to make peace. Instead, Fath Khan opened secret negotiations with Shah Jahan and, at his instance, murdered the Nizam Shah and put a puppet on the throne. He also read the *khutba*, and struck the *sikka* in the name of the Mughal emperor. As a reward, Fath Khan was taken in Mughal service, and the *jagir* around Poona previously allotted to Shahji was transferred to him. As a result, Shahji defected from the Mughal side. These events took place in 1632.

After the surrender of Fath Khan, Shah Jahan appointed Mahabat Khan as Mughal viceroy of the Deccan and returned to Agra. Mahabat Khan, faced with the combined opposition of Bijapur and the local Nizam Shahi nobles including Shahji, found himself in a very difficult situation. Parenda surrendered to Bijapur. Bijapur made a strong bid for the fort of Daulatabad as well, offering a large sum of money to Fath Khan for surrendering the fort. Elsewhere also, the Mughals found it difficult to hold on to their positions.

It will thus be seen that the Mughals and Bijapur were, in reality, engaged in a contest for dividing between themselves the prostrate body of Ahmadnagar. The Adil Shah sent a large army under Randaula Khan and Murari Pandit for the surrender of Daulatabad and for provisioning its garrison. Shahji also was enrolled in Bijapur's service to harass the Mughals and cut off their supplies. But the combined operations of the Bijapuri forces and Shahji were of no avail. Mahabat Khan closely invested Daulatabad, and forced the garrison to surrender (1633). The Nizam Shah was sent to prison in Gwaliyar. This marked the end of the Nizam Shahi dynasty.

However, even this did not solve the problems facing the Mughals. Following the example of Malik Ambar, Shahji found a Nizam Shahi prince, and raised him as a ruler. The Adil Shah sent a force of seven to eight thousand horsemen to aid Shahji, and induced many of the Nizam Shahi nobles to surrender their forts to Shahji. Many disbanded Nizam Shahi soldiers joined Shahji whose force swelled to 20,000 horses. With these he harassed the Mughals and took control of large portions of the Ahmadnagar state.

Shah Jahan now decided to give personal attention to the problems of the Deccan. He realised that the crux of the situation was the

attitude of Bijapur. He, therefore, deputed a large army to invade
Bijapur, and also sent feelers to the Adil Shah, offering to revive the
earlier accord of dividing the territory of Ahmadnagar between
Bijapur and the Mughals.

The policy of the stick and the carrot, and the advance of Shah
Jahan to the Deccan brought about another change in Bijapur politics.
The leaders of the anti-Mughal group including Murari Pandit were
displaced and killed, and a new treaty or *ahdnama* was entered into
with Shah Jahan. According to this treaty, the Adil Shah agreed to
recognise Mughal suzerainty, to pay an indemnity of twenty lakhs of
rupees, and not to interfere in the affairs of Golconda which was
brought under Mughal protection. Any quarrel between Bijapur and
Golconda was, in the future, to be referred to the Mughal emperor
for his arbitration. The Adil Shah agreed to cooperate with the
Mughals in reducing Shahji to submission and, if he agreed to join
Bijapuri service, to depute him in the south, away from the Mughal
frontier. In return for these, territory worth about 20 lakh *huns* (about
eighty lakh rupees) annually belonging to Ahmadnagar was ceded
to Bijapur. Shah Jahan also sent to Adil Shah a solemn *farman*
impressed with the mark of the emperor's palm that the terms of this
treaty would never be violated.

Shah Jahan completed the settlement of the Deccan by entering
into a treaty with Golconda as well. The ruler agreed to include the
name of Shah Jahan in the *khutba* and to exclude the name of the
Iranian emperor from it. The Qutb Shah was to be loyal to the
emperor. The annual tribute of four lakh *huns* which Golconda was
previously paying to Bijapur was remitted. Instead, it was required
to pay two lakh *huns* annually to the Mughal emperor in return for
his protection.

The treaties of 1636 with Bijapur and Golconda were
statesmanlike. In effect, they enabled Shah Jahan to realise the
ultimate objectives of Akbar. The suzerainty of the Mughal emperor
was now accepted over the length and breadth of the country. Peace
with the Mughals enabled the Deccani states to expand their
territories towards the south.

In the decade following the treaties of 1636, Bijapur and Golconda
overran the rich and fertile Karnataka area from the river Krishna to

Tanjore and beyond. This area was ruled over by a number of petty pricipalities. Many of them, such as the Nayaks of Tanjore, Jinji and Madurai, owed nominal allegiance to the Rayal, the former ruler of Vijayanagara. A series of campaigns were conducted by Bijapur and Golconda against these states. With the help of Shah Jahan, they agreed to divide the territories and the spoils gained by their armies in the proportion of 2/3 to Bijapur and 1/3 to Golconda. Despite frequent quarrels between the two, the task of conquest went ahead. Thus, in a short span of time, the territories of these two states were more than doubled and they reached the climax of their power and prosperity. If the rulers had been able to consolidate their hold over the areas they had conquered, the Deccan would have seen a long era of peace. However, rapid expansion weakened whatever internal cohesion these states had. Ambitious nobles such as Shahji, and his son Shivaji, in Bijapur, and Mir Jumla the leading noble in Golconda, started carving out spheres of influence for themselves. The Mughals, too, found that the balance of power in the Deccan had been upset and demanded a price for their benevolent neutrality during the expansionist phase of these states. These developments came to a head in 1656 following the death of Muhammad Adil Shah, and the arrival of Aurangzeb as the Mughal viceroy of the Deccan. These developments would be dealt with in a subsequent chapter.

Cultural Contribution of the Deccan States

The Deccani states had a number of cultural contributions to their credit. Ali Adil Shah (d. 1580) loved to hold discussions with Hindu and Muslim saints and was called a Sufi. He invited Catholic missionaries to his court, even before Akbar had done so. He had an excellent library to which he appointed the well-known Sanskrit scholar, Waman Pandit. Patronage of Sanskrit and Marathi was continued by his successors.

The successor of Ali Adil Shah, Ibrahim Adil Shah II (1580–1627), ascended the throne at the age of nine. He was very solicitous to the poor, and had the title of *'abla baba'*, or 'Friend of the Poor'. He was deeply interested in music, and composed a book called *Kitab-i-Nauras* in which songs were set to various musical modes or *ragas*.

He built a new capital, Nauraspur, in which a large number of musicians were invited to settle. In his songs, he freely invoked the goddess of music and learning, Saraswati. Due to his broad approach he came to be called '*Jagat Guru*'. He accorded patronage to all, including Hindu saints and temples. This included grants to Pandharpur, the centre of the worship of Vithoba, which became the centre of the Bhakti movement in Maharashtra. The broad, tolerant policy followed by Ibrahim Adil Shah II was continued under his successors.

The important role played by Maratha families in the service of the Ahmadnagar state has already been mentioned. The Qutb Shahs, too, utilised the services of both Hindus and Muslims for military, administrative and diplomatic purposes. Under Ibrahim Qutb Shah (d. 1580), Murahari Rao rose to the position of Peshwa in the kingdom, a position which was second only to that of Mir Jumla or wazir. The Nayakwaris, who formed the military-cum-landed elements, remained a power in the kingdom ever since the foundation of the dynasty. From 1672 till its absorption by the Mughals in 1687, the administrative and military affairs of the state were dominated by the brothers, Madanna and Akkanna.

Golconda was the intellectual resort of literary men. Sultan Muhammad Quli Qutb Shah, a contemporary of Akbar, was very fond of literature and architecture. The sultan was not only a great patron of art and literature but was a poet of no mean order. He wrote in Dakhini Urdu, Persian and Telugu and has left an extensive *diwan* or collection. He was the first to introduce a secular note in poetry. Apart from the praise of God and the Prophet, he wrote about nature, love, and the social life of his day. The growth of Urdu in its Dakhini form was a significant development during the period. The successors of Muhammad Quli Qutb Shah and many others poets and writers of the time adopted Urdu as a literary language. In addition to Persian, these writers drew on Hindi and Telugu for forms, idioms and themes as well as vocabulary. Urdu was patronized at the Bijapuri court also. The poet laureate Nusrati who flourished during the middle of the seventeenth century wrote a romantic tale about Prince Manohar, ruler of Kanak Nagar, and Madhu Malati. From the Deccan, Urdu came to north India in the eighteenth century.

In the field of architecture, Muhammad Quli Qutb Shah constructed many buildings, the most famous of which is the Char Minar. Completed in 1591–92, it stood at the centre of the new city of Hyderabad founded by Muhammad Quli Qutb Shah. It has four lofty arches, facing the four directions. Its chief beauty are the four minarets which are four-storeyed and are 48 metre high. The double screen of arches has fine carvings.

The rulers of Bijapur consistently maintained a high standard and an impeccable taste in architecture. The most famous Bijapuri buildings of the period are the Ibrahim Rauza and the Gol Gumbaz. The former was a mausoleum for Ibrahim Adil Shah and shows the style at its best. The Gol Gumbaz which was built in 1660 has the largest single dome ever constructed. All its proportions are harmonious, the large dome being balanced by tall, tapering minarets at the corner. It is said that a whisper at one side of the huge main room can be heard clearly at the other end. Painting also flourished in the Deccan, and reached a high state during the reign of Ibrahim Adil Shah (1580–1627).

It will thus be seen that the Deccani states were able to overcome the phase of sectarian violence during the sixteenth century, and maintain fine standards of communal harmony, and also contributed in the fields of music, literature, architecture and painting.

FIFTEEN

India in the First Half of the Seventeenth Century

POLITICAL AND ADMINISTRATIVE DEVELOPMENTS IN INDIA

The first half of the seventeenth century in India was, on the whole, an era of progress and growth. During the period, the Mughal empire was ruled by two capable rulers, Jahangir (1605–27), and Shah Jahan (1628–1658). In southern India, too, as we have seen, the states of Bijapur and Golconda were able to provide conditions of internal peace and cultural growth. The Mughal rulers consolidated the administrative system which had developed under Akbar. They maintained the alliance with the Rajputs, and tried to further broaden the political base of the empire by allying with powerful sections such as the Afghans and the Marathas. They embellished their capitals with beautiful buildings, many of them in marble, and tried to make the Mughal court the centre of the cultural life in the country. The Mughals played a positive role in stabilising India's relations with neighbouring Asian powers such as Iran, the Uzbeks, and the Ottoman Turks, thereby opening up greater avenues for India's foreign trade. Trade concessions given to various European trading companies were also aimed at promoting India's foreign trade. But a number of negative features came to the surface during the period. The growing prosperity of the ruling classes did not filter down to peasants and workers whose lives remained hard and miserable. The Mughal ruling class remained oblivious of the growth of science and technology in the West. The problem of succession to the throne created instability, thus posing a threat to the political system as well as to economic and cultural growth.

Jahangir, the eldest son of Akbar, succeeded to the throne without any difficulty, his younger brothers having died during the life-time of Akbar due to excessive drinking. However, shortly after Jahangir's succession, his eldest son, Khusrau, broke out into rebellion. Tussle between father and son for the throne was not unusual in those time. Jahangir himself had rebelled against his father, and kept the empire disturbed for some time. However, Khusrau's rebellion proved to be short-lived. Jahangir defeated him at a battle near Lahore and soon afterwards he was captured and imprisoned.

We have already seen how Jahangir brought to an end the conflict with Mewar which had continued for four decades, and the struggle in the Deccan with Malik Ambar who was not prepared to accept the settlement made by Akbar. There was conflict in the east, too. Although Akbar had broken the back of the power of the Afghans in this region, Afghan chiefs were still powerful in various parts of east Bengal. They had the support of many Hindu rajas of the region, such as the rajas of Jessore, Kamrup (western Assam), Cachar, etc. Towards the end of his reign, Akbar had recalled Raja Man Singh, the governor of Bengal, to the court, and during his absence the Afghan chief, Usman Khan, and others found an opportunity to raise a rebellion. Jahangir sent back Man Singh for some time but the situation continued to worsen. In 1608, Jahangir posted to Bengal, Islam Khan, the grandson of Shaikh Salim Chishti, the famous Sufi saint who was the patron saint of the Mughals. Though young in years, Islam Khan handled the situation with great energy and foresight. He won over many of the zamindars including the Raja of Jessore to his side, and fixed his headquarters at Dacca, which was strategically located, to deal with the rebels. To keep the area under full control, soon the provincial capital was transferred from Rajmahal to Dacca which began to develop rapidly. Islam Khan first directed his efforts to the conquest of Sonargaon which was under the control of Musa Khan and his confederates who were called the *Barah* (twelve) *Bhuiyan*. After three years of campaigning, Sonargaon was captured. Soon afterwards, Musa Khan surrendered and he was sent to the court as a prisoner. Usman Khan's turn came next, and he was defeated in a fierce battle. The back of the Afghan resistance was now broken and the other rebels soon surrendered. The principalities of Jessore and Kamrup were annexed. Thus Mughal power was firmly entrenched in east Bengal.

Like Akbar, Jahangir realised that conquest would be lasting on the basis not of force but of securing the goodwill of the people. He, therefore, treated the defeated Afghan chiefs and their followers with consideration and sympathy. After some time, many of the princes and zamindars of Bengal detained at the court were released and allowed to return to Bengal. Even Musa Khan was released and his estates restored. Thus after a long spell, peace and prosperity returned to Bengal. To cap the process, more Afghans now began to be inducted into the Mughal nobility. The leading Afghan noble under Jahangir was Khan-i-Jahan Lodi who rendered distinguished service in the Deccan.

By 1622, Jahangir had brought Malik Ambar to heel, patched up the long drawn out tussle with Mewar, and pacified Bengal. Jahangir was still fairly young (51), and a long era of peace seemed to be ahead. But the situation was changed radically by two developments—the Persian conquest of Qandhar which was a blow to Mughal prestige, and the growing failure of Jahangir's health which unleashed the latent struggle for succession among the princes, and led to jockeying for power by the nobles. These developments pitch-forked Nur Jahan into the political arena.

NUR JAHAN

The story of Nur Jahan's life, her first marriage with an Iranian, Sher Afghan, and his death in a clash with the Mughal governor of Bengal, Nur Jahan's stay in Agra with an elderly relation of Jahangir, and her marriage with Jahangir four years later (1611) are too well known to be repeated in detail here. Sober historians do not believe that Jahangir was responsible for the death of her first husband. Jahangir's chance meeting with her in the Meena Bazar and marrying her was not so unusual. Her family was a respectable one, and her father, Itimaduddaula, had been made joint *diwan* by Jahangir in the first year of his reign. After a brief eclipse due to the involvement of one of his sons with Khusrau's rebellion, he had been restored to his position. Having been tested in this office, and following Nur Jahan's marriage with Jahangir, he was raised to the office of the chief *diwan*. Other members of the family also benefited from this alliance, their *mansabs* being augmented. Itimaduddaula proved to be able, competent and loyal, and wielded considerable influence in the affairs of the state till his death ten years later. Nur Jahan's brother, Asaf Khan, was also a learned and able man. He was appointed the *khan-i-saman*, a post reserved for nobles in whom the emperor had full confidence. He married his daughter to Khurram (Shah Jahan) who was his father's favourite following the rebellion and imprisonment of Khusrau.

Some modern historians are of the opinion that along with her father and brother, and in alliance with Khurram, Nur Jahan formed a group or 'junta' which 'managed' Jahangir so that without its backing and support no one could advance in his career, and that this led to the division of the court into two factions—the Nur Jahan, 'junta' and its opponents. It is further argued that Nur Jahan's political ambitions ultimately resulted in a breach between her and Shah Jahan, and that this drove Shah Jahan into rebellion against his father in 1622, since he felt that Jahangir was completely under Nur Jahan's influence. However, some other historians do not agree with this view. They point out that till 1622 when Jahangir's health broke down, all the important political decisions were taken by Jahangir himself as is clear from his autobiography. The precise political role of Nur Jahan during this period is not clear. Coins were issued in her name, and she was given the title of Badshah Begum. Important nobles used to call on her to apprise her of events, and to secure her intervention with the emperor. She dominated the royal household and set new fashions based on Persian traditions. On account of her position, Persian art and culture acquired great prestige at the court. Nur Jahan was the constant companion of Jahangir, and even joined him in his hunting expeditions since she was a good rider and a sure shot. As such, she could influence Jahangir, and many people approached her to intercede with the king on their behalf. Under Mughal rule, no woman had reached such an important position earlier. But Jahangir was not dependent on the 'junta' or on Nur Jahan, as is also borne out by the fact that nobles who were not favourites of the 'junta' continued to get their normal promotions. The rise of Shah Jahan was due to his personal qualities and achievements rather than the backing of Nur Jahan. Shah Jahan had his own ambitions of which Jahangir was not unaware. In any case, in those times, no ruler could afford to allow a noble or a prince to become too powerful lest he challenge his authority. This was the basic reason for the conflict between Jahangir and Shah Jahan.

SHAH JAHAN'S REBELLION

The immediate cause of the rebellion was Shah Jahan's refusal to proceed to Qandhar which had been besieged by the Persians. Shah Jahan was afraid that the campaign would be a long and difficult one and that intrigues would be hatched against him during his absence from the court. Hence, he put forward a number of demands such as full command of the army which included the veterans of the Deccan, complete sway over the Punjab, control over a number of important forts, etc. Jahangir was enraged by this attitude. Convinced that the prince was meditating rebellion, he wrote harsh letters, and took punitive steps which only made the situation worse, and resulted in an open breach. From Mandu, where he was stationed, Shah Jahan made a sudden dash on Agra in order to capture the treasures lodged there. Shah Jahan had the full backing of the Deccan army and all the nobles posted there. Gujarat and Malwa had declared for him, and he had the support of his father-in-law, Asaf Khan, and a number of important nobles at the court. However, in the battle near Delhi, Shah Jahan was defeated by the forces led by Mahabat Khan. He was saved from complete defeat by the valiant stand of the Mewar contingent. Another army was sent to wrest Gujarat from Shah Jahan. Shah Jahan was hounded out of the Mughal territories and compelled to take shelter with his erstwhile enemies, the Deccani rulers. However, he crossed the Deccan into Orissa, took the governor by surprise, and soon Bengal and Bihar were under his control. Mahabat Khan was again pressed into service. He took energetic steps, and compelled Shah Jahan to retreat in to the Deccan again. This time, he made an alliance with Malik Ambar who was once again at war with the Mughals. However, soon Shah Jahan wrote abject letters of apology to Jahangir. Jahangir also felt that it was time to pardon and conciliate his ablest and most energetic son. As part of the agreement, two of Shah Jahan's sons, Dara and Aurangzeb, were sent to the court as hostages, and a tract in the Deccan was assigned for Shah Jahan's expenses. This was in 1626.

MAHABAT KHAN

Shah Jahan's rebellion kept the empire distracted for four years, resulted in the loss of Qandhar, and emboldened the Deccanis to recover all the territories surrendered to the Mughals during Akbar's time and in subsequent campaigns. It also pointed to a basic weakness of the system—a successful prince tended to become a rival focus of power, particularly when it was felt that the monarch was not able or willing to wield the supreme power himself. Shah Jahan's constant charge was that following Jahangir's failing health, all effective power had slipped into the hands of Nur Jahan Begum—a charge which is difficult to accept since Shah Jahan's father-in-law, Asaf Khan, was the imperial *diwan*. Also, though in poor health, Jahangir was still mentally alert and no decisions could be taken without his concurrence. Jahangir's illness created the further danger that an ambitious noble might try to use the situation to gather supreme power in his hands. An unexpected episode brought this to the fore. Mahabat Khan who had played a leading role in dealing with Shah Jahan's rebellion, had been feeling disgruntled because certain elements at the court were eager to clip his wings following the end of the prince's rebellion. Summoned to the court to render accounts, Mahabat Khan came with a trusted body of Rajputs and seized the emperor at an opportune moment when the royal camp was crossing the river Jhelum on its way to Kabul. Nur Jahan, who had not been apprehended, escaped across the river but an assault against Mahabat Khan failed. Nur Jahan now tried other ways. She surrendered herself to Mahabat Khan in order to be close to Jahangir. Within six months, taking advantage of the mistakes committed by Mahabat Khan, who was a soldier but not a diplomat or an administrator, and due to the growing unpopularity of his Rajput soldiers, Nur Jahan was able to wean away most of the nobles from Mahabat Khan's side. Realising his precarious position, Mahabat Khan abandoned Jahangir and fled from the court. Some time later, he joined Shah Jahan in the Deccan where he was biding his time.

The defeat of Mahabat Khan was the greatest victory attained by Nur Jahan, and it was due, in no small measure, to her cool courage and sagacity. However, Nur Jahan's triumph was shortlived, for in less than a year's time, Jahangir breathed his last, not far from Lahore (1627). The wily and shrewd Asaf Khan who had been appointed *wakil* by Jahangir, and who had been carefully preparing the ground for the succession of his son-in-law, Shah Jahan, now came into the open. Supported by the *diwan*, the chief nobles and the army, he made Nur Jahan a virtual prisoner, and sent urgent summons to Shah Jahan. Shah Jahan reached Agra and was enthroned amidst great rejoicing. Earlier, at his instance, all his rivals including his imprisoned brother, cousins, etc., were done to death. This precedent and the earlier precedent of a son rebelling against his father, which was begun by Jahangir and was followed by Shah Jahan, was to lead to bitter consequences for the Mughal dynasty. Shah Jahan himself was to reap the bitter seeds he had sown. As for Nur Jahan, after attaining the throne, Shah Jahan fixed a settlement upon her. She lived a retired life till her death 18 years later, and was buried at Lahore.

Shah Jahan's reign (1628–58) was full of many-sided activities. We have already studied his Deccan policy. We shall now turn to the foreign policy of the Mughals which reached a high watermark under Shah Jahan.

Foreign Policy of the Mughals

We have seen how following the break up of the Timurid empire in the second half of the fifteenth century, three powerful empires—the Uzbek, the Safavid and the Ottoman—established themselves in Trans-Oxiana (Central Asia), Iran, and Turkey. The Uzbeks were the natural enemies of the Mughals, having been responsible for the expulsion of Babur and the other Timurid princes from Samarqand and the adjoining area, including Khurasan. At the same time, the Uzbeks clashed with the rising power of the Safavids who claimed Khurasan. The Khurasanian plateau linked Iran with Central Asia, and the trade routes to China and India passed across it. It was natural for the Safavids and the Mughals to ally against the Uzbek danger, especially as there were no frontier disputes between them with the exception of Qandhar. The Uzbeks tried to exploit the sectarian differences with the Safavid rulers of Iran who had ruthlessly persecuted the Sunnis. Both the Uzbek and the Mughal rulers were Sunnis. But the Mughals were too broadminded to be swayed by sectarian differences. Annoyed at the alliance of the Mughals with a Shia power viz., Iran, the Uzbeks occasionally stirred up the fanatic Afghan and Baluchi tribesmen living in the northwest frontier tracts between Peshawar and Kabul against the Mughals.

The most powerful empire in West Asia at the time was that of the Ottoman Turks. The Ottoman or the Usmanli Turks, so called after the name of their first ruler, Usman (d. 1326), had overrun Asia Minor and eastern Europe, and also conquered Syria, Egypt and Arabia by 1529. They had received the title 'Sultan of Rum' from the shadowy caliph living at Cairo. Later, they also assumed the title of *Padshah-i-Islam*.

The rise of a Shiite power in Iran made the Ottoman Sultans conscious of the danger to their eastern flank, and that the rise of the Safavids would encourage Shiism in their own territories. In 1514 the Turkish sultan defeated the shah of Iran in a famous battle. The Ottomans clashed with Iran for the control of Baghdad, and also for the areas in north Iran, around Erivan. They gradually extended their control on the coastal areas around Arabia and made a bid to oust the Portuguese from the Persian Gulf and the Indian waters.

The Ottoman threat from the west made the Persians keen to befriend the Mughals, particularly when they had to face an aggressive Uzbek power in the east. The Mughals refused the Uzbek proposals for a tripartite Ottoman-Mughal-Uzbek alliance against the Persians as it would have upset the Asian balance of power and left them alone to face the might of the Uzbeks. Alliance with Iran was also helpful in promoting trade with Central Asia. If the Mughals had a stronger navy, they might, perhaps, have sought a closer alliance with Turkey which was also a naval power and was engaged in a struggle against the navies of the European powers in the Mediterranean. As it was, the Mughals were chary of a closer relationship with Turkey since they were not prepared to countenance the claim to superiority made by the Turkish sultan as successor to the caliph. These were some of the factors which shaped the foreign policy of the Mughals.

Akbar and the Uzbeks

In 1510, following the defeat of the Uzbek chief, Shaibani Khan, by the Safavids, Babur had briefly regained Samarqand. Although Babur had to leave the city after the Uzbeks had inflicted a sharp defeat on the Persians, the help extended to him by the Persian monarch established a tradition of friendship between the Mughals and the Safavids. Later, Humayun too, received help from the Safavid monarch, Shah Tahmasp, when he had sought refuge at his court after being ousted from India by Sher Shah.

The territorial power of the Uzbeks grew rapidly in the 1570s under Abdullah Khan Uzbek. In 1572–73, Abdullah Khan Uzbek seized Balkh which, along with Badakhshan, had served as a kind of buffer between the Mughals and the Uzbeks. In 1577, Abdullah Khan sent an embassy to Akbar, proposing to partition Iran. After the death of Shah Tahmasp (1576), Iran was passing through a phase of anarchy and disorder. Abdullah Uzbek urged that Akbar 'should lead an expedition from India to Iran in order that they may, with united efforts, release Iraq, Khurasan and Fars from the innovators (Shias)'. Akbar was not moved by this appeal to sectarian narrowness. A strong Iran was essential to keep the restless Uzbeks in their place. At the same time, Akbar had no desire to get embroiled with the Uzbeks, unless they directly threatened Kabul or the Indian possessions. This was the key to Akbar's foreign policy. Abdullah Uzbek also approached the Ottoman sultan and proposed a tripartite alliance of Sunni powers against Iran. As if in reply to this, Akbar sent a return embassy to Abdullah Uzbek in which it was pointed out that differences in law and religion could not be regarded as sufficient ground for conquest. Regarding difficulties faced by pilgrims to Mecca, he pointed out that with the conquest of Gujarat, a new route had been opened for *haj* pilgrims. He also emphasised the old friendship with Iran, and admonished Abdullah Khan Uzbek for making insulting references to the Safavids.

Akbar's growing interest in Central Asian affairs was reflected in his giving refuge at his court to the Timurid prince, Mirza Sulaiman, who had been ousted from Badakhshan by his grandson. Abdul Fazl says that the Khyber Pass was made fit for wheeled traffic, and that due to fear of the Mughals, the gates of Balkh were usually kept closed. In order to forestall invasion of Badakhshan, Abdullah Uzbek fomented trouble among the tribesmen of the northwest frontier through his agent, Jalal, who was a religious fanatic. The situation became so serious that Akbar had to move to Attock. It was during these operations that Akbar lost one of his best friend, Raja Birbal in a battle in the Khyber Pass.

In 1585, Abdullah Uzbek suddenly conquered Badakhshan. Both Mirza Sulaiman and his grandson sought refuge at Akbar's court and were given suitable *mansabs*. Meanwhile, with the death of his half-brother, Mirza Hakim (1585), Akbar annexed Kabul to his dominions. Thus, the Mughal and the Uzbek frontiers ran side by side.

Abdullah Khan Uzbek now sent another embassy which Akbar received while he was at Attok on the river Indus. Akbar's continued presence so near the frontier had made Abdullah Uzbek uneasy. Meanwhile, the Uzbeks succeeded in capturing from Iran most of the areas they had coveted in Khurasan.

In this situation, it appeared best to Akbar to come to terms with the Uzbek chief. Hence, he sent one of his agents to Abdullah Khan Uzbek with a letter and a verbal message. It seems that an agreement was made defining the Hindukush as the boundary between the two. It implied the Mughals giving up their interest in Badakhshan and Balkh which had been ruled by Timurid princes till 1585. But it also implied the Uzbeks not claiming Kabul and Qandhar. Though neither party gave up its claims formally, the agreement gave the Mughals a defensible frontier on the Hindukush. Akbar completed his objective of establishing a scientific defensible frontier by acquiring Qandhar in 1595. In addition to this, from 1586 Akbar stayed at Lahore in order to watch the situation. He left for Agra only after the death of Abdullah Khan Uzbek in 1598. After the death of Abdullah, the Uzbeks broke up into warring principalities, and ceased to be a threat to the Mughals for a considerable time.

Relations with Iran and the Question of Qandhar

The dread of Uzbek power was the most potent factor which brought the Safavids and the Mughals together, despite the Uzbek attempt to raise anti-Shia sentiments against Iran, and the Mughal dislike of the intolerant policies adopted by the Safavid rulers. The only trouble spot between the two was Qandhar the possession of which was claimed by both on strategic and economic grounds, as well as on considerations of sentiment and prestige. Qandhar had been a part of the Timurid empire and had been ruled over by Babur's cousins, the rulers of Herat, till they were ousted by the Uzbeks in 1507.

Strategically, Qandhar was vital for the defence of Kabul. The fort of Qandhar was considered to be one of the strongest forts in the region, and was well provided with water. Situated at the junction of roads leading to Kabul and Herat, Qandhar dominated the whole southern Afghanistan, and occupied a position of immense strategic importance. A modern commentator has observed, 'The Kabul-Ghazni-Qandhar line represented a strategic and logical frontier; beyond Kabul and Khyber, there was no natural line of defence. Moreover, the possession of Qandhar made it easier to control the Afghan and Baluch tribes.'

After the conquest of Sindh and Baluchistan by Akbar, the strategic and economic importance of Qandhar for the Mughals increased. Qandhar was a rich and fertile province and was the hub of the movement of men and goods between India and Central Asia. The trade from Central Asia to Multan via Qandhar, and thence down the river Indus to the sea steadily gained in importance, because the roads across Iran were frequently disturbed due to wars and internal commotions. Akbar wanted to promote trade on this route, and pointed out to Abdullah Uzbek that it was an alternative route for pilgrims and the goods traffic to Mecca. Taking all these factors into account, it would appear that Qandhar was not as important to the Persians as to the Mughals. For Iran, Qandhar was 'more of an outpost, an important one no doubt, rather than a vital bastion in a defence system.'

In the early phase, however, the dispute over Qandhar was not allowed to affect good relations between the two countries. Qandhar came under Babur's control in 1522 when the Uzbeks were threatening Khurasan once again.

Shah Tahmasp captured Qandhar taking advantage of the confusion following Humayun's death. Akbar made no effort to regain it till the Uzbeks under Abdullah Uzbek posed a renewed threat to Iran and to the Mughals. The Mughal conquest of Qandhar (1595) was not a part of an agreement between Akbar and the Uzbeks to partition the Persian empire as some modern historians have argued. It was more to establish a viable defensive line in the northwest against possible Uzbek invasion, since Khurasan had passed under Uzbek control by that time, and Qandhar was cut off from Persia.

Relations between Iran and the Mughals continued to be cordial, despite the Mughal conquest of Qandhar. Shah Abbas I (ruled 1588–1629), who was perhaps the greatest of the Safavid rulers, was keen to maintain good relations with the Mughals. There was a regular exchange of embassies and costly gifts, including rarities, between him and Jahangir. Shah Abbas also established close diplomatic and commercial relations with the Deccani states but this was not objected to by Jahangir. Neither side felt threatened, and there is an imaginary portrait by a court artist showing Jahangir and Shah Abbas embracing each other, with a globe of the world beneath their feet. Culturally, too, the two countries came even closer to each other during the period with the active help of Nur Jahan. But the alliance proved to be more useful to Shah Abbas than to Jahangir, for it led the latter to neglect cultivating friendship with the Uzbek chiefs, as he felt secure in the friendship of his 'brother', Shah Abbas. In 1620, Shah Abbas sent a polite request for the restoration of Qandhar, and made preparations for attacking it. Jahangir was taken by surprise, for he was diplomatically isolated and militarily unprepared. Hasty preparations for the relief of Qandhar were undertaken, but prince Shah Jahan put forward impossible demands before he would march. As a result, Qandhar passed into the hands of the Persians (1622). Although Shah Abbas tried to erase the bitterness over the loss of Qandhar by sending a lavish embassy to Jahangir, and offered facile explanations which were accepted by Jahangir formally, the cordiality which had marked the Mughal relations with Iran came to an end.

After the death of Shah Abbas (1629), there were disturbances in Iran. Taking advantage of this, and after being free of Deccan affairs, Shah Jahan induced Ali Mardan Khan, the Persian governor of Qandhar, to defect to the side of the Mughals (1638).

SHAH JAHAN'S BALKH CAMPAIGN

But the conquest of Qandhar was only the means to an end. Shah Jahan was more concerned with the serious danger of recurrent Uzbek attacks on Kabul, and their intrigues with the Baluch and Afghan tribes. At the time, both Bokhara and Balkh had come under the control of Nazr Muhammad. Nazr Muhammad and his son, Abdul Aziz, were ambitious and had launched a series of attacks with the help of Afghan tribesmen for gaining control of Kabul and Ghazni. However, soon afterwards Abdul Aziz headed a rebellion against his father, and only Balkh remained under the control of Nazr Muhammad who appealed to Shah Jahan for help. Secure from the side of the Persians, Shah Jahan accepted the appeal with alacrity. He moved from Lahore to Kabul, and deputed a large army under prince Murad to help Nazr Muhammad. The army which consisted of 50,000 horses and 10,000 footmen including musketeers, rocketeers and gunners, and a contingent of Rajputs, left Kabul in the middle of 1646. Shah Jahan had carefully instructed prince Murad to treat Nazr Muhammad with great consideration and to restore Balkh to him if he behaved with modesty and submission. Further, if Nazr Muhammad expressed a desire to regain Samarqand and Bokhara, the prince was to do everything to help him. Obviously, Shah Jahan wanted a friendly ruler at Bokhara who looked to the Mughals for help and support. But Murad's impetuosity ruined the plan. He marched on Balkh without waiting for instructions from Nazr Muhammad, and ordered his men to enter the fort of Balkh in which Nazr Muhammad was residing. Uncertain of the prince's intentions, Nazr Muhammad fled. The Mughals were forced to occupy Balkh, and hold it in the face of a sullen and hostile population. Nor was an alternative to Nazr Muhammad easily available. Abdul Aziz, son of Nazr Muhammad, raised the Uzbek tribes against the Mughals in Trans-Oxiana, and mustered an army of 1,20,000 men across the river

Oxus. Meanwhile, prince Murad, who had been pining for home, was replaced by prince Aurangzeb. The Mughals made no effort to defend the Oxus, since it was easily fordable. Instead, they placed pickets at strategic places, and kept the main force together so that it could march easily to any threatened point. Abdul Aziz crossed the Oxus, but in a running battle, the Mughals routed the Uzbeks outside the gates of Balkh (1647).

The victory of the Mughals at Balkh paved the way for negotiations with the Uzbeks. The Uzbek supporters of Abdul Aziz melted away and he now made overtures to the Mughals. Nazr Muhammad who had taken refuge in Persia also approached the Mughals for the restoration of his empire. After careful consideration, Shah Jahan decided in favour of Nazr Muhammad. But Nazr Muhammad was first asked to make an apology and humble submission to prince Aurangzeb. This was a mistake since the proud Uzbek ruler was unlikely to demean himself in this way, particularly when he knew that it was impossible for the Mughals to hold on to Balkh for any length of time. After waiting vainly for Nazr Muhammad to appear personally, the Mughals left Balkh in October 1647 since winter was fast approaching and there were no supplies in Balkh. The retreat nearly turned into a rout with hostile bands of Uzbeks hovering around. Though the Mughals suffered grievous losses, the firmness of Aurangzeb prevented a disaster.

The Balkh campaign of Shah Jahan has led to considerable controversy among modern historians. From the foregoing account, it should be clear that Shah Jahan was not attempting to fix the Mughal frontier on the so-called 'scientific line', the Amu Darya (the Oxus). The Amu Darya, as we have seen, was hardly a defensible line. Nor was Shah Jahan motivated by the desire to conquer Samarqand and Farghana, the Mughal 'homelands', though the Mughal emperors frequently talked about it. Shah Jahan's objective, it seems, was to secure a friendly ruler in Balkh and Badakhshan, the areas which bordered Kabul, and which had been ruled over by Timurid princes till 1585. This, he believed, would also help in controlling the disaffection of the Afghan tribes living around Ghazni and in the Khyber Pass. The campaign was a success in the military sense—the Mughals conquered Balkh, and defeated Uzbek attempts to oust them. This was the first significant victory of Indian arms in the region, and Shah Jahan had reason to celebrate it. However, it was beyond the strength of the Mughals to maintain their influence at Balkh for any length of time. Politically also, it was difficult to do so in the face of sullen Persian hostility and an unfriendly local population. All in all, while the Balkh campaign raised the prestige of Mughal arms for a time, it gained them little political advantage. Perhaps, it would have been more advantageous to the Mughals, and would have saved considerable expenditure of men and money, if Shah Jahan had firmly adhered to the Kabul-Ghazni-Qandhar line so laboriously established by Akbar. As ruler of Balkh, Nazr Muhammad remained friendly to the Mughals as long as he was alive and there was a constant exchange of envoys between the two. Thus, the Balkh expedition did prevent the rise of a united Uzbek state which would have been a danger to the Mughals at Kabul.

MUGHAL-PERSIAN RELATIONS—THE LAST PHASE

The setback in Balkh led to a revival of Uzbek hostility in the Kabul region and Afghan tribal unrest in the Khyber-Ghazni area, and emboldened the Persians to attack and conquer Qandhar (1649). This was a big blow to Shah Jahan's pride and he launched three major campaigns, one by one, under princes of blood to try and recover Qandhar. The first attack was launched by Aurangzeb, the hero of Balkh, with an army of 50,000. Though the Mughals defeated the Persians outside the fort, they could not conquer it in the face of determined Persian opposition.

A second attempt led by Aurangzeb three years later also failed. The most grandiloquent effort was made the following year (1653) under Dara, the favourite son of Shah Jahan. Dara had made many boastful claims, but he was unable to starve the fort into a surrender with the help of his large army, and an attempt at capturing it with the help of two of the biggest guns in the empire which had been towed to Qandhar was also of no avail.

The failure of the Mughals at Qandhar did not reflect the weakness of Mughal artillery, as has been asserted by some historians. It rather showed the inherent strength of Qandhar fort if held by a determined commander, and the ineffectiveness of medieval artillery against strong forts. (This was also the Mughal experience in the Deccan). It may, however, be argued that Shah Jahan's attachment to Qandhar was more sentimental than realistic. With the growing enfeeblement of both the Uzbeks and the Safavids, Qandhar no longer had the same strategic importance as it had earlier. It was not so much the loss of Qandhar as the failure of the repeated Mughal efforts which affected the Mughal prestige. But even this should not be unduly exaggerated for the Mughal empire remained at the height of its power and prestige during Aurangzeb's reign. Even the proud Ottoman sultan sent an embassy to Aurangzeb in 1680 to seek his support.

Aurangzeb decided not to continue the futile contest over Qandhar, and quietly resumed diplomatic relations with Iran. However, in 1668, Shah Abbas II, the ruler of Iran, insulted the Mughal envoy, made disparaging remarks against Aurangzeb, and even threatened an invasion. There was a flurry of Mughal activity in the Punjab and Kabul. But before any action could take place, Shah Abbas II died. His successors were non-entities, and all Persian danger to the Indian frontier disappeared till a new ruler, Nadir Shah, came to power more than fifty years later.

It will thus be seen that on the whole, the Mughals succeeded in maintaining a scientific frontier in the northwest, based on the Hindukush, with Qandhar as its outer bastion. Thus, their foreign policy was based basically on the defence of India. The defence of this frontier-line was further buttressed by diplomatic means. Friendship with Persia was its keynote, despite temporary setbacks over the question of Qandhar. The oft-proclaimed desire of recovering the Mughal homelands was really used as a diplomatic ploy, for it was never seriously pursued. The military and diplomatic means adopted by the Mughals were remarkably successful in giving India security from foreign invasions for a long time.

Secondly, the Mughals insisted on relations of equality with leading Asian nations of the time, both with the Safavids, who claimed a special position by virtue of their relationship with the Prophet, and with the Ottoman sultans who had assumed the title of *Padshah-i-Islam* and claimed to be the successors of the caliph of Baghdad.

Thirdly, the Mughals used their foreign policy to promote India's commercial interests. Kabul and Qandhar were the twin gateways of India's trade with Central Asia.

GROWTH OF ADMINISTRATION: MANSABDARI SYSTEM AND THE MUGHAL ARMY

The administrative machinery and revenue system developed by Akbar was maintained under Jahangir and Shah Jahan with minor modifications. Important changes were, however, effected in the functioning of the *mansabdari* system.

Under Akbar, for the maintenance of his contingent, the *mansabdar* was paid at the average rate of Rs 240 per annum per *sawar*. Later, in the time of Jahangir it was reduced to Rs 200 per annum. The *mansabdar* was allowed to retain 5% of the total salary bill of the *sawars* in order to meet various contingent expenses. The Mughals favoured mixed contingents, with men drawn in fixed proportions from Irani and Turani Mughals, Indian Afghans and Rajputs. This was to break the spirit of tribal or ethic exclusiveness. However, in special circumstances, a Mughal or a Rajput *mansabdar* was allowed to have a contingent drawn exclusively from Mughals or Rajputs, as we have noted.

A number of other modifications were also carried out during the period. There was a tendency to reduce *zat* salaries. Jahangir introduced a system whereby selected nobles could be allowed to maintain a large quota of troopers, without raising their *zat* rank. This was the *du-aspah sih-aspah* system (literally, trooper with 2 or 3 horses) which implied that a *mansabdar* holding this rank had to maintain and was paid for double the quota of troopers indicated by his *sawar* rank. Thus, a *mansabdar* holding a *zat* rank of 3000, and 3000 *sawars du-aspah sih-aspah* would be required to maintain 6000 troopers. Normally, no *mansabdar* was given a *sawar* rank which was higher than his *zat* rank.

A further modification, which comes to our notice during Shah Jahan's reign, was aimed at drastically reducing the number of *sawars* a noble was required to maintain. Thus, a noble was expected to maintain a quota of only one-third of his *sawar* rank, and in some circumstances, one-fourth. Thus, a noble who had the rank of 3000 *zat*, 3000 *sawar*, would maintain not more than 1000 troopers. But this would be doubled, i.e., he would maintain 2000 troopers, if his rank was 3000 *sawar du-aspah sih-aspah*.

Although the salaries of the *mansabdars* were stated in rupees, they were generally not paid in cash, but by assigning them a *jagir*. *Mansabdars* preferred a *jagir* because cash payments were likely to be delayed and sometimes entailed a lot of harassment. Also, control over land was a mark of social prestige. By devising a careful scale of gradations and laying down meticulous rules of business, the Mughals bureaucratized the nobility. But they could not take away their feudal attachment to land. This, as we shall see, was one of the dilemmas facing the Mughal nobility.

For purposes of assigning *jagirs*, the revenue department had to maintain a register indicating the assessed income (*jama*) of various areas. The account, however, was not indicated in rupees but in *dams* which was calculated at the rate of 40 *dams* to a rupee. This document was called the *jama-dami* or assessed income based on *dams*.

As the number of *mansabdars* kept growing and the financial resources of the state were strained on account of a number of reasons, even the modifications mentioned above were not found adequate. Drastic cuts in salaries all round would have created disaffection among the nobles which the rulers could ill afford. Hence, the quota of troopers and horses a noble had to maintain out of his *sawar* rank was further reduced by a new scaling device. The salaries of the *mansabdars* were put on a month-scale—10 months, 8 months, 6 months or even less than that—and their obligations for the maintenance of a quota of *sawars* were brought down accordingly. Thus, a *mansabdar* who had a rank of 3000 *zat*, 3000 *sawar* and maintained 1000 *sawars* under the rule of one-third mentioned above, would normally have had to maintain 2200 horses under the rule introduced by Akbar. But if he was put on a 10 months scale, he would maintain only 1800 horses, and for 5 months only 1000 horses. It was rare for any one to get allowances for less than 5 months or for more than 10 months.

The month-scale had little to do with decline in the income of the *jagir*. For the month-scale was applied not only to *jagirs*, but also to those who were paid in cash. During Shah Jahan's reign, the area under cultivation increased. Production of cash crops also increased. The *jama-dami* that is, the income of the *jagir*, also increased. But the increase kept pace broadly with the price rise during the period. It may be noted that most of the Marathas who were inducted into the Mughal service, were assigned *mansabs* on a 5 monthly basis or even less. In this way, while they were given a high rank in the hierarchy, the actual number of horses and effective *sawars* was much less than was indicated by their rank. The availability of remounts was, as we have seen, vital for an efficient cavalry force. The drastic reduction of remounts during Shah Jahan's reign must, therefore, have adversely affected the efficiency of the Mughal cavalry.

The *mansabdari* system of the Mughals was a complex system. Its efficient functioning depended upon a number of factors, including the proper functioning of the *dagh* (branding) system and of the *jagirdari* system If the *dagh* system worked badly, the state would be cheated. If the *jama-dami* was inflated, or the *jagirdar* was not able to get the salary due to him, he would be disaffected and he would not maintain his due contingent. On balance, the *mansabdari* system worked properly under Shah Jahan, on account of his meticulous attention to administration and selection of men including the appointment of highly competent persons as *wazirs*. Careful attention to the choice of right persons for the service, strict discipline and a definite system of promotion and rewards made the Mughal nobility a loyal and, on the whole, a highly dependable body which was able to discharge the duties of administration and to defend and expand the empire.

THE MUGHAL ARMY

The cavalry, as we have noted, was the principal arm of the Mughal army and the *mansabdars* provided the overwhelming proportion of it. In addition to the *mansabdars*, the Mughal emperors used to entertain individual troopers, called *ahadis*. The *ahadis* have been called gentlemen-troopers and received much higher salaries than other troopers. They were a highly trusted corps, being recruited directly by the emperors and having their own muster-master. An *ahadi* mustered up to five horses, though sometimes two of them shared a horse. The duties of *ahadis* were of a miscellaneous character. Most clerks of the imperial offices, the painters of the court, the foremen in the royal *karkhanas* belonged to this corps. Many were appointed as adjutants and carriers of imperial orders. In Shah Jahan's reign, they numbered 7000 and were often sent into the fighting line, where they were well distributed over the different parts of the army. Many of them worked as skilled musketeers (*baraq-andaz*) and bowmen (*tir-andaz*).

In addition to the *ahadis*, the emperors maintained a corps of royal bodyguards (*walashahis*) and armed palace guards. They were cavalrymen but served on foot in the citadel and the palace.

The footmen (*piyadgan*) formed a numerous but miscellaneous body. Many of them consisted of matchlock-bearers (*banduqchi*) and received salaries ranging between three and seven rupees a month. This was the infantry proper. But the foot soldiers also included porters, servants, news runners, swordsmen, wrestlers and slaves. The slaves, though not as numerous as during the Sultanat period, were clothed and fed by the emperor or by a prince. Sometimes a slave could become a gentleman trooper. But generally foot soldiers had a low status.

The Mughal emperors had a large stable of war elephants, and also a well-organised park of artillery. The artillery consisted of two sections—heavy guns which were used for defending or assaulting forts; these were often clumsy and difficult to move. The second was the light artillery which was highly mobile and moved with the emperor whenever he wanted. The Mughals were solicitous of improving their artillery and, at first, many Ottomans and Portuguese were employed in the artillery department. By the time of Aurangzeb, Mughal artillery had improved considerably, and foreigners found employment in the artillery department with difficulty.

The big guns were sometimes extravagantly large in size but, as a modern writer says, 'These huge guns made·more noise than they did harm; they could not be fired many times in a day, and were very liable to burst and destroy the men in charge.' However, the Frenchman, Bernier, who accompanied Shah Jahan to Lahore and Kashmir, found the light artillery, called 'artillery of the stirrup', to be extremely well appointed. He says: 'It consisted of fifty small field pieces, all of brass; each piece mounted on a well-made and handsomely painted carriage, containing two ammunition boxes, and drawn by two fine horses, with a third horse in reserve.' Artillery or swivel-guns were also mounted on elephants and camels.

It is difficult to estimate the strength of the Mughal army. It consisted, under Shah Jahan, of about 2,00,000 cavalry, excluding the men working in the districts and with *faujdars*. It rose to 2,40,000 under Aurangzeb. The infantry under Shah Jahan excluding the non-fighting people, was placed at 40,000 and may have been maintained at a similar figure under Aurangzeb.

How efficient was the Mughal army as compared to the neighbouring West and Central Asian states and the European states of the time? It is difficult to answer this question, though a number of European travellers, such as Bernier, have made adverse remarks about the efficiency of the Mughal army. A careful analysis shows that his remarks were really directed towards the Mughal infantry, which had no drill or discipline, was ill-organised and ill-led, and resembled a rabble. The development of the infantry had taken a different road in Europe. With the development of the flint-gun, the infantry became a formidable fighting force during the seventeenth century, and could even outclass the cavalry, as the Indian powers were to realise to their cost during the eighteenth century.

The success of the Mughals against the Uzbeks who could match themselves with the Persians at the time of the Balkh campaigns suggests that the Mughal army was not inferior to the Central Asian and Persian armies in an open contest. But the armies of these states were backward as compared to the Europeans, particularly in the fields of infantry and artillery. Though somewhat deficient in the field of artillery, by the time of Aurangzeb, the Mughals had apparently caught up with the Asian powers—though not with the European sea-going powers. The Mughals, including the Asian powers, except Turkey and the Sultanat of Oman, were deficient in the naval sphere, particularly in the field of sea-warfare. The army as a whole, particularly the cavalry, was closely linked with the *jagirdari* system which, in turn, was based on the feudal system of land relations prevalent in the country. Ultimately the strength and efficiency of one depended on the other.

SIXTEEN

Economic and Social Life under the Mughals

ECONOMIC AND SOCIAL CONDITIONS

The Mughal empire reached its territorial zenith by the end of the seventeenth century. During the period it had to face many political and administrative problems, some of which we have already discussed. In the economic and social spheres, the period from the advent of Akbar to the end of the seventeenth century may be treated as one since there were no fundamental changes although there were important social and economic developments which we shall try to analyse.

STANDARD OF LIVING: PATTERN OF VILLAGE LIFE AND THE MASSES

During the period, many European traders and travellers came to India, and some of them have left accounts about the social and economic conditions of the country. In general, they have emphasized the wealth and prosperity of India and the ostentatious life-style of the ruling classes, on the one hand, and on the other the grinding poverty of the ordinary people—the peasants, the artisans and the labourers. Babur was struck by the scanty clothes worn by the ordinary people. He observed that 'peasants and people of low standing go about naked.' He then goes on to describe the *langota* or decency cloth worn by men, and the *sari* worn by women. His impression has been corroborated by later European travellers. Ralph Fitch, who came to India towards the end of the sixteenth century, says that at Banaras 'the people go naked save a little cloth bound about their middle.' De Laet wrote that the labourers had insufficient clothing to keep themselves warm and cozy during winter. However, Fitch observed, 'In the winter which is our May, the men wear quilted gowns of cotton, and quilted caps.'

Similar remarks have been made about the use of footwear. Nikitin observed that the people of the Deccan went bare-footed. A modern author, Moreland, says that he did not find a shoe mentioned anywhere north of the Narmada river, except Bengal, and ascribes it to the high cost of leather.

As far as housing and furniture were concerned, little need be said. The mud houses in which the villagers lived were not different from those at present. They had hardly any furniture except cots and bamboo mats, and earthen utensils which were made by the village potter. Copper and bell-metal plates and utensils were expensive and were generally not used by the poor.

Regarding food, rice, millet and pulses (what Pelsaert and De Laet called *khicheri*) formed the staple diet, along with fish in Bengal and the coasts, and meat in the southern peninsula. In north India, *chapatis* made of wheat or coarse grains, with pulses and green vegetables were common. The ordinary people, it is said, ate their main meal in the evening, and chewed pulse or other parched grain in the day. Ghee and oil were much cheaper than foodgrains then, and seem to have been a staple part of the poor man's food. But salt and sugar were more expensive.

Thus, while people had less clothes to wear and shoes were too costly, on balance they ate better. With more grazing land, they could keep more cattle, so more milk and milk products must have been available.

The standard of living ultimately depended upon income and wages. It is difficult to determine the income of the large mass of the peasants in real terms, for money hardly entered into transactions in the villages. The village artisan were paid for their services by means of commodities which were fixed by custom. It is difficult to compute the average size of the holding of the peasant. The information available to us shows that there was a great deal of inequality in the villages. The peasant who did not have his own ploughs and bullocks often tilled the land of the zamindars or the upper castes, and could eke out a bare existence. The landless peasants and labourers often belonged to the class of people called 'untouchables' or *kamin*.

Whenever there was a famine—and famines were frequent—it was this class of peasants and the village artisans who suffered the most. The peasants who owned the land they tilled were called *khudkasht*. They paid land revenue at customary rates. Some of them had many ploughs and bullocks which they let out to their poorer brethren, the tenants or *muzarian* who generally paid land revenue at a higher rate. These two groups were the largest section among the cultivators in the village.

Thus, the village society was highly unequal. The *khudkasht* who claimed to be the original settlers of the village often belonged to a single dominant caste or castes. These castes not only dominated the village society, they exploited the other or weaker sections. In turn, they were often exploited by the zamindars.

It has been estimated that the population of India at the beginning of the seventeenth century was about 125 million. Hence, there was plenty of cultivable land available, and it may be surmised that a peasant would cultivate as much land as his means and family circumstances would allow, subject to social restraints. Unlike many other countries in Asia and Africa, India had a well diversified economy, with the cultivation of a large variety of crops such as wheat, rice, gram, barley, pulses, bajra, etc., as also crops which were used for manufacture and could be processed locally. These were cotton, indigo, *chay* (the red dye), sugarcane, oil-seeds, etc. These crops paid land revenue at a higher rate, and had to be paid for in cash. Hence, they are often called cash crops or superior crops. The peasant not only shifted his cultivation from one crop to the other depending on prices, but was also willing to adopt new crops, if he found it profitable to do so. Thus, during, the seventeenth century, two new crops were added—tobacco and maize. Silk and tusser cultivation became so widespread in Bengal during the period that there was no need to import silk from China. The adoption of potato and red chillies happened in the eighteenth century. Regarding efficiency of production, it should be noted that the countryside was able to feed a growing city population during the seventeenth century. India also exported food grains, especially rice and sugar to some of the neighbouring countries. It was also able to provide the raw materials needed for the expansion of manufactured goods during the period,

especially the manufacture of textiles. The Mughal state provided
incentives and loans (*taccavi*) to the peasants for expansion and
improvement of cultivation. But the expansion and growth would
hardly have been possible without local efforts, initiative and
investment.

Thus, the Indian cultivator was not as conservative and resistant
to change as he has often been made out to be. Although no new
agricultural techniques were introduced, Indian agriculture was, on
balance, efficient and played a definite role in the growth of the
manufacturing sector and trade during the period.

In medieval times, a peasant was not dispossessed from his land
as long as he paid the land revenue. He could also sell his land if he
could find a buyer, and if the rest of the community raised no
objections. His children inherited his land as a matter of right after
his death. The state dues were heavy, sometimes amounting to nearly
half of his produce so that the ordinary peasant was left only with
barely enough to keep body and soul together, and was in no position
to invest anything for the improvement of land or extension of
cultivation. Although the life of the peasant was hard, he had enough
to eat and to meet his simple requirements, i.e., production and
reproduction. The pattern of his life was fixed partly by the seasons
and partly by custom and tradition in which fairs, pilgrimages,
ceremonies, etc., had their due place. The condition of the landless
and a section of the artisans including the menials, must have been
much harder. However, not all peasants lived at this low level.
Resident cultivators (*khudkasht*) had generally larger lands to cultivate,
and a small section among them had large areas of land, and many
ploughs and oxen for cultivation. They could also let out a part of
their lands to the ordinary cultivators (*muzarian*) on profitable terms.
These sections and village zamindars could and did invest in the
expansion and improvement of cultivation.

As far as the cities were concerned, the largest section consisted of
the poor—the artisans, the servants and slaves, the soldiers, manual
workers, etc.

The salary of the lowest grade of a servant, according to European
travellers, was less than two rupees a month. The bulk of the workers
and foot soldiers began at less than three rupees a month. It has been

calculated that a man could feed his family on two rupees a month. Moreland, who wrote in the early part of the twentieth century, observed that during the period there was little change in the real wages of workers—they had a more balanced diet but clothes, sugar, etc., were more expensive. Moreland concluded from this that the conditions of the Indian people had not worsened under the British rule. But the matter has to be seen in a wider context. While there was a vast increase in wealth and rise in real wages in Europe during the period, there was overall stagnation, if not decline, of living standards in India under the British rule.

THE RULING CLASSES: THE NOBLES AND ZAMINDARS

The nobility, along with the landed gentry, the zamindars, formed what may be called the ruling class in medieval India. Socially and economically, the Mughal nobility formed a privileged class. Theoretically, the doors of the Mughal nobility were open to everyone. In practice, persons belonging to aristocratic families, whether they were Indians or foreigners, had a decided advantage. To begin with, the bulk of the Mughal nobles were drawn from the homeland of the Mughals— Turan and from its neighbouring areas, Tajikistan, Khurasan, Iran, etc. Although Babur was a Turk, the Mughal rulers never followed a narrow racist policy. Babur tried to win the leading Afghan nobles to his side, but they proved to be restless and untrustworthy and soon defected. The tussle between the Mughals and the Afghans continued in Bihar and Bengal even under Akbar. But from the time of Jahangir, more Afghans began to be recruited in the nobility. Indian Muslims who were called Shaikhzadas or Hindustani were also given service.

From the time of Akbar, Hindus also began to be inducted into the nobility on a regular basis. The largest section among them consisted of the Rajputs. At first, among the Rajputs, the Kachhwahas predominated. According to a modern calculation, the proportion of Hindus in the nobility under Akbar in 1594 was about 16 per cent only. But these figures do not give any adequate idea of the position and influence of the Hindus. Both Raja Man Singh and Raja Birbal were the personal friends and boon companions of Akbar, while in

the spheres of revenue administration, Raja Todar Mal had a place
of great influence and honour. The Rajputs who were recruited to
the nobility were either hereditary rajas or belonged to aristocratic
families related to or allied to the raja. Thus, their incorporation into
the nobility strengthened its aristocratic character. Despite this, the
nobility did provide an avenue of promotion and distinction to persons
drawn from the lower section of society. Thus, many *kayasthas* and
khatris were employed at various levels in the central and provincial
governments. A few of them were elevated to the position of a noble.
We even find some persons of humble origins as *mansabdars*.

The nobility attained a considerable measure of stability under
Jahangir and Shah Jahan. Both these monarchs paid careful attention
to the organization of the nobility (the *mansabdari* system). Rules
and regulations were worked out for the orderly promotions, discipline
and the recruitment of competent people into the imperial service.

The Mughal nobles, as we have seen, received salaries which were
extremely high by any standards. This, as well as the liberal policy of
the Mughal emperors in matters of faith, and the stable political
conditions in India attracted many talented persons from foreign
lands to the Mughals court. Thus, there was a brain drain in reverse.
On account of the influx into India of Iranis, Turanis and many others
in search of service at the Mughal court, a French traveller, Bernier,
has stated that the Mughal nobility consisted of 'foreigners who
enticed each other to the court'. Modern research has shown this
statement to be fallacious. While talented people continued to come
to India, and many of them rose to prominence in the service of the
Mughals, all of them settled down in India and made it their
permanent home. Thus, during medieval times as during earlier
times, India continued to provide a home to many people who came
from outside. But these immigrants rapidly assimilated themselves
into the Indian society and culture, while at the same time, retaining
some of their special traits. This accounts for the richness and diversity
which has been a special feature of Indian culture. Under Jahangir
and Shah Jahan, the bulk of the nobles already consisted of those
who had been born in India. Simultaneously, the proportion of
Afghans, Indian Muslims (Hindustanis), and Hindus in the nobility
continued to rise. A new section among the Hindus which entered

the nobility during the period were the Marathas. Jahangir was the first monarch who realised that the Marathas were 'the hub of affairs' in the Deccan, and tried to win them over to his side. The policy was continued by Shah Jahan. Among the Maratha sardars who served Shah Jahan was Shahji, the father of Shivaji, though he soon defected. Aurangzeb also gave service to many Marathas and Deccani Muslims. We shall discuss Mughal relations with the Marathas in a later section. However, it may be noted that while the Hindus formed roughly 24 per cent of the nobility under Shah Jahan, they accounted for about 33 per cent of the nobles during the second half of Aurangzeb's reign, while their total number rose by four and half times. Of the Hindus nobles, the Marathas formed more than half during Aurangzeb's reign.

Although the Mughal nobles received extremely high salaries, their expenses were also very high. Each noble maintained a large train of servants and attendants, and a large stable of horses, elephants, etc., and transport of all types. Many of them maintained a large *haram* of women, which was considered normal for a man of status in those times. The nobles aped the Mughal emperors in leading a very ostentatious life. They lived in fine houses containing gardens with fruit trees and running water. They wore the finest clothes and spent a lot on their table expenses. According to an account, 40 dishes used to be prepared for each meal for Akbar. A lot of money was spent on fruits, the choicest being imported from Samarqand and Bokhara. Ice, which was an item of luxury, was used the year round by the privileged classes. Jewels and ornaments which were worn both by men and women was another costly item. Jahangir introduced the fashion of men wearing costly jewels in their ears after piercing them. To some extent, jewellery was also meant to be a reserve to be used in an emergency. Another item of expenditure was presents to the emperor which had to be made twice a year. However, it should be remembered that the value of presents to be given was fixed according to the status of the individual. Also, the nobles received presents from the emperor in return.

Although spending, not hoarding was the dominant characteristic of the ruling class of the time, with only a few nobles remaining out of debt and bequeathing large sums of money to their children, the nobility did, directly or indirectly, contribute to the development of the economy. This took several directions. Many nobles bought land, or land was gifted to them by the emperor in places where they wanted to settle down and make it their home. In these places, they developed orchards, or built covered markets (*mandis*) which could bring them income from rent and sales. They also lent money on interest to traders, or participated in trade, often in the name of traders or in partnership with them. In a remarkable passage, Abul Fazl had advised nobles 'to invest a little in commercial speculation and engage in remunerative undertaking'. Although usury was condemned by Islamic laws, Abul Fazl told the nobles not to hesitate in investing money on interest, thus reflecting contemporary values.

It is not easy to compute the precise share of the nobility in the commercial undertakings of the period. Sometimes, some nobles, even royal princes, tried to misuse their position to engross the sale and purchase of certain commodities, or to force the artisans and traders to sell their services and commodities cheap. But such instances were not as large as to seriously affect trade, commerce and artistic production. The English factor at Surat remarked in 1614 that 'large and small are merchants'. Even members of the royal family, including princes, princesses and royal ladies, took part in freighting goods on foreign ships, and even owned ships for trade. Mir Jumla, a leading nobleman during the reign of Aurangzeb, owned a fleet of ships which carried extensive commerce with Persia, Arabia and countries of Southeast Asia. The lure for money from commerce had reached such a stage that even the chief *qazi* of Aurangzeb had substantial commercial undertakings which he tried to conceal from the emperor.

Thus, the Mughal nobility had a number of unusual features. Though often divided on ethnic lines, it formed a composite ruling class representing different regions and religions. It also tried to promote a composite culture by extending patronage to painters, musicians, poets, both of Persian and Hindawi, and to scholars. Though essentially feudal in character, since land was its main source of income, it had developed many characteristics of a bureaucracy. It was also becoming more commerce and money-minded.

Thus, the Mughal state and ruling class did not act as a barrier to the economic development of India. Whether this development could, by itself, have taken India to the capitalist path is doubtful, but we need not enter into this debate here. Our main concern is to see whether there was a continued growth of the economy during this period, and if so, the direction of development.

Rapid growth in the number of the nobility during the seventeenth century, tensions between different groups, individuals and sections, and a crisis in the working of the *jagirdari* system had an adverse effect on the discipline and proper functioning of the nobility under Aurangzeb and during the reign of his successors. Some of these aspects are dealt with in greater detail in a subsequent chapter.

ZAMINDARS AND THE RURAL GENTRY

From the writings of Abul Fazl and other contemporary authors, it is clear that personal ownership of land was very old in India. The right of ownership in land depended mainly on heredity. But new rights of ownership in land were being created all the time. The tradition was that any one who first brought land under cultivation was considered its owner. There was plenty of cultivable wasteland (*banjar*) available in medieval times. It was not difficult for an enterprising group of people to settle a new village or to bring under cultivation the wastelands belonging to a village and become the owners of these lands. In addition to owning the lands they cultivated, a considerable section of the zamindars had the hereditary right of collecting land revenue from a number of villages. This was called his *talluqa* or his *zamindari*. For collecting the land revenue, the zamindars received a share of the land revenue which could go up to 25 per cent in some areas. The zamindar was not the 'owner' of all the lands comprising his *zamindari*. The peasants who actually cultivated the land could not be dispossessed as long as they paid the land revenue. Thus, the zamindars and the peasants had their own hereditary rights in land.

Above the zamindars were the rajas who dominated larger or smaller tracts and enjoyed varied degrees of internal autonomy. These rajas are also called zamindars by the Persian writers to emphasise their subordinate status, but their position was superior to that of the zamindars who collected land revenue. Thus medieval society, including rural society, was highly segmented or hierarchical.

The zamindars, rajas and chiefs had their own armed forces, and generally lived in forts or *garhis* which was both a place of refuge and a status symbol. The combined forces of these sections, called zamindars in medieval sources, were considerable. According to the *Ain*, in Akbar's reign they had 3,84,558 *sawars*, 42,77,057 foot soldiers, 1,863 elephants, and 4,260 cannons. But the zamindars were dispersed and could never field such large forces at any time or at one place.

The zamindars generally had close connections on a caste, clan or tribal basis with the peasants settled in their *zamindaris*. They had considerable local information also about the productivity of land. The zamindars formed a very numerous and powerful class which was to be found all over the country under different names such as *deshmukh, patil, nayak*, etc. Thus, it was not easy for any central authority to ignore or alienate them.

It is difficult to say anything about the living standards of the zamindars. Compared to the nobles, their income was limited; the smaller ones may have lived more or less like the peasants. However, the living standards of the larger zamindars might have approached those of petty rajas or nobles. Most of the zamindars apparently lived in the countryside and formed a kind of loose, dispersed local gentry.

It would not be correct to look upon the zamindars merely as those who fought for control over land, and exploited the cultivators in the area they dominated. Many of the zamindars had close caste and kinship ties with the land-owning cultivating castes in their zamindari. These zamindars not only set social standard, they also provided capital and organization for settling new villages, or extending and improving cultivation.

THE MIDDLE STRATA

There has been a lot of discussion on whether during the medieval period, India had a middle class or not. The Frenchman, Bernier, said that in India there was no 'middle state', a person was either extremely rich, or lived miserably. It is, however, not possible to agree with this statement. If the word 'middle class' means traders and shop keepers, India had a large class of rich traders and merchants, some of them being amongst the richest merchants of the world at that time. These merchants also had rights based on tradition, such as protection of life and property. But they did not have the right to administer any of the towns. Such rights had been acquired in Europe by the merchants in special circumstances. Also, these rights tended to be abridged whenever strong territorial states grow up, as in France and Britain.

If by 'middle state' is meant a section whose standard of living was between the rich and the poor, such sections were large in Mughal India. They included the small *mansabdars*, petty shop-keepers and a small, but important section of master craftsmen. It also included the class of professionals—*hakims*, leading musicians and artists, historians, scholars, *qazis* and theologians, and the large class of petty officials or pen-pushers, who ran the large and growing Mughal administrative apparatus. While the petty officials were generally paid in cash, and supplemented their income by means of corruption, many of the others, especially the scholars, religious divines, etc., were granted small tracts of land for maintenance. Such grants were called *madad-i-maash* in Mughal terminology, or *sasan* in Rajasthan. In addition to the Mughal emperor, local rulers and zamindars, and even nobles made such grants. Although these grants were to be renewed by every ruler, they often became hereditary in practice. These sections often became part of the rural gentry, and a link between the village and the town. Writers, historians and theologians often belonged to the class. The 'middle strata' did not form a class: the interests of different sections being different. They were also drawn from various religious groups and castes.

ORGANIZATION OF TRADE AND COMMERCE

The Indian trading classes were large in numbers, spread out all over the country, well organized and highly professional. Some specialized in long distance, inter-regional trade, and some in local, retail trade. The former were called *seth*, *bohra* or *modi*, while the latter was called *beoparis* or *banik*. In addition to retailing goods, the *baniks* had their own agents, in the villages and townships, with whose help they purchased foodgrains and cash crops. There was a special class of traders, the *banjaras*, who specialized in carrying bulk goods. The *banjaras* used to move over long distances, sometimes with thousands of oxen carrying foodgrains, pulses, ghee, salt, etc. The more expensive goods, such as textiles, silks, etc., were laden on camels and mules, or in carts. But it was cheaper to move bulk goods through the rivers on boats. Boat traffic on waterways, and coastal trade along the seashore was more highly developed than now. The trade in food stuffs and a wide range of textile products were the most important components of inter-regional trade during the period. Bengal exported sugar and rice as well as delicate muslin and silk. The coast of Coromandel had become a centre for textile production, and had a brisk trade with Gujarat, both along the coast and across the Deccan. Gujarat was the entry point of foreign goods. It exported fine textiles and silks (*patola*) to north India, with Burhanpur and Agra as the two nodal points of trade. It received foodgrains and silk from Bengal, and also imported pepper from Malabar. North India imported luxury items and also exported indigo and foodgrains. Lahore was another centre of handicraft production. It was also the distribution centre for the luxury products of Kashmir—shawls, carpets, etc. The products of the Punjab and Sindh moved down the river Indus. It had close trade links with Kabul and Qandhar, on the one hand, and with Delhi and Agra on the other.

It will thus be seen that India's inter-regional trade was not in luxuries alone. The movement of these goods was made possible by complex networks linking wholesalers with merchants down to the regional and local levels through agents (*gumashtas*) and commission agents (*dalals*). The Dutch and English traders who came to Gujarat during the seventeenth century found the Indian traders to be active and alert. There was keen competition for inside information, and whenever there was demand for goods in one part of the country, it was rapidly made good.

Movement of goods was also facilitated by the growth of a financial system which permitted easy transmission of money from one part of the country to another. This was done through the use of *hundis*. The *hundi* was a letter of credit payable after a period of time at a discount. The *hundis* often included insurance which was charged at different rates on the basis of value of the goods, destination, means of transport (land, river or sea), etc. The *sarrafs* (*shroffs*) who specialized in changing money, also specialized in dealing with *hundis*. In the process, they also acted as private banks: they kept money in deposit from the nobles, and lent it. By means of *hundis*, they created credit which supplemented the money in circulation, since the merchant could cash his *hundi* after he had sold his goods at the point of his destination. Thus, movement of money which was always a risky enterprise could be reduced, especially when the rich traders such as Virji Vohra set up agency houses in different parts of India, and also in West Asia and Southeast Asia.

The trading community in India did not belong to one caste or religion. The Gujarati merchants included Hindus and Jains, and Muslims who were mostly Bohras. In Rajasthan, Oswals, Maheshwaris and Agarwals began to be called Marwaris. Overland trade to Central Asia was in the hands of Multanis, Afghans and Khatris. The Marwaris spread out to Maharashtra and Bengal during the eighteenth century. The Chettis on the Coromandel coast and the Muslim merchants of Malabar, both Indian and Arab, formed the most important trading communities of south India.

The trading community in India, especially in the port towns, included some of the richest merchants who are comparable in wealth and power to the merchant princes of Europe. Thus, Virji Vohra dominated the Surat trade for several decades. He owned a large fleet of ships and was reputed to be amongst the wealthiest men of his time. Abdul Ghafur Bohra left 55 lakh rupees in cash and goods and a fleet of 17 sea-going ships at the time of his death in 1718. Similarly, Malay Chetti of the Coromandel coast, Kashi Viranna and Sunca Rama Chetti were reputed to be extremely wealthy, and had extensive commercial dealings in India and abroad. There were many wealthy merchants at Agra, Delhi, Balasore (Orissa), and Bengal also. Some of these merchants, especially those living in the coastal towns, lived in an ostentatious manner and aped the manners of the nobles.

European travellers mention the commodious and well-built houses in which the wealthy merchants of Agra and Delhi lived. But the ordinary sorts lived in houses above their shops. The French traveller, Bernier, says that the merchants tried to look poor because they were afraid that they would be used like 'fill'd sponges', i.e., squeezed of their wealth. This does not appear to be fully correct. Emperors from the time of Sher Shah passed many laws for protecting the property of the merchants. The laws of Sher Shah are well known. Jahangir's ordinances included a provision that 'if anyone, whether unbeliever or Musalman should die, his property and effects should be left for his heirs, and no one should interfere with them. If he should have no heirs, they should appoint inspectors and separate guardians to guard the property, so that its value might be expended in a lawful expenditure, such as the building of mosques and sarais, repair of broken bridges and the digging of tanks and wells.' However, local officials could always abuse their power to harass traders.

Despite some harassments, the property of the merchants was generally safe. Means of transport were cheap and adequate for their needs. Despite complaints by some European travellers, safety on the roads was satisfactory, and could be covered by insurance. The means of travel with sarais at the distance of 5 *kos* on the principal highways was a good as in Europe at the time. Nevertheless, trade and the traders continued to have a low social status. The influence of the merchants on political processes is a matter of controversy. Merchants in India were not without influence in political quarters where their own interests were concerned. Thus, each community of merchants had its leader or *nagarseth* who could intercede with the local officials on their behalf. We do have instances of strikes (*hartal*) by merchants in Ahmedabad and elsewhere to stress their points of view. We have also noted the involvement of members of the Mughal royal family, and prominent nobles, such as Mir Jumla, in trade.

Thus, the Mughal ruling class was not unconcerned with business and protection of the commercial interests of the country and the trading classes, though it was not as actively involved in pushing its business interests as some European states such as Britain, France and Holland were.

Trade and commerce expanded in India during the seventeenth century due to a number of factors. An important factor was the political integration of the country under Mughal rule and establishment of conditions of law and order over extensive areas. The Mughals paid attention to roads and sarais. Taxes were levied on goods at the point of their entry into the empire. Road cesses or *rahdari* was declared illegal, though it continued to be collected by some of the local rajas. The Mughals minted silver rupees of high purity from mints scattered all over the empire. Any trader could carry silver to the royal mint, and have coins in exchange on payment of a *batta* (discount). The Mughal rupee became a standard coin in India and abroad and thus helped India's trade.

Some of the Mughal policies also helped in the commercialization of the economy, or the growth of a money economy. Salaries to the standing army as well as to many of the administrative personnel (but not to the nobles) were paid in cash. Under the *zabti* system, the land revenue was assessed and required to be paid in cash. Even when the peasant was given the option of choosing other methods of assessment, such as crop-sharing, the share of the state was, generally, sold in the villages with the help of grain dealers. It has been estimated that about 20 per cent of the rural produce was marketed, which was a high proportion. The growth of the rural grain markets led to the rise of small townships or *qasbas*. The demand for all types of luxury goods by the nobles led to the expansion of handicraft production and to the growth of towns.

Already during the sixteenth century, a number of major towns had developed in the country. According to Ralph Fitch, Agra and Fatehpur Sikri were larger than London, then one of the biggest town in Europe. Monserrate, the Jesuit priest who came to Akbar's court, says that Lahore was second to none of the cities in Europe or Asia. A recent study shows that Agra was more than doubled in size during the seventeenth century. Bernier, who wrote in the middle of the seventeenth century, says that Delhi was not less than Paris, and that Agra was bigger than Delhi. During the period, Ahmadnagar and Burhanpur in the west, Multan in the northwest, and Patna, Rajmahal and Dacca in the east grew to become big towns. Thus, Ahmedabad was as large as London and its suburbs, and Patna had a population of two lakhs—a large size by the standard of those times. These towns were not only administrative centres, but developed as centres of trade and manufacture.

The Mughal ability to collect a high share of the rural produce, which was commuted into money, and its concentration in the hands of the nobility, stimulated the demand for all kinds of luxury goods, including building materials for residential houses, sarais, *baolis*, etc. The growth of arms manufactures—guns of all types, cannons, armour, etc., and of shipping—are two primary examples of the result of direct government intervention in the matter. Both Akbar and Aurangzeb were deeply interested in the manufacture of guns of all types, including mobile guns, and took steps to improve their production. Indian steel swords were also in demand outside India. In 1651, Shah Jahan initiated a programme of building sea-going vessels, and four to six ships were built each year for voyages to West Asia. In the following year, six ships were put into commission. This was part of a ship-building programme of many wealthy merchants and nobles. In consequence Indian shipyards were soon in a position to produce ships based on European models, and freight rates to West Asia were reduced.

FOREIGN TRADE AND THE EUROPEAN TRADERS

We have already mentioned that there was a number of ports and towns from which brisk trade between India and the outer world was carried on. India not only supplied food stuffs, such as sugar, rice, etc., to many countries of Southeast and West Asia, but Indian textiles also played a very important role in the trade of the region. As an English agent observed, 'From Aden to Achin from head to foot, everyone was clothed in Indian textiles'. This statement, even though a little exaggerated (for Egypt and Ottoman Turkey also produced cotton and exported textiles), was essentially true. It was this which made India the virtual manufactory of the Asian world (excluding China). The only articles which India needed to import were certain metals, such as tin and copper, production of which was insufficient (tin was used for making bronze), certain spices for food and medicinal purposes, war horses and luxury items (such as ivory). The favourable balance of trade was met by import of gold and silver. As a result of the expansion of India's foreign trade, the import of silver and gold into India increased during the seventeenth century;

so much so that Bernier says that 'gold and silver, after circulating over every part of the world, is finally buried in India which is the sink of gold and silver.' This statement is also based on exaggeration for in those days every country tried to hold on to gold and silver. However, India and China were more successful in doing so because of the scale of their economies, and their being largely self-sufficient.

We have already mentioned the advent of the Portuguese into India towards the end of the fifteenth century. During the seventeenth century, many other European traders, specially the Dutch, the English and later the French came to India for purposes of trade. This enterprise was a direct result of the growth of the European economy consequent upon a rapid expansion in the fields of agriculture and manufactures.

The Portuguese power had begun to decline during the second half of the sixteenth century. Despite vehement Portuguese opposition, the Dutch established themselves at Masulipatam, obtaining a *farman* from the ruler of Golconda in 1606. They also established themselves in the Spice Islands (Java and Sumatra) so that by 1610 they predominated in the spice trade. The Dutch had originally come to the coast for the sake of the spice trade. But they quickly realized that spices could be obtained most easily in exchange for Indian textiles. The cloth produced on the Coromandel coast was the most acceptable in Southeast Asia, and also cheapest to carry. Hence, the Dutch spread south from Masulipatam to the Coromandel coast, obtaining Pulicat from the local ruler and making it a base of their operations.

Like the Dutch, the English also had come to the east for the spice trade, but the hostility of the Dutch who had more resources and had already established themselves in the Spice Islands forced the English to concentrate on India. After defeating a Portuguese fleet outside Surat, they were able, at last, to set up a factory there in 1612. This was confirmed in 1618 by a *farman* from Jahangir, obtained with the help of Sir Thomas Roe. The Dutch followed, and soon they too established a factory at Surat.

The English quickly realized the importance of Gujarat as a centre for India's export trade in textiles. They tried to break into India's trade with the Red Sea and the Persian Gulf ports. In 1622, with the help of the Persian forces, they captured Ormuz, the Portuguese base at the head of the Persian Gulf. (See Map B, Appendix)

Thus, by the first quarter of the seventeenth century, both the Dutch and the English were well set in the Indian trade, and Portuguese control of the sea was broken for ever. The Portuguese remained at Goa and also at Daman and Diu, but their share in India's overseas trade declined continuously.

Recent research has shown that despite their domination of the seas, the Europeans were never able to oust the Indian traders from the Asian trade. In fact, the share of the European trading companies from any part of India—Gujarat, Coromandel or Bengal, remained a fraction of India's foreign trade. The reason why the Indian traders were able to maintain themselves were several: when it came to textile trade, the Indian traders knew both the domestic and foreign markets better. Also, the Indians were willing to work at a lower profit, of 10 to 15 per cent as against 40 to 50 per cent which was considered the minimum by the Dutch to meet their overhead costs: costs of factories, war ships, etc. The English approach must have been similar. The Dutch and the English found that they could not trade in India, or even feed the people in their factories without the cooperation of the Mughal government and Indian traders. For these reasons, and to reduce their cost of operations, they started freighting the goods of Indian merchants on their ships. The Indian traders had little objection to this for it made their own operations safer. At the same time, Indian shipping grew such that from about 50 ships in the middle of the seventeenth century at Surat, many of them well built, its numbers rose to at least 112 by the end of the century. This was another index of the growth of India's foreign trade and domestic manufactures.

Apart from sharing in the Asian trade, the English and Dutch searched for articles which could be exported from India to Europe. At first, 'the prime trade', apart from pepper, was indigo which was used to colour the woollens. The indigo found most suitable was that produced at Sarkhej in Gujarat and Bayana near Agra. Soon the English developed the export of Indian textiles, called 'calicoes', to Europe. At first, the produce of Gujarat was sufficient for the purpose. As the demand grew, the English sought the cloth produced in Agra and its neighbourhood. Even this was not enough. Hence the Coromandel was developed as an alternate source of supply. By 1640, export of cloth from the Coromandel equalled that from Gujarat, and by 1660 it was three times that from Gujarat. Masulipatam and Fort St. George which later developed into Madras were the chief ports for this trade.

The Dutch joined the English in their new venture, exporting both calico and indigo from the Coromandel.

The English also explored Lahri Bandar at the mouth of the river Indus which could draw the produce of Multan and Lahore by transporting goods down the river Indus. But the trade there remained subsidiary to the Gujarat trade. More important were their efforts to develop the trade of Bengal and Orissa. The activities of the Portuguese and the Magh pirates in east Bengal made this development slow. However, by 1650, the English had set themselves up at Hoogly and at Balasore in Orissa, exporting from there raw silk and sugar in addition to textiles. Another item which was developed was the export of salt petre which supplemented the European sources for gun powder. It was also used as a ballast for ships going to Europe. The best quality salt petre was found in Bihar. Exports from the eastern areas grew rapidly, and were equal in value to the exports from the Coromandal by the end of the century.

Thus, the English and the Dutch companies opened up new markets and articles of export for India. Indian textiles became a rage in England by the last quarter of the seventeenth century. As an English observer wrote, 'Almost everything that used to be made of wood or silk, relating either to dress of the women or the furniture of our houses was supplied by the Indian trade'. As a result of agitations, in 1701, 'all calicoes painted, dyed, printed or stained' from Persia, China or the East Indies (i.e., India) were banned. But these and other laws imposing severe penalties had little effect. In place of printed cloth, the export of white Indian calicoes which had risen to 9½ lakh pieces in 1701, jumped to 20 lakhs in 1719.

Although India's trade with Europe grew rapidly during the second half of the seventeenth and the early part of the eighteenth century, intra-Asian trade still remained much more lucrative. Thus, it has been estimated, of the spices produced, only 14 per cent went to

Europe, the largest part being consumed in India and China. During the seventeenth century, India's textile exports to West Asia and East Africa also grew. A new item of trade was, coffee, produced in Yemen (Southern Arabia).

Lahore and Multan were the major centres for India's overland trade. We are told that a large colony of traders, amounting to 10,000 lived in different parts of Iran. From Iran they spread to Bokhara and Samarqand and also to South Russia. Thus, there was a large colony of Indian traders at Baku and at Astrakhan at the mouth of the river Volga, who traded upto Moscow. There were colonies of Indian traders at 'Yarkand and Khotan' (modern Sinkiang) who helped in the trade from Punjab via Kashmir and Ladakh to China. The overland trade declined only with the break up of the Safavid empire, followed by the disintegration of the Mughal empire.

The growth of India's foreign trade, the influx of gold and silver into the country, and the linking of India more closely with the rapidly expanding European markets had a number of important consequences. While the Indian economy grew, the influx of silver and gold into the country was even faster. As a result, during the first half of the seventeenth century, prices almost doubled. The effect of this price rise on different sections of society has yet to be worked out in detail. It probably weakened the old, traditional ties in the villages, and made the nobility more money-minded, greedy and demanding.

Secondly, the European nations searched for alternatives to the export of gold and silver to India. One method was to enter the Asian trade network by trying to monopolize the spice trade, and trying to capture the Indian trade in textiles. As we have seen, they had only limited success in these fields. Hence, they tried to acquire empires in India and its neighbourhood so that they could pay from the revenues of these territories for the goods exported to Europe. The Dutch were able to conquer Java and Sumatra. But the key was India. Both the English and the French competed for the conquest of India, but they could not succeed as long as India remained strong and united, first under Mughal rule and then under able provincial governors. They could only succeed when internal and external factors weakened even these states.

SEVENTEEN

Cultural and Religious Developments

There was an outburst of many-sided cultural activity in India under the Mughal rule. The traditions in the field of architecture, painting, literature and music created during this period set a norm and deeply influenced the succeeding generations. In this sense, the Mughal period can be called a second classical age following the Gupta age in northern India. In this cultural development, Indian traditions were amalgamated with the Turko-Iranian culture brought to the country by the Mughals. The Timurid court at Samarqand had developed as the cultural centre of West and Central Asia. Babur was conscious of this cultural heritage. He was critical of many of the cultural forms existing in India and was determined to set proper standards. The development of art and culture in various regions of India during the fourteenth and fifteenth centuries had led to a rich and varied development from which it was possible to draw upon. But for this, the cultural efflorescence of the Mughal age would hardly have been possible. Peoples from different areas of India, as well as peoples belonging to different faiths and races contributed to this cultural development in various ways. In this sense, the culture developed during the period was tending towards a composite national culture.

ARCHITECTURE

The Mughals built magnificent forts, palaces, gates, public buildings, mosques, *baolis* (water tank or well), etc. They also laid out many formal gardens with running water. In fact use of running water even in their palaces and pleasure resorts was a special feature of the Mughals. Babur was very fond of gardens and laid out a few in the neighbourhood of Agra and Lahore. Some of the Mughal gardens, such as the Nishat Bagh in Kashmir, the Shalimar at Lahore, the Pinjore garden in the Punjab foothills, etc., have survived to this day.

A new impetus to architecture was given by Sher Shah. His famous mausoleum at Sasaram (Bihar) and his mosque in the old fort at Delhi are considered architectural marvels. They form the climax of the pre-Mughal style of architecture, and the starting point for the new.

Akbar was the first Mughal ruler who had the time and means to undertake construction on a large scale. He built a series of forts, the most famous of which is the fort at Agra. Built in red sandstone, this massive fort had many magnificent gates. For their forts, the Mughals drew on the developed Indian tradition of fort-building, such as the ones at Gwaliyar, Jodhpur, etc. The climax of fort-building was reached at Delhi where Shah Jahan built his famous Red Fort.

In 1572, Akbar commenced a palace-cum-fort complex at Fatehpur Sikri, 36 kilometres from Agra, which he completed in eight years. Built atop a hill, along with a large artificial lake, it included many buildings in the style of Gujarat and Bengal. These included deep eaves, balconies, and fanciful kiosks. In the Panch Mahal built for taking the air, all the types of pillars used in various temples were employed to support flat roofs. The Gujarat style of architecture is used most widely in the palace built probably for his Rajput wife or wives. Buildings of a similar type were also built in the fort at Agra, though only a few of them have survived. Akbar took a close personal interest in the work of construction both at Agra and Fatehpur Sikri. Persian or Central Asian influence can be seen in the glazed blue tiles used for decoration in the walls or for tiling the roofs. But the most magnificent building was the mosque and the gateway to it called the Buland Darwaza (the lofty gate) built to commemorate Akbar's victory in Gujarat. The gate is in the style of what is called a half-dome portal. What was done was to slice a dome into half. The sliced portion provided the massive outward facade of the gate, while smaller doors could be made in the rear wall where the dome and the floor meet. This devise, borrowed from Iran, became a feature in Mughal buildings later.

With the consolidation of the empire, the Mughal architecture reached its climax. Towards the end of Jahangir's reign began the practice of putting up buildings entirely of marble and decorating the walls with floral designs made of semi-precious stones. This method of decoration, called pietra dura, became even more popular under Shah Jahan who used it on a large scale in the Taj Mahal, justly regarded as a jewel of the builder's art. The Taj Mahal brought together in a pleasing manner all the architectural forms developed by the Mughals. Humayun's tomb built at Delhi towards the beginning of Akbar's reign, and which had a massive dome of marble, may be considered a precursor of the Taj. The double dome was another feature of this building. This devise enabled a bigger dome to be built with a smaller one inside. The chief glory of the Taj is the massive dome and the four slender minarets linking the platform to the main building. The decorations are kept to a minimum, delicate marble screens, pietra dura inlay work and kiosks (*chhatris*) adding to the effect. The building gains by being placed in the midst of a formal garden.

Mosque-building also reached its climax under Shah Jahan, the two most noteworthy ones being the Moti Masjid in the Agra fort, built like the Taj entirely in marble, and the other the Jama Masjid at Delhi built in red sandstone. A lofty gate, tall, slender minarets, and a series of domes are a feature of the Jama Masjid at Delhi.

Although not many buildings were put up by Aurangzeb who was economy-minded, the Mughal architectural traditions based on a combination of Hindu and Turko-Iranian forms and decorative designs, continued without a break into the eighteenth and early nineteenth centuries. Thus, Mughal traditions influenced the palaces and forts of many provincial and local kingdoms. Even the *Harmandir* of the Sikhs, called the Golden Temple at Amritsar which was rebuilt several times during the period was built on the arch and dome principle and incorporated many features of the Mughal traditions of architecture.

Painting

The Mughals made distinctive contribution in the field of painting. They introduced new themes depicting the court, battle scenes and the chase, and added new colours and new forms. They created a living tradition of painting which continued to work in different parts of the country long after the glory of the Mughals had disappeared.

The richness of the style, again, was due to the fact that India had an old tradition of painting. The wall-paintings of Ajanta are an eloquent indication of its vigour. After the eighth century, the tradition seems to have decayed, but palm-leaf manuscripts and illustrated Jain texts from the thirteenth century onwards show that the tradition had not died.

Apart from the Jains, some of the provincial kingdoms, such as Malwa and Gujarat extended their patronage to painting during the fifteenth century. But a vigorous revival began only under Akbar. While at the court of the shah of Iran, Humayun had taken into his service two master painters who accompanied him to India. Under their leadership, during the reign of Akbar, a painting workshop was set up in one of the imperial establishments (*karkhanas*). A large number of painters, many of them from the lower castes, were drawn from different parts of the country. From the beginning, both Hindus and Muslims joined in the work. Thus, Daswant and Basawan were two of the famous painters of Akbar's court. The school developed rapidly, and soon became a celebrated centre of production. Apart from illustrating Persian books of fables, the painters were soon assigned the task of illustrating the Persian text of the *Mahabharata*, the historical work *Akbar Nama*, and others. Indian themes and Indian scenes and landscapes, thus, came in vogue and helped to free the school from Persian influence. Indian colours, such as peacock blue, the Indian red, etc., began to be used. Above all, the somewhat flat effect of the Persian style began to be replaced by the roundedness of the Indian brush, giving the pictures a three-dimensional effect.

Mughal painting reached a climax under Jahangir who had a very discriminating eye. It was a fashion in the Mughal school for the faces, bodies and feet of the people in a single picture to be painted by different artists. Jahangir claims that he could distinguish the work of each artist in a picture.

Apart from painting hunting, battle and court scenes, under Jahangir special progress was made in portrait painting and paintings of animals. Mansur was the great name in this field. Portrait painting also became fashionable.

Under Akbar, European painting was introduced at the court by the Portuguese priests. Under their influence, the principles of foreshortening, whereby near and distant people and things could be placed in perspective was quietly adopted.

While the tradition continued under Shah Jahan, Aurangzeb's lack of interest in painting led to a dispersal of the artists to different places of the country. This helped in the development of painting in the states of Rajasthan and the Punjab hills. The Mughal tradition of painting was, however, revived during the eighteenth century under the patronage of the successors of Aurangzeb.

The Rajasthan style of painting combined the themes and earlier traditions of western India or Jain school of painting with Mughal forms and styles. Thus, in addition to hunting and court scenes, it had paintings on mythological themes, such as the dalliance of Krishna with Radha, the *barah-masa* (seasons) or the *ragas* (melodies). The Pahari school continued these traditions.

LANGUAGE, LITERATURE AND MUSIC

The important role of Persian and Sanskrit as vehicles of thought and government at the all-India level, and the development of regional languages, largely as a result of the growth of the Bhakti Movement, have already been mentioned. Regional languages also developed due to the patronage extended to them by local and regional rulers.

These trends continued during the sixteenth and seventeenth centuries. By the time of Akbar, knowledge of Persian had become so widespread in north India that he dispensed with the tradition of keeping revenue records in the local language (*Hindawi*) in addition to Persian. However, the tradition of keeping revenue records in the local language continued in the Deccani states till their extinction in the last quarter of the seventeenth century.

Persian prose and poetry reached a climax under Akbar's reign. Abul Fazl who was a great scholar and a stylist, as well as the leading historian of the age, set a style of prose-writing which was emulated for many generations. The leading poet of the age was his brother, Faizi, who also helped in Akbar's translation department. The translation of the *Mahabharata* was carried out under his supervision. Utbi and Naziri were the two other leading Persian poets. Though born in Persia, they were among the many poets and scholars who migrated from Iran to India during the period and made the Mughal court one of the cultural centres of the Islamic world. Hindus also contributed to the growth of Persian literature. Apart from literary and historical works a number of famous dictionaries of the Persian language were also compiled during the period.

Although not much significant and original work was done in Sanskrit during the period, the number of Sanskrit works produced during the period is quite impressive. As before, most of the works were produced in south and east India under the patronage of local rulers, though a few were produced by Brahmans employed in the translation department of the Mughal emperors.

Regional languages acquired stability and maturity and some of the finest lyrical poetry was produced during this period. The dalliance of Krishna with Radha and the milkmaids, pranks of the child Krishna and stories from the *Bhagawat Puran* figure largely in lyrical poetry in Bengali, Oriya, Hindi, Rajasthani and Gujarati during this period. Many devotional hymns to Rama were also composed, and the *Ramayana* and the *Mahabharata* were translated into the regional languages, especially if they had not been translated earlier. A few translations and adaptations from Persian were also made. Both Hindus and Muslims contributed in this. Thus, Alaol composed in Bengali and also translated from Persian. In Hindi, the *Padmavat*, the story written by the Sufi saint, Malik Muhammad Jaisi, used the attack of Alauddin Khalji on Chittor as an allegory to expound Sufi ideas on the relations of soul with God, along with Hindu ideas about *maya*.

Medieval Hindi in the Brij form, that is the dialect spoken in the neighbourhood of Agra, was also patronised by the Mughal emperor and Hindu rulers. From the time of Akbar, Hindi poets began to be attached to the Mughal court. A leading Mughal noble, Abdur Rahim Khan-i-Khanan, produced a fine blend of Bhakti poetry with Persian ideas of life and human relations. Thus, the Persian and the Hindi literary traditions began to influence each other. But the most influential Hindi poet was Tulsidas who venerated Rama as a god and hero, and he used a dialect of Hindi spoken in the eastern parts of Uttar Pradesh. Pleading for a modified caste system based not on birth but on individual qualities, Tulsidas was essentially a humanistic poet who upheld family ideals and complete devotion to Rama as a way of salvation open to all, irrespective of caste.

In south India, Malayalam started its literary career as a separate language in its own right. Marathi reached its apogee at the hands of Eknath and Tukaram. Asserting the importance of Marathi, Eknath exclaims: 'If Sanskrit was made by God, was Prakrit born of thieves and knaves? Let these errings be of vanity alone. God is no partisan of tongues. To Him Prakrit and Sanskrit are alike. My language Marathi is worthy of expressing the highest sentiments and is rich, laden with the fruits of divine knowledge.'

This undoubtedly expresses the sentiments of all those writing in local languages. It also shows the confidence and the status acquired by these languages. Due to the writings of the Sikh gurus, Punjabi received a new life.

MUSIC

Another branch of cultural life in which Hindus and Muslims cooperated was music. Akbar patronised Tansen of Gwaliyar who is credited with composing many new melodies (*ragas*). Jahangir and Shah Jahan as well as many Mughal nobles followed this example. There are many stories about the burial of music by the orthodox Aurangzeb. Recent research shows that Aurangzeb banished singing from his court, but not playing of musical instruments. In fact, Aurangzeb himself was an accomplished *veena* player. Music in all forms continued to be patronised by Aurangzeb's queens in the *haram* and by the princes and nobles. That is why the largest number of books on classical Indian music in Persian were written during Aurangzeb's reign. But some of the most important developments in the field of music took place later on in the eighteenth century during the reign of Muhammad Shah (1719–48) who was a great patron of music and musicians.

RELIGIOUS IDEAS AND BELIEFS, AND PROBLEMS OF INTEGRATION

The Bhakti Movement continued apace during the sixteenth and seventeenth centuries. Amongst the new movements was the Sikh movement in the Punjab, and what is called Maharashtra Dharma in Maharashtra. The Sikh movement had its origin with the preachings of Nanak. But its development is closely linked with the institution of Guruship. The first four gurus continued the tradition of quiet meditation and scholarship. The fifth guru, Arjun Das, completed the compilation of the Sikh scriptures called the *Adi-Granth* or *Granth Sahib*. To emphasize that the guru combined both spiritual and worldly leadership in his person, Guru Arjun began to live in an aristocratic style. He erected lofty buildings at Amritsar, wore fine clothes, kept fine horses procured from Central Asia and maintained retainers in attendance. He also started a system of collecting offerings from the Sikhs at the rate of one-tenth of their income to promote the movement.

Akbar had been deeply impressed with the Sikh gurus and, it is said, visited them at Amritsar. However, a clash began with the imprisonment and death of Guru Arjun by Jahangir on a charge of helping rebel prince, Khusrau, with money and prayers. His successor, Guru Har Govind, was also imprisoned for some time, but he was soon set free and developed good relations with Jahangir, and accompanied him in his journey to Kashmir just before his death.

Guru Har Govind came into clash with Shah Jahan on a hunting incident. While the Emperor was hunting near Amritsar, one of his favourite hawks flew into the guru's camp, and his refusal to give it up led to a series of clashes. However, the matter was hushed up at the intervention of some well-wishers at the court.

A second conflict took place a little later when the guru's attempt to build a new city on the river Beas near Jallandhar was objected to.

A third conflict took place when two horses of 'surpassing beauty and swiftness' being brought to the guru from Central Asia were seized by the royal officials. A follower of the guru, Bidhi Chand, stole these horses and presented them to the guru. By this time the guru had a sizeable following, and in the series of skirmishes the guru acquitted himself well. The guru was supported for some time by a Pathan, Painda Khan. Ultimately, Guru Har Govind retired to the Punjab foot-hills and was not interfered with.

All these conflicts were of an 'inconsequential nature', according to the well-known historian, R.P. Tripathi who ascribes them to personal and political factors rather than religion. The gurus assuming a rich lifestyle and being called *sachcha padshah* or 'true sovereign' by his followers does not seem to have been a cause of concern to the rulers because some of the Sufi saints led a rich life style, and were given similar titles by their followers to emphasise their spiritual eminence.

There was no atmosphere of confrontation between the Sikhs and the Mughal rulers during this period. Nor was there any systematic persecution of the Hindus, and hence, no occasion for the Sikhs or any group or sect to stand forth as the champion of the Hindus against religious persecution. Despite some display of orthodoxy by Shah Jahan at the beginning of his reign and a few acts of intolerance, such as the demolition of 'new' temples, he was not narrow in his outlook which was further tempered towards the end of his reign by the influence of his liberal son, Dara. Dara, the eldest son of Shah Jahan, was by temperament a scholar and a Sufi who loved to discourse with religious divines. With the help of the Brahmans of Kasi, he got the *Gita* translated into Persian. But his most significant work was an anthology of the *Vedas* in the introduction to which Dara declared the *Vedas* to be 'heavenly books in point of time' and 'in conformity with the holy *Quran*'. Thus, he underlined the belief that there were no fundamental differences between Hinduism and Islam.

Another saint, Dadu, born in Gujarat but who seems to have lived mostly in Rajasthan preached a non-sectarian (*nipakh*) path. He refused to identify himself with either the Hindus or the Muslims, or to bother with the revealed scriptures of the two, asserting the indivisibility of the *Brahma* or the Supreme Reality.

The same liberal trend can be seen in the life and works of Tukaram, the supreme exponent of Bhakti in Maharashtra at Pandharpur, which had become the centre of the Maharashtra Dharma and where worship of Vithoba, a form of Vishnu, had become popular. Tukaram, who states that he was born a shudra used to do *puja* to the god with his own hand.

It was not be expected that such ideas and practices would be easily accepted by the orthodox elements belonging to the two leading faiths, Hinduism or Islam, and thus give up the entrenched positions of power and influence which they had enjoyed for a long time. The sentiments of the orthodox Hindus were echoed by Raghunandan of Navadwipa (Nadia) in Bengal. Considered to be the most influential writer on the *Dharmashastras* during the medieval period, Raghunandan asserted the privileges of the Brahmans stating that none other except the Brahmans had the right to read the scriptures or to preach. Hĕ ends by saying that in the *Kali* age there were only two *varnas*, Brahmans and Shudras, the true Kshatriyas having disappeared long ago and the Vaishyas and others having lost their caste status due to the non-performance of appropriate duties. Ram Das of Maharashtra, who was later the spiritual.guru of Sivaji, and who put forward a philosophy of activism, was equally vehement in assertion of the privileges of the Brahmans.

Among the Muslims, too, while the trend of *tauhid* continued apace, and was supported by many leading Sufi saints, a small group of the orthodox *ulama* denounced it, as also the liberal policies of Akbar. The most renowned figure in the Muslim orthodox and revivalist movement of the time was Shaikh Ahmad Sirhindi. A follower of the orthodox Naqshbandi school of Sufis which had been introduced in India during Akbar's reign, Shaikh Ahmad Sirhindi opposed the concept of pantheistic mysticism (*tauhid*) or unity of God and the created being, denouncing it as un-Islamic. He also opposed all those practices and beliefs which he held were due to the influence of Hinduism, such as the use of music in religious gatherings (*sama*), excessive meditation, visiting tombs of saints, etc. In order to assert the Islamic character of the state, he demanded re-imposition of *jizyah*, a stern attitude towards the Hindus, and the minimum association of Muslims with them. In order to implement this programme, he started centres and also wrote letters to the emperor and to many nobles to win them over to his side.

However, the ideas of Shaikh Ahmad had little impact. Jahangir imprisoned him for claiming a status beyond that of the Prophet and only released him after his retraction. Nor did Aurangzeb pay any special attention to his son and successor.

It will thus be seen that the influence of the orthodox thinkers and preachers was limited, being necessarily confined to narrow circles. Their chief hope was that their ideas would receive the support and backing of those who held positions of wealth and power in society and the state. On the other hand, the liberal thinkers made their appeal to the broad masses.

The recurrent cycles of liberalism and orthodoxy in Indian history should be seen against the situation which was rooted in the structure of Indian society. One aspect of the struggle was between entrenched privilege and power on the one hand, and the egalitarian and humanistic aspirations of the mass of the people on the other.

The prestige and influence of the narrow, orthodox elements and their re-assertion of narrow ideas and beliefs was a barrier to the growing process of rapproachement and tolerance among the votaries of the two dominant religions, Hinduism and Islam, and a hindrance to the process of cultural integration. The clash between the two trends came to the surface during Aurangzeb's reign. However, the broad, liberal religious policy of Akbar was revived, and became the norm during the eighteenth century.

EIGHTEEN

Climax and Disintegration of the Mughal Empire—I

PROBLEMS OF SUCCESSION

The last years of Shah Jahan's reign were clouded by a bitter war of succession among his sons. There was no clear tradition of succession among the Muslims or the Timurids. The right of nomination by the ruler had been accepted by some of the Muslim political thinkers. But it could not be asserted in India during the Sultanat period. The Timurid tradition of partitioning had not been successful either and was never applied in India.

Hindu traditions were also not very clear in the matter of succession. According to Tulsidas, a contemporary of Akbar, a ruler had the right of giving the *tika* to any one of his sons. But there were many cases among the Rajputs where such a nomination had not been accepted by the other brothers. Thus, Sanga had to wage a bitter struggle with his brothers before he could assert his claim to the *gaddi*.

Towards the end of 1657, Shah Jahan was taken ill at Delhi and for some time, his life was despaired of. But he rallied and gradually recovered his strength under the loving care of Dara. Meanwhile, all kinds of rumours had gained currency. It was said that Shah Jahan had already died, and Dara was concealing the reality to serve his own purposes. After some time, Shah Jahan slowly made his way by boat to Agra. Meanwhile, the princes, Shuja in Bengal, Murad in Gujarat and Aurangzeb in the Deccan, had either been persuaded that these rumours were true, or pretended to believe them, and made preparations for the inevitable war of succession.

Anxious to avert a conflict between his sons, which might spell ruin to the empire, and anticipating his speedy end, Shah Jahan now decided to nominate his eldest son Dara as his successor (*wali-ahd*). He raised Dara's *mansab* from 40,000 *zat* to the unprecedented rank of 60,000. Dara was given a chair next to the throne, and all the nobles were instructed to obey Dara as their future sovereign. But these actions, far from ensuring a smooth succession as Shah Jahan had hoped, convinced the other princes of Shah Jahan's partiality to Dara. It thus strengthened their resolve of making a bid for the throne.

It is not necessary for us to follow in detail the events leading to the ultimate triumph of Aurangzeb. There were many reasons for Aurangzeb's success. Divided counsel and under-estimation of his opponents by Dara were two of the major factors responsible for Dara's defeat. On hearing of the military preparations of his sons and their decision to march on the capital, Shah Jahan had sent an army to the east led by Dara's son, Sulaiman Shikoh, aided by Mirza Raja Jai Singh, to deal with Shuja who had crowned himself. Another army was sent to Malwa under Raja Jaswant Singh, the ruler of Jodhpur. On his arrival in Malwa, Jaswant found that he was faced with the combined forces of Aurangzeb and Murad. The two princes were intent on a conflict and invited Jaswant to stand aside. Jaswant could have retreated but deeming retreat to be a matter of dishonour, he decided to stand and fight, though the odds were definitely against him. The victory of Aurangzeb at Dharmat (15 April 1658) emboldened his supporters and raised his prestige, while it dispirited Dara and his supporters.

Meanwhile, Dara made a serious mistake. Over-confident of the strength of his position, he had assigned for the eastern campaign some of his best troops. Thus, he denuded the capital, Agra. Led by Sulaiman Shikoh, the army moved to the east and gave a good account of itself. It surprised and defeated Shuja near Banaras (February 1658). It then decided to pursue him into Bihar—as if the issue at Agra had been already decided. After the defeat at Dharmat, express letters were sent to these forces to hurry back to Agra. After patching up a hurried treaty (7 May 1658), Sulaiman Shikoh started his march to Agra from his camp near Monghyr in eastern Bihar. But it was hardly likely that he could return to Agra in time for the conflict with Aurangzeb.

After Dharmat, Dara made frantic efforts to seek allies. He sent repeated letters to Jaswant Singh who had retired to Jodhpur. The rana of Udaipur was also approached. Jaswant Singh moved out tardily to Pushkar near Ajmer. After raising an army with the money provided by Dara, he waited there for the rana to join him. But the rana had already been won over by Aurangzeb with a promise of a rank of 7000, and the return of the *parganas* seized by Shah Jahan and Dara from him in 1654 following a dispute over the re-fortification of Chittor. Aurangzeb also held out to the rana a promise of religious freedom and 'favours equal to those of Rana Sanga'. Thus, Dara failed to win over even the important Rajput rajas to his side.

The battle of Samugarh (29 May 1658) was basically a battle of good generalship, the two sides being almost equally matched in numbers (about 50,000 to 60,000 on each side). In this field, Dara was no match for Aurangzeb. The Hada Rajputs and the Saiyids of Barha upon whom Dara largely depended could not make up for the weakness of the rest of the hastily recruited army. Aurangzeb's troops were battle hardened and well led.

Aurangzeb had all along pretended that his only object of coming to Agra was to see his ailing father and to release him from the control of the 'heretical' Dara. But the war between Aurangzeb and Dara was not between religious orthodoxy on the one hand, and liberalism on the other. Both Muslim and Hindu nobles were equally divided in their support to the two rivals. We have already seen the attitude of the leading Rajput rajas. In this conflict, as in so many others, the attitude of the nobles depended upon their personal interests and their association with individual princes.

After the defeat and flight of Dara, Shah Jahan was besieged in the fort of Agra. Aurangzeb forced Shah Jahan into surrender by seizing the source of water supply to the fort. Shah Jahan was confined to the female apartments in the fort and strictly supervised though he was not ill-treated. There he lived for eight long years, lovingly nursed by his favourite daughter, Jahanara, who voluntarily chose to live within the fort. She re-emerged into public life after Shah Jahan's death and was accorded great honour by Aurangzeb who restored her to the position of the first lady of the realm. He also raised her annual pension from twelve lakh rupees to seventeen lakhs.

According to the terms of Aurangzeb's agreement with Murad, the kingdom was to be partitioned between the two. But Aurangzeb had no intention of sharing the empire. Hence, he treacherously imprisoned Murad and sent him to the Gwaliyar jail. He was killed two years later.

After losing the battle at Samugarh, Dara had fled to Lahore and was planning to retain control of its surrounding areas. But Aurangzeb soon arrived in the neighbourhood, leading a strong army. Dara's courage failed him. He abandoned Lahore without a fight and fled to Sindh. Thus, he virtually sealed his fate. Although the civil war dragged on for more than two years, its outcome was hardly in doubt. Dara's move from Sindh into Gujarat and then into Ajmer on an invitation from Jaswant Singh, the ruler of Marwar, and the subsequent treachery of the latter are too well known. The battle of Deorai near Ajmer (March 1659) was the last major battle Dara fought against Aurangzeb. Dara might well have escaped into Iran, but he wanted to try his luck again in Afghanistan. On the way, in the Bolan Pass, a treacherous Afghan chief made him a prisoner and handed him over to his dreaded enemy. A panel of jurists decreed that Dara could not be suffered to live 'out of necessity to protect the faith and Holy law, and also for reasons of state (and) as a destroyer of the public peace'. This is typical of the manner in which Aurangzeb used religion as a cloak for his political motives. Two years after Dara's execution, his son, Sulaiman Shikoh, who had sought shelter with the ruler of Garhwal was handed over by him to Aurangzeb on an imminent threat of invasion. He soon suffered the same fate as his father.

Earlier, Aurangzeb had defeated Shuja at Khajwah near Allahabad (December 1658). Further campaigning against him was entrusted to Mir Jumla who steadily exerted pressure till Shuja was hounded out of India into Arakan (April 1660). Soon afterwards, he and his family met a dishonourable death at the hands of the Arakanese on a charge of fomenting rebellion.

The civil war which kept the empire distracted for more than two years showed that neither nomination by the ruler, nor plans of division of the empire were likely to be accepted by the contenders for the throne. Military force became the only arbiter for succession and the civil wars became steadily more destructive. After being seated securely on the throne, Aurangzeb tried to mitigate, to some extent, the effects of the harsh Mughal custom of war unto death between brothers. At the instance of Jahanara Begum, Siphir Shikoh, son of Dara, was released from prison in 1673, given a *mansab* and married to a daughter of Aurangzeb. Murad's son, Izzat Bakhsh, was also released, given a *mansab* and married to another daughter of Aurangzeb. Earlier, in 1669, Dara's daughter, Jani Begum, who had been looked after by Jahanara as her own daughter, was married to Aurangzeb's third son, Muhammad Azam. There are many other marriages between Aurangzeb's family and the children and grandchildren of his defeated brothers. Thus, in the third generation, the families of Aurangzeb and his defeated brothers became one.

Aurangzeb's Reign—His Religious Policy

Aurangzeb ruled for almost 50 years. During his long reign, the Mughal empire reached its territorial climax. At its height, it stretched from Kashmir in the north to Jinji in the south, and from the Hindukush in the west to Chittagong in the east. Aurangzeb proved to be a hardworking ruler, and never spared himself or his subordinates in the tasks of government. His letters show the close attention he paid to all affairs of the state. He was a strict disciplinarian who did not spare his own sons. In 1686, he imprisoned prince Muazzam on a charge of intriguing with the ruler of Golconda, and kept him in prison for 12 long years. His other sons also had to face his wrath on various occasions. Such was the awe of Aurangzeb that even late in his life when Muazzam was the Governor of Kabul, he trembled every time he received a letter from his father who was then in south India. Unlike his predecessors, Aurangzeb did not like ostentation. His personal life was marked by simplicity. He had the reputation of being an orthodox, God-fearing Muslim. In course of time, he began to be regarded as a *zinda pir*, or 'a living saint'.

Historians are, however, deeply divided about Aurangzeb's achievements as a ruler. According to some, he reversed Akbar's policy of religious toleration and thus undermined the loyalty of the Hindus to the empire. According to them, this, in turn, led to popular uprisings which sapped the vitality of the empire. His suspicious nature added to his problems so that in the words of Khafi Khan, 'all his enterprises were long drawn out' and ended in failure. Another set of historians think that Aurangzeb has been unjustly maligned, that the Hindus had become disloyal due to the laxity of Aurangzeb's predecessors, so that Aurangzeb had no option but to adopt harsh methods and to try to rally the Muslims on whose support in the long run the empire had to rest.

A new trend has, however, emerged as shown in the research work on Aurangzeb. In these works, efforts have been made to assess Aurangzeb's political and religious policies in the context of social, economic and institutional developments. There is little doubt about his being orthodox in his beliefs. He was not interested in philosophical debates or in mysticism—though he did occasionally visit Sufi saints for their blessings, and did not debar his sons from dabbling in Sufism. While taking his stand on the Hanafi school of Muslim law which had been traditionally followed in India, Aurangzeb did not hesitate in issuing secular decrees, called *zawabit*. A compendium of his decrees, and government rules and regulations had been collected in a work called *Zawabit-i-Alamgiri*. Theoretically, the *zawabits* supplemented the *sharia*. In practice, however, they sometimes modified the *sharia*, in view of the conditions obtaining in India which were not provided for in the *sharia*.

Thus, apart from being an orthodox Muslim, Aurangzeb was also a ruler. He could hardly forget the political reality that the overwhelming population of India was Hindu, and that they were deeply attached to their faith. Any policy which meant the complete alienation of the Hindus and of the powerful Hindu rajas and zamindars was obviously unworkable.

In analysing Aurangzeb's religious policy, we may take note first of what have been called moral and religious regulations. At the beginning of his reign, he forbade the *kalma* being inscribed on coins—lest a coin be trampled underfoot or be defiled while passing from hand to hand. He discontinued the festival of *Nauroz* as it was considered a Zoroastrian practice favoured by the Safavid rulers of Iran. *Muhtasibs* were appointed in all the provinces. These officials were asked to see that people lived their lives in accordance with the *sharia*. Thus, it was the business of these officials to see that wine and intoxicants such as *bhang* were not consumed in public places. They were also responsible for regulating the houses of ill repute, gambling dens, etc., and for checking weights and measures. In other words, they were responsible for ensuring that things forbidden by the *sharia* and the *zawabits* (secular decrees) were, as far as possible, not flouted openly. In appointing *muhtasibs*, Aurangzeb emphasised that the state was also responsible for the moral welfare of the citizens, especially the Muslims. But these officials were instructed not to interfere in the private lives of citizens.

Later, in the eleventh year of his reign (1669), Aurangzeb took a number of measures which have been called puritanical. They were designed to show that the emperor was opposed to all practices which were not in accordance with the *sharia*, or which could be considered superstitious. Some measures were of an economic and social nature. Thus, he forbade singing in the court and the official musicians were pensioned off. Instrumental music and *naubat* (the royal band) were, however, continued. Singing also continued to be patronized by the ladies in the haram, and by princes, and individual nobles. It is of some interest to note, as has been mentioned before, that the largest number of Persian works on classical Indian music were written in Aurangzeb's reign, and that Aurangzeb himself was proficient in playing the *veena*. Thus, the jibe of Aurangzeb to the protesting musicians that they should bury the bier of music they were carrying deep under the earth so 'that no echo of it may rise again' was only an angry remark.

Aurangzeb discontinued the practice of *jharoka darshan* or showing himself to the public from the balcony since he considered it a superstitious practice and against Islam. Similarly, he forbade the ceremony of weighing the emperor against gold and silver and other articles on his birthdays. This practice which was apparently started during Akbar's reign had become widespread and had become a burden on the smaller nobles. But the weight of social opinion was too much. Aurangzeb had to permit this ceremony for his sons when they recovered from illness. He forbade astrologers to prepare almanacs. But the order was flouted by everybody, including members of the royal family.

Many other regulations of a similar nature, some of a moral character and some to instill a sense of austerity, were issued. The throne room was to be furnished in a cheap and simple style; clerks were to use porcelain ink-stands instead of silver ones; silk clothes were frowned upon, the gold railings in the *diwan-i-am* were replaced by those of lapis lazuli set on gold. Even the official department of history-writing was discontinued as a measure of economy.

To promote trade among the Muslims who depended almost exclusively on state support, Aurangzeb at first largely exempted Muslim traders from the payment of cess on import of goods. But he soon found that the Muslim traders were abusing it, even passing off the goods of Hindu merchants as their own to cheat the state. So Aurangzeb re-imposed the cess on Muslim traders, but, kept it at half of what was charged from others.

Similarly, he tried to reserve the posts of *peshkars* and *karoris* (petty revenue officials) for Muslims but soon had to modify it in the face of opposition from the nobles and lack of qualified Muslims.

We may now turn our attention to some of the other measures of Aurangzeb which may be called discriminatory and showed a sense of bigotry towards people professing other religions. The most important was Aurangzeb's attitude towards temples, and the levying of *jizyah*.

At the outset of his reign, Aurangzeb reiterated the position of the *shara* regarding temples, synagogues, churches, etc., that 'long standing temple should not be demolished but no new temples allowed to be built.' Further, old places of worship could be repaired 'since buildings cannot last for ever'. This position is clearly spelt out in a number of extant *farmans* he issued to the Brahmans of Banaras, Vrindavan, etc.[1]

Aurangzeb's order regarding temples was not a new one. It reaffirmed the position which had existed during the Sultanat period and which had been reiterated by Shah Jahan early in his reign. In practice, it left wide latitude to the local officials as to the interpretation of the words, 'long standing temples'. The private opinion and sentiment of the ruler in the matter was also bound to weigh with the officials. For example, after the rise of the liberal-minded Dara as Shah Jahan's favourite, few temples had been demolished in pursuance of his order forbidding new temples. Aurangzeb, as

---

1 The Banaras *farman* is in the National Library, Calcutta, and the Vrindavan *farman* is presently in a temple at Jaipur.

governor of Gujarat, ordered a number of temples in Gujarat to be destroyed. In many cases, it meant disfiguring the images and closing down the temples. At the outset of his reign, Aurangzeb found that images in many of these temples had been restored and idol worship had been resumed. Aurangzeb, therefore, ordered again in 1665 that these temples be destroyed. The famous temple of Somnath which he ordered to be destroyed earlier in his reign was apparently one of the temples mentioned above.

It does not seem that Aurangzeb's order regarding ban on new temples led to a large-scale destruction of temples at the outset of the reign. Later, as Aurangzeb encountered political opposition from a number of quarters, such as the Marathas, Jats, etc., he seems to have adopted a new stance. In case of conflict with local elements, he now considered it legitimate to destroy even long-standing Hindu temples as a measure of punishment and as a warning. Further, he began to look upon temples as centres of spreading subversive ideas, that is, ideas which were not acceptable to the orthodox elements. Thus, he took strict action when he learnt in 1669 that in some of the temples in Thatta, Multan and especially at Banaras, both Hindus and Muslims used to come from great distances to learn from the Brahmans. Aurangzeb issued orders to the governors of all provinces to put down such practices and to destroy the temples where such practices took place. As a result of these orders, a number of temples such as the famous temple of Vishwanath at Banaras and the temple of Keshava Rai at Mathura built by Bir Singh Deo Bundela in the reign of Jahangir were destroyed and mosques erected in their place. The destruction of these temples had a political motive as well. Mustaid Khan author of the *Maasir-i-Alamgiri* says, with reference to the destruction of the temple of Keshava Rai at Mathura, 'On seeing this instance of the strength of the Emperor's faith and the grandeur of his devotion to God, the proud rajas were stifled, and in amazement they stood like images facing the wall.'

It was in this context that many temples built in Orissa during the last ten to twelve years were also destroyed. But it does not seem that there were any orders for the general destruction of temples. Mustaid Khan, who wrote his history of Aurangzeb in the early eighteenth century and who had been closely associated with Aurangzeb, asserts that the motive of Aurangzeb's orders was to 'establish Islam' and that the Emperor ordered the governors to destroy all temples and to ban public practice of the religion of these misbelievers, that is, the Hindus. If Mustaid Khan's version was correct, it would have meant Aurangzeb going far beyond the position of the *sharia*, for the *sharia* did not ban the non-Muslims from practising their faiths as long as they were loyal to the ruler, etc. Nor have we found any *farmans* to the governors on the lines suggested by Mustaid Khan. However, the situation was different during periods of hostilities. Thus, during 1679–80 when there was a state of war with the Rathors of Marwar and the rana of Udaipur, many temples of old standing were destroyed at Jodhpur and its *parganas*, and at Udaipur.

In his policy toward temples, Aurangzeb may have remained formally within the framework of the *sharia*, but there is little doubt that his stand in the matter was a setback to the policy of broad toleration followed by his predecessors. It led to a climate of opinion that destruction of temples on any excuse would not only be condoned but would be welcomed by the emperor. While we do have instances of grants to Hindu temples and *maths* by Aurangzeb, on the whole, the atmosphere generated by Aurangzeb's policy towards Hindu temples was bound to create disquiet among large sections of Hindus. However, it seems that Aurangzeb's zeal for the destruction of temples abated after 1679, for we do not hear of any large-scale destruction of temples in the south between 1681 and his death in 1707. But a new irritant, the *jizyah* or the poll tax, was introduced in the interval.

We have already explained the background of the *jizyah* and its introduction in India by the Arab and Turkish rulers. According to the *sharia*, in a Muslim state, the payment of *jizyah* was obligatory (*wajib*) for the non-Muslims. Akbar had abolished it for reasons that we have noted. However, a section of orthodox theologians had been agitating for the revival of *jizyah*, so that the superior position of Islam, including that of the theologians, could be made manifest to all. We are told that after accession to the throne, Aurangzeb contemplated revival of the *jizyah* on a number of occasions but did not do so for fear of political opposition. Ultimately, in 1679, in the twenty-second year of his reign, he finally re-imposed it. There has been a considerable discussion among historians regarding Aurangzeb's motives for the step. Let us first see what it was not. It was *not* meant to be an economic pressure for forcing the Hindus to convert to Islam for its incidence was light—women, children, the disabled and the indigent, that is those whose income was less than the means of subsistence were exempted, as were those in government service. Nor, in fact, did any significant section of Hindus change their religion in earlier times due to this tax. Secondly, it was not a means of meeting a difficult financial situation. Although the income from *jizyah* is said to have been considerable, Aurangzeb had sacrificed a considerable sum of money by giving up a large number of cesses called *abwabs* which were not sanctioned by the *sharia* and were hence considered illegal. However, the money from *jizyah* did not go to the royal treasury, but was ear-marked for use by the theological classes. The re-imposition of *jizyah* was, in fact, both political and ideological in nature. It was meant to rally the Muslims for the defence of the state against the Marathas and the Rajputs who were up in arms, and possibly against the Muslim states of the Deccan, especially Golconda which was in alliance with the infidel Marathas. Moreover, *jizyah* was to be collected by honest, God-fearing Muslims, who were especially appointed for the purpose, and its proceeds were reserved for the *ulama*. It was thus a big bribe for the theologians among whom there was a lot of unemployment. But the disadvantages out-weighed the possible advantages of the step. It was bitterly resented by the Hindus who considered it as a mark of discrimination. Its mode of collection also had some negative features. The payee was required to pay it personally and sometimes he suffered humiliation at the hands of the theologians in the process. Since in the rural areas *jizyah* was collected along with the land revenue, well-to-do Hindus in the cities were affected more by these practices. We, therefore, hear of a number of occasions when Hindu traders shut their shops and observed *hartal* against the measure. Also, there was a lot of corruption, and in a number of instances, the *amin* or collector of *jizyah* was killed. But Aurangzeb was unrelenting, and was reluctant to grant exemption for payment of *jizyah* to the peasants, even when remission in land revenue had to be given on account of natural calamities. Finally, he had to suspend *jizyah* in 1705 'for the duration of the war in the south' (for which no end was in sight). This could hardly influence his negotiations with the Marathas. Gradually *jizyah* fell into disuse all over the country. It was formally abolished in 1712 by Aurangzeb's successors.

Some modern writers are of the opinion that Aurangzeb's measures were designed to convert India from a *dar-ul-harb*, or a land of infidels, into *dar-ul-Islam*, or a land inhabited by Muslims. But this has no basis, in fact, a state in which the laws of Islam prevailed and where the ruler was a Muslim is *dar-ul-Islam*. In such a state, the Hindus who submitted to the Muslim ruler, and agreed to pay *jizyah* were *zimmis* or protected people according to the *sharia*. Hence, the state in India had been considered a *dar-ul-Islam* since the advent of the Turks. Even when Mahadji Sindhia, the Maratha general, occupied Delhi in 1772, and the Mughal emperor became a puppet in his hands, the theologians decreed that the state remained a *dar-ul-Islam* since the laws of Islam were allowed to prevail and the throne was occupied by a Muslim. Although Aurangzeb considered it legitimate to encourage conversion to Islam, evidence of systematic or large-scale attempts at forced conversion is lacking.[1] Nor were Hindu nobles discriminated against. A recent study has shown that the number of Hindus in the nobility during the second half of Aurangzeb's reign steadily increased, till the Hindus including Marathas formed about one-third of the nobility as against one-fourth under Shah Jahan. On one occasion, Aurangzeb wrote on petition in which a post was claimed on religious grounds 'what connection and what right have wordly affairs with religion? And what right have matters of religion to enter into bigotry? For you is your religion, for me is mine. If this rule (suggested by you) were established it would be my duty to extirpate all (Hindu) rajas and their followers.'

Thus, Aurangzeb's attempt was not so much to change the nature of the state, but to re-assert its fundamentally Islamic character. Aurangzeb's religious beliefs cannot be considered the basis of his political policies. While as an orthodox Muslim he was desirous of upholding the strict letter of the law, as a ruler he was keen to

---

1 The conversion of large sections of the population to Islam in Kashmir had taken place apparently during the fourteenth-fifteenth centuries, as has been noted in an earlier chapter.

strengthen and expand the empire. Hence, he did not want to lose the support of the Hindus to the extent possible. However, his religious ideas and beliefs on the one hand, and his political or public policies on the other, clashed with each other on many occasions so that Aurangzeb was faced with difficult choices. Sometimes this led him to adopt contradictory policies which harmed the empire.

POLITICAL DEVELOPMENTS—NORTH INDIA

During the war of succession, many local zamindars and rajas had withheld revenue, or started plundering the neighbouring areas including Mughal territories and royal highways. After seating himself on the throne formally, Aurangzeb embarked upon an era of strong rule. In some cases, such as the northeast and the Deccan, the imperial frontier was advanced. However, in general, Aurangzeb did not embark upon a forward policy. His first attempt immediately after his succession was to re-assert imperial authority and prestige. This included recovery of areas which had been lost during the war of succession and to which the Mughals felt they had legal claim. To begin with, Aurangzeb was more concerned with consolidation than conquest and annexation. Thus, he sent an army to Bikaner to enforce obedience to the Mughal emperor, but made no effort to annex it. But in another case, such as Palamau in Bihar, the ruler who was accused of disloyalty was dispossessed, and the bulk of his state annexed. The rebel Bundela chief, Champat Rai, who had been an ally of Aurangzeb at first but had taken to a life of plunder, was relentlessly hunted down. But Bundela lands were not annexed.

NORTHEAST AND EAST INDIA

We have mentioned in an earlier chapter the rise of the Ahom power in Assam valley and their conflict with the rulers of Kamata (Kamrup) on the one hand and with the Afghan rulers of Bengal on the other. The kingdom of Kamata declined by the end of the fifteenth century and was replaced by the kingdom of Kuch (Cooch Bihar) which dominated north Bengal and western Assam, and which continued the policy of conflict with the Ahoms. However, internal disputes led to the division of the kingdom in the early seventeenth century and to the entry of the Mughals in Assam at the instance of the Kuch ruler. The Mughals defeated the split-away kingdom and in 1612 occupied the western Assam valley up to the Bar Nadi with the help of Kuch armies. The Kuch ruler became a Mughal vassal. Thus, the Mughals came into contact with the Ahoms who ruled eastern Assam across the Bar Nadi. After a long war with the Ahoms who had harboured a prince of the defeated dynasty, a treaty was made with them at last in 1638 which fixed the Bar Nadi as the boundary between them and the Mughals. Thus Guwahati came under Mughal control.

There was a long-drawn out war between the Mughals and the Ahoms during the reign of Aurangzeb. The war began with the attempt of the Ahom rulers to expel the Mughals from Guwahati and the neighbouring area and thus complete their control over Assam. Mir Jumla, who had been appointed the governor of Bengal by Aurangzeb, wanted to make his mark by bringing Cooch Bihar and the entire Assam under Mughal rule. He first assaulted Cooch Bihar which had repudiated Mughal suzerainty and annexed the entire kingdom to the Mughal empire. He next invaded the Ahom kingdom. Mir Jumla occupied the Ahom capital, Garhgaon, and held it for six months. Next, he penetrated up to the limit of the Ahom kingdom, finally forcing the Ahom king to make a humiliating treaty (1663). The raja had to send his daughter to the Mughal haram, pay a larger war indemnity and an annual tribute of 20 elephants. The Mughal boundary was extended from the Bar Nadi to the Bharali river.

Mir Jumla died soon after his brilliant victory. However, the advantages of a forward move in Assam were doubtful since the area was not rich and was surrounded by warlike tribes, such as the Nagas, living in the mountains. It was found that the back of Ahom power had not been broken, and that it was beyond Mughal power to enforce the treaty. In 1667, the Ahoms renewed the contest. They not only recovered the areas ceded to the Mughals, but also occupied Guwahati. Earlier, the Mughals had also been expelled from Cooch Bihar. Thus, all the gains of Mir Jumla were rapidly lost. A long, desultory warfare with the Ahoms lasting a decade and a half followed. For a long period the command of the Mughal forces were with Raja Ram Singh, the ruler of Amber. But he hardly had the resources for the task. Finally, the Mughals had to give up even Guwahati, and to fix a boundary west of it.

The events in Assam showed the limits of Mughal power in far-flung areas, and also the skill and determination of the Ahoms who avoided pitched battles and adopted a mode of guerrilla warfare. Similar tactics were to be adopted with similar success by the opponents of the Mughals in other areas. However, the shock of the Mughal invasion and the subsequent warfare undermined the strength of the Ahom monarchy and led to the decline and disintegration of the Ahom empire.

The Mughals had more success elsewhere. Shaista Khan, who succeeded Mir Jumla as the governor of Bengal after his setback at the hands of Shivaji, proved to be a good administrator and an able general. He modified Mir Jumlas forward policy. First, he patched up an agreement with the ruler of Cooch Bihar. Next, he gave his attention to the problem of south Bengal, where the Magh (Arakanese) pirates, had been terrorizing the area up to Dacca from their headquarters at Chittagong. The land up to Dacca had become desolate and trade and industry had suffered a setback. Shaista Khan built up a navy to meet the Arakanese pirates and captured the island of Sondip as a base of operations against Chittagong. Next, he won the Firingis to his side by inducements of money and favours. The Arakan navy near Chittagong was routed and many of their ships captured. Chittagong was next assaulted and captured early in 1666. The destruction of the Arakanese navy opened the seas to free commerce. This was no minor factor in the rapid growth of Bengal's foreign trade during the period and the expansion of cultivation in east Bengal.

In Orissa, the rebellion of the Pathans was put down and Balasore reopened to commerce.

POPULAR REVOLTS AND MOVEMENTS FOR REGIONAL INDEPENDENCE: JATS, AFGHANS AND SIKHS

Within the empire, Aurangzeb had to deal with a number of difficult political problems, such as the problems of the Marathas in the

Deccan, the Jats and Rajputs in north India, and that of the Afghans and Sikhs in the northwest. Some of these problems were not new, and had to be faced by Aurangzeb's predecessors. But they assumed a different character under Aurangzeb. The nature of these movements also varied. In the case of the Rajputs, it was basically a problem of succession. In the case of the Marathas, it was a question of local independence. The clash with the Jats had a peasant-agrarian background. The only movement in which religion played a powerful role was the Sikh movement. Both the Jat and the Sikh movements ultimately culminated in setting up independent regional states. The struggle of the Afghans was tribal in character, but there also the sentiment of setting up a separate Afghan state was at work. Thus, economic and social factors, as well as the sentiment of regional independence which continued to be strong were major factors in shaping these movements. Religion also played an undoubted role.

It has sometimes been argued that all these movements, excluding the Afghan one, represented a Hindu reaction against Aurangzeb's narrow religious policies. In a country where the overwhelming section of the people consisted of Hindus, any movement which came into conflict with the predominantly Muslim central government could be dubbed a challenge to Islam. Likewise, the leaders of these 'rebel' movements could use religious slogans or symbols to broaden their appeal. Hence, religion must be seen as part of societal and political movements.

Jats and Satnamis

The first section to come into conflict with the Mughal government were the Jats of the Agra-Delhi region living on both sides of the river Yamuna. The Jats were mostly peasant cultivators, only a few of them being zamindars. With a strong sense of brotherhood and justice, the Jats had often come into conflict with the government and taken to rebellion, taking advantage of their difficult terrain. Thus, conflict with the Jats of the area had taken place during the reigns of Jahangir and Shah Jahan over collection of land revenue. Since the imperial road to the Deccan and the western seaports passed through the Jat area, the Mughal government had taken a serious view of these rebellions and taken stern measures.

In 1669, the Jats of the Mathura region broke out in rebellion under the leadership of a local zamindar, Gokla. The rebellion spread rapidly among the peasants of the area, and Aurangzeb decided to march in person from Delhi to quell it. Although the Jat levies had swelled to 20,000, they were no match for the organised imperial army. In a stiff battle the Jats were defeated. Gokla was captured and executed.

However, the movement was not completely crushed and discontent continued to simmer. Meanwhile, in 1672, there was another armed conflict between the peasants and the Mughal state at Narnaul, not far from Mathura. This time the conflict was with a religious body called Satnamis. The Satnamis were mostly peasants, artisans and low caste people, called 'goldsmiths, carpenters, sweepers, tanners and other ignoble beings' by a contemporary writer. They did not observe distinctions of caste and rank or between Hindus and Muslims, and followed a strict code of conduct. Starting from a clash with a local official, it soon assumed the character of an open rebellion. Again, the emperor had to march in person to crush it. It is interesting to note that the local Hindu zamindars, many of whom were Rajputs, sided with the Mughals in this conflict.

In 1685, there was a second uprising of the Jats under the leadership of Rajaram. The Jats were better organised this time and adopted the methods of guerrilla warfare, combining it with plunder. Aurangzeb approached Raja Bishan Singh, the Kachhwaha ruler to crush the uprising. Bishan Singh was appointed *faujdar* of Mathura and the entire area was granted to him in *zamindari*. Conflict between the Jats and the Rajputs over *zamindari* rights complicated the issue, most of the primary zamindars, that is the cultivating peasants who owned the land being Jats, and the intermediary zamindars, that is those who collected the land revenue being Rajputs. The Jats put up stiff resistance, but by 1691, Rajaram and his successor, Churaman, were compelled to submit. However, unrest among the Jat peasants continued and their plundering activities made the Delhi-Agra road unsafe for travellers. Later, in the eighteenth century, taking advantage of Mughal civil wars and weakness in the central government, Churaman was able to carve out a separate Jat principality in the area and to oust the Rajput zamindars. Thus, what apparently started as a peasants' uprising, changed its character, and culminated in a state in which Jat chiefs formed the ruling class.

The Afghans

Aurangzeb came into conflict with the Afghans also. Conflict with the hardy Afghan tribesmen who lived in the mountain region between the Punjab and Kabul was not new. Akbar had to fight against the Afghans and, in the process, lost the life of his close friend and confidant, Raja Birbal. Conflict with the Afghan tribesmen had taken place during the reign of Shah Jahan also. These conflicts were partly economic and partly political and religious. With little means of livelihood in the rugged mountains, the Afghans had no option but to prey on the caravans or to enrol in the Mughal armies. Their fierce love of freedom made service in the Mughal armies difficult. The Mughals generally kept them content by paying them subsidies. But growth of population or the rise of an ambitious leader could lead to a breach of this tacit agreement.

During the reign of Aurangzeb, we see a new stirring among the Pathans. In 1667, Bhagu, the leader of the Yusufazai tribe, proclaimed as king a person named Muhammad Shah who claimed descent from an ancient royal lineage, and proclaimed himself his *wazir*. It would appear that among the Afghans, as among the Jats, the ambition of setting up a separate state of their own had begun to stir. A religious revivalist movement called the Raushanai, which emphasised a strict ethical life and devotion to a chosen *pir* had provided an intellectual and moral background to the movement.

Gradually, Bhagu's movement spread till his followers started ravaging and plundering the Hazara, Attock and Peshawar districts and brought the traffic in the Khyber to a standstill. To clear the Khyber and crush the uprising, Aurangzeb deputed the chief bakhshi, Amir Khan. A Rajput contingent was posted with him. After a series of hard-fought battles, the Afghan resistance was broken. But to watch over them, in 1671, Maharaja Jaswant Singh, the ruler of Marwar, was appointed as *thanedar* of Jamrud.

There was a second Afghan uprising in 1672. The leader of the opposition this time was the Afridi leader, Akmal Khan, who proclaimed himself king and read *khutba* and struck *sikka* in his name. He declared war against the Mughals and summoned all the Afghans to join him. According to a contemporary writer, with a following 'more numerous than ants and locusts', they closed the Khyber Pass.

Moving forward to clear the Pass, Amir Khan advanced too far and suffered a disastrous defeat in the narrow defile. Amir Khan managed to escape with his life, but 10,000 men perished, and cash and goods worth two crores were looted by the Afghans. This defeat brought other tribesmen into the fray including Khushhal Khan Khattak, a sworn enemy of Aurangzeb in whose hands he had suffered imprisonment for some time.

In 1674, another Mughal noble Shujaat Khan, suffered a disastrous rout in the Khyber. But he was rescued by a heroic band of Rathors sent by Jaswant Singh. At last, in the middle of 1674, Aurangzeb himself went to Peshawar and remained in the neighbourhood till the end of 1675. By force and diplomacy, the Afghan united front was broken, and peace was slowly restored.

The Afghan uprising shows that sentiments of resistance to the Mughal rule and the urge for regional freeedom were not confined to sections of Hindus, such as Jats, Marathas, etc. Also, the Afghan uprising helped to relax Mughal pressure on Shivaji during a crucial period. It also made difficult, if not impossible, a forward policy by the Mughals in the Deccan till 1676 by which time Shivaji had crowned himself and entered into an alliance with Bijapur and Golconda.

The Sikhs

Although there had been some clashes between the Sikh guru and the Mughals under Shah Jahan, there was no clash between the Sikhs and Aurangzeb till 1675. In fact, conscious of the growing importance of the Sikhs, Aurangzeb had tried to engage Ram Rai, the elder son of Guru Har Rai, at the court. However, Guru Har Rai was displeased with Ram Rai, and nominated as his successor a younger son, Har Kishan, who was only six years old at the time. Har Kishan died soon after, and was succeeded in 1664 by Guru Tegh Bahadur. Ram Rai put forward his claims to the *gaddi* both before the accession of Guru Har Kishan, and after his death. Aurangzeb did not interfere and gave a grant of land at Dehra Dun to Ram Rai to build his gurudwara there. But most of the time Ram Rai remained at Delhi, and continued to intrigue against the guru, and to try and poison the mind of the emperor against him. After his succession, Guru Tegh Bahadur had come to Delhi, but to escape the intrigues of Ram Rai he journeyed to Bihar, and served with Raja Ram Singh of Amber in Assam till 1671. However, in 1675, Guru Tegh Bahadur was brought to Delhi from his head-quarters with five of his followers. Various accusations were made against him, and he was asked to recant his faith which he refused. As a punishment, he was beheaded.

Various reasons have been put forward to account for Aurangzeb's action. According to a poetic work of Guru Goving Singh, the son and successor of Guru Tegh Bahadur, he gave up his life in defence of Hindu faith following his meeting with some Brahmans of Kashmir who had sought his support. However, we do not have any details of this meeting. According to a separate and later tradition, the guru was protesting against the oppression of the Governor of Kashmir, Sher Afghan, and large scale forcible conversion of Hindus there. However, the Mughal Governor of Kashmir till 1671 was Saif Khan. He is famous as a builder of bridges. He was a liberal and broad-minded person who had appointed a Hindu to advise his on matters of administration. His successor after 1671 was Iftekhar Khan. He was anti-Shia, but there are no references of his persecution of Hindus. In fact, this is not mentioned in any of the local histories of Kashmir, including one written by Narayan Kaul in 1710.

There is another tradition that the guru was beheaded because some of the enemies and rivals of Guru Tegh Bahadur, such as Ram Rai, had suggested to Aurangzeb that he should ask the guru to show a miracle to prove his claim of divine powers, and that action could be taken against him if he failed to do so. But this does not appear likely. Aurangzeb had been out of Delhi from the beginning of 1675 to March 1676, in pursuit of action against the Afghan rebels. Hence, he could not have called the guru to Delhi at the suggestion of Ram Rai.

An explanation has been put forward by later Persian sources which appear to be a defence of the official action. It has been said that the guru who had a large following moved about the Punjab, in association with one Hafiz Adam, who was a follower of Shaikh Ahmad Sirhindi, extorting money by force from the villagers. It is further said that the local *waqia navis*, or intelligence reporter, told the emperor that if action was not taken against the guru, it could lead to disturbances, and even to a rebellion.

We do not know the sources of the Persian account. It mentions Hafiz Adam as an associate of the guru, but Hafiz Adam had died much earlier. Also, the execution of the guru is placed at Lahore, not Delhi. An account does, however, say that the guru was executed at the orders of the emperor.

It would appear that for Aurangzeb, the beheading of the guru was primarily a law and order question. However, according to another Persian source, whenever any peasants came into conflict with the local revenue collector, *jagirdar* or zamindar, they resorted to the guru who looked after them. Thus, far from extorting money by force from the peasants, as alleged, the guru was emerging as a champion against injustice and oppression.

An atmosphere of heightened religious tensions had been brought about in large measure by Aurangzeb's emphasis on the *sharia*, his destruction of newly built temples, and even of some temples of old standing at Mathura, Varanasi, etc., as punishment for local rebellions, or complaints by the *qazis* of opening their doors and teachings to Muslims also. In such a situation, any conflict with a distinguished religious leader was bound to have larger repurcussions.

Whatever the reasons, Aurangzeb's action was unjustified from any point of view and betrayed a narrow approach. The execution of Guru Tegh Bahadur forced the Sikhs to go back to the Punjab hills. It also led to the Sikh movement gradually turning into a military brotherhood. A major contribution in this sphere was made by Guru Govind Singh. He showed considerable organizational ability and founded the military brotherhood or the *khalsa* in 1699. Before this, Guru Govind Singh had made his headquarters at Makhowwal or Anandpur in the foothills of the Punjab. At first, the local Hindu hill rajas had tried to use the guru and his followers in their internecine quarrels. But soon the guru became too powerful and a series of clashes took place between the hill rajas and the guru, who generally triumphed. The organization of the *khalsa* further strengthened the hands of the guru in this conflict. However, an open breach between the guru and the hill rajas took place only in 1704, when the combined forces of a number of hill rajas attacked the guru at Anandpur. The rajas had again to retreat and they pressed the Mughal government to intervene against the guru on their behalf.

The struggle which followed was thus not primarily a religious struggle. It was partly an offshoot of local rivalries among the Hindu hill rajas and the Sikhs, and partly an outcome of the Sikh movement as it had developed. Aurangzeb was concerned with the growing power of the guru and had earlier asked the Mughal *faujdar* 'to admonish the guru'. He now wrote to the governor of Lahore and the *faujdar* of Sirhind, Wazir Khan, to aid the hill rajas in their conflict with Guru Govind Singh. The Mughal forces assaulted Anandpur but the Sikhs fought bravely and beat off all assaults. The Mughals and their allies now invested the fort closely. When starvation began inside the fort, the guru was forced to open the gate, apparently on a promise of safe conduct by Wazir Khan. But when the forces of the guru were crossing a swollen stream, Wazir Khan's forces suddenly attacked. Two of the guru's sons were captured, and on their refusal to embrace Islam, were beheaded at Sirhind. The guru lost two of his remaining sons in another battle. After this, the guru retired to Talwandi and was generally not disturbed.

It is doubtful whether the dastardly action of Wazir Khan against the sons of the guru was carried out at the instance of Aurangzeb. Aurangzeb, it seems, was not keen to destroy the guru and wrote to the governor of Lahore 'to conciliate the guru'. When the guru wrote to Aurangzeb in the Deccan, apprising him of the events, Aurangzeb invited him to meet him. Towards the end of 1706, the guru set out for the Deccan and was on the way when Aurangzeb died. According to some, he had hoped to persuade Aurangzeb to restore Anandpur to him.

Although Guru Govind Singh was not able to withstand Mughal might for long, or to establish a separate Sikh state, he created a tradition and also forged a weapon for its realization later on. It also showed how an egalitarian religious movement could, under certain circumstances, turn into a political and militaristic movement, and subtly move towards regional independence.

RELATIONS WITH THE RAJPUTS—BREACH WITH MARWAR AND MEWAR

We have seen how Jahangir settled in 1613 the long drawn out conflict with Mewar. Jahangir continued Akbar's policy of giving favours to the leading Rajput rajas and of entering into matrimonial relations with them. Shah Jahan maintained the alliance with the Rajputs. During his reign, Rajput contingents served with distinction in such far-flung areas as the Deccan, Balkh in Central Asia, and Qandhar. However, no Rajput raja was appointed governor of a province, and no further matrimonial relations were made with the leading Rajput rajas—though Shah Jahan himself was the son of a Rathor princess.[1] Perhaps, alliance with the Rajputs having been consolidated, it was felt that matrimonial relations with the leading rajas were no longer necessary. However, Shah Jahan accorded high honour to the heads of the two leading Rajputs houses, Jodhpur and Amber. Raja Jaswant Singh, the ruler of Marwar, was high in Shah Jahan's favour. Both he and Jai Singh held the ranks of 7000/7000 at the time of Aurangzeb's accession.

Aurangzeb attached great value to the alliance with the Rajputs. He tried to secure the active support of the maharana of Mewar and raised his *mansab* from 5000/5000 to 6000/6000. Although Jaswant Singh had fought against him at Dharmat and defected from his side during the campaign against Shuja, and invited Dara to his dominions, Aurangzeb pardoned him and restored him to his previous *mansab*. He was also appointed to important commands, including the governorship of Gujarat. Jai Singh remained the close friend and confidant of Aurangzeb till his death in 1667.

Jaswant Singh who had been deputed to look after the affairs of the Afghans in the northwest died towards the end of 1678. The maharaja had no surviving male issue and hence the question of succession to the *gaddi* immediately arose. There was a longstanding Mughal tradition that in case of a disputed succession, the state was brought under Mughal administration (*khalisa*) to ensure law and order, and then handed over to the chosen successor. Thus, in 1650, when there was a dispute about succession in Jaisalmer, Shah Jahan first took the state under *khalisa* and then sent Jaswant Singh at the

---

1 Tradition persists in naming Jodha Bai as the mother of Jahangir. But the only marriage of a Rathor princess we know of was the marriage in 1585 of the daughter of Mota Raja Udai Singh with Salim (Jahangir). Jahangir's mother was a Kachhwaha princess.

head of an army to install the candidate chosen by the emperor. There was another reason also for bringing Marwar under the *khalisa*. The Maharaja, like most Mughal nobles, had large sums of money due to the state which he had not been able to pay back. Many Rajputs, whom Jaswant Singh had annoyed, or whose territories had been granted to him in *jagir* by the emperor, were eager to use the absence of a ruler on the *gaddi* of Jodhpur to create disturbances.

Anticipating resistance from the Rathors, Aurangzeb had allotted two *parganas* in Marwar for the maintenance of the family and supporters of Jaswant Singh. He also assembled a strong army and marched to Ajmer to enforce his orders. Rani Hadi, the chief queen of Jaswant Singh, who had been objecting to handing over charge of Jodhpur to the Mughals, since it was the *watan* (homeland) of the Rathors, had no option but to submit. A diligent search was now made for any hidden treasures that Jaswant Singh might have possessed. Mughal officials were posted all over Marwar. Large numbers of temples, including old temples, were demolished or bricked up.

Thus, the Mughals behaved as conquerors and treated Marwar as hostile territory. It is difficult to find a justification for this. However, Aurangzeb had no intention of retaining control of the territory of Marwar on account of its strategic importance in linking Delhi with the Gujarat seaports, as has been asserted by the modern historian Jadunath Sarkar. Two sons were born at Lahore to two ranis of Jaswant Singh after his death. Their claim to the *gaddi* was strongly canvassed. However, before returning to Delhi, Aurangzeb decided to award the *tika* of Jodhpur to Inder Singh, the grandson of Jaswant Singh's elder brother, Amar Singh, in return for a succession fee of thirty-six lakhs of rupees. Perhaps, Aurangzeb was moved by the argument that Shah Jahan had done a great injustice in passing over the claims of Amar Singh, in giving the *tika* to his younger brother, Jaswant Singh. He may also have wanted to avoid a minority administration in Marwar.

According to some modern historians, Aurangzeb offered Jodhpur to Ajit Singh, the posthumous son of Jaswant Singh, on condition of his becoming a Muslim. There is no such suggestion in contemporary sources. According to a contemporary Rajasthani work, *Hukumat-ri-Bahi*, Aurangzeb offered a *mansab* to Ajit Singh when he was presented at the court in Agra and declared that the two *parganas* in

Marwar, Sojat and Jaitaran, would continue as his *jagir*. Thus, Aurangzeb was virtually contemplating a division of the state of Marwar between the two branches of the family.

The Rathor sardars led by Durgadas, rejected this proffered compromise which they felt would be against the best interests of the state. Angered at the rejection of his offer by the sardars, Aurangzeb ordered that the princes and their mothers be put in confinement at the fort of Nurgarh. This alarmed the Rathor sardars who, after a valiant fight, made their escape from Agra along with one of the princes, and crowned him as Ajit Singh at Jodhpur amidst great rejoicing.

Aurangzeb might have gracefully accepted the fact that Inder Singh had no following among the Rathors. He set aside Inder Singh for 'incompetence' but adopted a stern, unbending attitude towards Ajit Singh, declaring him to be a 'pretender'. Strong forces were summoned from all parts of the empire and, once again, Aurangzeb marched to Ajmer. The Rathor resistance was crushed and Jodhpur occupied. Durgadas fled with Ajit Singh to Mewar where the rana sent him to a secret hide-out.

It was at this stage that Mewar entered the war on the side of Ajit Singh. Rana Raj Singh who at one stage had supported Aurangzeb had been gradually alienated. He had sent a force of 5000 men under one of his leading men to Jodhpur to back up the claim of Rani Hadi. Apparently, he was deeply opposed to Mughal interference in the internal affairs of the Rajputs, such as questions of succession. Apart from this, he nursed a grievance at Mughal efforts to detach from Mewar the states to its south and west, Dungarpur, Banswara, etc., which had been at one time tribute-paying, dependent rulers under Mewar. But the immediate cause was his unease at the Mughal military occupation of Marwar, and Aurangzeb's rejection of Ajit Singh's claim of succession.

Aurangzeb struck the first blow. In November 1679 he attacked Mewar. A strong Mughal detachment reached Udaipur and even raided the camp of the rana who had retreated deep into the hills to conduct a harassing warfare against the Mughals. The war soon reached a stalement. The Mughals could neither penetrate the hills, nor deal with the guerrilla tactics of the Rajputs. The war now became highly unpopular, Aurangzeb's admonitions and warnings to his commanders having little effect. At last, the eldest son of Aurangzeb, prince Akbar, tried to take advantage of this situation by turning his arms against his father. In alliance with the Rathor chief, Durgadas, he marched on Ajmer (January 1681) where Aurangzeb was helpless, all his best troops being engaged elsewhere. But prince Akbar delayed, and Aurangzeb was able to stir up dissensions in his camp by false letters. Prince Akbar had to flee to Maharashtra and Aurangzeb heaved a sigh of relief.

The campaign of Mewar now became secondary for Aurangzeb. He patched up a treaty with Rana Jagat Singh, Rana Raj Singh having died in the meantime. The new rana was forced to surrender some of his *parganas* in lieu of *jizyah*, and was granted a *mansab* of 5000 on a promise of loyalty and of not supporting Ajit Singh. Regarding Ajit Singh, all that Aurangzeb would promise was that *mansab* and *raj* would be given to him when he came of age.

This agreement and the promise regarding Ajit Singh satisfied none of the Rajputs. The Mughals kept their control on Marwar and desultory warfare continued till 1698 when at last, Ajit Singh was recognised as the ruler of Marwar. But the Mughals refused to relax their hold on the capital, Jodhpur. The rana of Mewar, too, remained dissatisfied at the surrender of his *parganas* to the Mughals. There was no change in this situation till Aurangzeb died in 1707.

Aurangzeb's policy towards Marwar and Mewar was clumsy and blundering, and brought no advantage of any kind to the Mughals. On the other hand, Mughal failure against these states damaged Mughal military prestige. It is true that the warfare in Marwar after 1681 involved only a few troops, and were not of much consequence militarily. It is also true that Hada and Kachhwaha and other Rajput contingents continued to serve the Mughals. But the results of the Marwar policy of Aurangzeb cannot be judged solely by these. The breach with Marwar and Mewar weakened the Mughal alliance with the Rajputs at a crucial time. Above all, it created doubts about the firmness of Mughal support to old and trusted allies and the ulterior motives of Aurangzeb. It showed the rigid and obstinate nature of Aurangzeb. It did not, however, amount to a fixed determination on his part to subvert Hinduism, as has been alleged, because during the period after 1679, large numbers of Marathas were allowed entry into the nobility.

Aurangzeb's conflicts in the northeast and with the Jats, Afghans, Sikhs and Rajputs put a strain on the empire. However, the real conflict lay in the Deccan.

NINETEEN

Climax and Disintegration of the Mughal Empire—II

THE RISE OF THE MARATHAS

We have already seen that the Marathas had important positions in the administrative and military systems of Ahmadnagar and Bijapur, and that their power and influence in the affairs of government had grown as the Mughals advanced towards the Deccan. Both the Deccani sultans and the Mughals made a bid for their support, and Malik Ambar used them in his army in large numbers as loose auxiliaries. Although a number of influential Maratha families—the Mores, the Ghatages, the Nimbalkars, etc., exercised local authority in some areas, the Marathas did not have any large, well-established states as the Rajputs had. The credit for setting up such a large state goes to Shahji Bhonsale and his son, Shivaji. As we have seen, for some time, Shahji acted as the kingmaker in Ahmadnagar, and defied the Mughals. However, by the treaty of 1636, Shahji yielded the territories he was dominating. He joined the service of Bijapur and turned his energies to Karnataka. Taking advantage of the unsettled conditions, Shahji tried to set up a semi-independent principality at Bangalore, just as Mir Jumla, the leading noble of Golconda, tried to carve out such a principality on the Coromandel coast. A number of other chiefs, such as the Abyssinian chiefs on the western coast, the Sidis, behaved in a similar manner. This forms the background to Shivaji's attempt to carve out a large principality around Poona.

EARLY CAREER OF SHIVAJI

Shahji had left the Poona *jagir* to his neglected senior wife, Jija Bai, and his minor son, Shivaji. Shivaji showed his mettle when at the young age of 18, he overran a number of hill forts near Poona—

Rajgarh, Kondana and Torna in the years 1645–47. With the death of his guardian, Dadaji Kondadeo in 1647, Shivaji became his own master, and the full control of his father's *jagir* passed to him.

Shivaji began his real career of conquest in 1656 when he conquered Javli from the Maratha chief, Chandra Rao More. The Javli kingdom and the accumulated treasure of the Mores were important, and Shivaji acquired them by means of treachery. The conquest of Javli made him the undisputed master of the Mavala area, or the highlands, and freed his path to the Satara area and to the coastal strip, the Konkan. Mavali foot soldiers became a strong part of his army. With their help, he strengthened his position by acquiring a further series of hill forts near Poona.

The Mughal invasion of Bijapur in 1657 saved Shivaji from Bijapuri reprisal. Shivaji first entered into negotiations with Aurangzeb, then changed sides and made deep inroads into Mughal areas, seizing rich booty. When Aurangzeb came to terms with the new Bijapur ruler in preparation for the civil war, he pardoned Shivaji also. But he distrusted Shivaji, and advised the Bijapur ruler to expel him from the Bijapuri area he had seized, and if he wanted to employ him, employ him in Karnataka, away from the Mughal frontiers.

With Aurangzeb away in the north, Shivaji resumed his career of conquest at the expense of Bijapur. He burst into the Konkan, the coastal strip between the Ghats and the sea, and seized its northern part. He also overran a number of other hill forts. Bijapur now decided to take stern action. It sent against Shivaji a premier Bijapuri noble, Afzal Khan, at the head of 10,000 troops, with instructions to capture him by any means possible. Treachery was common in those days, and both Afzal Khan and Shivaji had resorted to treachery on a number of occasions. Shivaji's forces were not used to open fighting and shrank from an open contest with this powerful chief. Afzal Khan sent an invitation to Shivaji for a personal interview, promising to get him pardoned from the Bijapuri court. Convinced that this was a trap, Shivaji went prepared, and murdered the Khan (1659) in a cunning but daring manner. Shivaji put his leaderless army to rout and captured all his goods and equipment including his artillery. Flushed with victory, the Maratha troops overran the powerful fort of Panhala and poured into south Konkan and the Kolhapur districts, making extensive conquests.

Shivaji's exploits made him a legendary figure. His fame grew and he was credited with magical powers. People flocked to him from the Maratha areas to join his army; and even Afghan mercenaries who had been previously in the service of Bijapur, joined his army.

Meanwhile, Aurangzeb was anxiously watching the rise of a Maratha power so near the Mughal frontiers. Aurangzeb instructed the new Mughal governor of the Deccan, Shaista Khan, who was related to Aurangzeb by marriage, to invade Shivaji's dominions.

At first, the war went badly for Shivaji. Shaista Khan occupied Poona (1660) and made it his headquarters. He then sent detachments to wrest control of the Konkan from Shivaji. Despite harassing attacks from Shivaji, and the bravery of Maratha defenders, the Mughals secured their control on north Konkan. Driven into a corner, Shivaji made a bold stroke. He infiltrated into the camp of Shaista Khan at Poona, and at night attacked the Khan in his haram (1663), killing his son and one of his captains, and wounding the Khan. This daring attack put the Khan into disgrace and Shivaji's stock rose once again. In anger, Aurangzeb transferred Shaista Khan to Bengal, even refusing to give him an interview at the time of transfer as was the custom. Meanwhile, Shivaji made another bold move. He attacked Surat, which was the premier Mughal port, and looted it to his heart's content (1664), returning home laden with treasure.

TREATY OF PURANDAR AND SHIVAJI'S VISIT TO AGRA

After the failure of Shaista Khan, Aurangzeb deputed Raja Jai Singh of Amber, who was one of the most trusted advisers of Aurangzeb, to deal with Shivaji. Full military and administrative authority was conferred on Jai Singh so that he was not in any way dependent on the Mughal viceroy in the Deccan, and dealt directly with the emperor. Unlike his predecessors, Jai Singh did not underestimate the Marathas. He made careful diplomatic and military preparations. He appealed to all the rivals and opponents of Shivaji, and even tried to win over the sultan of Bijapur in order to isolate Shivaji. Marching to Poona, Jai Singh decided to strike at the heart of Shivaji's territories— Fort Purandar where Shivaji had lodged his family and his treasure. Jai Singh closely besieged Purandar (1665), beating off all Maratha attempts to relieve it. With the fall of the fort in sight, and no relief likely from any quarter, Shivaji opened negotiations with Jai Singh. After hard bargaining, the following terms were agreed upon:

(i) Out of 35 forts held by Shivaji, 23 forts with surrounding territory which yielded a revenue of four lakhs of *huns* every year were to be surrendered to the Mughals, while the remaining 12 forts with an annual income of one lakh of *huns* were to be left to Shivaji 'on condition of service and loyalty to the throne'.

(ii) Territory worth four lakhs of *huns* a year in the Bijapuri Konkan, which Shivaji had already held, was granted to him. In addition, Bijapur territory worth five lakhs of *huns* a year in the uplands (Balaghat), which Shivaji was to conquer, was also granted to him. In return for these, he was to pay 40 lakhs *huns* in instalments to the Mughals.

Shivaji asked to be excused from personal service. Hence, a *mansab* of 5000 was granted in his place to his minor son, Sambhaji. Shivaji promised, however, to join personally in any Mughal campaign in the Deccan.

Jai Singh cleverly threw a bone of contention between Shivaji and the Bijapuri ruler. But the success of Jai Singh's scheme depended upon Mughal support to Shivaji in making up from Bijapur territory the amount he had yielded to the Mughals. This proved to be the fatal flaw. Aurangzeb had not lost his reservations about Shivaji, and was doubtful of the wisdom of a joint Mughal-Maratha attack on Bijapur. But Jai Singh had larger ideas. He considered the alliance with Shivaji the starting point of the conquest of Bijapur and the entire Deccan. And once this had been done, Shivaji would have no option but to remain an ally of the Mughals since, as Jai Singh wrote to Aurangzeb, 'We shall hem Shivaji in like the centre of a circle.'

However, the Mughal-Maratha expedition against Bijapur failed. Shivaji who had been deputed to capture Fort Panhala was also unsuccessful. Seeing his grandiose scheme collapsing before his eyes, Jai Singh persuaded Shivaji to visit the emperor at Agra. If Shivaji and Aurangzeb could be reconciled, Jai Singh thought, Aurangzeb might be persuaded to give greater resources for a renewed invasion of Bijapur. But the visit proved to be a disaster. Shivaji felt insulted when he was put in the category of *mansabdars* of 5000—a rank which had been granted earlier to his minor son. Nor did the emperor, whose birthday was being celebrated, find time to speak to Shivaji. Hence, Shivaji walked off angrily and refused imperial service. Such an episode had never happened, and a strong group at the court argued that exemplary punishment should be meted out to Shivaji in order to maintain and assert imperial dignity. Since Shivaji had come to Agra on Jai Singh's assurance, Aurangzeb wrote to him for advice. Jai Singh strongly argued for a lenient treatment for Shivaji. But before any decision could be taken, Shivaji escaped from detention (1666). The manner of Shivaji's escape is too well known to be repeated here.

Aurangzeb always blamed himself for his carelessness in allowing Shivaji to escape. There is little doubt that Shivaji's Agra visit proved to be the turning point in Mughal relations with the Marathas— although for two years after his return home, Shivaji kept quiet. The visit proved that, unlike Jai Singh, Aurangzeb attached little value to the alliance with Shivaji. For him, Shivaji was just a 'petty *bhumia*' (land-holder). As subsequent developments proved, Aurangzeb's stubborn reservations about Shivaji, refusal to recognize his importance and attaching a low price to his friendship were among the biggest political mistakes made by Aurangzeb.

FINAL BREACH WITH SHIVAJI—SHIVAJI'S ADMINISTRATION AND ACHIEVEMENTS

Aurangzeb virtually goaded Shivaji into resuming his career of conquest by insisting upon a narrow interpretation of the treaty of Purandar, although with the failure of the expedition against Bijapur, the bottom had dropped out of the treaty. Shivaji could not be reconciled to the loss of 23 forts and territory worth four lakhs *huns* a year to the Mughals without any compensation from Bijapur. He renewed the contest with the Mughals, sacking Surat a second time in 1670. During the next four years, he recovered a large number of his forts, including Purandar, from the Mughals and made deep inroads into Mughal territories, especially Berar and Khandesh. Mughal preoccupation with the Afghan uprising in the northwest helped Shivaji. He also renewed his contest with Bijapur, securing

Panhala and Satara by means of bribes, and raiding the Kanara country at leisure.

In 1674, Shivaji crowned himself formally at Raigarh. Shivaji had travelled far from being a petty *jagirdar* at Poona. He was by now the most powerful among the Maratha chiefs, and by virtue of the extent of his dominions and the size of his army could claim a status equal to the effete Deccani sultans. The formal coronation had, therefore, a number of purposes. It placed him on a pedestal much higher than any of the Maratha chiefs, some of whom had continued to look upon him as an upstart. To strengthen his social position further, Shivaji married into some of the leading old Maratha families—the Mohites, the Shirkes, etc. A formal declaration was also made by the priest presiding over the function, Gaga Bhatta, that Shivaji was a high class kshatriya. Finally, as an independent ruler it now became possible for Shivaji to enter into treaties with the Deccani sultans on a footing of equality and not as a rebel. It was also an important step in the further growth of Maratha national sentiment.

In 1676 Shivaji undertook a bold new venture. With the active aid and support of the brothers, Madanna and Akhanna at Hyderabad, Shivaji undertook an expedition into the Bijapuri Karnataka. Shivaji was given a grand welcome by the Qutb Shah at his capital, and a formal agreement was arrived at. The Qutb Shah agreed to pay a subsidy of one lakh *huns* (five lakhs of rupees) annually to Shivaji and a Maratha ambassador was to live at his court. The territory and the booty gained in Karnataka was to be shared. The Qutb Shah supplied a contingent of troops and artillery to aid Shivaji and also provided money for the expenses of his army. The treaty was very favourable to Shivaji and enabled him to capture Jinji and Vellore from Bijapuri officials and also to conquer much of the territories held by his half-brother, Ekoji. Although Shivaji had assumed the title of '*Haindava-Dharmoddharak*' (Protector of the Hindu faith), he plundered mercilessly the Hindu population of the area. Returning home laden with treasure, Shivaji refused to share anything with the Qutb Shah, thus straining his relations with him.

The Karnataka expedition was the last major expedition of Shivaji. The base at Jinji built up by Shivaji proved to be a haven of refuge for his son, Rajaram, during Aurangzeb's all-out war on the Marathas.

Shivaji died in 1680, shortly after his return from the Karanataka expedition. Meanwhile, he had laid the foundations of a sound system of administration. Shivaji's system of administration was largely borrowed from the administrative practices of the Deccani states. Although he designated eight ministers, sometimes called the *Ashtapradhan*, it was not in the nature of a council of ministers, each minister being directly responsible to the ruler. The most important ministers were the Peshwas who looked after the finances and general administration, and the *sar-i-naubat* (*senapati*) which was a post of honour and was generally given to one of the leading Maratha chiefs. The *majumdar* was the accountant, while the *wakenavis* was responsible for intelligence, posts and household affairs. The *surunavis* or *chitnis* helped the king with his correspondence. The *dabir* was master of ceremonies and also helped the king in his dealings with foreign powers. The *nyayadhish* and *panditrao* were in charge of justice and charitable grants.

More important than the appointment of these officials was Shivaji's organisation of the army and the revenue system. Shivaji preferred to give cash salaries to the regular soldiers, though sometimes the chiefs received revenue grants (*saranjam*). Strict discipline was maintained in the army, no women or dancing girls being allowed to accompany the army. The plunder taken by each soldier during campaigns was strictly accounted for. The regular army (*paga*) consisting of about 30,000 to 40,000 cavalry, as distinct from the loose auxiliaries (*silahdars*), were supervised by *havaldars* who received fixed salaries. The forts were carefully supervised, Mavali foot soldiers and gunners being appointed there. We are told that three men of equal rank were placed in charge of each fort to guard against treachery.

The revenue system seems to have been patterned on the system of Malik Ambar. A new revenue assessment was completed by Annaji Datto in 1679. It is not correct to think that Shivaji abolished the *zamindari* (*deshmukhi*) system, or that he did not award *jagirs* (*mokasa*) to his officials. However, Shivaji strictly supervised the *mirasdars*, that is, those with hereditary rights in land. Describing the situation, Sabhasad, who wrote in the eighteenth century, says that these sections paid to the government only a small part of their collections. 'In consequence, the *mirasdars* grew and strengthened themselves by building bastions, castles and strongholds in the villages, enlisting footmen and musketeers... This class had become unruly and seized the country.' Shivaji destroyed their bastions and forced them to submit.

Shivaji supplemented his income by levying a contribution on the neighbouring Mughal territories. This contribution which came to one-fourth of the land revenue, began to be called *chauthai* (one-fourth) or *chauth*.

Shivaji not only proved to be an able general, a skilful tactician and a shrewd diplomat, he also laid the foundation of a strong state by curbing the power of the *deshmukhs*. The army was an effective instrument of his policies, rapidity of movement being the most important factor. The army depended for its salaries to a considerable extent on the plunder of the neighbouring areas. But the state cannot thereby be called just a 'war-state'. It was regional in character, no doubt, but it definitely had a popular base. To that extent, Shivaji was a popular king who represented the assertion of popular will in the area against Mughal encroachments.

AURANGZEB AND THE DECCANI STATES (1658–87)

It is possible to trace three phases in the relations of Aurangzeb with the Deccani states. The first phase lasted till 1668 during which the main attempt was to recover from Bijapur the territories belonging to the Ahmadnagar state surrendered to it by the treaty of 1636; the second phase lasted till 1684 during which the major danger in the Deccan was considered to be the Maathas, and efforts were made to pressurize Bijapur and Golconda into joining hands with the Mughals against Shivaji and then against his son, Sambhaji. The Mughals nibbled at the territories of the Deccani states and at the same time tried to bring them under their complete domination and control. The last phase began when Aurangzeb despaired of getting the cooperation of Bijapur and Golconda against the Marathas, and decided that to destroy the Marathas it was necessary to conquer Bijapur and Golconda first.

The treaty of 1636, by which Shah Jahan had given one-third of the territories of Ahmadnagar state as a bribe for withdrawing support to the Marathas, and the promise that the Mughals would 'never ever' conquer Bijapur and Golconda, had been abandoned by Shah Jahan himself. In 1657–58, Golconda and Bijapur were threatened with extinction. Golconda had to pay a huge indemnity, and Bijapur had to agree to the surrender of the Nizam Shahi territories granted to it in 1636. The 'justification' for this was that both these states had made extensive conquests in Karnataka and that 'compensation' was due to the Mughals on the ground that the two states were Mughal vassals, and that their conquests had been made possible due to benevolent neutrality on the part of the Mughals. In reality the cost of maintaining the Mughal armies in the Deccan was high, and the income from the Deccani areas under the control of the Mughals was insufficient to meet it. For a long time, the cost was met by subsidies from the treasuries of Malwa and Gujarat.

The resumption of a policy of limited advance in the Deccan had far-reaching implications which, it seems, neither Shah Jahan nor Aurangzeb adequately appreciated: it destroyed for all times confidence in the Mughal treaties and promises, and made impossible 'a union of hearts' against the Marathas—a policy which Aurangzeb pursued with great perseverance for a quarter of a century, but with little success.

THE FIRST PHASE (1658–68)

On coming to the throne, Aurangzeb had two problems in the Deccan: the problem posed by the rising power of Shivaji, and the problem of persuading Bijapur to part with the territories ceded to it by the treaty of 1636. Kalyani and Bidar had been secured in 1657. Parenda was secured by bribe in 1660. Sholapur still remained. After his accession, Aurangzeb asked Jai Singh to punish both Shivaji and Adil Shah. This shows Aurangzeb's confidence in the superiority of the Mughal arms and the underestimation of his opponents. But Jai Singh was an astute politician. He told Aurangzeb, 'It would be unwise to attack both these fools at the same time.'

Jai Singh was the only Mughal politician who advocated an all-out forward policy in the Deccan during this period. Jai Singh was of the opinion that the Maratha problem could not be solved without a forward policy in the Deccan—a conclusion to which Aurangzeb finally came 20 years later.

While planning his invasion of Bijapur, Jai Singh had written to Aurangzeb, 'The conquest of Bijapur is the preface to the conquest of all Deccan and Karnataka.' But Aurangzeb shrank from this bold policy. We can only guess at the reasons: the ruler of Iran had adopted a threatening attitude in the northwest; the campaign for the conquest of the Deccan would be long and arduous and would need the presence of the emperor himself for large armies could not be left in charge of a noble or an ambitious prince, as Shah Jahan had discovered to his misfortune. Also, as long as Shah Jahan was alive, Aurangzeb could not afford to go away on a distant campaign.

With his limited resources, Jai Singh's Bijapur campaign (1665) was bound to fail. The campaign recreated the united front of the Deccani states against the Mughals, for the Qutb Shah sent a large force to aid Bijapur. The Deccanis adopted guerilla tactics, luring Jai Singh on to Bijapur while devastating the countryside so that the Mughals could get no supplies. Jai Singh found that he had no means to assault the city since he had not brought siege guns, and to invest the city was impossible. The retreat proved costly, and neither money nor any additional territory was gained by Jai Singh by this campaign. This disappointment and the censures of Aurangzeb hastened Jai Singh's death (1667). The following year (1668), the Mughals secured the surrender of Sholapur by bribery. The first phase was thus over.

THE SECOND PHASE (1668–84)

The Mughals virtually marked time in the Deccan between 1668 and 1676. A new factor during the period was the rise to power of Madanna and Akhanna in Golconda. These two gifted brothers virtually ruled Golconda from 1672 almost till the extinction of the state in 1687. The brothers followed a policy of trying to establish a tripartite alliance between Golconda, Bijapur and Shivaji. This policy was periodically disturbed by faction fights at the Bijapur court, and by the overweening ambition of Shivaji. The factions at Bijapur could not be depended upon to follow a consistent policy. They adopted a pro or anti-Mughal stance depending upon their immediate interests. Shivaji looted and alternately supported Bijapur against the Mughals. Although seriously concerned at the growing Maratha power, Aurangzeb, it seems, was keen to limit Mughal expansion in the Deccan. Hence, repeated efforts were made to install and back a party at Bijapur which would cooperate with the Mughals against Shivaji, and which would not be led by Golconda.

In pursuit of this policy, a series of Mughal military interventions were made, the details of which are of little interest.

The only result of Mughal diplomatic and military efforts was the re-assertion of the united front of the three Deccani powers against the Mughals. A last desperate effort of Diler Khan, the Mughal Viceroy, in 1679–80 to capture Bijapur also failed, largely because no Mughal viceroy had the means to contend against the united forces of the Deccani states. A new element which was brought into play was the matchlock armed Karnataki foot soldiers. Thirty thousand of them sent by the Berar chief, Prem Naik, were a major factor in withstanding the Mughal siege of Bijapur in 1679–80. Shivaji, too, sent a large force to relieve Bijapur and raided the Mughal dominions in all directions. Thus, Diler Khan could achieve nothing except laying Mughal territories open to Maratha raids. Hence, he was recalled by Aurangzeb.

THE THIRD PHASE (1684–87)

Thus, the Mughals achieved little during 1676–80. When Aurangzeb reached the Deccan in 1681 in pursuit of his rebel son, prince Akbar at first, he concentrated his forces against Sambhaji, the son and successor of Shivaji while making renewed efforts to detach Bijapur and Golconda from the side of the Marathas. His efforts did not have an outcome different from those of the earlier ones. The Marathas were the only shield against the Mughals, and the Deccani states were not prepared to throw it away.

Aurangzeb now decided to force the issue. He called upon the Adil Shah as a vassal to supply provision to the imperial army, to allow the Mughal armies free passage through his territory, and to supply a contingent of 5000 to 6000 cavalry for the war against the Marathas. He also demanded that Sharza Khan, the leading Bijapuri noble opposed to the Mughals, be expelled. An open rupture was now inevitable. The Adil Shah appealed for help both to Golconda and Sambhaji, which was promptly given. Even the combined forces of the Deccani states could not withstand the full strength of the Mughal army, particularly when it was commanded by the Mughal emperor himself. However, it took 18 months of siege, with Aurangzeb being personally present during the final stages, before Bijapur fell (1686). This provides ample justification for the earlier failures of Jai Singh (1665), and Diler Khan (1679–80) against Bijapur.

A campaign against Golconda was inevitable following the downfall of Bijapur. The 'sins' of the Qutb Shah were too many to be pardoned. He had given supreme power to the infidels, Madanna and Akhanna, and helped Shivaji on various occasions. His latest 'treachery' was sending 40,000 men to aid Bijapur, despite Aurangzeb's warnings. Earlier in 1685, despite stiff resistance, the Mughals had occupied Golconda. The emperor had agreed to pardon the Qutb Shah in return for a huge subsity, the ceding of some areas and the ousting of Madanna and Akhanna. The Qutb Shah had agreed. Madanna and Akhanna had been dragged out into the streets and murdered (1686). But even this crime failed to save the Qutb Shah. The Mughals opened the siege of Golconda early in 1687 and after more than six months of campaigning the fort fell on account of treachery and bribery.

Aurangzeb had triumphed but he soon found that the extinction of Bijapur and Golconda was only the beginning of his difficulties. The last and the most difficult phase of Aurangzeb's life began now.

AURANGZEB, THE MARATHAS AND THE DECCAN—
THE LAST PHASE (1687–1707)

After the downfall of Bijapur and Golconda, Aurangzeb was able to concentrate all his forces against the Marathas.

In 1689, Sambhaji was surprised at his secret hide-out at Sangameshwar by a Mughal force. He was paraded before Aurangzeb and executed as a rebel and an infidel. This was undoubtedly another major political mistake on the part of Aurangzeb. He could have set a seal on his conquest of Bijapur and Golconda by coming to terms with the Marathas. By executing Sambhaji, he not only threw away this chance, but provided the Marathas a new cause. At the same time, in the absence of a single rallying point, the Maratha sardars were left free to plunder the Mughal territories, disappearing at the approach of the Mughal forces, and rallying again. Instead of having destroyed the Maratha state, Aurangzeb made the Maratha opposition all-pervasive in the Deccan. Rajaram, the younger brother of Sambhaji, was crowned as king, but had to escape when the Mughals attacked his capital. Rajaram sought shelter at Jinji on the east coast and continued the fight against the Mughals from there. Thus, Maratha resistance spread from the west to the east coast.

However, for the moment, Aurangzeb was at the height of his power, having triumphed over all his enemies. Some of the nobles were of the opinion that Aurangzeb should return to north India, leaving to others the task of mopping-up operations against the Marathas. Earlier, there was an opinion which, it appears, had the support of the heir-apparent, Shah Alam, that the task of ruling over Karnataka should be left to the vassal rulers of Bijapur and Golconda. Aurangzeb rejected all these suggestions, and imprisoned Shah Alam for daring to negotiate with the Deccani rulers. Convinced that the Maratha power had been crushed after 1690, Aurangzeb, concentrated on annexing to the empire the rich and extensive Karnataka tract. However, Aurangzeb bit off more than he could chew. He unduly extended his lines of communications which became vulnerable to Maratha attacks. This resulted in his failure to provide a sound administration to Bijapur which was the hub of Maratha activities.

During the period between 1690 and 1703, Aurangzeb stubbornly refused to negotiate with the Marathas. Rajaram was besieged at Jinji, but the siege proved to be long drawn out. Jinji fell in 1698, but the chief prize, Rajaram, escaped. Maratha resistance grew and the Mughals suffered a number of serious reverses. The Marathas recaptured many of their forts and Rajaram was able to come back to Satara.

Undaunted, Aurangzeb set out to win back all the Maratha forts. For five and half years, from 1700 to 1705, Aurangzeb dragged his weary and ailing body from the siege of one fort to another. Floods, disease and the Maratha roving bands took fearful toll of the Mughal army. Weariness and disaffection steadily grew among the nobles and in the army. Demoralization set in, and many *jagirdars* made secret pacts with the Marathas and agreed to pay *chauth* if the Marathas did not disturb their *jagirs*.

In 1703, Aurangzeb opened negotiations with the Marathas. He was prepared to release Shahu, the son of Sambhaji, who had been captured at Satara along with his mother. Shahu had been treated well. He had been given the title of raja and the *mansab* of 7000/7000. On coming of age he had been married to two Maratha girls of respectable families. Aurangzeb was prepared to grant to Shahu, Shivaji's swarajya and the right of *sardeshmukhi* over the Deccan, thus recognising his special position. Over 70 Maratha sardars actually assembled to receive Shahu. But Aurangzeb cancelled the arrangements at the last minute, being uncertain about the intentions of the Marathas.[1]

By 1706, Aurangzeb was convinced of the futility of his effort to capture all the Maratha forts. He slowly retreated to Aurangabad while an exulting Maratha army hovered around and attacked the stragglers.

Thus, when Aurangzeb breathed his last at Aurangabad in 1707, he left behind an empire which was sorely distracted, and in which all the various internal problems were coming to a head.

DECLINE OF THE MUGHAL EMPIRE—RESPONSIBILITY OF AURANGZEB

The Mughal empire declined rapidly after the death of Aurangzeb. The Mughal court became the scene for faction fighting among the nobles, and soon ambitious provincial governors began to behave in an independent manner. The Maratha depredations extended from the Deccan to the heartland of the empire, the Gangetic plains. The weakness of the empire was proclaimed to the world when Nadir Shah imprisoned the Mughal emperor and looted Delhi in 1739.

---

1 It has been said that Aurangzeb offered the kingdom to Shahu on condition of his turning a Muslim. Contemporary records do not support this. If Aurangzeb had wanted to convert Shahu to Islam, he could have done so while he was his captive during the preceding 13 years. Normally, a converted Hindu prince, lost the right to his kingdom.

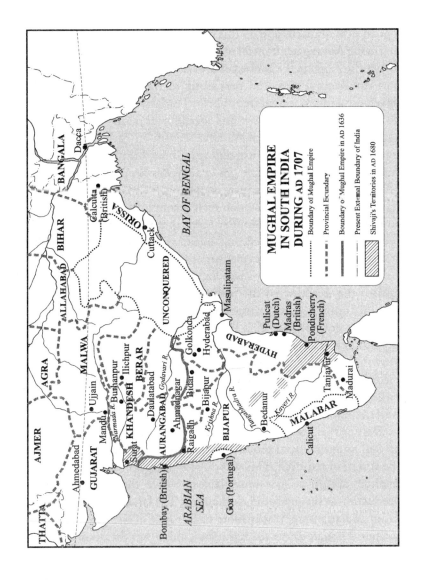

The map titles within the legend read:

MUGHAL EMPIRE
IN SOUTH INDIA
DURING AD 1707

Boundary of Mughal Empire
Provincial Boundary
Boundary of Mughal Empire in AD 1636
Present External Boundary of India
Shivaji's Territories in AD 1680

To what extent was the downfall of the Mughal empire due to developments after the death of Aurangzeb, and to what extent was it due to the mistaken policies adopted by Aurangzeb? There has been a good deal of discussion on this point among historians. While not absolving Aurangzeb from all responsibility, the recent trend has been to view his reign in the context of the economic, social, administrative and intellectual situation prevailing in the country, as also the developing international trends before and during his reign.

The working of economic and social forces in medieval India has yet to be fully understood. We have seen in an earlier chapter that trade and commerce were expanding in India during the seventeenth century and that handicraft production was keeping pace with the growing demand. This, in turn, could only have been made possible if the production of raw materials such as cotton, indigo, etc., expanded simultaneously. The area under *zabti*, that is, where the system of measurement was followed, expanded, according to official Mughal statistics. There is some evidence, in fact, that the total area under cultivation expanded. This was due not only to population growth, and to the working of the economic forces but, in part, to the administrative policies pursued by the Mughals. Every noble, even a religious grantee was expected to take personal interest in the expansion and improvement of cultivation, and careful records of such growth were maintained. Historians are surprised at the detailed records that were maintained regarding the number of ploughs, bullocks and wells in each village, the increase in their numbers as well the number of cultivators and the area under cultivation.

Despite this, there is reason to believe that trade and manufacture, as well as agricultural production were not expanding as rapidly as the situation required. This was due to a number of factors. No new methods of cultivation were available to counter the trend of declining production as the soil became exhausted. The land revenue was heavy. From Akbar's time, it was more or less half of the produce,[1] if we include the share due to the zamindars and to the other local elements.

---

1 Under Akbar, the standrd rate was one third of the average produce, but the share of the zamindar and other local elements was not included in it. From the middle of the seventeenth century, the state share generally rose to half, but it included the share of the zamindar and local elements (village headman etc.)

The state demand varied from area to area, being less in the less fertile areas of Rajasthan and Sindh, and more in such fertile areas as the saffron-producing areas in Kashmir. However, it was not, generally speaking, so heavy as to drive the peasant away from land. In fact, figures from eastern Rajasthan show that new villages were continuously being founded during the second half of the seventeenth and the early part of the eighteenth century. (We do not have figures for the earlier period.) The basic reasons for the limited expansion, it appears, were social and partly administrative. Since the population of the country during the period is estimated to be about 125 million, there was plenty of surplus cultivable land available. However, we hear of landless labourers in many villages. The bulk of these people, it seems, can be broadly classified as untouchables or Dalits. The cultivating communities, and the zamindars who often belonged to the general (*Shudra*) and upper castes, had little desire or incentive for making it possible for the Dalits to settle new villages and thus acquire proprietary right in land. They had, in fact, a vested interest in keeping them in the village as a reserve labour force, and for performing various menial jobs for them, such as skinning the dead animals, making leather ropes, etc. The rural landless and poor (i.e. those who had very small holdings) had neither the necessary capital nor the organisation needed for settling new villages or breaking uncultivated lands on their own. The state did, sometimes, take the initiative in settling new lands, but had to depend on the local zamindars and the village headmen (*muqaddams*) in the enterprises. Often, these sections belonged to specific caste groups and had their own vested interests, as we have noted.

While agricultural production increased slowly, the demands and expectations of the ruling classes expanded rapidly. Thus, the number of *mansabdars* rose from 2069 at the time of Jahangir's accession in 1605, to 8000 in 1637 during Shah Jahan's reign, and to 11,456 during the latter half of Aurangzeb's reign. While the number of nobles rose five times, the revenue resources of the empire increased only slowly. During the reigns of Jahangir and Shah Jahan, the empire hardly expanded. Moreover, Shah Jahan inaugurated what may be called an age of magnificence. The opulence of the nobles who already enjoyed the highest salaries in the world increased further during the period.

Though many nobles took part in trade and commerce directly or through merchants acting on their behalf, income from trade and commerce could only supplement their income which continued to be mainly from land. Their problems worsened by the fact that the prices rose considerably during the first half of the 17th century. Hence, they tried to increase their income from land by squeezing the peasants and the zamindars as far as they could.

We know very little about the number of zamindars and their living standards. Mughal policy towards the zamindars was contradictory. While on the one hand, the zamindars were considered the main threat to the internal stability of the empire, on the other hand, efforts were made to draw them into the task of local administration. Many of them—Rajputs, Marathas and others—were given *mansabs* and political offices in an effort to broaden the political base of the empire. The zamindars, who as a class had become more powerful and influential in the process, were in no mood to submit to the illegal exactions of the nobles. Nor was it easy to increase the exactions on the peasantry still further, especially when there was plenty of surplus cultivable land and the zamindars, and the village headmen vied with each other to try to attract new cultivators to their lands. The movement of these migrant peasants called *pahis* or *uparis* from village to village in search of better conditions is a little noticed feature of medieval rural life.

Thus attempts to realize more from the *jagirs*, often by means not sanctioned by the state, brought to the surface all the internal contradictions of medieval rural society. It led to peasant discontent in some areas, uprisings led by zamindars in some others, and attempts to carve out independent local kingdoms in still others. At the administrative level, it led to growing dissatisfaction and factionalism in the nobility and to the growth of what has been called the crisis of the *jagirdari* system. The nobles were unable to get from their *jagirs* the income indicated on paper. In consequence, many of them were unable to maintain their stipulated quota of troops. The position in the Deccan was particularly bad. Due to the disturbed conditions, and the lack of a proper contingent on the part of the nobles, we are told by a contemporary observer, Bhim Sen, they were sometimes unable to realize even a farthing. According to him, in consequence many of the *mansabdars* entered into private agreements with the Maratha sardars to pay *chauth*, i.e. share a quarter of their income if they did not create disturbances in the *jagirs*.

Another problem was shortage of *jagirs*. Following the annexation of Bijapur and Golconda, the best and most easily manageable *jagirs* had been kept by Aurangzeb in the *khalisa*, i.e., direct management in order to pay for the war. *Jagirs* in the newly conquered areas, i.e. the Karnataka yielded little income since the area was still unsettled. Hence, there were no takers for *jagirs* in the area. Even the existing *jagirdars*, especially those holding small *jagirs*, were harassed by the corruption of the clerks and other office holders who demanded bribes, and were often transferred to poorer, less paying *jagirs* if they failed to pay the bribes.

The crisis of the *jagirdari* system put the nobility under pressure. In order to grant *jagirs* to larger and larger numbers, and also to meet the gap between the paper income of the *jagir* and its realization, Shah Jahan had reduced the number of horses and *sawars* a *mansabdar* was expected to maintain. This was expressed in the formula that the salary would be equivalent to six or five months' salary in a year. But the problem of shortage of *jagirs* persisted, and became specially acute during the latter part of Aurangzeb's reign. The conquest of the Deccan did not solve the problem because Aurangzeb was keen to accommodate the officials of the former Deccani kingdom, as also the Marathas, who were active and influential in the area.

To conserve resources, Aurangzeb put a virtual ban on new recruitment. This led to acute disappointment to the sons and sons-in-law of the old nobles who had been awaiting long for the grant of a *mansab* and *jagir*. In the picturesque language of the historian, Khafi Khan, grant of a *jagir* became like "one pomegranate among a hundred sick."

The nobility was one of the most important institutions which developed under the Mughals. We have seen how the Mughals were able to attract to their services some of the most competent people irrespective of race or creed, from various sections within the country, and also from outside. The nobility functioned successfully in a system which emphasized accessibility and attention to grievances, public or personal. It also helped to maintain a fair state of security and peace in the country. But this role the nobility played as the service to the emperor served their own interests. It is wrong to argue, as some historians have done, that the nobility decayed because the 'vivifying' stream of immigrants from Central Asia stopped after the death of Aurangzeb. By the time Aurangzeb ascended the throne, the bulk of the Mughal nobility consisted of those who had been born in India. The belief that there was something wrong in the Indian climate which led to the decline of character was really a racialist argument put forward later by the British historians to justify India's domination by people coming from colder climates. Such an argument cannot be accepted by us.

It has also been argued that the Mughal nobility acted in an anti-national manner, because it was drawn from diverse communities and ethnic and racial groups and hence lacked a national character. A sense of nationalism, as we understand the term today, did not exist in medieval times. But the concept of loyalty to the salt was effective enough to ensure loyalty to the Mughal dynasty and a broad sense of patriotism. As we have seen, the nobles who came from abroad had few links left with the country of their origin and shared the Indo-Mughal cultural values and outlook.

The Mughals had devised a careful system of checks and balances at various levels in the administrative machinery and tried to balance various ethnic and religious groups in such a way that the ambitions of individual nobles or groups of them could be kept under control. Nobles began to assume independent airs only when the administrative machinery was allowed to decay by the successors of Aurangzeb, and on account of the steady accentuation of the crisis of the *jagirdari* system. Thus, disintegration was speeded up not because of but as a result of the breakdown of the Mughal administrative system. The Mughal administrative system was highly centralized and needed a competent monarch to run it. In the absence of such monarchs, *wazirs* tried to fill the bill, but they failed. Thus, individual failures and the breakdown of the system reacted on each other.

It has been argued that by the time Aurangzeb came to the throne, the Mughal army had become outmoded, on account of neglect of the infantry armed with flint guns, and a mobile field artillery. Such forces might also have enabled Aurangzeb to deal more effectively with Maratha held forts in the Deccan. But such a development needed larger resources, and would have been resisted by the nobles since decline of the cavalry would have influenced their prestige as well.

In the political field, Aurangzeb committed a number of serious mistakes. We have already referred to his inability to understand the true nature of the Maratha movement, and his disregard of Jai Singh's advise to befriend Shivaji. The execution of Sambhaji was another mistake, for it deprived Aurangzeb of a recognised Maratha head to negotiate with. Apparently, Aurangzeb had no desire to negotiate with the Marathas. He was convinced that after the extinction of Bijapur and Golconda, the Marathas were at his mercy and that they had no option but to accept his terms—a truncated *swarajya* (the term used by Maratha writers for the state carved out by Shivaji) and promise of loyalty and service to the Mughal emperor. When Aurangzeb realised his mistake and opened negotiations with the Marathas, the demand for *chauth* and *sardeshmukhi* proved a serious obstacle. Even this had been, by and large, surmounted. In 1703, agreement had been, more or less arrived at, but Aurangzeb could not bring himself to trust Shahu and the Maratha sardars.

Aurangzeb failed to solve the Maratha problem and thus left an open sore. He did give *mansabs* to many Maratha sardars; in fact, Maratha sardars had more *mansabs* at the highest levels than the Rajputs ever had. Yet, the Maratha sardars were not trusted. Unlike the Rajputs, they were never given offices of trust and responsibility. Thus, the Marathas could not be integrated into the Mughal political system. Here again, a political settlement with Shivaji, or Sambhaji or Shahu might have made a big difference.

Aurangzeb has been criticized for having failed to unite with the Deccani states against the Marathas, or for having conquered them thereby making the empire 'so large that it collapsed under its own weight.' A unity of hearts between Aurangzeb and the Deccani states was 'a psychological impossibility' once the treaty of 1636 was abandoned, a development which took place during the reign of Shah Jahan himself. After his accession, Aurangzeb desisted from pursuing a vigorous forward policy in the Deccan. In fact, he postponed as long as possible the decision to conquer and annex the Deccani states.

Aurangzeb's hand was virtually forced by the growing Maratha power, the support extended to Shivaji by Madanna and Akhanna from Golconda, and his fear that Bijapur might fall under the domination of Shivaji and the Maratha-dominated Golconda. Later, by giving shelter to the rebel prince Akbar, Sambhaji virtually threw a challenge to Aurangzeb who quickly realised that the Marathas could not be dealt with without first subduing Bijapur and possibly Golconda.

The attempt to extend Mughal administration over Golconda, Bijapur and Karnataka, stretched the Mughal administration to a breaking point. It also laid Mughal lines of communications open to Maratha attacks, so much so, that the Mughal nobles in the area found it impossible to collect their dues from the *jagirs* assigned to them and sometimes made private pacts with the Marathas, as has been noted above. This, in turn, raised the power and prestige of the Marathas, led to demoralisation in the nobility, and a setback to the imperial prestige. Perhaps, Aurangzeb might have been better advised to accept the suggestion put forward by his eldest son, Shah Alam, for a settlement with Bijapur and Golconda, annex only a part of their territories, and let them rule over Karnataka which was far away and difficult to manage.

The impact of the Deccani and other wars on the Mughal empire and of the prolonged absence of Aurangzeb from northern India, should not be overestimated. Despite the mistakes of policy and some of the personal shortcomings of Aurangzeb, such as his excessive suspiciousness and his narrow and cold temperament, the Mughal empire was still a powerful and vigorous military and administrative machinery. The Mughal army might fail against the elusive and highly mobile bands of Marathas in the mountainous region of the Deccan. Maratha forts might be difficult to capture and still more difficult to retain, but in the plains of northern India and the vast plateau extending up to the Karnataka, the Mughal artillery was still master of the field. Thirty or forty years after Aurangzeb's death, when the Mughal artillery had declined considerably in strength and efficiency, the Marathas could still not face it in the field of battle. Continuous anarchy, wars and the depredations of the Marathas may have depleted the population of the Deccan and brought its trade, industry and agriculture to a virtual standstill, but in northern India which was the heart of the empire and was of decisive economic and political importance in the country, the Mughal administration still retained much of its vigour, and trade and industry not only continued to flourish, but expanded. The administration at the district level proved amazingly tenacious, and a good deal of it survived and found its way indirectly into the British administration.

Politically, despite the military reverses and the mistakes of Aurangzeb, the Mughal dynasty still retained a powerful hold on the mind and imagination of the people.

As far as the Rajputs are concerned, we have seen that the breach with Marwar was not due to an attempt on Aurangzeb's part to undermine the Hindus by depriving them of a recognized head, but due to a miscalculation on his part; he wanted to divide the Marwar state between the two principal claimants, and in the process alienated both, including the ruler of Mewar who considered Mughal interference in such a delicate matter to be a dangerous precedent. The breach with Mewar and the long drawn-out war which followed damaged the moral standing of the Mughal state. However, the fighting was not of much consequence militarily after 1681. It may be doubted whether the presence of Rathor Rajputs in larger numbers in the Deccan between 1681 and 1706 would have made much difference in the outcome of the military conflict with the Marathas. The demands of the Rajputs related to grant of high *mansabs* as before and restoration of their homelands. These demands having been accepted within half a dozen years of Aurangzeb's death, the Rajputs ceased to be a problem for the Mughals. They played little active role in the subsequent disintegration of the empire, nor help in arresting the process of decline.

Aurangzeb's religious policy should be seen in the social, economic and political context. Aurangzeb was orthodox in his outlook and tried to remain broadly within the framework of the Islamic law. But this law had developed outside India under vastly different circumstances, and could hardly be applied rigidly to India. His failure to respect the susceptibilities of his non-Muslim subjects on many occasions, his enunciation of a policy which led to the destruction of many temples of old standing, and re-imposition of *jizyah* as laid down by the Islamic law did not help him to rally the Muslims to his side, or to generate a greater sense of loyalty towards a state based on Islamic law. On the other hand, it alienated segments of the Hindus and strengthened the hands of those section which were opposed to the Mughal empire for political or other reasons. By itself, religion was not a point at issue. *Jizyah* was scrapped within half a dozen years of Aurangzeb's death, and restrictions on building new temples eased. But these, again, had no effect on the rapidly accelerating decline and disintegration of the empire in the 18th century.

In the ultimate resort, the decline and downfall of the empire was due to economic, social, political and institutional factors. Akbar's measures helped to keep the forces of disintegration in check for some time. But it was impossible for him to effect fundamental changes in the structure of society. By the time Aurangzeb came to the throne, the socio-economic forces of disintegration were already strong. Aurangzeb lacked the foresight and statesmanship necessary to effect fundamental changes in the socio-political structure, or to pursue policies which could, for the time being, reconcile the various competing elements.

Thus, Aurangzeb was both a victim of circumstances, and helped to create the circumstances of which he became a victim.

TWENTY

Assessment and Review

The thousand years from the beginning of the eighth century to the end of the seventeenth century saw important changes in the political, economic and cultural life of the country and also, to a smaller extent, in its social life.

In the field of social life, the caste system continued to dominate, despite the challenge posed to it by Islam and loss of political power by the Rajput rulers who were duty bound to protect *dharma* which implied, among other things, the upholding of the four-fold division of society (*varnashrama-dharma*). Although the Nath Panthi Jogis and the Bhakti saints vehemently criticised the caste system, they could hardly make a dent in it. A tacit agreement was arrived at in course of time. The criticism of the caste system by saints did not, with some notable exceptions, extend to day-to-day or secular life, while the Brahmans acquiesced in the advocacy of the path of devotion as the way for salvation for all castes, specially for the Shudras. Many women saints, such as Mira, and others such as Surdas opened the way of *bhakti* for women also, and their rising above the task of service and duty to a husband. However, the Brahmans continued to claim a privileged position for themselves, including the exclusive right to preach and educate.

Within the framework of caste, new subgroups arose, due in parts to the absorption of tribal groups into Hinduism, the growth of new professional groups, and also the local and regional feelings. At the same time, the *varna* status of castes rose or fell, according to the economic and political power of the groups concerned. Rajputs, Marathas and Khatris may be mentioned in this context.

The Bhakti and Sufi saints gradually brought about a better understanding of the fundamental tenets of Hinduism and Islam, underlining the fact that they had a great deal of similarity. This resulted in a greater spirit of mutual harmony and toleration, although forces advocating a narrow, intolerant approach continued to be strongly entrenched and sometimes influenced state policies. But such occasions were, on the whole, limited.

The Bhakti and Sufi saints also brought about important changes in the approach to religion, laying greater emphasis on true faith than to the formal observances. They also contributed to the growth of regional languages and literature. But the excessive concern with religious and spiritual affairs resulted in a setback to the growth of rational sciences, especially to the cultivation of science and technology.

On balance, the position of women worsened. Seclusion of women or purdah became more widespread, while Hindu women were not able to claim the right of remarriage or a share in their father's property which Muslim women had. In fact, these rights tended to be denied more and more even to Muslim women.

In the political and economic fields, the most important development was the political and administrative integration of the country brought about by the Turks and later consolidated by the Mughals. Although the Turkish and Mughal system of administration remained largely confined to northern India, indirectly it affected other parts of India also. The institution of a well-minted currency based on silver, the development of roads and sarais and the preference for city life had a direct effect on the growth of trade and handicrafts which reached its climax during the seventeenth century. Under the Mughals, political integration was accompanied by a deliberate effort to create a unified ruling class consisting of Muslims and Hindus. However, the ruling class remained strongly aristocratic in character, with only limited opportunities of career being open to the people of talent from lower classes. It also remained largely northern in character. Aurangzeb did try to induct large numbers of Marathas and Deccani nobles into the services. The Deccanis were integrated, but not the Marathas. Perhaps, regional as well as religious and social prejudices played a role in this because, unlike the Rajputs in north India, the Maratha sardars were drawn from social sections which had never exercised political power, or been a ruling class. Nor were they considered Kshtriyas.

The Mughal nobility was organised as a bureaucracy dependent on the monarch. However, it derived its income mainly from lands cultivated by peasant proprietors. For the collection of land revenue from peasants, the nobility depended partly on its military following and partly on the strength of the zamindars whose rights and privileges were defended and maintained by the state in return for their support. That is why many historians argue that the state in medieval India remained essentially feudal.

A significant contribution of the Turks was the defence of the country from Mongol onslaughts during the thirteenth and fourteenth centuries. Later, for 200 years, the Mughals were able to secure the northwest frontiers of India from foreign invasions. For this purpose, the defence of India was fixed on the Kabul-Ghazni line with the Hindukush mountains to the north. The politics of Central and West Asia were closely followed and sometimes an active part was taken.

India's reputation as a land of spices, and its position as the textile manufactory of the eastern world including East Africa, led the European nations to try to establish direct trade relations with India. The richness of the oriental trade further whetted the appetite of the European nations and quickened their economic and technological growth. Since they had hardly any commodities to offer which were in demand in the oriental world, except the silver and gold procured from Central and South America, the European traders, backed by their governments sought an entry into the internal trade of India and Asia. On a number of occasions, they desired to control Indian territories whose income could be used for the purchase of Indian goods, just like the Dutch who had been able to bring the East Indies (modern Indonesia) under their control. As long as the Mughal empire was strong, the European nations were not successful in this objective. The decline of the Mughal empire and important political events in India during the eighteenth century, such as the entry of Nadir Shah and later, the Afghans, as well as the rapid economic development of the European nations enabled them to establish their dominations in India as also in many other Asian countries.

While scholars have tried to explain the causes of the decline and downfall of the Mughal empire, the reasons why India, like many other Asian nations, could not develop as rapidly as the European nations in the economic and scientific fields, needs further detailed study and research. The Mughal ruling classes had no traditions of connection with the sea. While the Mughal rulers were quick to recognize the importance of foreign trade, and for that reason gave patronage and support to the European trading companies, they had little understanding of the importance of naval power in the economic development of a nation.

India's lagging behind in the field of naval power was a part of its growing backwardness in the field of science and technology. Even the mechanical clock which brought together all the European inventions in the field of dynamics was not produced in India during the seventeenth century. The superiority of the Europeans in the field of artillery was freely acknowledged. Even where Indian craftsmen were able to copy European developments—as for example in the field of ship-building—little ability to innovate was displayed. Apart from the attitude of the ruling class to which we have referred, the social structure, historical traditions and the outlook of various sections are important in this context. There was too much emphasis on past learning, and of showing deference to those who were supposed to be the repositories of this knowledge—the Brahmans and the mullahs. Akbar's efforts to modernize the syllabus by introducing more science subjects of secular interest were defeated due to the pressure of these elements. The very skill of the Indian artisans and their availability in large number inhibited the efforts to develop and apply machine power to productive enterprises. The effect of the caste system in breeding an attitude of insularity and conservatism is, however, a matter of discussion.

Thus, India lagged behind the world in the field of science and technology and the Mughal ruling class remained singularly blind to this development. Like all ruling classes on their way out, the Mughal ruling class was more concerned with matters of immediate concern, including its creature comforts, than matters which would shape the future.

Despite this, the developments in various fields in India during the period should not be lost sight of. The growth of political integration was paralleled by cultural integration. Indian society was one of the few societies in the world which was able to develop a more or less unified culture despite differences in race, religion and language. This unified culture was reflected in an outburst of creative activity which makes the seventeenth century a second classical age. In the south, the traditions of the Cholas were continued by the Vijayanagara kingdom. The Bahmani kingdom and its successor states also contributed to cultural developments in various fields. The rich cultural developments in the various regional kingdoms during the fifteenth century were, to some extent, integrated in the new cultural forms developed by the Mughals. However, this integrated culture came under pressure from the religious dogmatists of the two faiths, as well as from the competing and conflicting interests of various sections in the ruling classes. But that it survived, on the whole, till the middle of the nineteenth century is no mean tribute to all those saints, scholars and enlightened rulers who had helped to build it.

The period was also marked by economic development and growth. Trade and manufactures expanded and there was expansion and improvement of cultivation also. However, the growth was uneven in different areas and during different phases. Apart from the Ganga valley where the Mughals spent a substantial part of the revenue resources of the empire, the areas which developed rapidly during the seventeenth century were Gujarat, the Coromandel coast and Bengal. Perhaps, it is no accident that these have been the areas in the forefront of economic development of India in the modern period, particularly in the post-independence era.

Would India have continued to progress economically and even attained an industrial revolution of its own, if the Mughal empire had continued? While trade and manufactures continued to expand during the eighteenth century, despite the downfall of the Mughal empire, it remained backward compared to Europe, not only in the field of science and technology, but in other fields as well. Thus, most of the manufactures remained small in scale, with hardly any machinery, with the workers using the simplest tools. In consequence, howsoever skilful a craftsman might be, his productivity and efficiency remained low. Nor could the artisans develop into traders and entrepreneurs as in the West, both because of caste and because most artisans had little by way of capital. This was a reflection of the extremely uneven distribution of money and resulted in the domestic market being limited. During the seventeenth and eighteenth centuries, there was a growth of the putting out (*dadni*) system. This increased production, but made the artisans more and more dependent on the merchants, Indian or foreign.

It was in these circumstances that the British were able to conquer India and convert it into a colony, supplying raw materials in place of being the manufactory of the east as it was earlier. It is this ebb and flow which makes the study of history both interesting and rewarding.

Appendix

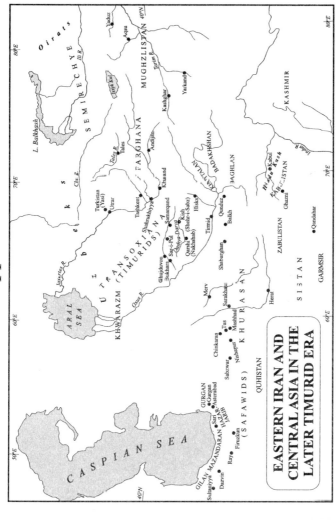

MAP A. Eastern Iran and Central Asia in the later Timurid era

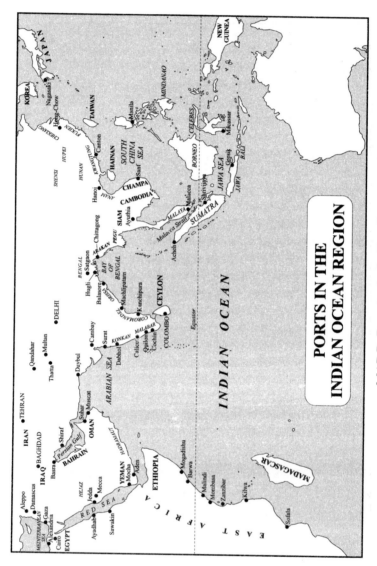

MAP B. Ports in the Indian Ocean

Books for Further Reading
(Select List)

General

A. A Comprehensive History of India Series

Habib, M., and K. A. Nizami, eds. *The Delhi Sultanat*. Vol. 5, 2 parts. New Delhi: People's Publishing House, 1992.

Majumdar, R. C., ed. *The Gupta Empire and After*. Vol. 4, 2 parts. New Delhi: People's Publishing House, 1981.

Sharma, R. S., ed. *The Cholas, Chalukyas and Rajputs, AD 985–1206*. Vol. 4, part 1. New Delhi: People's Publishing House, 1992.

B. The History and Culture of the Indian People Series

Majumdar, R. C., A. D. Pusalkar, and A. K. Majumdar. *The Delhi Sultanat*. Vol. 6. Bombay: Bharti Vidya Bhawan, 1960.

Majumdar, R. C., and K. K. Dasgupta, eds. *The Struggle for Empire*. Vol. 5. Bombay: Bharti Vidya Bhawan, 1955.

Majumdar, R. C., J. N. Chaudhri, and S. Chaudhuri. *The Mughal Empire*. Vol.7. Bombay: Bharti Vidya Bhavan, 1960.

C. Other Books

Chandra, S. *Medieval India: From Sultanat to the Mughals*. 2 vols. New Delhi: Har Anand, 2004 (3rd edition).

Richards, J. F. *The Mughal Empire*. New Delhi: Foundation Books, 1993.

Sastri, K. A. Nilakanta. *A History of South India*. New Delhi: OUP, 1976 (4th edition).

Sherwani, H. K., and P. M. Joshi, eds. *History of Medieval Deccan (1295–1724)*. 2 vols. Hyderabad: Government of Andhra Pradesh, 1973–74.

Tripathi, R. P. *Rise and Fall of the Mughal Empire*. Allahabad: Central Book Depot, 1956.

Political History

Early Period and the Sultanat

Altekar, A. S. *The Rashtrakutas and their Times*. Poona: Oriental Books, 1966 (revised edition).

Basak, R. G. *History of North Eastern India*. Calcutta: Firma KLM, 1934.

Habibullah, A. B. M. *The Foundation of Muslim Rule in India*. Allahabad: Central Book Depot, 1967.

Husain, A. Mehdi. *Tuglaq Dynasty*. New Delhi: S. Chand & Company, 1976 (reprint).

Lal, K. S. *History of the Khaljis 1290–1320*. Allahabad: The Indian Press, 1967 (2nd edition).

Sarkar, J. N. *History of Bengal (1200–1757)*. Patna: Academica Asiatica, 1973.

Sastri, K. A. Nilakanta. *The Cholas*. 2 vols. New Delhi: University of Madras, 1976 (4th edition).

Sherwani, H. K. *The Bahmanis of Deccan*. New Delhi: Munshiram Manoharlal, 1985 (2nd edition).

Stein, Burton. *Vijayanagara*. Cambridge: CUP, 1989.

Mughals

Prasad, Beni. *History of Jahangir*. London: OUP, 1922.

Prasad, Ishwari. *The Life and Times of Humayun*. Calcutta: Orient Longman, 1955.

Saksena, B. P. *History of Shah Jahan of Dihli*. Allahabad: Central Book Depot, 1973.

Sarkar, J. N. *History of Aurangzeb*. 5 vols. Calcutta: J. Sarkar & Sons, 1912–1914 (Also the one volume of *History of Aurangzeb*).

————. *Shivaji and His Time*. Calcutta: J. Sarkar & Sons, 1948 (4th edition).

Srivastava, A. L. *Akbar the Great*. 2 vols. Agra: Shiv Lal Agarwal & Co., 1962, 1967.

Williams, Rushbrooke. *Babur: An Empire Builder of the Sixteenth Century*. New Delhi: S. Chand & Co, n.d. (reprint).

Administration

Aziz, A. *The Mansabdari Systems and the Mughal Army*. New Delhi: Idarah-i-Adabiyat, 1954.

Habib, Irfan. *The Agrarian System of Mughal India, 1526–1707*. New Delhi: OUP, 1999 (2nd edition).

Moreland, W. H. *The Agrarian System of Moslem India*. Allahabad: Central Books, 1920 (Indian Edition).

Quereshi, I. H. *The Administration of the Mughal Empire*. Karachi: OUP, 1966.

———. *The Administration of the Sultanate of Delhi*. Karachi: Pakistan History Society, 1958.

Economic, Social and Cultural Life

Asher, Catherine B. *Mughal Architecture*. Cambridge: CUP, 1992.

Beach, Milo C. *Mughal Painting*. Cambridge: CUP, 1992.

Brown, Percy. *Indian Architecture (Islamic Period)*. Bombay: Taraporevala,1958 (3rd edition).

Chandra, S. *Essays on Medieval Indian History*. New Delhi: OUP, 2003.

Chaudhuri, K. N. *Trade and Civilization in the Indian Ocean*. New Delhi: Munshiram Manoharlal, 1985 (Indian edition).

Ojha, P. N. *Some Aspects of North Indian Social Life, 1556–1707*. Patna: Nagari Prakashan, 1961.

Raychaudhari, T., and Irfan Habib, eds. *The Cambridge Economic History of India, 1200–1700*. Vol 1. Cambridge: CUP, 1982.

Index